# Global Energy Security
# and American Hegemony

*Themes in Global Social Change*

Christopher Chase-Dunn, *Series Editor*

*Consulting Editors*
Janet Lippman Abu-Lughod
Giovanni Arrighi
Jonathan Friedman
Keith Griffin

# Global Energy Security and American Hegemony

Doug Stokes and Sam Raphael

The Johns Hopkins University Press
*Baltimore*

© 2010 The Johns Hopkins University Press
All rights reserved. Published 2010
Printed in the United States of America on acid-free paper
9 8 7 6 5 4 3 2 1

The Johns Hopkins University Press
2715 North Charles Street
Baltimore, Maryland 21218-4363
www.press.jhu.edu

Library of Congress Cataloging-in-Publication Data

Stokes, Doug, 1972–
    Global energy security and American hegemony / Doug
Stokes and Sam Raphael.
        p. cm.—(Themes in global social change)
    Includes bibliographical references and index.
    ISBN-13: 978-0-8018-9496-1 (hardcover : alk. paper)
    ISBN-10: 0-8018-9496-4 (hardcover : alk. paper)
    ISBN-13: 978-0-8018-9497-8 (pbk. : alk. paper)
    ISBN-10: 0-8018-9497-2 (pbk. : alk. paper)
    1. Power resources—Government policy—United States.
2. Energy policy—United States.   3. United States—Foreign
economic relations—Developing countries.   4. Developing
countries—Foreign economic relations—United States.
I. Raphael, Sam, 1977–   II. Title.
    HD9502.U52S829 2010
    333.790973—dc22        2009038860

A catalog record for this book is available from the British
Library.

*Special discounts are available for bulk purchases of this book. For
more information, please contact Special Sales at 410-516-6936 or
specialsales@press.jhu.edu.*

The Johns Hopkins University Press uses environmentally
friendly book materials, including recycled text paper that is
composed of at least 30 percent post-consumer waste, whenever
possible. All of our book papers are acid-free, and our jackets
and covers are printed on paper with recycled content.

*To the memory of my grandparents, Albert and Doris Hahn* DS

*To Vanessa, of course* SR

*And to the memory of Peter Gowan (1946–2009)*

# Contents

# Acknowledgments

We would like to thank the many individuals who read, commented on, or helped with the development of this book. These include Ken Booth, Vanessa Cooke, Michael Cox, Eric Herring, Jonathon Joseph, Michael Klare, Columba Peoples, Richard Saull, and Richard Sakwa. The British Academy funded a substantial amount of the research in this book, so our thanks to them.

# Abbreviations

| | |
|---|---|
| AFRICOM | U.S. Africa Command |
| BP | British Petroleum |
| CAFTA | Central American Free Trade Agreement |
| CENTCOM | U.S. Central Command |
| CI | counterinsurgency |
| CINC | commander-in-chief |
| CN | counternarcotics |
| CSIS | Center for Strategic and International Studies |
| CT | counterterrorism |
| EUCOM | U.S. European Command |
| FDI | foreign direct investment |
| FMF | foreign military financing |
| FMS | foreign military sales |
| FOL | forward operating location |
| FY | fiscal year |
| GDP | gross domestic product |
| HN | host nation |
| IFI | international financial institution |
| IMET | International Military Education and Training |
| IMF | International Monetary Fund |
| IOC | international oil company |
| mbpd | million barrels per day |
| NAFTA | North American Free Trade Agreement |
| NEPD | National Energy Policy Development |
| NGO | nongovernmental organization |
| NOC | national oil company |
| NPC | National Petroleum Council |
| NSC | National Security Council |
| OECD | Organisation for Economic Co-operation and Development |
| OPEC | Organization of the Petroleum Exporting Countries |
| PMC | private military company |
| SOUTHCOM | U.S. Southern Command |
| USSOCOM | U.S. Special Operations Command |

# Global Energy Security
# and American Hegemony

# Global Oil Supplies and US Intervention

At heart, this book is about the ways in which American power has been used in the postwar era to construct and defend a globalized economic order under US hegemony and the role played by Washington's military power to shore up this order when threatened. In particular, it examines an important aspect of American "grand strategy": namely, the attempt to secure control over global oil supplies, primarily through coercive intervention into the key oil-rich regions of the global South. The core themes of the book—the construction of a US-led global order, the role of American military power to sustain it, and the necessity of controlling vital oil supplies—are closely related, and we do not treat them otherwise. In other words, although we provide a detailed account of US interventions in the oil-rich South, and chart Washington's long-standing attempt to maintain hegemony in these zones, this is not a book simply about the United States and oil. We also explore the interrelation between US "energy security," coercive power, and wider US grand strategy. Ultimately, we are concerned with revealing how US global power plays out in the case of oil and how the control of oil sustains this power.

Energy security was a declared priority for the Bush administration and is a declared priority for the Obama administration. Of course, this is partly because of the immense energy requirements of the US economy, which is responsible for a significant proportion of the world's daily consumption. However, American concerns over energy security range far wider than this: in an era marked by a globalized economy that is heavily dependent upon plentiful supplies of energy—and upon oil in particular—Washington has sought to control the conditions under which *all* core powers receive oil from the South. This is so because of the integrated nature of energy markets—where US energy security cannot be disaggregated from global energy security—and because such control provides Washington with immense *structural* power. By acting as the ultimate guarantor of global energy security, US hegemony over the international system is consolidated, with potential rivals to its position forced to be (and in some instances content to be) reliant upon American power. These wider objectives characterize US statecraft in relation to oil; American planners are not just concerned with ensuring that enough foreign oil reaches US shores. In this light, the eventual destination of individual shipments is of less concern for planners than the smooth functioning of the global oil market. And given the preferred mode of wider global rule by Washington, this has led the United States to focus on the "free marketization" of oil-rich political economies in the South.

Washington has worked, where possible, to create an environment conducive to the investment by private oil capital. That this capital is increasingly *transnational* in nature—with international oil companies owned and run by executives and shareholders from many countries—only goes to demonstrate the positive-sum characteristics of the US-led order. By "transnationalizing" oil-rich political economies and further integrating them into the global economy Washington plays a managerial role for the capitalist order as a whole. Yet this is not a consequence of altruism on behalf of US planners. Nor is it, as some would have it, the result of fundamental changes in the structure of global politics, with the United States the lead example of an emerging "transnational state," replacing the traditional "nation-state" and acting primarily on behalf of a "transnational capitalist class."[1] Rather, US planners seek to affect this transnational outcome for distinctly national ends: it is through the management of a positive-sum liberal order, through the extension of that order to oil-rich zones, and through guaranteeing the provision of oil to all players within the order, that American hegemony over the international system is maintained.

The overt drive to transnationalize the oil-rich South is central to Washington's strategy to cement its global hegemony. Achieving this objective, however, has required successive US administrations to deploy military force—most often in the guise of counterinsurgency (CI) training and equipping to friendly security forces—in order to stabilize crucial oil-rich zones. Through the application of CI, American planners have often sought to militarize state-society relations, with the aim of disciplining those social forces that have the potential to organize against US oil hegemony. In this way, the American state has worked to "armor" processes of transnationalization and globalization through the use of coercive statecraft. This is a key element of overall US strategy and will be seen at play throughout the book. Furthermore the armoring of free market relations in the oil-rich South has had profound consequences for the development of political order. Human security has been a regular casualty as the United States has insulated ruling elites from internal pressures for reform, with wider strategic imperatives trumping, time and again, a principled stance regarding human rights and democracy.

These themes in American strategy toward the oil-rich South—transnationalization bolstered by militarization—will be explored in this book at three levels. In the first two chapters, we will look at the ways in which US power is exercised at the global level, in relation to the extension of the liberal order under conditions of American strategic primacy (chapter 1), and in relation to Washington's parallel drive to stabilize important regions in the global South (chapter 2). In particular, by examining how this strategy plays out in oil-rich zones, we shall reveal how control over important energy reserves is maintained and how this underpins the wider project of global hegemony. Subsequently (in chapter 3), we shall examine how these themes manifest in relation to the most significant oil-rich region in the world: the Persian Gulf. The success (or otherwise) of American strategy in the Persian Gulf will, to no small extent, determine the future of US global power. As such, the United States has a long history of exercising its power in this region, with its overwhelming military dominance translating into repeated attempts to stabilize oil production under favorable conditions. In this light, the invasion of Iraq in 2003 was a natural (although not inevitable) outcome of an American strategy toward the region which has evolved since 1945. Finally, and in some depth, we shall explore how these themes manifest in three other oil-rich regions: the Caspian Basin (chapter 4), West Africa (chapter 5), and Latin America (chapter 6). Diversification away from the Persian Gulf has become an increasing concern for US planners, with accelerated efforts to open up, and to stabilize, favorable state formations in these regions. In turn, this has had profound consequences for notions of human security and democracy.

Before we go any further, however, it would be useful to locate our argument in relation to wider debates about the nature of US power today. This will occupy the remainder of this introduction, as we seek to set out our broader position.

## Debating US Power in the Contemporary Age

Debates over the nature and consequences of American power have moved to the forefront of academic and popular discourse in recent years, largely as a result of the response by the US state to the attacks of September 11, 2001. When the hijacked planes smashed into the Twin Towers in New York and the Pentagon in Washington, D.C., in 2001, international politics was ruptured in a myriad of ways. Amongst Western government officials, media and academic commentators, and popular imagination, consensus quickly built around the claim that the world had fundamentally changed and that the peaceful "interregnum" between the Cold War and September 11, 2001, had all but dissolved. Those who had predicted the fast-approaching end of the peace dividend that came with the collapse of the Berlin Wall had been proved correct, and none more so than those who had urged that greater attention be paid to radical Islamist forces plotting large-scale destruction on the American homeland.[2] The declaration of war by al Qaeda, according to most, was a truly defining moment, on a par with very few other events in modern times. Public discourse in the "post-9/11 era" quickly settled on an understanding of contemporary times as strikingly new, where old orders and established truths were rapidly crumbling in the face of a new and deadly threat. Crucially, this viewpoint was sustained and amplified by the rhetoric of the Bush administration in the United States. In just one of many instances of threat construction in the months following the attacks, National Security Advisor Condoleezza Rice made clear that "this period is analogous to 1945 to 1947 in that the events so clearly demonstrated that there is a big global threat . . . That has started shifting the tectonic plates in international politics." In this light, Rice argued, the "fall of the Berlin Wall and the fall of the World Trade Center were the bookends of a long transition period" and, as the world entered a new era, there was "no longer any doubt that today America faces *an existential threat to our security*—a threat as great as any we faced during the Civil War, the so-called 'Good War,' or the Cold War."[3]

Justified in this way, the White House moved quickly to declare a "global war on terror" as a response to the attacks on 9/11. This Pentagon-led battle was to be fought on several fronts across the world, amounting to "a lengthy campaign, unlike any we have ever seen."[4] The enduring nature of the threat, and therefore the necessity of a prolonged response, remained central to the political positioning of the Bush administration throughout its two terms in office. As Defense Secretary Donald Rumsfeld declared during the release of the 2006 *Quadrennial Defense Review* (the four-yearly planning document setting out the Pentagon's strategic vision for the US military), the United States was engaged in a "generational conflict" that "might last decades as allies work to root out terrorists across the globe and battle extremists who want to rule the world."[5] The Bush administration declared a "Long War," which was global in scope and limitless in duration.

With this declaration of a war on terror, Washington under President Bush embarked upon its most interventionist path in a generation. Under the banner of a global "counterterrorist" campaign, the United States launched a number of coercive interventions, most notably in Afghanistan and Iraq. Forcible regime change in both of these countries captured most of the headlines during the Bush years, given that, even as the administration was entering its last days at the end of 2008, the Pentagon was still deploying around 150,000 troops in Iraq and over 30,000 in Afghanistan. Casualties in both theaters (predominantly civilian) had reached staggering levels, with regional instability in many ways of far greater concern than in the years prior to US action.[6] Bush's military-led war on terror, however, stretched far wider than Iraq and Afghanistan. There was a radical escalation of intelligence and defense spending across the board, and a proliferation of covert operations by US forces, matched by increased security assistance programs to "counterterrorist allies." And although the Pentagon's budget reached levels unseen since World War II, with annual appropriations nearing $600 billion, this global projection of force remained largely unseen, and the sheer scale of US intervention rarely appreciated.[7] Cloaked in secrecy, with a lack of accountability for both funding and execution, a wide range of US security agencies became engaged in unconventional warfare against the "terrorist" threat. Central Intelligence Agency (CIA) operations were at the front line of the war on terror, as it coordinated a hidden global internment network across a wide range of countries.[8] Likewise, the size of US Special Forces grew by 15 percent, with an additional 3,700 personnel deployed for "psychological operations" against perceived enemies.[9] Such forces received covert military authorization to conduct wide-ranging strikes in states across the world, none of which were at war with the United States. Teams were inserted into more than a dozen countries during Bush's second term in order to carry out attacks, in violation of their formal sovereignty.[10]

The increased militarization of US policy in the years following 9/11 was facilitated by a shift toward a unilateral foreign policy, with the United States increasingly bypassing the established rules and norms of the international system. Most significantly, the broad consensus of international legal opinion understands the decision to invade Iraq, in the absence of explicit authorization by the UN Security Council, to have been a clear violation of the UN Charter regulating the use of force in international affairs.[11] Similarly, the construction of a detention facility at the US naval base at Guantanamo Bay, Cuba, saw the US imprison and try "suspected terrorists" outside of the framework of the Geneva Conventions. And although this move toward a more assertive policy stance was greeted by outcry from many quarters, the Bush administration remained unrepentant, resolute in its claim that the scale of the threat necessitated a firm response unhindered by the constraints of multilateral diplomacy and international law.

In the months and years after 9/11, the foreign policy formulated by the Bush team was both controversial and highly significant, recasting the debate over US-global relations in ways likely to endure far beyond its term in office. In particular, this period reignited the debate over whether American strategy formed part of an "imperial project," with many commentators adopting the language of "empire" to describe the Bush administration's war on terror. As Michael Ignatieff asked provocatively in the *New York Times:* "This may come as a shock to Americans, who don't like to think of their country as an empire. But what else can you call America's legions of soldiers, spooks and Special Forces straddling the globe? These garrisons are by no means temporary."[12]

## The Bush Administration and the War on Terror: An Imperial Moment?

A preeminent US historian once declared that one of the central "themes of American historiography is that there is no American Empire."[13] During the Bush administration, this sentiment became less prescient than in previous eras, as a "new imperial discourse" took off in the academy.[14] Vast military expenditures, numerous interventions throughout the globe, and a disregard for established norms and international law; surely such a posture was indicative of more profound trends in the Bush strategy than simply a reaction to the threat posed by al Qaeda? Indeed, many could point to the intellectual foundations of neoconservatism and the subsequent appointment to high office of prominent members of the now-infamous Project for the New American Century (including Vice President Dick Cheney, Defense Secretary Donald Rumsfeld, and his deputy, Paul Wolfowitz).[15] This group, active during the Clinton administration, had argued explicitly for a reinvigorated "American global leadership," exercised primarily through "a military that is strong and ready to meet both present and future challenges." Crucially, for those pinning the charge of imperialism on the motivations of Cheney, Rumsfeld, Wolfowitz, and the others, they had stressed that this US leadership was to be exercised *specifically* in order to "shape a new century favorable to American principles and interests."[16] These overt policy statements, married to the concrete action on the ground once key members of the group were in power, led many to reinterpret the war on terror as a long-awaited exercise in imperialism.

As analyses of US strategy in these terms became more commonplace, and were no longer limited to left-wing critics of American power, debate increasingly turned on the question of the *desirability* of US empire under the Bush administration. In fact, not all commentators were averse to the idea of US imperialism, and many began to look past the negative connotations traditionally associated with the term. As Michael Cox made clear, many writers argued that we should "drop the pretense that America is not an Empire, and accept that if the world was going to be a stable place, the US had to act in much the same imperial fashion as the British and Romans had done several centuries before."[17] And within this new proempire discourse, the events of 9/11—and Bush's counterterror response—were central to understanding the contours of an emerging American imperialism.

Thomas Friedman, for example, echoed Bush administration officials when he equated the significance of 9/11 with World War II and the end of the Cold War and claimed that it had radically altered the context within which US foreign policy operated: "9/11 has set off World War III, and it, too, is defining a new international order." As a result, Friedman explicitly called for an imperial turn in US policy toward the South, since the post-9/11 era, like the earlier Cold War era, was "also bipolar, but instead of being divided between East and West it is divided between the World of Order and the World of Disorder." The mission of the World of Order, led by the overwhelming power of the United States, was to dominate the South—to help "stabilize and lift up the World of Disorder"—because too "little American power will only lead to the World of Disorder expanding."[18] In this reading, US empire was an essentially benign entity. According to Michael Ignatieff: "America's Empire is not like empires of times past, built on colonies, conquest and the white man's burden . . . The 21st century imperium is a new invention in the annals of political science, an Empire lite, a global hegemony whose grace notes are free markets, human rights and democracy, enforced by the most awesome military power the world has ever known."[19]

Likewise, Robert Kaplan explained that there was "a positive side to Empire . . . It's in some ways the most benign form of order," as a globally hegemonic United States provided the best hope for peace and stability.[20] And as Sebastian Mallaby argued, "anti-imperialist restraint is becoming harder to sustain," because "the disorder in poor countries grows more threatening." In response, he argued, the United States and its allies must "learn to love imperialism—again."[21] Themes of empire's necessity, and its benign nature in the American context, were further matched by an assumption of the reluctance with which the United States had taken up this mantle. America's empire was neither desired nor sought, with the overwhelming superiority of US power established by default.[22]

This supposed "turn to empire" by Washington during the Bush administration attracted critics from across the political spectrum. Amongst the more perceptive of theorists from a liberal perspective, John Ikenberry argued that management of the global order under the Bush administration had moved away from consensual rule *within* the system and toward a new dominance *over* the system, underpinned by military primacy. This shift represented a turn to what he called Washington's new "imperial grand strategy," which sought to utilize its current preponderance of global power to forge a "world order in which it runs the show." The evolution of this "grand strategic vision" under Bush was, according to Ikenberry, a dangerous development, which could ultimately have led to other states seeking to "work around, contain and retaliate against US power" and which could potentially have left the world "more dangerous and divided—and the United States less secure." The main fear was that, if the imperial foreign policy was pursued too vigorously, balancing behavior may have occurred amongst other states, with the formation of anti-US coalitions designed to counter American power. In turn, this could have fractured the international system and the forms of strategic, political, and economic interdependence which have brought peace and order to the realm of global politics in the postwar era. As a result, Ikenberry urged a post-Bush return to the traditional *hegemonic* role for the United States, sharply distinct in his eyes from an imperial role, based as it was on leadership in accordance with the rules of the system.[23]

Similar criticisms of the "Bush turn" emerged from within the realist school of international relations. Traditionally adopting a more conservative stance, realist scholars have tended to guard against overemphasis on the moral considerations of US foreign policy and instead seek to make core national interests central. But in doing so, many became distinctly uneasy with Bush's foreign policy. As a consequence, high-profile realists such as John Mearsheimer, Stephen Walt, and Kenneth Waltz joined the Coalition for a Realistic Foreign Policy (CRFP) in 2003 to argue that "American foreign policy is moving in a dangerous direction toward empire." According to a "Statement of Principles" by the group, "worrisome imperial trends are apparent in the Bush administration's National Security Strategy," and this "move toward empire must be halted immediately." Unlike Ikenberry's focus on the effects that US empire may have on the international system of interstate cooperation, and the vitality of institutions such as the United Nations, these scholars refracted their criticism through a more naked reference to US national interests: American national security policy needed to be turned away from imperial domination through the use of military force and "toward realistic and sustainable measures for protecting US vital interests."[24]

For both sets of critics, Washington under the guidance of the Bush administration had erred from—and needed to be pulled back toward—its traditional, benign role of global hegemon, whereby it guides and works within (rather than imposes) global order. And for many across the world, this is exactly what has occurred with the election of Barack Obama. Writing during the first months of Obama's time in office, critics of US policy under the Bush administration breathed a collective sigh of relief and celebrated the ascendancy of leaders who will shape Washington's foreign policy away from the perceived excesses of the neocons. Indeed, the declared desire of the Obama administration to end the combat mission in Iraq, to close Guantanamo Bay, to abandon the use of "coercive interrogations" against terror suspects, and to adopt a softer line on Bush's remaining "axis of evil" states (especially Iran), would seem to point to a new direction in US foreign policy. This shift was exemplified by the early decision to drop the term "war on terror," and thus signal a substantially different approach to counterterrorism.[25] Given these announcements by the Obama administration, common talk of American imperialism has ceased, with the language of empire ditched as quickly as it was adopted. In retrospect, US imperialism was nothing more than an unfortunate historical moment; Washington had now returned to its rightful role of global guarantor, upholding and defending the framework within which peaceful international politics can take place.[26]

A central theme of our argument is a rejection of these supposed disconti-nuities in the direction of US foreign policy during the years of the Bush administration. Whilst we would certainly acknowledge the unprecedented degree of unilateralism and militarism that characterized the Bush years, and whilst we do not deny the historically unique nature of Obama's presidency, we are less sanguine about the supposedly profound break that either administration made (or is making) with the past. Indeed, there are deeper forces at play in the making of US strategy. These arise from structural processes at work in the postwar global political and economic system, and as such it is possible to identify a great deal of commonality across the direction taken by consecutive occupants of the White House. Of course, individual policies shift all the time, sometimes in interesting or unexpected ways, and the justificatory language used to legitimate these certainly evolves from administration to administration. But ultimately during the postwar era, and even during times where American leadership was passed from one political bedrock to the other (such as from Carter to Reagan, from Clinton to Bush, or from Bush to Obama), the objectives of the US state have remained largely unchanged. Washington's relations with the world since World War II have, we would argue, been shaped by a deep and abiding continuity in relation to its core interests and therefore its grand strategy. In this context, it is our bet that Obama's new perspectives on current global issues—refreshing and inspiring although they often are—will in turn be constrained in fundamental ways by the necessity of pursuing these abiding interests.

## A Continuity of Interests, a Continuity of Strategy

We would agree with realist Stephen Walt that "the overriding goal of US foreign policy is, of course, to protect US citizens and promote US prosperity. Our primary strategic objective has long been to prevent challenges to our dominant position."[27] Given this, the question then becomes, how has the US state acted to promote American prosperity and remove challenges to its dominance? In his account of Washington's strategy in the postwar era, Christopher Layne succinctly provided the answer: "US policymakers repeatedly have stated their global hegemonic ambitions," and the United States "has consistently sought to expand its power and attain a position of hegemony in the international system—not only after 1989 but from the early 1940s and throughout the Cold War as well." Layne attributes this to a grand strategy that he calls "extraregional hegemony":

> Following World War II, the United States possessed overwhelming material ca-pabilities relative to all other states in the international system (including the Soviet Union). The regional hegemony of the United States in the Western Hemi-sphere provided a secure geopolitical platform from which it could seek extra-regional hegemony. Moreover, World War II caused an important shift in the distribution of power between the United States and Western Europe. As a result, the United States had both the means and the opportunity to impose its hege-mony over postwar Western Europe. Similar factors—overwhelming US material capabilities plus the Soviet Union's demise—created the opportunities for an-other round of hegemonic expansion after 1989.[28]

We would agree that extraregional hegemony—in other words, military, political, and economic dominance over the world's important regions—has represented the grand strategic objective of the US state in the postwar era; not for reasons of preserving international peace and security, nor for promot-ing democracy and human rights, but for the purposes of maintaining its extraordinary levels of prosperity and power vis-à-vis the rest of the world. To be clear: the primary logic which drives US statecraft has been a desire to se-cure and maintain the conditions which best serve its own economic and political interests, and Washington has consistently prioritized the defense of these interests above those of others and above any notion of being a "force for good." In this context, the effort by the Bush administration to ensure that US global hegemony was maintained—and even extended—in the post-9/11 era should be understood as a continuation (albeit an acceleration) of long-standing strategy. The uniquely unilateralist tendencies of the Bush team gave rise to a particular set of policies that differed only in the means used to achieve the same strategic ends that have guided US statecraft since 1945. And crucially, US strategy should be understood not just as the desire to establish military primacy over other *states;* the driving logic runs deeper than this. Underpinning Washington's posture toward other powers has been a desire to consolidate a unique structural position within the global order, and it has needed to defend this position from a wide range of challenges. These have often been states or, as in the Cold War, a "bloc" of states opposed to the free reign of American power. But in addition, Washington has had to intervene at numerous points to remove armed and unarmed *nonstate* threats to its position, whether these are packaged up as "communist subversives," "international drug traffickers," or "global terrorists." In fact, challenges to American interests have regularly appeared "from below." In turn, defending these interests has often necessitated the imposition of "order" and "stability" from above, acting through preexisting state forms.

In this light, we find to be problematic those analyses of US grand strategy that understand it to be driven by the benevolent desire to act as a "world policeman" or "global sheriff" in the international sphere, preserving order and peace for the benefit of all. This is not to say that there aren't government officials acting for altruistic reasons (clearly there are) or to deny that programs—often funded to the tune of millions of dollars—exist which are designed to provide basic humanitarian aid or to protect universally recognized human rights. But it *is* to challenge the fundamental underlying claim of liberal international theory as it applies to the United States: namely, that Washington has acted (indeed, should act and will act under Obama) to build a global society for the benefit of all (bar the odd "rogue state" or "international terrorist group," which simply refuses to play by the civilized world's rules).

The consistent prioritization of US interests comes as no surprise to us, and we do not consider it to be a wildly contentious point. However, putting this fact center stage leads one to a particular understanding—clearly borne out, we believe, by the empirical record—of the objectives of US planners and of how these have played into the construction of global order. Specifically, we view the current liberal order to be profoundly hierarchical. Although debates over labeling the United States an "empire" have often generated more heat than light, the term does capture a fundamental characteristic of its global rule. The United States is not simply the most powerful state within the current order; it has structured that order itself so as to reinforce its preponderance in the system and to ensure that no rival power (state or otherwise) has the capacity to challenge its position. Time and again throughout this book, we will see this imperial logic at work. And, we would predict that significant changes to this underlying logic during the Obama administration are highly unlikely. The United States has adopted an imperial grand strategy throughout the postwar era, with a remarkable degree of success, and it will continue to do so into the future. This will be the case even as emerging "counterhegemonic" powers in the system (such as China) increasingly present a challenge to American global rule, and the twenty-first century begins to look less like an American era than did the twentieth.

Hierarchy in the system isn't enough to mark out imperial relations. A further condition of empire is the defense of this hierarchical order through a violation of its rules, most clearly through the use of military force. For John Ikenberry, it is this unilateral use of power by the dominant state, *acting outside the order which has been established for the benefit of that state*, which marks out an empire: "The key difference between empire and hegemony is that in an empire, the lead state operates unilaterally and outside the order, whereas in a hegemonic order, the lead establishes multilateral rules and institutions *that it itself operates within.*"[29] It is the repeated exercise of US power outside of these rules since 1945, combined with the particular understanding of long-standing US strategic objectives, that underpins our framing of contemporary US foreign policy within the language of empire.[30] And in doing so, of course, we take issue with the "new imperial discourse" that emerged during the Bush administration and which looked to explain the rise of empire simply by reference to the assertive, openly imperial brand of neoconservatism that gained power in Washington for eight years. The inherent "periodization" that characterizes much of the recent work on US imperialism is misleading and fails to capture the enduring nature of the US imperial project.[31]

In continuing to make use of an imperial discourse, we need to take care. This is not least because of the pejorative connotations traditionally associated with it, and not least because the US imperium—the form that Washington's rule takes—exhibits manifestly different characteristics when compared with past empires. In particular, the lack of significant territorial expansion on behalf of the American state marks out its global rule as substantially new. As Simon Bromley acknowledges: "The *differentia specifica* of [US] imperialism is that it is exercised indirectly through, between and among states that maintain their *de jure* sovereignty, rather than through direct—that is, colonial—imposition. It is an empire fully attuned to the post-colonial world."[32]

This characteristic of US rule does not preclude it from being considered imperial in nature. In fact, although territorial acquisition has historically been a common method for imperial rule, it is far from necessary. To paraphrase Michael Cox, the real issue is not the means employed to consolidate the desired rule, but the form of desired rule itself.[33] Historically, empires have achieved this through a particular mix of strategies. These range, on the one hand, from direct colonial rule and forcible subjugation under military and political conquest to the consolidation of indirect rule through preexisting state forms and local, co-opted elite structures on the other.[34] With this in mind, we find that Alejandro Colás and Rick Saull's definition of "empire" captures the concept's core essence: it needs to be understood as a "hierarchical and exploitative [form] of rule over diverse territories and peoples from and for a metropolitan centre."[35] And as we will see, US planners not only desire American power to be assured vis-à-vis allies and rivals, and work not only to hedge against and destroy all significant threats to this preponderance. Crucially, they also seek to entrench this power within a hierarchical order that best serves US interests (albeit within a system comprised of formally equal and sovereign states), and they do so through a repeated violation of the rules of this order.

## Imperial Logics?

If the United States is rightfully considered to be at the helm of an imperial project, then it is certainly an empire like no other. Washington's rule is decidedly postcolonial, with few attempts to acquire territory for direct rule. Instead, the asymmetric patterns of relations that exist at the heart of the US empire are largely sustained through the co-option of preexisting elite structures in key states, with US personnel (civilian and military) taking on a supportive, advisory role. Similarly, the current order clearly benefits more than just the United States. The global economy has become increasingly transnationalized, with barriers to trade and investment falling and capital becoming less constrained by state boundaries. Moreover, these features are bound to characterize the global economy well into the future, regardless of the severity of the financial crisis that erupted in late 2008. Washington plays a vital role in directing the path of global economic development and acts to provide a form of political and economic stability for the benefit of globalized capital flows and core states (committed, as they all now are, to preserving and acting within a globalized capitalist economy). It is simply untenable to suggest that the entire world is subjugated under an American imperial yoke, given the positive-sum benefits provided by the liberal economic order to core (capitalist) powers.

How, then, to square our claim of the hierarchy built into the current order—and the intention by US planners to preserve this disparity in power— with the evidently positive-sum nature of the US-led order? For some, the very fact that most within the capitalist core derive benefits from the liberal order is enough to preclude the United States from being considered an empire at all.[36] For others, American empire does exist in an era of globalization and transnationalized capitalist economies, although in a radically different form from past imperial projects, with Washington acting not for its own, national interests, but for the interests of an emergent class of "transnational capitalists."[37] The US state, in this reading, remains the most powerful actor in the system, but globalized capital in the form of transnational corporations is now, in this latest capitalist stage of development, the primary manifestation of the bourgeoisie. Such accounts have much to commend them, and they provide a welcome corrective to works that downplay the positive-sum nature of the contemporary order.

However, in contrast to these scholars, we argue that US empire continues to be a distinctly national project, albeit in an increasingly globalized order. Here we come to one of our central observations: that US strategy in the postwar era has been driven by a dual logic. By this, we mean that the American state has worked to maintain an open global economy within which other core powers and agents of globalized capital (transnational corporations) can participate—a transnational logic—whilst simultaneously ensuring that its own, national interests are pursued within this. For us, reading US strategy as narrowly focused on American national interests, to the exclusion of those of other powers, simply ignores the most fundamental contours of the global order. However, the national logic of US empire remains at the heart of Washington's strategic thinking, and the positive-sum order has been constructed specifically in order to sustain American hegemony over other powers. That is, the liberal global order both reinforces US primacy whilst also delivering critical public goods for other core powers. By promoting and maintaining an order wherein all major powers are content, the United States works to integrate *and thereby pacify* any potential challenges to its privileged position. Moreover, it is granted a unique role within (or even above) this order by other core powers. Eager to maintain a status quo, potential rivals to the US mantle of global hegemony in fact delegate to Washington the task of "systems-maintenance." US hegemony is in turn reinforced and the set of asymmetric relations are consolidated, as the American state gets to play a guiding, managerial role over others. Of course, as the Cold War showed (and as fears of renewed geopolitical rivalry with Russia and China, and even the European Union, remind us), this ability to pacify rival powers is never complete. But to the extent that core states are willing to operate within the US-led liberal order, then US hegemony over that order (and the unique benefits that accrue) is assured.

US hegemony is far from absolute and will no doubt come to an end at some point in the future. There are distinct limits to American power: limits that were discovered in Vietnam several decades ago and limits that have been rediscovered in Iraq. Indeed, the United States may have an overwhelming preponderance of power, but it is far from able to apply that power unimpeded in all locations of the globe and at any point in time. Labeling the American state as an empire does not mean viewing it as omnipotent. Likewise, whether or not the twenty-first century will be as "American" as the twentieth, US dominance is not an immutable fact of global politics. History is not predetermined, and as some have argued (bolstered by the financial crisis of 2008 and thereafter), the very forces that have brought the United States such unprecedented global superiority may contain within them the seeds of its destruction. In this light, we do not seek to reduce the entirety of global politics down to the actions of the American state. However, with all appropriate caveats noted, it remains undeniably the case that the United States has—since the depths of World War II and the dissolution of the European imperial project—retained an immense power within the current global order. Washington has had a unique role in the construction of this order, and it has ensured that its reconstitution from the ashes of the 1940s has served a set of interests that are distinctly American. In this book, we will place a consideration of these interests central to the analysis and chart the ways in which US power has been used to further these through the construction of the postwar liberal order.

Likewise, we will examine the ways in which US global hegemony has been—and remains—underpinned by unchallenged control over vast quantities of oil. This has been so not only because of the direct needs of the US economy, although this goes quite some way to explaining the direction of American strategy. In addition, controlling the conditions under which oil is received by other core powers gives Washington a significant political lever to be operated (or threatened) should the current conditions of intracore peace break down. In the meantime, however, energy supplies flow from producing to consuming economies via an international market, and the US state has been granted (and grants itself) the unique role of providing the ultimate guarantee that this market will continue to function smoothly. We will see this "transnational logic" at play throughout the book, as we chart the ways in which the United States works to "open up" and transnationalize oil-rich economies in the global South, integrating them into the wider global economy. Yet in playing this role on behalf of the capitalist core, Washington is able to pursue its own, national interests, further entrenching its privileged position within the current order. In this sense, the dual logic that drives US strategy overall can be seen clearly at play when examining the control of oil.

In order to ensure that its hegemonic position in the global order remains unchallenged and that the flow of oil onto international markets is stabilized, the United States has long deployed military force across strategic regions of the global South. This was most clearly revealed, of course, during the invasion and occupation of Iraq. The move to secure this vital oil-rich region has thrown into stark relief many of the core dilemmas surrounding the extent and nature of US power. Indeed, the intervention in Iraq represents a nexus of the core themes that animate this book: the role of oil in sustaining American power; the role of American power in securing oil flows; the interrelation between oil and US coercion; the ways in which each of these has been vital to the preservation of a liberal economic order and the smooth transmission of globalized capital; and the imperial logics that drive US strategy in this regard. However, the case of Iraq is just one of many examples of the exercise of US power in the oil-rich South, and this book will chart both the historical evolution of US strategic dominance in the Persian Gulf and the ways in which this strategy has been supplemented by an attempt to open up and stabilize oil-rich zones in the Caspian Basin, West Africa, and Latin America. These regions are crucial to the success (or otherwise) of American global hegemony and so have been the recipients of intense levels of US coercive intervention.

Before we turn to look at these concrete case studies, we must engage in a fuller discussion of the nature of US power, the role that coercive interventions play in sustaining this, and the ways in which the control of oil underpins Washington's global rule. It is to this subject that we turn in the first two chapters.

# CHAPTER ONE

# US Hegemony and Global Energy Security

Dominant themes in American politics and historiography stress the underlying benevolence and principled nature of US foreign policy since 1945, whereby Washington has acted in the world in order to preserve freedom, democracy, and prosperity for Americans and non-Americans alike. We would disagree with this analysis. Without denying that the promotion of such principles for their own sake has formed one of the drivers of US policy, we argue in this chapter that the American state has acted consistently in the world since 1945 in pursuit of its own, very particular interests. As such, the US has deployed its power in the postwar era in order to construct a hierarchical world order with American economic and political interests at its apex. However, unlike the past imperial projects of European powers, this order has not been pursued at the expense of the interests of other core states. Rather, Washington has taken the lead role in establishing a framework within which other major powers can pursue their interests, without the threat of armed attack from neighbors and rivals. This framework—based on an open door trading regime underpinned by American military might—has evolved steadily throughout the postwar era, and it is an unwavering commitment to the policing and reproduction of this particular form of global-capitalist political economy that has allowed the US to consolidate its position within the system.

This commitment has required the US to adopt a complex strategy to achieve its objectives. First and most obviously, it has worked to establish and maintain American primacy in the international sphere. Overwhelming global military and economic dominance—established by default at the end of World War II and actively maintained ever since—ensures that the US can exert influence throughout the liberal order and places it in a privileged position when it comes to protecting it from major challenge. The pursuit of primacy has required a strategy to contain existing or emerging rivals and to dissuade others from engaging in competition for hegemony over key regions. Second, and in stark contrast to past imperial projects, Washington has worked to integrate other core powers—both allied and otherwise—within the liberal order, thereby pacifying potential competitors for hegemony and neutralizing the perceived need by others to "balance" against American power. In so doing, it has driven the liberalization of the global economy, so as to provide "public goods" for the capitalist core through the promotion of positive-sum trade whilst also cementing its position as the global hegemon. Third, American planners have worked to open up key economies in the global South in order to facilitate the smooth transmission and operation of transnational capital for the benefit of the liberal core. The first half of this chapter examines US strategy in the postwar era in this regard and outlines the national and transnational logics that drive Washington's relations with the world. This dual logic seeks both to directly enhance US national interests in the world and to maintain a world order conducive to the generic reproduction of global capitalism, given that this in turn underpins US hegemony. It is this logic that explains the unique (and relatively benign) characteristics of the American empire, wherein previously rival powers are overwhelmingly pacified (for now) by the overdetermining nature of US power.[1]

In the second half of the chapter, we will explore how Washington's global strategy plays out in relation to its energy security agenda. We will see that concerns over energy security are increasingly prevalent amongst US planners and that the Bush administration focused particular effort on prioritizing this issue, with the Obama administration continuing this theme. Consequently, the US has long acted to retain dominance over, and uninterrupted access to, the world's major oil supplies, principally in the Persian Gulf. However, the many energy interventions in the oil-rich South, discussed at length in later chapters, have not been designed to extract oil for the sole benefit of the United States, or even primarily for US oil companies. Instead, such interventions have been intended to facilitate integration of oil-rich political economies into the wider global economy, for the benefit of all major players within it. And in addition, the assumption by Washington of a managerial role over this integrative process gives it significant structural power vis-à-vis its rivals, because of the position it holds as the ultimate guarantor of (or, dependent on one's position, the ultimate threat to) world energy supplies. In other words, the importance accorded by Washington to energy security is due both to the fact that a large proportion of America's oil is imported from foreign sources and, crucially, to the power that control of oil provides the US in relation to other players within the system.

## US Grand Strategy in the Postwar Era: American Hegemony and the Liberal Order

US planners have long worked to shape the international sphere in such a way as to allow its interests to be pursued as far as possible. In the postwar era, this strategy has been implemented within the context of unsurpassed American global supremacy. Even at the height of the Cold War, US power in almost every sphere was unmatched by its opponents in the Communist Bloc, notwithstanding the existence of a Soviet nuclear arsenal that constrained certain policy pathways. This supremacy was granted, to a large extent, by the cataclysm of World War II and the consequent decline of British hegemony. Washington's preeminence in the immediate postwar era was underwritten by its unrivaled military, political, and economic power, with the US owning almost half of the world's manufacturing capacity, the majority of its food supply, and nearly all of its capital reserves.[2] And US interests quickly coalesced around maintaining this position. This was captured clearly in 1948 by George Kennan, a central architect of the US-led order during the Cold War. According to Kennan, the US had "about 50% of the world's wealth, but only 6.3% of its population . . . In this situation, we cannot fail to be the object of envy and resentment. Our real task in the coming period is to devise a pattern of relationships that will permit us to maintain this position of disparity."[3]

The pursuit of US interests in this way became the cornerstone of strategy during the Cold War from its earliest years. This is, we should say, a relatively unorthodox reading of US Cold War strategy. Whilst we acknowledge that "containment" of Soviet power was one of the primary objectives of American strategy, it was by no means the only one.[4] Rather than simply reacting against an aggressive Soviet Union, as the standard reading of American policy suggests, US planners often inflated the threat from Moscow in order to legitimate various policies and worked actively to construct a global system within which US power would predominate. Although this objective necessarily took account of a hostile Soviet Union, Washington's strategic rationale was far from driven by this consideration alone. According to NSC 68, perhaps the most important national security document laying out Washington's strategy during the Cold War, "we must make ourselves strong . . . in the development of our military and economic strength" so as to "foster a world environment *in which the American system can survive and flourish.*" And, crucially, this was a policy "we would probably pursue even if there were no Soviet threat."[5] Throughout the Cold War, US objectives included the deterrence of military attack and political gains by the USSR, but also a strengthening of US influence throughout the world, specifically in order to "ensure the US access to foreign markets, and to ensure the US and its allies and friends access to foreign energy and mineral resources."[6]

US grand strategy has sought to establish primacy within the system in a very different way from earlier hegemonic projects. Specifically, it has not relied upon locking rival centers of power out of zones of economic production and prosperity as the old mercantilist powers had done but, in fact, quite the contrary: it has sought the integration of close allies, neutral powers, and emerging rivals alike within a global order structured to provide substantial benefits to all. This order is organized around an economically open liberal international system, highly conducive for capital penetration and circulation within the capitalist core.[7] The centrality of the United States in underwriting global capitalism was recognized early on by US planners. In 1942, Secretary of State Cordell Hull argued that leadership "towards a new system of international relations in trade and other economic affairs will devolve largely on the United States because of our great economic strength." He went on to assert that the US "should assume this leadership and the responsibility that goes with it, primarily for the reasons of pure national self-interest."[8]

The central role to be played by the US state was encapsulated with the development of the "Grand Area" strategy during the early 1940s. Orchestrated by the influential Council on Foreign Relations and senior US policymakers, the strategy emerged from an analysis of the causes of World War II, which were attributed to the disintegration of the interwar international order in the face of the Depression, and the resulting emergence of rival spheres of influence and protectionist economic blocs amongst capitalist powers. The lesson to be drawn was that, in order to prevent future depressions and the possibility of war between the core capitalist powers, Western planners should seek to foster forms of economic interdependency between their respective economies, thereby eliminating the potential for interimperial rivalry.[9]

To this end, the US sought to open up what had been hitherto-closed territories for investors and traders and pursued the incorporation of rival capitalist nations under US economic, political, and military hegemony: what has been termed the "open door" strategy.[10] Moreover, it required the breakup of the old European empires, as Washington sought to include what had been under British imperial control, as well as great swaths of the Western Hemisphere, the Middle East, and East Asia.[11] The promotion of an open liberal trading system under US hegemony was put into stark effect when US Marshall Plan loans to the United Kingdom were made conditional upon the liberalization of the relatively closed Sterling Bloc that had developed under the British empire.[12] According to John Ikenberry, the suppression of rivalry between the core capitalist economies under US hegemony was designed to "solve the internal problems of Western industrial capitalism" and so ensure the long-term "economic and military viability" of the US by securing "markets and supplies of raw materials in Asia and Europe."[13] Echoing the earlier postwar planners, for example, the Nixon administration underlined Washington's commitment to a "secure and friendly environment for American investments in Europe and for the operation of transnational corporations based on American capital, and the assurance of a mutually profitable trade relationship with Western Europe in the first instance but encompassing in time the entire continent."[14]

This was further concretized with the emergence of the US dollar as the global currency of trade in the face of the unilateral abandonment of the gold standard by the Nixon administration. It was in this context that the US led a drive to fundamentally change economic policy throughout the core, via a newly emergent neoliberal model that heavily circumscribed the role of the state in economic affairs and that privileged the open market as the primary mechanism for provision of universal wealth and security. The rise of a neoliberal doctrine sought to rebalance the power between capital and organized labor whilst freeing an increasingly internationally orientated capital from the shackles of the postwar Keynesian framework.[15] And with this in mind, the task of consolidating and underwriting a capitalist global political economy internationalized the American state in relation to its "national" interests and its subsequent obligations. Henry Kissinger captured this new reality when he reminded the former European colonial powers that the "United States [had] global interests and responsibilities" whilst "our European allies" merely "have regional interests."[16]

## US Grand Strategy in an "Age of Globalization": Continuity in the Post–Cold War Era

In contrast to orthodox readings of international history, which stress the discontinuity in global politics at the end of the Cold War, we would argue that the core themes of US grand strategy during the Cold War continued to drive policy after 1991. Since US Cold War strategy was driven by a desire to establish unparalleled hegemony in the international sphere, as opposed to simply contain and destroy the Soviet Union, it is unsurprising that the USSR's demise did not significantly alter Washington's underlying objectives. Of course, the policies enacted to attain these objectives were often subject to change as particular contingencies arose and as competing readings on the best use of American power in the so-called new world order became concretized within various administrations. But overall, US planners continued to seek integration of other core powers within the US-led order as well as the ability to dissuade and destroy rivals to American primacy.

The Cold War saw the removal of significant constraints to economic integration that accompanied the collapse of the Soviet Union, and this led to a further acceleration of the globalizing tendencies of the capitalist world under US hegemony. Standard readings of "globalization" interpret it as, in Joseph Stiglitz's words, "the closer integration of the countries and peoples of the world [through] the breaking down of artificial barriers to the flows of goods, services, capital, knowledge and (to a lesser extent) people."[17] This understanding of barriers as "artificial" is immensely powerful, because it makes a laissez-faire global economy appear natural, desirable, and inevitable. In fact, processes of economic globalization derive from a highly directed set of policies and strategies, devised and enacted throughout treasuries of the core powers and the international financial institutions (IFIs) and operationalized through a very particular global trade architecture. In the post–Cold War era, the result has been the tearing down of barriers to the circulation of international finance, with a wave of privatizations and neoliberal reforms sweeping the globe.[18] In this sense, economic globalization marked a decisive shift from a *world* economy to a *global* economy, with national markets, linked together by international trade and with nation-states providing a mediating role, giving way to an increasingly transnationalized market wherein global capital was free to operate.

Aside from the continued commitment to the ongoing globalization of capitalism, Washington also sought to consolidate its strategic and geopolitical power throughout the 1990s. This objective was seen quite starkly in a leaked draft of the 1992 *Defense Planning Guidance* (*DPG*). Authored within the Pentagon, and cleared by Colin Powell (then chair of the Joint Chiefs of Staff) and Paul Wolfowitz (then undersecretary of defense for policy), the *DPG* argued for the US to extend its global hegemony and to continue to pacify rivalries emerging in the core, through the maintenance of key US-led defense structures. Specifically, the document insisted that the US needed to "refocus on precluding the emergence of any potential future global competitor" and guard against "other potential nations or coalitions that could, in the further future, develop strategic aims and a defense posture of region-wide or global domination."[19] The resulting outcry from US public and allied governments led to the redrafting of the guidance, although the essence of the strategy remained the same.[20]

Indeed, whilst many assumed that the key ideas were abandoned after the furor caused by the leaked version, the changes made were in fact relatively insignificant. According to James Mann, working at the influential Center for Strategic and International Studies (CSIS), US planners "recognized that the notion of America blocking a rival power was the part that had engendered controversy" and so "dropped the language about competitors" in later drafts. However, this did not signal that the idea had been abandoned; in fact, the rewrite "encompassed a more breathtaking vision: the United States would build up its military capabilities *to such an extent that there could never be a rival.*" US military superiority would be so overwhelming that any state even contemplating a challenge to US primacy would realize that it would be self-defeating to try.[21] The report was released publicly in largely unchanged form by Dick Cheney at the end of the elder Bush administration's term in office:

> Simply put, it is the intent of the new Regional Defense Strategy to enable the US to lead in shaping an uncertain future so as to preserve and enhance [the] strategic depth won at such great pains . . . Together with our allies, we must preclude hostile nondemocratic powers from dominating regions critical to our interests and otherwise work to build an international environment conducive to our values. Yet, even as we hope to increasingly rely on collective approaches to solve international problems, we recognize that a collective effort may not always be timely and, in the absence of US leadership, may not gel. Where the stakes so merit, we must have forces ready to protect our critical interests.

And importantly, the regions seen to be "critical to our interests"—and within which the US would work to preclude the emergence of oppositional hegemonic forces—encompassed virtually the entire globe, including "Europe, East Asia, the Middle East / Persian Gulf and Latin America."[22] As the United States stood on the edge of unrivaled global supremacy for the first time, influential defense and foreign policy intellectuals—Republican and Democrat alike—increasingly coalesced around the theme of US world "leadership" through unparalleled strength.[23] Throughout the 1990s, as American military and economic strength continued to expand, US planners actively sought to make sure that this power continued to underpin the liberal order and so maintain Washington's position within it. And it is in the context of this fundamental continuity in US grand strategy—spanning both Cold War and post–Cold War eras—that we should understand the main elements of American policy since 2001.

## US Grand Strategy and the War on Terror

As we saw in the introduction, the US state under George W. Bush responded to the attacks of 9/11 with an increased militarization of American foreign policy and a wide-ranging set of coercive interventions across the world. But although this response was justified by reference to the severity of the global terrorist threat facing the American people, US strategy during the Bush administration was not all that it might seem. It was *not* principally designed to defend the US from the threat of Islamist terrorism and "terrorist supporting" states (the so-called axis of evil).[24] Rather, secondary and subsidiary objectives aside, it was designed to expand and entrench American global hegemony in line with Washington's longstanding strategic objectives. And to the extent that terrorist groups with a global reach *were* considered to pose a significant threat to core US interests, of concern was the threat they posed to Washington's ability to establish and maintain its hegemony within the present order. In this reading, we would agree with Peter Gowan that the invasions of Afghanistan and Iraq primarily represented "tactical steps" in a "larger strategic turn to change US-*global* relations," with 9/11 utilized as a "legitimating mechanism" for this goal. For Gowan: "The attacks on Afghanistan and Iraq were to be *tactical* means in a global strategy for global programmatic goals . . . The war on Afghanistan and then Iraq as well as the other campaigns against the axis of evil and the Palestinian armed resistance should thus be seen as steps toward the goals of asserting *US disciplinary power at the global level.*"[25]

We are not arguing that US planners were engaged in a coordinated conspiracy to defraud the American public and the world at large regarding their concerns over the threat posed by global terrorism to US interests (although at points officials clearly lied in order to mobilize support for a particular policy).[26] Al Qaeda surely did (and still does) pose a threat to the core interests of the American state and, insofar as it represents a symbolic challenge to US global hegemony, it is understandable that US planners in the Bush administration desired the group's destruction. However, it remains the case that—and this is a point passed over by many analysts—the ultimate strategic objective of the United States in the post-9/11 era has remained the maintenance of its hegemonic position and the regulation and pacification of emerging rival powers. In this sense, the rhetoric of the war on terror served a wider purpose: it provided the political room for maneuver necessary for achieving fundamental and long-term geostrategic objectives.

On occasions, this functional aspect of the war on terror was acknowledged by those in power. According to Condoleezza Rice, the opportunities presented by the events of 9/11 had to be capitalized upon and harnessed to the advantage of Washington. Through the war on terror, the United States may have been seeking to remove the capacity of global jihadist forces and "rogue states" to threaten its interests; but it was also incumbent upon the administration to use the moment to *fundamentally change the shape of the world and America's relations to it.* Rice stated that, as the international order underwent major changes, it was "important to try to seize on that and position American interests and institutions and all of that before they harden again."[27]

These deeper currents were also captured by several strategic documents released by the Bush administration. The publication of the 2002 *National Security Strategy (NSS)* was a milestone in setting out the thinking of the Bush team. With its release, significant attention was paid by many to the section focused on the triad of threats posed by terrorism, rogue states, and weapons of mass destruction (WMD) and on the necessity of adopting a policy of preventative strikes to counter the threat.[28] This was especially true given the legal consequences of this policy and the unprecedented declaration by Washington of its intent to bypass international norms regarding the use of force.[29] However, this new assertiveness over the *means* of US statecraft in the post-9/11 era only attained full significance when married to the equally brash declaration of policy *goals*. In this context, global terrorism actually represented just one form of threat to US interests and, overall, America's strategic posture needed to "maintain the capability to defeat *any attempt* by an enemy . . . to impose its will on the United States, our allies or our friends . . . Our forces will be strong enough to dissuade potential adversaries from pursuing a military build up in the hopes of surpassing, or equalling, the power of the United States."[30]

It is this theme of ensuring superiority over *all* potential rivals and other threats, combined with an explicit determination to deploy military force to achieve this end (in direct and acknowledged violation of standing international law) that formed the centerpiece of US grand strategy post-9/11. And nor was the *NSS* an anomalous publication. Indeed, rather than marking a high tide in US unilateralism, its themes were echoed throughout later planning documents. For example, alongside a detailed exposition of US strategy for dealing with global terrorism in the "Long War," the 2006 *Quadrennial Defense Review* (QDR) argued that the US "will also seek to ensure that no foreign power can dictate the terms of regional or global security. It will attempt to dissuade any military competitor from developing disruptive or other capabilities that could enable regional hegemony or hostile action against the United States or other friendly countries, and it will seek to deter aggression or coercion. Should deterrence fail, the United States would deny a hostile power its strategic and operational objectives."[31]

This objective was spelled out in further detail in the 2008 *National Defense Strategy*, which saw threats to US power and interests stemming not just from al Qaeda but also from "the rising military power of other states," which "may actively seek to counter the United States in some or all domains of traditional warfare or to gain an advantage by developing capabilities that offset our own." In response, the strategy was clear that "for the foreseeable future, we will need to hedge against [rivals'] growing military modernization and the impact of [their] strategic choices upon international security," specifically in order to "mitigate near term challenges while preserving and enhancing US national advantages over time."[32]

It is this wider understanding of US strategic posture during the Bush administration that helps explain the size of the US military budget. US defense expenditure at the end of the Bush term represented no less than 45 percent of total global military spending, more than ten times the size of any potential challenger.[33] It is also this understanding, rather than the immediate needs of the war on terror, which primarily explained the global positioning of US forces in over two-thirds of the world's states with, on any given day during the mid-2000s, almost 350,000 personnel deployed in around 130 countries to "protect and advance US interests and values."[34] This vast array of bases exemplifies the Pentagon's post–Cold War thinking, which has driven a change in US military presence from large, static bases in relatively few locations to a so-called lily pad basing structure, designed to enable rapid and sustained projection of power throughout the globe. As Peter Pace, then vice chairman of the Joint Chiefs of Staff, stated: "Our [global basing] concept is framed to position US forces optimally to influence the threats we now face and create a [worldwide] presence and capacity."[35] US naval posture has been designed explicitly to "control the seas, assure access, and project power beyond the sea, to influence events and advance American interests across the full spectrum of military operations." This control is to be truly global, exercised "anywhere, anytime, around the world, around the clock," with a vast array of sea bases designed to "project direct and decisive power around the globe."[36] Significantly, this posture is designed to "project the sovereignty of the United States globally" and ties in with a defense strategy that views "full spectrum dominance" as the ultimate goal: an ability to "defeat any adversary and control any situation across the range of military operations."[37]

Despite several high-profile policy shifts with regard to individual military campaigns, the Obama administration looks set to support this defense posture; the underlying doctrine of global military presence and unsurpassed supremacy remains central to Washington's strategy. Obama himself has been clear that the US retains the unilateral right to "maintain the strongest, best-equipped military in the world in order to defeat and deter conventional threats" and that he supports the expansion of ground forces by over 90,000 personnel. Indeed, Obama has explicitly rejected "the notion that the American moment has passed. I dismiss the cynics who say that this new century cannot be another when, in the words of President Franklin Roosevelt, we lead the world in battling immediate evils and promoting the ultimate good."[38] To this end the Obama administration has in fact *increased* military spending over that of the previous Bush administration. In Bush's last year in power, the Pentagon asked for a $515 billion baseline with an additional $70 billion for ongoing operations in the war on terror. A year later, with Obama in office, the request was 20 percent higher and stood at $534 billion with an additional $130 billion.[39] In this way, the centrality of overwhelming US military power continues to form a cornerstone of Obama's foreign policy, with a common strategic framework underpinning the change in mood-music. As the 2010 budget request made clear:

> While today's strategic environment is characterized by a high degree of uncertainty—particularly given the global economic crisis—what remains clear is America's enduring core interest in the health and security of the broader international system. From the end of World War II to the conclusion of the Cold War with the Soviet Union, the United States remained committed to sustaining an international system whose very existence was commensurate with America's desire to maintain open commerce, ensure the security of its friends and allies, and help further the spread of liberty and peace. In this respect, the touchstone of American strategy during last century's Cold War remains relevant to today's challenges.[40]

US planners have since 1945 helped to construct a liberal international free trade order integrated with (and largely beneficial to) other leading capitalist powers under the tutelage of the US state. Geir Lundestad has termed this process an "empire by invitation" in relation to the major European capitalist powers, with many European capitals welcoming the inward investment of American finance and the security of living under its strategic umbrella.[41] The form of order that developed under Washington's auspices has been consolidated through pulling both firm allies and potential peer competitors alike within its desired global order. As Leo Panitch and Sam Gindin argue, in the new, US-centric order, "the densest imperial networks and institutional linkages, which had earlier run north-south between imperial states and their formal or informal colonies, now came to run between the US and the other major capitalist states." Washington has succeeded where past empires had failed, by "integrating all the other capitalist powers into an effective system of coordination under its aegis."[42] This has been a central goal of US grand strategy in the postwar era and continues to be so during the Obama presidency.

## US Empire and the Global South

If the US-led order has been sustained throughout the postwar era by the high degree of consent from core powers, the picture outside of the capitalist core has been markedly different. Throughout the global South, the workings and consequences of the liberal economic order have often brought its imperial nature into stark relief. Indeed, the durability of this order has been built largely upon the widespread exploitation of important economic zones in the South. Structural underdevelopment has characterized many of these regions, with the US (as the lead capitalist state) leading the integration of the South on terms beneficial to the core.

US strategy toward the South has been largely based upon devising mechanisms for expropriating vital resources and opening up further markets for transnational investment. Whilst US rule in this context rarely involves formal imperial control in the fashion of past European empires, it has nevertheless been designed to establish a clear global hierarchy. In this, we would agree with Susanne Soederberg that American imperialism is based upon "a historically specific expression of domination and exploitation of the US vis-à-vis other countries" with the US state in particular needing to "constantly re-create the conditions of its power by ensuring, *inter alia,* that all states, particularly subordinate or poorer states, adhere to the international rules and laws in order to facilitate the reproduction of capitalist social relations."[43] The reorientation of political economies in the South toward the requirements of the core has required a co-option of local elites willing to undertake drastic economic restructuring under the tutelage of the US Treasury, the World Bank, and the International Monetary Fund (IMF). These institutions have been accorded primary responsibility for guiding economic "development" in the South throughout the postwar era and where necessary have exerted devastating economic coercion toward certain regions. In this way, they have had a long record in forcibly opening up economic zones in the South for penetration by global capital and disciplining (or even liquidating) those elites who do not prove suitably responsive to the interests of the wider order.[44]

This drive to break down the "artificial" barriers to trade and investment has often entailed a dramatic reconfiguration of local political economies. Because economic and political conditions on the ground are often not conducive to the free movement of capital, it has become a vital requirement to alter such conditions if need be. By acting to remove these barriers in the South (so-called distortions to the economy), the United States and the IFIs have worked to transform prevailing economic conditions into a form more conducive to wider integration.[45] Through this restructuring process, suitable investment climates for foreign corporations are cultivated through a variety of means. Since the mid-1970s, such efforts have been organized under what has been termed the "Washington Consensus"; essentially a blueprint for a suitably globalized economy, structured along neoliberal lines. These include the opening up of new markets with the privatization of state-owned enterprises; an extensive process of deregulation to abolish those "excessive" regulations that impede competition; the abolition of barriers to the entry of foreign direct investment (FDI) from abroad; the reduction of trade restrictions; financial liberalization; and, crucially, the cementing of a legal system geared toward defending the sanctity of contracts and private property.[46] Economies that undergo this form of neoliberal restructuring present an attractive site for foreign investment, since transnational corporations are guaranteed a free movement of capital into and out of individual regions at will and have their profit-making operations within each country secured through force of law.

Despite the fact that proponents of neoliberal globalization argue that the opening up of local economies represents the most powerful engine for social and economic progress within the South,[47] the global economic order has in fact been constructed to serve the interests of transnational capital over and above the interests of local populations. US-led economic globalization is, in many ways, the continuation of an age-old imperial strategy—accumulation by dispossession—with the privileged position of global capitalist elites irrevocably tied to the economic exploitation of the South.[48] Globalization has developed in a "lopsided way," with trade liberalization proceeding far more slowly in economic sectors where developing countries are more competitive and reform efforts have focused on removing restrictions on the freedom of movement of capital (given that this is where industrialized countries have a distinct comparative advantage).[49] Free trade and investment agreements clearly seek to benefit core-based exporters and firms at the expense of those in the South.[50]

Perhaps unsurprisingly, such imbalances in globalization have had profound consequences for poverty levels and rates of socioeconomic development across regions experiencing "integration." According to one high-level UN official, speaking just within the context of the agricultural sector, liberalization of trade and investment across the South has caused "greater hunger and poverty, as peasants have been pushed off their land to make way for large-scale plantations," leading to widespread poverty as "the production of basic staple foods has been hit by competition from cheap imports." In fact, while processes of economic globalization clearly benefit those entities with substantial capital, primarily large corporations, "the poor are finding it increasingly difficult to subsist, particularly in a context of lack of alternative employment."[51] The social consequences for many of traveling down the "adjustment road" has even been noted in research sponsored by the World Bank: "The problem is not that the reform process has failed to generate economic benefits. It is that these benefits have tended to be concentrated in a relatively few hands, both domestic and foreign, while millions of other people have increasingly been deprived of the resources and opportunities they require to move out of poverty."[52]

The process of transnationalizing critical economic zones in the South has not always proceeded smoothly. Chronic instability characterizes much of the South, often as a result of weak governance and large wealth disparities. In turn, this has meant that global capital has in many cases lacked the confidence to invest where it would otherwise hope to. As Colin Powell stated when he was US secretary of state, "Capital is a coward. It is only drawn to places where there is the clarity of law, where the society and the government rest on a body of law . . . Capital in this globalized world, where you can move capital instantaneously by the flick of a mouse switch, capital will go to where it is going to be safe, where it can find a return on its investment."[53]

In addition, the presence of a range of social and political forces actively organized against US-led economic integration—and against US hegemony more broadly—has in many instances led to "counterhegemonic" struggles throughout the South. Whether armed or unarmed, these have posed a major threat to political and economic stability, to continued investment by global capital, and to the sustained projection of American power. As such, the US has needed to defend the global order from a variety of challenges emerging from the South, often by force of arms. "Stabilizing" capitalist social relations in these regions has been a core strategic objective of the US state throughout the postwar era and plays a prominent role in Washington's policy toward the oil-rich South. The means by which it attempts to achieve this will be examined in detail in chapter 2.

## The Logics of American Power

We would caution against developing an overly "reductive" understanding of global politics, whereby core states in the international system are engaged in a geopolitical struggle with each other for access to resources, markets, and influence, with the US dominant over all others. In its realist variant, this reductive position has a tendency to focus on relative power distribution in the system and the geopolitical dominance of Washington in these terms. In its more Marxian variant, the US state is primarily a *tool* to be manipulated and utilized by the nationally based (i.e., American) capitalist class in order to maximize its specific economic interests at the expense of others. As John Foster has argued, "Intercapitalist rivalry remains the hub of the imperialist wheel . . . In the present period of global hegemonic imperialism the United States is geared above all to expanding its imperial power to whatever extent possible and subordinating the rest of the capitalist world to its interests."[54]

Such accounts, we believe, miss out on a crucial aspect of US hegemony. The sheer durability of US rule in the postwar era is based in no small part upon its ability to establish significant consent amongst core powers. The integrative process is reliant upon states "buying in" to a rules-based global order underpinned by American power, and the US has adopted a distinct *managerial* role in this capitalist order. In this way, there is an obvious transnational logic driving US strategy. William Robinson has done much to explore this aspect of American power and has argued that the United States has "taken the lead in developing policies and strategies on behalf of the global capitalist agenda." For Robinson, globalization "has emerged in the period of worldwide US dominance, and the concentration of resources and coercive powers within the US national state allows it to play a leadership role on behalf of a transnational elite," whilst "US military conquest does not result in the creation of exclusive zones for the conquerors' exploitation . . . but the colonization and recolonization of the vanquished for the new global capitalism and its agents." In this context, "the US military apparatus is the ministry of war in the cabinet of an increasingly globally integrated ruling class," and US military preponderance acts not to secure American hegemony vis-à-vis potential geopolitical rivals but rather for the interests of transnational capital as a whole.[55]

This account provides a welcome corrective to traditional "interimperial rivalry" analyses of global politics under US hegemony. Robinson's work on the active role played by the US state in creating an environment conducive to the interests of global capital stands out as a nuanced understanding of the logic of American power. We would also warn against moving too far in this direction, and see a counterproductive tendency amongst some to downplay (or ignore altogether) the continuing *national* logic underpinning US strategy.[56] Epitomized by Michael Hardt and Antonio Negri's work *Empire,* such global capitalist approaches argue that, in important ways, nation-states and the rivalry between them have been superseded by a new, nonlinear form of rule that enmeshes all within its sphere of influence. For Hardt and Negri, "conflict or competition among several imperialist powers has in many important respects been replaced by the idea of a single power that over determines them all, structures them in a unitary way, and treats them under one common notion of right that is decidedly postcolonial and post imperialist."[57]

Similarly, Leslie Sklair has argued that "British or French or Japanese or US imperialism" has tended to be viewed incorrectly in "state-centrist terms," because a new, transnational capitalist class is emerging that renders obsolete the notion of national (or nationally based class) interests. Indeed, with the advent of a "genuinely globalising capitalist system dominated by a transnational capitalist class, the ideas of national interest and national economy were revealed for the ideological tools that they were."[58] Robinson himself has picked up on this idea of a new, deterritorialized, transnational state (TNS): nation-states have not withered away but have been transformed into units that are responsive primarily to the needs of transnational capital. In this sense, the nascent TNS comprises transnational institutions that "maintain, defend, and advance the emergent hegemony of a global bourgeoisie and its project of constructing a new global capitalist historical bloc."[59]

Both the interstate rivalry and global capitalist approaches capture core elements of the nature of contemporary international relations. In isolation, however, they each miss out on crucial aspects of US statecraft that have developed under forms of globalization in the postwar period. Just as traditional interstate rivalry theorists pay insufficient attention to the positive-sum, *transnational* logic of US power, global capitalist theorists such as Robinson fail to take sufficient account of Washington's *national* agenda to ensure that no other power has the means to dictate or significantly influence the terms of the current system. Importantly, these two logics cannot be reduced to independent instruments of power. It is not simply the case that the transnational logic can be equated to Washington's economic policy, based around the integration of the global economy under the tutelage of the US state. Similarly, the national logic does not simply speak to a Pentagon policy for unilateral military superiority. Instead, each of these instruments of power—

economic and military—is in turn driven by a dual national and transnational logic.[60]

## The Dual Logics of American Power

US military power is not merely a tool for global dominance over all other powers. As the 2001 Department of Defense *Annual Report* served to remind observers, US military strategic presence throughout the globe serves to provide a "general sense of stability and confidence, which is crucial to the economic prosperity that benefits much of the world" and which "underpin[s] the political stability on which the prosperity of civilized nations is built."[61] This positive-sum logic to the deployment of US military power was reiterated by the 2008 version of the Pentagon's *National Defense Strategy,* which declared that the US "required freedom of action in the global commons and strategic access to important regions of the world [not only] to meet our national security needs." In addition: "For more than sixty years, the United States has secured the global commons for the benefit of all. Global prosperity is contingent on the free flow of ideas, goods and services. The enormous growth in trade has lifted millions of people out of poverty by making locally produced goods available on the global market. Low barriers to trade also benefit consumers by reducing the cost of goods." As a result, the Pentagon has been designated a unique role in ensuring that the conditions for "global prosperity" are met, with top military objectives including the promotion of stability to "foster economic growth and [secure] the global commons and with them access to world markets and resources."[62]

However, it is also incorrect to regard US military power merely as a tool for an increasingly globalized capitalism, with no nationally based logic at play. Rather, as we have seen, coercive force is utilized by Washington to both enable global markets to function and to maintain direct US primacy among other powers. This dual logic has seen Washington play a systems-maintaining role, which in turn has reinforced US hegemony as other core powers have looked to Washington to sustain the liberal order. In this way, the US gets to "mediate" the relationship between the global order and those forces that would bring it down. By defining the threat facing the core—whether this be a rival state (the USSR, Iran), a nonstate group of global reach (al Qaeda), or a nonpersonified understanding of challenges to "international" security ("instability," "popular nationalism")—Washington is granted the authority to employ its political, economic, and military power in "response" and so defend the system for all.

Likewise, US attempts to build an open door economic order, and to integrate capitalist powers within it, cannot be read simply as a state-led strategy enacted on behalf of a transnational capitalist class. The US may consciously act to create global outcomes that directly benefit transnational capital; as Robinson argues, the United States "has taken the lead in developing policies and strategies *on behalf of the global capitalist agenda.*"[63] However, in this context, the very drive to free capital from all significant constraints in itself benefits *territorialized* US capital over and above that from other regions, given the overwhelming preponderance that it has within the global market system. This is why Washington has pursued the establishment of an open door global order for so long: not because it is engaged in a continual act of global benevolence, but because open doors, free markets, and level playing fields provide distinct advantages for the American economy over and above all others. Indeed, the specifically *national* logic driving Washington's economic agenda has been well noted by US officials: for instance, President Clinton's national security advisor, Sandy Berger, stated that the US was "best placed to benefit from globalization" and Clinton himself reassured audiences that "you know, we're going to do very, very well, as the world becomes more interdependent."[64]

In particular, the strategy of negotiating free trade agreements (FTAs) in order to tie regions across the world more closely to the American economy provides the framework for the smooth operation of all capital but is also specifically designed to guarantee wider foreign access for US capital. As the Office of the US Trade Representative has made clear, trade is "critical to America's prosperity" and the US faces a problem, because "markets abroad are too closed and US goods, farm products and services face numerous barriers." The US is therefore committed to "actively opening markets abroad for Americans with FTA negotiations in Latin America, Asia, the Middle East, and Africa." The reduction of foreign trade barriers is designed to "give our farmers, ranchers, manufacturers and service providers better access to the 95 percent of the world's customers living outside our borders."[65]

The open door liberal regime constructed under US guidance benefits US-based capital over and above capital from other locations. This is due to the sheer preponderance of US capital but is also a consequence of Washington explicitly according a privileged position to its own economy within the free trade regime. In other words, although an open door order benefits the US more than most, the lead state has worked to retain a firm hand on that door and can close it whenever its core economic interests appear unduly threatened. This can be seen most starkly within the context of the US Congress's ratification of the World Trade Organization Treaty. The WTO is one of the key institutions of global governance and is seen by Robinson specifically, and the global capital school more generally, as one of the principal institutional forms for the emergent TNS. However, Section 301 of the 1974 US Trade Act allows the US Congress to unilaterally reject WTO provisions that may threaten American industries or economic interests. Under this act, the US government reserves the right to identify any practice by a foreign country that restricts US commerce and threatens American economic interests. Interestingly, such practices may "not necessarily [be] in violation of, or inconsistent with, the international legal rights of the United States"—in other words, they may be perfectly legal under the free trade system—as long as Washington determines them to be "otherwise unfair and inequitable." And when such threats are identified, the US is empowered to "suspend, withdraw, or prevent the application of, benefits of trade agreement concessions" or otherwise "impose duties or other import restrictions."[66]

In other words, Washington has reserved the right to act unilaterally outside of the rules of open trade should its national economic interests be threatened, even when such "threats" are fully complying with international trade law. As Gowan has argued, the US has participated in international economic regimes when it suits economic interests, with acceptance of WTO jurisdiction "conditional upon the WTO's being 'fair' to US interests. And all who follow international trade policy know that the word 'fair' in this context means serving and defending US economic interests."[67] Similarly, early indications point to the fact that the Obama administration is continuing to pursue economic protectionism for key sectors of American business that are vulnerable to market competition from non-American corporations, with privileged status being given to American iron and steel corporations as part of a multi-billion-dollar bailout of American capital by American taxpayers.[68]

Instead of arguing that the US state now acts through its unparalleled economic and military power in order to secure a transnational outcome on behalf of transnational capital, it would be more correct to view the US state as acting so as to secure transnational outcomes *and* to ensure that these outcomes primarily benefit US capital. Washington seeks to underwrite and police the liberal international order within which it enjoys a hegemonic position and in so doing develops specific capacities to act for global capitalism as a whole (not just for American capitalism), thereby serving both national and transnational interests.[69] As Simon Bromley has succinctly argued, the twin objectives of the American state are "first, 'making the world safe' for capitalism, and second, ensuring its hegemony within the capitalist world," both of which reinforce one another.[70]

## US Hegemony and Global Energy Security

US hegemony within the postwar international order era has been reliant to no small extent upon Washington's ability to exert control over oil reserves in the global South as well as the conditions under which those reserves are released onto international markets. Access to reliable, cheap, and bountiful energy supplies is a core requirement of every industrialized economy, and the US economy is no exception. The US consumes a staggering amount of energy, running at around 100 quadrillion British thermal units (qBtu) per annum and comprising over 20 percent of the global total. As part of this, US oil consumption is simply vast, representing around 40 percent of all energy used in America. Oil use amounts to 21 million barrels per day (mbpd) out of a global consumption of 85 mbpd. In other words, the US consumes no less than 24 percent of all the oil used in any one day; a level that is comparable to the consumption from all European states and Japan combined.[71]

Despite the fact that the US remains the world's third largest oil producer, consumption by the American economy is so great that the majority of the oil has to be imported from foreign sources. In 2006, no less than 60 percent of oil consumption was based on imports, and this proportion is set to rise. The US Department of Energy has forecast that, left unchecked, imports will make up 75 percent of US oil supply by 2030; a situation that clearly presents a fundamental challenge to core US energy security.[72] As this energy gap—the difference between demand and domestic supply—has continued to grow, the problem of ensuring American energy security has steadily worked its way up the agenda of US planners. Although the potential consequences of this energy gap have been forecast by analysts for several decades, they were brought home in vivid style to Americans in the summer of 2000 and again in early

2001, as energy shortages in California led to rolling blackouts affecting tens of thousands of households.[73] As the nation struggled to cope with the idea of energy shortages, tackling this problem became an early priority of the Bush administration and efforts to resolve the growing gap took on an urgency not seen in previous years. Within just one week of his inauguration, President Bush had directed Vice President Dick Cheney to chair the National Energy Policy Development (NEPD) Group: a high-level team that included the secretary of state (Colin Powell), the secretary of the treasury (Paul O'Neill), and several other cabinet-level officials and which was tasked with developing "a national energy policy designed to . . . promote dependable, affordable, and environmentally sound production and distribution of energy for the future."[74]

As the Group conducted its work in the early months of 2001, top officials were dispatched to publicly advertise energy security as a pressing challenge. Bush himself declared that the US faced "an energy shortage, which has caused rising prices and growing uncertainty" and that Washington needed to bolster energy security by ensuring "a steady supply of affordable energy for America's homes and businesses and industry" until "the day America achieves energy independence."[75] Crucial to all this was, according to the final NEPD report, the "fundamental imbalance between supply and demand" within the US, with "our projected energy needs [projected to] far outstrip expected levels of production."[76] Bush's secretary of energy, Spencer Abraham, was clear about what this meant: the US faces "a major energy supply crisis" over the next two decades, and "failure to meet this challenge will threaten our nation's economic prosperity, compromise our national security, and literally alter the way we live our lives."[77]

Much of the final report was wrapped up in the language of energy conservation, the promotion of energy efficiency through developing new technologies, and diversification away from oil and toward renewable sources of energy. According to Bush, the plan was designed to reduce demand without impacting upon levels of economic growth, through harnessing the "American entrepreneurial system" to promote innovation and technology and to "make us the world leader in efficiency and conservation."[78] Much of this rhetoric was in fact an attempt to hide a more significant recommendation of the report: a drive to work "with key countries and institutions to expand the sources and types of global energy supplies," with an *increase* in levels of imported oil through maximizing production levels across the oil-rich South.[79] In this way, ensuring that adequate supplies of foreign oil are produced and exported from oil-rich regions remains a central plank of US energy security strategy.

With the election of Barack Obama, a new emphasis has been placed on reducing American dependency on oil, with Obama himself declaring that US appetite for oil "comes at a tremendous price—a price measured by our vulnerability to volatile oil markets, which send gas prices soaring and families scrambling."[80] In response, Obama echoed Bush's early pronouncements over the urgency of reducing dependency on oil, declaring that "at a time of such great challenge for America [as the financial crisis of 2008–2009], no single issue is as fundamental to our future as energy. America's dependence on oil is one of the most serious threats that our nation has faced."[81] It is too early to make a full assessment of the direction of policy under Obama, although his administration looks to be investing vastly more sums into sustainable energy than his predecessor's and he has declared a target of full energy independence within ten years.[82] However, the sheer scale of American dependency on oil (including, crucially, on foreign oil), and the pervasive nature of this dependency, means that US planners will undoubtedly continue to forge strategies to secure unfettered access to global reserves.

This likely continuity in American strategy toward the oil-rich South is also driven by the fact that the need for access to foreign oil reserves is more than a consequence of the high level of demand for oil from the American economy. In addition, Washington's strategic posture and the sustained projection of military power is fully predicated upon receiving an uninterrupted supply of vast quantities of oil, and this will not change for many years to come. According to a 2007 study commissioned by the Pentagon's Office of Force Transformation and Resources, entitled *Transforming the Way DoD Looks at Energy,* the Pentagon is by far the largest single consumer of oil in the world, with US soldiers now using sixteen times the amount they did during World War II, as military systems become more reliant on fossil fuels. In fact, of all the cargo transported by the US military, more than half consists of fuel, whilst on the battlefield this figure leaps to 80 percent of all transport. Furthermore, the extension and consolidation of the Pentagon's global military footprint through the Bush administration—and the likely continuation of this theme during the Obama administration and beyond—itself necessitates substantive increases in energy use: "The US military will have to be even more energy intense, locate in more regions of the world, employ new technologies, and manage a more complex logistics system. Simply put, more miles will be travelled, both by combat units and the supply units that sustain them, which will result in increased energy consumption."[83]

This reliance on oil for American global military dominance understandably means that US defense planners are concerned with ensuring uninterrupted access to reserves. This is especially the case given the future predictions over reductions and instabilities in global supply, where demand for oil will almost certainly outstrip supply at some point in the near to medium term. In the context of a likely fall in supply, Milton Copulos, president of the National Defense Council Foundation, said: "We have to wake up. We are at the edge of a precipice and we have one foot over the edge." In light of the predicted rises in the military's oil requirements just as supply starts to falter, Copulos stated, the US was "rushing headlong into disaster," with grave consequences for the future of American power.[84] As a result of such concerns, Pentagon officials have moved to reduce the military's reliance on oil.[85] In the near to medium term this goal will undoubtedly be difficult to achieve in any meaningful way, since the bulk of the Pentagon's inventory is dependent on fossil fuels and that the service-life for these tend to be decades-long. As former secretary of defense James Schlesinger testified in 2005: "Until such time as new technologies, *barely on the horizon,* can wean us from our dependence on oil and gas, we shall continue to be plagued by energy insecurity. We shall not end dependence on imported oil."[86]

Even if the US economy and military were able to significantly reduce their reliance on imported oil—a distinctly unlikely possibility despite Bush's, and now Obama's, public pronouncements—its global hegemonic position would still be premised upon playing the foremost role in ensuring the stable supply of oil from the South. This is so because of the *derivative structural power* that US dominance in oil-rich zones affords the US state in relation to other core powers. In this context, controlling access to global oil stocks affirms Washington's relative power vis-à-vis potential and actual rivals. Since any serious challenger to US primacy would require unfettered access to vast quantities of oil and preventing the emergence of any such challenge is a core theme of US strategy, control of this commodity has long been a key objective for the American state. As we have seen, this is an important logic of US hegemony: by establishing an environment beneficial to all core capitalist powers, it also strengthens US primacy over those potential rivals.

Almost every powerful state in the current order (with the exception of Russia, Canada, and the United Kingdom) requires large volumes of imported oil to sustain the demand from its domestic economies. Along with the United States, China and India need to import over half of their oil requirements, whereas members of the G8 such as Japan, France, Germany, and Italy are almost wholly reliant on foreign oil. Moreover, this reliance is set to grow, as increased demand from powerful states is not matched by rises in their domestic production. In fact, the shortfall between consumption and production for the core powers—the extent to which they are reliant upon imports—is set to almost double by 2030. For China, this rise is even more dramatic: as annual oil consumption more than doubles by 2030, relatively static levels of domestic production will cause the resulting energy gap to grow massively. Chinese leaders will need to source an additional 8.6 mbpd from foreign sources by 2030, almost quadrupling the amount of oil needing to be imported into the country. It is in this context that Washington's political and military dominance over oil-rich political economies generates enormous structural power for the American state. And this remains the case regardless of Obama's declared desire to reduce dependency. Zbigniew Brzezinski, President Carter's national security advisor, captured this wider logic when he argued: "America has major strategic and economic interests in the Middle East that are dictated by the region's vast energy supplies. Not only does America benefit economically from the relatively low costs of Middle Eastern oil, but America's security role in the region gives it indirect but politically critical leverage on the European and Asian economies that are also dependent on energy exports from the region."[87]

The role that oil plays in underpinning American supremacy within the international system has driven the formation of a long-term, proactive strategy to ensure that Washington controls access to, and therefore the supply from, oil-rich zones across the South. The mismatch between the geographical distribution of global energy stocks and the location of the largest energy consumers—and the growing energy gap as demand from key consumers continues to outstrip domestic supplies—creates what can be called an "energy security nexus" that animates US planners. For Washington, energy security has become irretrievably entwined with wider foreign and security policies, and controlling the conditions under which this resource is produced, exported, and delivered to consumers has become a major strategic concern. This was articulated plainly by the Bush administration, with the NEPD report recommending that the US should make "energy security a priority of our trade and foreign policy," since vital national interests are ultimately reliant, "in all cases, [on] long-term reliable supply relationships."[88] And in a future where US reliance on imported oil will inevitably rise—to sustain the economy at home and the military footprint abroad—control is needed not only to stabilize existing supplies but to boost production across the board.

Simply put, more oil needs to be extracted in order to meet rising demand, and the NEPD report calls for Washington to develop strategies to make this happen. However, whilst the NEPD Group put the case for US oil hegemony in its most explicit terms thus far—and was interesting especially because of the high public profile accorded to its final report—successive US administrations have long regarded control over oil reserves in the South to be a fundamental priority of strategic planning. We will see this long-term focus play out in chapter 3, in relation to US strategy toward the Persian Gulf. Then, in chapters 4, 5, and 6, we will show how interest in control of oil reserves in the three other key oil-rich zones significantly predates the Bush administration. As we shall see, it is undeniably the case that the NEPD Group brought an increased focus on the need to diversify oil production away from the Persian Gulf and consequently provided the intellectual foundations for an acceleration of US interventions in these zones. We also chart a clear focus amongst US planners in the Clinton administration and before to exert control over these regions as part of a wider project to sustain American hegemony. Likewise, as US strategy under Obama begins to emerge, we will show that early indicators suggest a fundamental continuity of strategy toward these regions is likely to characterize the post-Bush years, even as major policy shifts (such as in Iraq) are put into effect.

## US Control of Oil and the Liberal Order

In relation to oil, the transnational, positive-sum organizational role played by the American state has long been clear. The wider liberal economic order fully encompasses the trade in oil, with an international market mediating the relationship between producers and consumers. Private capital—in the form of international oil companies (IOCs)—is granted freedom across much of the oil sector to make independent decisions over where to invest, based almost purely upon commercial considerations. In turn, the role of the US remains one of maintaining the international environment required for private capital to operate with security and profits.[89] By ensuring that conditions within the oil-rich South are conducive to investment by private capital, US policy has *not* sought to carve out exclusive zones within the global economy. Rather, it has sought to reconfigure oil-rich political economies and transnationalize them as part of a global project of defending and deepening market relations. As the final report of the NEDP Group stated: "Longstanding US policy supports a liberalized global energy sector that is open to international trade and investment," and "promoting such investment will be a core element of our engagement with major foreign oil producers."[90]

The fact that the flow of oil from producers to consumers is mediated by an international market further enmeshes the interests of all core powers and ensures that US energy security cannot be divorced from the energy security of others. This is a point well understood by US military planners such as General Charles Wald, deputy commander of US European Command (EUCOM), who has been clear that European energy security is "a strategic issue for us as well. The European Union economy helps drive the United States economy . . . And the reason I say that is we're connected. We're connected with Europe economically. We all have the same interests. Whether we like it or not, we're interconnected."[91] This is a hugely significant characteristic of the international political economy of oil, and it means that the specific destination of oil exports from any particular region is of less relevance than the overall stability of flow onto the market.

These aspects of the current energy order are well recognized by policymakers and related experts. For example, the National Petroleum Council (NPC)—an organization consisting of top-level oil industry executives that provides advice to the US government—released a government-commissioned report on the subject in 2007. In this, the group maintained that there "can be no US energy security without global energy security" and that the only way to achieve both is through "free and open markets [which] should be relied upon wherever possible to produce efficient solutions."[92] Likewise, an influential Council on Foreign Relations task force on oil dependency concluded that "even if the United States were self-sufficient in oil . . . US foreign policy would remain constrained as long as US allies and partners remained dependent on imports because of their mutual interdependence. Thus, while reducing US imports is desirable, the underlying problem is the high and growing demand for oil worldwide."[93] Similar understandings were echoed in the NEPD report: "We should not . . . look at energy security in isolation from the rest of the world. In a global energy marketplace, US energy and economic security are directly linked not only to our domestic and international energy supplies, but to those of our trading partners as well. A significant disruption in world oil supplies could adversely affect our economy and our ability to promote important foreign and economic policy objectives, *regardless of the level of US dependence on oil imports.*"[94]

In practice, Washington has not always found it easy to implement this project to open oil-rich zones for investment by IOCs. Several oil-exporting governments have resisted calls to grant private capital a major role in the exploration and production of their reserves and have in fact reduced the power of IOCs by shifting control over to national oil companies (NOCs). With the OPEC revolution in ownership, the bulk of the world's oil reserves are in countries where NOCs now have majority control. This trend is exemplified throughout the Persian Gulf, where the major producers have full national ownership and control of their reserves and where the top four NOCs own no less than 60 percent of the world's reserves.[95] In this context, Washington's desired model of a free market–oriented sector has had to take account of realities on the ground. US planners have had to accommodate oil nationalism as it relates to ownership and production whilst attempting to work around this as much as possible. This strategy was summed up in a report by the James A. Baker III Institute for Public Policy: "If the United States were able to wish into existence a world that would favor its terms of trade and superpower status, all NOCs would be privatized, foreign investors would be treated the same as local companies and OPEC would be disbanded, allowing free trade and competitive markets to deliver the energy that is needed worldwide at prices determined solely by the market."[96]

Our analysis of the role played by the United States, as a stabilizer of the international market in oil and as the driving force for opening up oil-rich economies for transnational investment, stands in contrast to a particular strand of Marxist analysis. For some scholars, the United States (as the predominant capitalist state) acts primarily as an instrument for its economic elite and works to secure nationally based corporate interests (especially those of oil giants). The role of American capitalist intervention in oil-rich regions is therefore one of securing these interests. This form of analysis gained huge impetus from the invasion of Iraq in 2003, where many commentators highlighted the multifarious links between senior figures in the Bush administration and US-based oil and construction corporations.[97]

In contrast to such analyses, and whilst certainly acknowledging the reality of these links, we argue here that the United States has ultimately acted in the oil-rich South for the interests of the capitalist world order as a whole, even where such interests come into direct conflict with the narrow interests of the US oil sector. The US is not simply a tool for American oil capital, and it does not always act to maximize these profits. US planners have a relative autonomy in relation to specific capitalists, and long-term interests over maintaining an environment conducive to corporate activities takes a priority over ensuring commercial success for individual corporations. A good example of this can be seen in the context of the US-led sanctions regime against Iran and (until recently) Libya. Given the vast reserves of oil held in both countries, it would clearly be in the interests of US oil corporations to enter into negotiations with local elites over potential investment in exploration and production.[98] However, US sanctions against the two countries, embodied in Executive Orders 12957 and 12959, and in the Iran-Libya Sanctions Act (ILSA), serve as a powerful incentive for all oil companies to steer clear. Here, as elsewhere, US strategic concerns over containing regimes hostile to the wider US-led capitalist order decidedly trumps the specific interests of oil companies.[99] Where the prevailing political order *is* conducive to wider American hegemonic rule, though, US planners have sought to increase the production and exportation of oil reserves by encouraging and protecting investment by transnational capital in relevant energy sectors. In this way, Washington plays the same systems-maintaining role that we saw earlier, and American interests are served through the defense of the wider liberal order.

## A Return to Geopolitical Rivalry?

Whilst our above discussion sketches the contours of the contemporary international oil order and describes the role played by the US within it, some scholars point to what they see as a coming end to this system. Accordingly, predictions abound over the return to a more naked form of geopolitical rivalry over scarce resources, rivalry that has hitherto been pacified under US hegemony. Such arguments are based primarily on the growing urgency with which the problem of energy security is viewed across the industrialized and rapidly industrializing world and the increasing understanding of the need to secure enough supply for national economies and national security. Certainly, "energy security" is a term in vogue across the globe. The intersection of a number of trends—rising global demand for energy, fears of dwindling supplies, increased instability in many of the energy-rich regions, and concerns about the potential future devastation wrought by climate change—has made the sources, locations, and stability of world energy supplies a common subject for debate.

At one level, the growing perception of energy insecurity is simple to explain. Demand for energy use is growing—and in all likelihood will continue to grow for the foreseeable future—whilst it is not at all clear that reliable and stable sources of supply will continue to match this. In turn, the growing energy gap exacerbates concerns amongst leaders over the sources of future supply. Overall global consumption of "marketed energy" stood at just over 460 qBtu in 2005.[100] This level is forecast to rise by over 50 percent during the medium term, to nearly 700 qBtu by 2030. This is a truly staggering rate of increase, and it will significantly dictate the nature of the energy problem over the coming decades. Those states that are currently responsible for the majority of the world's energy consumption—the industrialized states of North America, Europe, East Asia, and Australasia that make up the Organisation for Economic Co-operation and Development (OECD)—are set to increase their consumption by almost 20 percent by 2030 as economic growth leads to sustained increases in energy demand.

However, it is the future rise in demand by the newly emergent major economies of the non-OECD (projected to grow by 85% by 2030) that will primarily account for increased global consumption. In particular, the rapid growth of the Chinese and Indian economies is drastically changing the energy map of the world: together, they accounted for less than 8 percent of overall consumption in 1980; by 2005 this share had grown to 18 percent; by 2030 it is projected to be no less than 25 percent. Indeed, by 2030 Chinese energy use is projected to considerably outstrip that of the United States. Unsurprising, therefore, that some have referred to an emerging "Chindia Challenge," destined to exacerbate the coming problem of energy insecurity.[101] Oil is crucial to the workings of industrialized and industrializing economies, providing the basis for much of the world's transportation, industrial production, and commercial activity. Current consumption of 84 mbpd is forecast to rise by 35 percent by 2030, ensuring that the production of an additional 29 mbpd will be required to meet growing demand: equivalent to three times current Saudi production. And although most government and industry analyses have tended to forecast rises in oil production sufficient to meet growing

demand, these have usually been based on a scarcity of hard data and a tendency of oil-rich countries and oil companies to overstate the size of reserves
in their possession. A recent report by the International Energy Agency suggested that the moment of "peak oil" may come far sooner than previously
thought. This moment—whereby the discovery and exploitation of new oil
reserves will no longer match or exceed the decline in production levels from
existing reserves, thus leading to an overall decline of production—may be
only several years away.[102]

The potential for geopolitical rivalries over control of oil to emerge has been
noted by several scholars, who chart the implications that this will have for
international security more broadly. In particular, Michael Klare's penetrating
work on the geopolitics of energy has developed the idea that the growing
"energy gap" is leading to a breakdown in cooperation and a reemergence of
Great Power competition. As a result of the zero-sum dynamic that characterizes control over resources, international conflict will become ever more common. For Klare, we are witnessing "the energy equivalent of an arms race to
secure control over whatever remaining deposits of oil and natural gas are up
for sale on the planet, along with reserves of other vital minerals. This resource
race is already one of the most conspicuous features of the contemporary landscape and, in our lifetimes, may become *the* most conspicuous one—a vora-
cious, zero-sum contest that, if allowed to continue along present paths, can
only lead to conflict among the major powers." Indeed, the upcoming " 'Great
Game' over energy, with all its potential for rivalries, alliances, conflicts,
schisms, betrayals and flash points, will surely be a pivotal—if not the central—
feature of world affairs for the remainder of this century." In this light, energy
scarcity is likely to lead to future disruptions in the global system and the
emergence of a "new international energy order" characterized less by liberal
free market trading than by statism and neomercantilism.[103] In this understanding, the US is attempting more and more to translate its current global
primacy into unfettered control over the world's energy stocks for its own,
national purposes. In an era of resource scarcity, the thrust of US policy toward
the South is increasingly subordinated to the chief objective of satisfying
America's energy needs, over and above those of its strategic rivals, with the US
military "slowly but surely . . . being converted into a global oil-protection
service."[104]

There is much to support this understanding of the national logic driving
interventions in the oil-rich South. Aside from the public proclamations made

by all recent US administrations as to the desirability of energy independence, the fact remains that there is currently no alternative or combination of alternatives that can replace oil as the primary energy resource for the industrialized powers. As fears over dwindling oil stocks combine with the rapidly growing energy needs of emerging powers such as China, Brazil, and India, ruling elites from across the world are understandably concerned about the implications this may have for national power and interests. The growing global energy gap will undoubtedly lead to instability within the system, and increasing levels of interstate conflict are likely as rival centers of power scramble to secure remaining reserves for their own use. In this context, we are currently witnessing a (re)emergence of strategic rivalries to US hegemony, primarily from a resurgent Russia and an emerging China: a feature of international politics that had been largely absent since the end of the Cold War.

The Great Game analysis does well to explain recent moves by powers outside the liberal core to circumvent the international market in energy. In the case of China, there is a sense of deep concern in Beijing about the extent of American dominance in the Persian Gulf and the ability of Washington to control the flow of oil in any future conflict. According to a major study on the issue by the US think tank RAND, the Chinese government "is uncomfortable with the fact that the US Navy dominates the sea-lanes stretching from the Persian Gulf to the South China Sea through which the bulk of China's oil imports must pass."[105] As a result, Chinese planners *are* to a certain extent acting to circumvent the US-led international order and the oil markets, primarily through direct, bilateral deals with oil-rich regimes across the world that result in the trade of oil outside of the global marketplace. Instead of purchasing this oil via the market, and therefore paying the market rate, China has increasingly entered into negotiations with oil-rich states over the price of a set amount of oil (be it any number of barrels) or over the rights to explore for, extract, and directly repatriate specific reserves.

It is too early to determine the extent to which Beijing's strategy is designed to undermine US global hegemony and the challenge it will present to US planners. But of crucial importance in this regard—and a point skated over by Klare and others—is that US government strategy is still tied irrevocably to extending, entrenching, and defending the global market system, because this provides the structures through which US hegemony is exercised. The US state has primarily acted, and continues to act, to secure the generic conditions for global capital, and the current challenge from emergent powers does not affect this. In other words, in the face of increased tension between major global powers, we are not seeing a return to interimperial rivalry, especially since the primary imperial power remains dedicated to a global order based on largely positive-sum, open door trading between key states. By far the most preferred future scenario for Washington is a China (and Russia and India) that remains pacified and subordinate to US hegemony within the liberal economic order. In fact, this can be seen most plainly in relation to US policy vis-à-vis China's activities in the energy sector. US planners are clearly concerned about the potential for Beijing to undermine the liberal economic order, and ultimately Washington remains dedicated to hedging against the possibility that Chinese "strategic choices" will impact negatively upon US hegemony.[106]

However, alongside this hedging strategy, Washington is exerting substantial energy in an attempt to pull China within the US orbit and thereby to integrate it fully within the liberal order. This has led to schizophrenic positioning in relation to Beijing, with US planners (in the Clinton, Bush, and Obama administrations) viewing China simultaneously as a strategic partner and as a strategic rival. In this light, the 2006 *National Security Strategy* stated that as China "becomes a global player, it must act as a responsible stakeholder that fulfills its obligations and works with the United States and others to advance the international system that has enabled its success." And Beijing was reprimanded for its "holding on to old ways of thinking and acting that exacerbate concerns throughout the region and the world": old ways that include "expanding trade, but acting as if they can somehow 'lock up' energy supplies around the world or seek to direct markets rather than opening them up—as if they can follow a mercantilism borrowed from a discredited era."[107] As Chinese president Hu Jintao visited Washington just weeks after the release of this *NSS*, Deputy Secretary of State Robert Zoellick stated that the United States desired to incorporate China more fully within the US-led order, especially with reference to the question of energy: "We are seeking to steer them from a *narrow perspective* to a recognition that *together* we need to expand sources of supply."[108]

In the early days of the Obama administration, efforts to further incorporate China within the liberal order have continued. With the global economy facing unprecedented turbulence, presidents Obama and Hu met at the sidelines of the G20 Financial Summit in London in April 2009. Committing publicly to deepen cooperation at all levels, the two sides pledged to "work together to resolutely support global trade and investment flows that benefit all," to "resist protectionism," and to "promote the smooth functioning of the international financial system and the steady growth of the world economy."[109]

Despite a partial reemergence of rivalry between core powers, therefore, we would argue that accounts that stress the coming fracture in global politics (apparently brought into stark relief by dwindling oil supplies) ultimately underplay the durability of the US-led international order. Washington will continue to play a coordinating role for the capitalist core, and it is this role which means that—to the extent that US hegemony over oil-rich regions remains untrammeled—overt competition for the world's oil stocks will continue to be overwhelmingly pacified, as rival centers of power opt primarily to work under the American strategic umbrella.

## Conclusion

As we have seen, the United States has attempted to achieve energy security by exerting control over significant portions of the world's oil supplies, and this objective has long been central to maintaining America's hegemonic position in the world. US strategy has been conducted within the context of the liberal economic order constructed in the postwar era under Washington's tutelage. The US has adopted a managerial role within the current order, whereby it acts to guide, extend, and defend a system of open trade for the benefit of capital (which in turn has become increasingly transnationalized in recent decades). This has translated into a strategy toward oil-rich regions in the periphery, where the promotion of a stable and attractive investment climate is the prime operational objective for US planners. It is this which will encourage private oil capital to increase production capacity and export rates at multiple sites (the requirement for a stable oil market), and it is the smooth operation of the international oil market that provides the mechanism through which US energy security—and, indirectly, global hegemony—is assured.

As we will see in later chapters, this operational objective drives the specific policies adopted by Washington in relation to the oil-rich South. First, though, it is necessary to explore an element of US strategy that has long been central to the defense of stable and attractive investment climates in the South: the use of coercive force by Washington to insulate pro-US elites from political instability and to contain or destroy any significant threats to the current order. Processes of transnationalizing oil-rich political economies have, in many cases, required "armoring" by the US so as to defend free market relations from substantive challenge. And as we shall see in the next chapter, the use of this coercive statecraft is not limited to campaigns against armed groups fighting to overturn existing political and economic orders; it is also used to discipline a range of unarmed social forces that seek to pursue alternative paths of economic development. It is the threat to Washington's preferred model of capitalist development, rather than the form that this threat takes, that is of central concern for US planners. It is in this context that counterinsurgency has been deployed worldwide to stabilize the farthest reaches of the American empire.

# CHAPTER TWO

# Counterinsurgency and the Stabilization of Order

As we saw in chapter 1, playing the key role in securing the flow of oil onto international markets has long formed a central plank of American grand strategy in the postwar era. Controlling oil-rich regions in the South provides Washington with unparalleled structural power vis-à-vis other states, since it offers the US a potential stranglehold over existing and emerging Great Powers.[1] However, this control has taken a very particular form, derived from the specific contours of the international order constructed under US leadership. The unique characteristics of American power, which is built upon managing and defending positive-sum intracore relations, has ensured the unprecedented durability of the US-centric global order. Many European and East Asian powers have consented (thus far) to US military and economic dominance over their respective regions in return for Washington's security guarantees that would preserve those public goods enjoyed by all. This logic of US global hegemony translates into the strategy adopted to control oil-rich regions in the South.

As we have seen, Washington does not seek to establish zones of exclusive control for delivering specifically American energy security, in direct competition with the energy needs of rival powers. Rather, Washington has adopted the same managerial role as for the global order overall and has taken the lead role in stabilizing global oil markets through transnationalizing and integrating oil-rich political economies as productive circuits of global capital. In practice, this strategy has necessitated the active promotion of an environment wherein global oil capital has the opportunity and confidence to make long-term investments. Working to maintain a stable and attractive investment climate within these regions provides, in effect, the means through which Washington guarantees the uninterrupted flow of necessary volumes of oil onto world markets. In turn, this sustains the smooth operation of the global economy, serves the interests of all core powers, and underwrites US global hegemony.

This strategy has led to the adoption of a highly interventionist posture by US planners in the postwar era, as Washington has worked to transform oil-rich zones in ways conducive to the wider order. In the absence of formal colonial control, intervention has been more indirect than during earlier imperial times. American control is predominantly exercised through preexisting elite structures in key regions, in order to ensure the stability and friendly orientation of important states. As we explored briefly in chapter 1, this integrative process has been far from smooth, with US-led globalization often exacerbating existing dislocations within societies. Widening levels of wealth inequality, falling standards of living, and increasing feelings of helplessness have often fed into widespread discontent across the South, with resulting instabilities presenting an obvious threat to US interests. In addition, a more active resistance to the US-led neoliberal agenda and wider American hegemony has emerged at many points across the South throughout the postwar era. Such counterhegemonic forces present an especially grave threat to US interests, since they often seek to pursue an alternative path of economic and political development outside of Washington's orbit.

Challenges to US hegemony are by no means limited to oil-rich zones, but of all the regions in the global South, they are often some of the most unstable. "Dutch disease"—whereby unintended side effects from substantial oil income drives up exchange rates and consequently makes the manufacturing sector less competitive—severely affects many of these economies, leading to slow overall growth and a "hollowing out" of non-oil sectors. With alternative industries stagnating or collapsing as a result, wealth becomes highly concentrated in the oil sector. And because of the close relations between the sector and political elites, and the relative ease with which central government can exert control over oil production and exports, this concentration leads in many cases to a consolidation of political power. Leaders have little incentive to share power when their legitimacy rests upon control of the state's natural resources (such as oil), rather than upon a democratic mandate.[2]

In this way, authoritarian state forms can be more easily sustained in oil-rich regions, with the centralization of wealth working to insulate the ruling strata from popular pressure for reform. And in turn, the reduction of legitimate political space for most of the population, combined with often-vast inequalities in wealth distribution as the oil "rents" are retained within a small circle of leaders, can breed domestic unrest. In regions where poverty is endemic, and there is a clear mismatch between the living standards for most and the wealth for a few, political instability can easily arise. Unsurprisingly, this often results in the emergence of social and political forces actively organized against the prevailing socioeconomic order. Often cast by US planners as "communist," "subversive," or "terrorist" and tied rhetorically into a "global conspiracy" against "international stability," such forces have in fact often had a distinctly local history, emerging as a response to pressures on the ground. We shall see this in later chapters, whether in relation to unionized oil workers in Iraq, religious leaders in Angola, or armed guerrillas in Colombia.

As such, Washington has to armor ongoing processes of free marketization against pressures for inimical social change. Coercive statecraft and economic policy are intimately interlinked in the minds of US planners as well as on the ground in the South. In the words of former secretary of defense Donald Rumsfeld, "security and economic opportunity" are closely related: "It is a truth. They're not separable. You can simply not create an environment that's hospitable to investment and enterprise and opportunity for people in a circumstance that lacks security and safety. It just doesn't happen." Expanding his thoughts, Rumsfeld was clear:

> I think that there are always going to be in this part of the world . . . people, movements, groups, interests that are different from those of us who believe in free political systems and free economic systems. And they will rise and fall over time . . . There will always be people who will try to weaken it and to put in its place some approach to governing that is fundamentally inconsistent with freedom . . . People have to recognize that freedom is under challenge fairly continuously in many parts of the world, *and that it does need to be defended* and it has to be nurtured and protected and allow it to flourish, and *those that oppose it have to be discouraged and ultimately lose heart.*[3]

In this light, the Pentagon has long been granted the lead role in stabilizing the environment within which economic integration and transnational investment can take place. US coercive power is regularly deployed across the South so as, in the words of one US commander-in-chief, to "help achieve the security conditions necessary to create the enduring basis for prosperity."[4]

In practice, creating the conditions for prosperity in this way has required Washington to insulate local pro-US elites for as long as they prove responsive to the needs of global capital and energy security. This chapter will explore how this insulation process takes place and how this has relied predominantly upon the overt militarization of state-society relations in important strategic regions. Washington has, throughout the postwar era and across the South, relied extensively on the provision of assistance to local security forces, which in turn have been trained and equipped to police their populations for signs of dissent and "subversion." This process has taken shape through the use of a particular form of warfare across the South: counterinsurgency (CI). We will therefore examine how CI has formed the centerpiece—or "keystone"—of assistance to pro-US militaries and how this strategy is orientated toward policing internal populations for signs of subversion and unrest and to responding to these through a process of identification, control, and, ultimately, destruction. US-led stabilization has by no means been limited to oil-rich zones, however, and the bulk of this chapter will examine the broad contours of Washington's coercive strategy. This will frame the remaining chapters of the book, which will explore in some depth how this has played out in the oil-rich regions of the South.

## Insulating Order

Given the potential for "radical" forces to attain power in vital areas, US planners concluded early on that the imposition of free market reforms could not happen in isolation from parallel attempts to stabilize favorable state formations. In response to challenges to US hegemony throughout the South, Washington has intervened on countless occasions in the postwar era in order to bolster certain developmental pathways for nascent state forms and thus make sure that ruling elites remain responsive to the needs of the wider liberal order. "Stability" runs throughout Washington's declaratory policy toward the South as a desirable end-state. As the Obama administration declared in the first months of power: "Promoting security abroad is central to the well-being of Americans at home [and] it is necessary to actively promote a healthy international system. The [Pentagon's] strategy for promoting security emphasizes building the capacity of a broad spectrum of partners. From helping to train and equip the security forces of states facing common threats, to maintaining close relationships with the militaries of America's strongest allies and partners, the Department helps to maintain the peace and bring stability to troubled regions."[5]

Depending on context, various state forms have been considered to be the best guarantor of stability. In an ideal world, liberal democratic-capitalist state formations have been preferred. European and Japanese economies, for example, have been highly receptive to the interests of global capital, generally enthusiastic about closer economic integration, and willing to submit themselves to American strategic dominance. However, to the extent that *authoritarian* regimes have also remained responsive to the needs of foreign corporations, and submissive to US hegemony, they have in turn been considered far more preferable than prospective alternatives that may not be so pliant. For US planners, the ideal state form in the South has been that which has maintained an open door economy coupled with a strong anticommunist, antinationalist, or antiterrorist strategic posture and has proved receptive to US hegemony and political guidance. If such state forms happen to be authoritarian in nature, then this is to be tolerated for the greater good of stability. Indeed, working through strong, centralized governments that are relatively unresponsive to popular pressures has often provided the clearest means to prevent undesirable social change. In practice, concerns expressed by Washington over the global promotion of democracy and human rights have been heavily moderated by a need to ensure that any institutionalization of popular democratic expression does not deliver the wrong result. Of constant concern for US planners has been the fear that universal suffrage, and forms of direct democracy, could result in forms of governance that subsequently pursue developmental paths inimical to US interests.

The need, in the final instance, to rely on undemocratic state forms has long been acknowledged by US planners. In the context of the Cold War, a 1959 State Department report argued that "authoritarianism is required to lead backward societies through their socio-economic revolutions" with the trend toward right-wing pro-US dictatorships needing to remain "the norm . . . for a long period." This was the case because military authoritarianism provides the best response "as developmental problems become more acute and the facades of democracy left by the colonial powers prove inadequate to the immediate tasks."[6] George Kennan summarized this logic when he explained that, in dealing with dissent during the Cold War, the final answer "may be an unpleasant one" but the US "should not hesitate before police repression by the local government." Along with other prominent figures in the foreign policy–making establishment, Kennan considered this repression to be strategically necessary, since "the Communists are essentially traitors." In fact, it "is better to have a strong regime in power than a liberal government if it is indulgent and relaxed and penetrated by Communists."[7]

Likewise, Reagan's foreign policy advisor and ambassador to the UN, Jeane Kirkpatrick, claimed that "only intellectual fashion and the tyranny of Right/ Left thinking prevent intelligent men of good will from perceiving the *facts* that traditional authoritarian governments are less repressive than revolutionary autocracies, that they are more susceptible to liberalization, and that they are more compatible with US interests." As such, and in the context of various popular-based insurgencies against pro-US dictatorships, Washington should provide economic and military support to friendly regimes and only encourage the "process of [political] liberalization and democratisation provided that the effort is not made at a time when the incumbent government is fighting for its life against violent adversaries, and that proposed reforms are aimed at producing gradual change rather than perfect democracy overnight."[8]

Such support has continued in the post–Cold War era, as authoritarian state forms are often still understood to be necessary (if regrettable) to prevent unfavorable social change. In particular, dictatorships throughout the South have received increased levels of support since 9/11, as their compliance with the wider interests of the United States (now refracted through the lens of the war on terror) has trumped concerns over the building of representative structures of governance.[9] We will see this with absolute clarity in chapters 3, 4, and 5, in the context of US attempts to provide stability in the Middle East, the Caspian Basin, and West Africa. Of course, US planners have increasingly declared the elevation of "democracy promotion" throughout the South to be a foreign policy priority. In turn, and as we will see in chapter 6 (on Latin America), this has undoubtedly led to increased rhetorical support for state forms structured around electoral democracy. In reality, Washington has continued to remain deeply hostile to democracies that deliver the wrong result, and the underlying objective has remained the same: the extension and defense of US regional and global hegemony and the parallel promotion of a set of outwardly looking capitalist social relations.[10]

In supporting pro-US state formations throughout the South, Washington has often relied heavily upon host nation security forces to insulate "friendly" elites from counterhegemonic forces. Militaries throughout the South that have been trained, funded, and equipped by the United States have long been the key institution for guaranteeing the necessary stability and have in many instances been the central conduits through which Washington exercises its power. These forces have provided both a bulwark against varying forms of internal reformism and—on occasion—a tool for (counter)revolution should incumbent regimes prove resistant to US-led reforms. Building the military capacities of allies throughout strategically vital regions has been a core objective of US policy since World War II. As early as 1947 the US secretary of war, Robert Patterson, was clear about the role played by US security assistance. In the context of Latin America, he stated that "the provision of United States equipment is the keystone since United States methods of training and organization must inevitably follow its adoption along with far-reaching concomitant benefits of permanent United States military missions and the continued flow of Latin American officers through our service schools. Thus will our ideals and way of life be nurtured in Latin America, to the eventual exclusion of totalitarian and other foreign ideologies."[11]

Through security assistance packages, the Pentagon and State Department have been able to deliver a wide range of benefits to host nation forces. These have ranged from loans or grants to purchase US weapons, to the provision of surplus or obsolete US weaponry at little or no cost, and to the direct training of officers and soldiers. Assistance programs are a critical foreign policy tool in the promotion of US global interests, by ensuring that allied militaries are equipped and trained to operate in missions defined as relevant and important by US planners. This assistance is designed to pull recipient militaries within the orbit of US strategy, with in-depth and sustained training to build a "long-term understanding of and support for US policies."[12] "Interoperability" has become vital, as the Pentagon works to ensure the smooth transition of its equipment, doctrine, and training practices to less-advanced militaries.[13] In a 2004 speech, Douglas Feith (undersecretary of defense for policy) made it known that security cooperation is a key means by which the US achieves its objectives. Accordingly, the Pentagon is focused on ensuring allied security forces share with Washington "a common appreciation of problems and solutions," with the US military working to "share technology, information, activities and a frame of mind about security issues." In this light, the goal is one of "helping our partners to increase their capabilities . . . to take on missions that serve our common interest."[14] In 2002, General Charles Holland, commander-in-chief (CINC) of US Special Operations Command (USSOCOM), stated that US Special Forces (SOF) should be engaged in "surrogate warfare," which involved "the training of surrogate forces to gain results favorable to our interests."[15]

A huge number of foreign military personnel undergo Pentagon-led training, much of which takes place in the host nation, supplemented by the 475 military training schools and installations within the United States itself.[16] According to the most recent joint report to Congress from the Pentagon and State Department, no fewer than 77,000 military officers received training in 2006, from 149 countries throughout the South. This is a staggering level of activity, with an annual cost of more than $430 million and arranged through more than 30,000 individual events. Moreover, this training is supplemented by the widespread transfer of weapons and other equipment necessary to operate effectively, with the US delivering $14 billion worth of arms in 2006. This represented 52 percent of the entire arms trade that year, and with shipments destined primarily for militaries in the South.[17] The provision of this aid is nothing new, and security assistance programs have been extensive throughout the postwar era. Over $180 billion has been provided in grants and loans to facilitate the transfer of US defense articles and associated services, with training a key plank of this aid. In just one example, the School of the Americas (SOA) was responsible for training over 40,000 Latin American military personnel by the end of the Cold War, whilst the highest-profile training program (International Military Education and Training, or IMET) has seen over 700,000 "friendly" officers pass through its courses since 1950, in an effort costing over $3 billion.[18]

Whilst this aid has traditionally been channeled through the State Department, funds in the post–Cold War era are increasingly run through the Pentagon budget. Crucially, this represents a shift toward far less oversight and legislative restriction, as Congress has much less say over the nature and scope of defense programs. As such, they can be used to achieve a wide variety of objectives with little or no external scrutiny. Programs such as JCET (Joint Combined Exchange Training) and CTFP (Counter Terrorism Fellowship Program) are used to train allied militaries in a wide variety of tasks, many of which have little to do with countering terrorism per se, and most of which are identical to broader State Department programs (but without the human rights restrictions and reporting requirements).[19] Hundreds of millions of dollars is now appropriated each year as part of the Pentagon's "Global Train and Equip Program," which is considered to be the "single most important tool for building partner operational capacity, shaping the environment, and countering terrorism outside Iraq and Afghanistan," so much so that the annual demand from combatant commanders has "significantly exceeded current authority," with more than $1.6 billion of proposals submitted.[20] The Pentagon now sees support to foreign military forces, once the preserve of foreign policy officials, to be a legitimate and core task of the US military. According to Robert Gates, defense secretary for both Bush and Obama: "Arguably the most important military component in the War on Terror is not the fighting we do ourselves, but how well we enable and empower others to defend and govern their own countries. The standing up and mentoring of indigenous armies and police—once the province of Special Forces—is now a key mission for the military as a whole."[21]

The Obama administration has in fact increased funding for several assistance programs, justified by the fact that they further "US interests around the world by ensuring that coalition partners and friendly foreign governments are equipped and trained to work toward common security goals."[22] Assistance on the ground to pro-US states is increasingly targeted at maintaining internal security against significant threats to economic and political stability.

## Counterinsurgency: Stabilizing Orders

One of the most important features of US assistance to pro-Washington militaries in the South has often been the reorientation of recipient forces away from an external defense posture to one of internal security, whereby they become charged with policing their own civilian populations for signs of subversion and internal unrest. This use of coercive statecraft to stabilize the liberal economic order has long been an explicit goal for US planners. Policing in this way has allowed Washington and its proxies to weed out and eliminate social forces that may threaten the continued penetration of foreign capital, as well as the stability of the wider order. In effect, US military aid has been used—and continues to be used—to armor processes of globalization. Where necessary, this support for security forces has also led to a long record of military-led coups and counterrevolutions, relying on pro-US elements within the security forces (which had generally been cultivated in close military-to-military ties with the Pentagon during a prerevolutionary era). In this light, Washington has supported counterdemocracy coups and interventions against Iran (1953), Guatemala (1954), Indonesia (1965), Chile (1973), Nicaragua (1984), and Venezuela (2002).[23]

Most often, though, the assistance provided to pro-US security forces has been designed, through intensive training and equipment programs, to provide local forces with the means and the know-how to prosecute counterinsurgency campaigns. CI has long formed a central plank of US coercive foreign policy and has often dominated the military relationship between Washington and its allies in the South. CI has its roots in a response to the Cuban Revolution, when President Kennedy established a Special Group (Counter-Insurgency) in 1962 to provide "unity of effort and the use of all available resources with maximum effectiveness in preventing and resisting subversive insurgency and related forms of indirect aggression in friendly countries."[24]

Since this date, the thrust of US support has been operationalized through the 1961 Foreign Assistance Act, which remains the centerpiece legislation governing US security assistance programs. This act commits Washington to provide "measures of support" to friendly countries "in the common defense against internal and external aggression, including the furnishing of military assistance." The US government is required by this law to focus on "assisting friendly countries to *maintain internal security, and creating an environment of security and stability* in the developing friendly countries essential to their more rapid social, economic, and political progress."[25] This has required addressing any "capability gap" within pro-US militaries to impose necessary order, with assistance programs targeted at bolstering local capacity for policing their populations. In a speech to West Point graduates in 1962, Kennedy stated that "subversive insurgency is another type of war" that requires, "in those situations where we must counter it . . . a whole new kind of strategy, a wholly different kind of force, and therefore a new and wholly different kind of training."[26] This new requirement filtered down to specific training schools; the 1962 mission statement of the SOA stated that "every course taught has definite application in the CI field . . . Currently, the Department provides instruction in every aspect of CI operations, be it military, paramilitary, political, sociological or psychological."[27]

CI training was fed through the assistance provided to allies during the Cold War, with literally tens of thousands of officers receiving CI instruction at the hands of the Pentagon.[28] Furthermore, it has continued as a central theme of foreign military training throughout the post–Cold War era. A review of several SOF training missions throughout the 1990s found that, rather than the official justification given by the Pentagon (training American troops through interaction with regional allies), they were in fact designed for "helping foreign armies fight drug traffickers [and] teaching counterinsurgency techniques in countries concerned about domestic stability."[29] And in the post-9/11 era, available evidence points to the fact that, whilst US SOF "sometimes provide training for humanitarian de-mining, medical first aid and triage, and veterinarian services . . . *the centerpiece of most training missions is foreign internal defence—training in counterinsurgency techniques.*"[30] Indeed, the 2007 posture statement by USSOCOM is clear that "foreign internal defense" is one of its core tasks, with the Command itself "aggressively collaborating with other government agencies and our international partners to build a global network to combat terrorism," including the provision of "training and assistance to the host countries to develop their indigenous capacity to combat terrorism and create a more secure and stable environment."[31]

The overall objective of US security assistance has been outlined in the 2008 *National Defense Strategy,* although its formulation could effectively be applied to any period since 1945: "Armed sub-national groups, including but not limited to those inspired by violent extremism, threaten the stability and legitimacy of key states. If left unchecked, such instability can spread and threaten regions of interest to the United States, our allies, and friends . . . Ungoverned, under-governed, misgoverned and contested areas offer fertile ground for such groups to exploit the gaps in governance capacity of local regimes to undermine local stability and regional security." In response, therefore, US military strategy "seeks to build the capacity of fragile or vulnerable partners to withstand internal threats" and the Pentagon works "with and through like-minded states to help shrink the ungoverned areas of the world . . . By helping others to police themselves and their regions, we will collectively address threats to the broader international system."[32]

In this way, CI warfare has become the central mechanism by which Washington has contained and ultimately rolled back social forces throughout the South committed to challenging the prevailing order. And this process is only accelerating under Obama. In an interview after unveiling his first defense budget under the new administration, Defense Secretary Robert Gates made it clear that Washington was seeking a major "rebalancing" of military strategy so as to recognize "the enduring requirement for the capabilities to fight these irregular or hybrid conflicts." Crucial for Gates, and important for understanding the future of US defense strategy, is to "get that capability into the base budgets so that it will continue and we don't forget, as we did after Vietnam, how to do what we're doing right now so successfully in both Iraq and Afghanistan."[33]

## CI Doctrine: Blueprint for Stabilization

Counterinsurgency warfare is designed primarily to achieve internal security by increasing the power of centralized authority to impose stability in the face of threats and challenges arising "from below." As generals David Petraeus and James Mattis stated in the most recent version of US doctrine, CI is at heart a war "amongst the people," with forces needing to be "ready each day to be greeted with a handshake or a hand grenade."[34] Many commentators have identified that this has profound implications for CI forces attempting to neutralize the threat from armed insurgents, because—unlike conventional forces—such opponents tend to reside and operate in close proximity to civilians. However, a careful reading of past and current US doctrine reveals a further, often-overlooked implication of operating within a CI framework. It suggests the need for security forces to take account of—and focus military effort upon—the opinions and actions of those civilians amongst whom armed insurgents find support and safe haven. And there is a fundamental continuity in this regard that runs through Cold War and post–Cold War counterinsurgency theory and practice. CI forces are directed to "win the hearts and minds" of the people. Although this "ideological" component of the CI effort is often couched in terms of providing social benefits to the population in order to win them to one's side, at its heart it maintains the possibility of—and the need to caution against—subversive elements of the population. As the 2009 US government *Counterinsurgency Guide* states:

> COIN [counterinsurgency] is a complex effort that integrates the full range of civilian and military agencies. It is often more *population-centric* (focused on securing and controlling a given population or populations) than enemy-centric (focused on defeating a particular enemy group) . . . The capabilities required for COIN may be very similar to those required for peacekeeping operations, humanitarian assistance, stabilization operations, and development assistance missions. However, the intent of a COIN campaign is to build popular support for a government while marginalizing the insurgents: it is therefore fundamentally an *armed political competition* with the insurgents. Consequently, control

(over the environment, the population, the level of security, the pace of events, and the enemy) is the fundamental goal of COIN, a goal that distinguishes it from peace operations or humanitarian intervention.[35]

As part of the effort to control populations in this way, the heart of CI doctrine has long been an identification of unarmed elements from within civil society—in clear distinction from armed insurgents—as a threat to desired stability. CI forces are not only in competition with insurgents *over* a population; they are also required to police and discipline various subversive elements *of* the population. In this light, civilians are viewed and assessed in terms of their potential support for the insurgency, and whole swaths of civil societies are often designated as potentially inimical and subversive. The Cold War US Army manual entitled *Stability Operations,* used extensively to train host nation security forces in CI, stated that civilian populations are central to any insurgent movement: "To succeed in his phased development the insurgent relies on the population as the major source for expansion and replacement of his military forces." The manual then extended its definition of subversion beyond armed insurgents and explicitly linked civil society organizations to the problem of insurgency. For example, the manual asked, "Are there any legal political organizations which may be a front for insurgent activities?" and then highlighted the education system as vulnerable to subversion: "Is the public education system vulnerable to infiltration by insurgent agents? What is the influence of politics on teachers, textbooks, and students, conversely, what influence does the education system exercise on politics?" The manual then asked: What "is the nature of the labor organizations; what relationship exists between these organizations, the government, and the insurgents?"[36]

Alongside the designation of certain sectors of the workforce as a potential threat to government forces, has been the blanket labeling of moves toward democratic reform, or criticism of the status quo, as inherently subversive. US CI doctrine has long identified patterns of political behavior as fundamentally linked to insurgent activity. For example, the 1970 manual stated that organizations that stress "immediate social, political, or economic reform may be an indication that the insurgents have gained a significant degree of control." It then moved on to detail a series of "Insurgent Activity Indicators," which were generic behavioral signs that allegedly indicated subversion:

Refusal of peasants to pay rent, taxes, or loan payments or unusual difficulty in their collection. Increase in the number of entertainers with a political message. Discrediting the judicial system and police organizations. Characterization of the armed forces as the enemy of the people. Appearance of questionable doctrine in the educational system. Appearance of many new members in established organizations such as labor organizations. Increased unrest among laborers. Increased student activity against the government and its police, or against minority groups, foreigners and the like. An increased number of articles or advertisements in newspapers criticizing the government. Strikes or work stoppages called to protest government actions. Increase of petitions demanding government redress of grievances. Proliferation of slogans pinpointing specific grievances. Initiation of letter-writing campaigns to newspapers and government officials deploring undesirable conditions and blaming individuals in power.[37]

We see, then, an unambiguous designation of civil society and the civilian population as a potential, and in some senses an inevitable, threat to stability. This designation has continued right up to the present day, with current CI doctrine—used in the training of numerous pro-US security forces—quoting earlier manuals verbatim. For example, in appendix E of the 2004 US Army manual *Counterinsurgency Operations* a section called "Intelligence Indicators" listed virtually the same indicators above but also added others, including:

Unusual gatherings among the population. Appearance of new organizations stressing grievances or interests of repressed or minority groups. Trends of demonstrated hostility toward government forces or mission force. Attempts to discredit or ridicule national or public officials. Characterization of government leaders as puppets. Agitation against government projects and plans. Character assassinations of mission, military, and law enforcement officials. Widespread hostile media coverage of even minor criminal violations or incidents involving mission force personnel. Accusations of brutality or ineffectiveness or claims that mission or government forces initiated violence following confrontations. Publication of photographs portraying repressive and violent acts by mission force or government forces.[38]

Ideas around, debate over, and critical scrutiny of government power—which in the context of "stable" liberal capitalist-democracies are understood to be normal (indeed, vital) elements of the political process—are, within the context of the "unstable" South, understood to be something very different. In this sense, CI warfare provides a blueprint for a campaign against civil society, with vocal critics of the government often viewed as a potential threat.

Perhaps unsurprisingly, this facet of CI warfare leads almost inevitably to an understanding of civil society as a legitimate target of counterinsurgency. This focus on directly countering the perceived threat from unarmed sections of civil society often comes under the rubric of "psychological operations" (psyops), justified by the need to "win hearts and minds." For example, an early CI manual outlined that the primary target "for tactical psychological operations is the local civilian population" and that "civilians in the operational area may be supporting their own government or collaborating with an enemy occupation force. Themes and appeals disseminated to this group will vary accordingly, but the psychological objectives will be the same as those for the enemy military. An isolation program designed to instill doubt and fear may be carried out."[39]

A second manual from the same period went on to list a series of measures that could be introduced to further control civilian populations. These included the suspension "of civil rights to permit search of persons . . . and arrest and confinement on suspicion"; the "establishment of a reporting system whereby absentee employees are immediately reported for investigation"; the confiscation of "property, real and personal, of those individuals adjudged guilty of collaboration"; press "censorship"; and the forced "relocation of entire hamlets or villages [or] suspected individuals and families to unfamiliar neighborhoods, away from relatives and friends who may be serving with the insurgents."[40] In particular, CI intelligence operations were to target "ordinary citizens who are typical members of organizations or associations which represent predominant local occupations, such as farming, industry, labor unions, farm cooperatives, social organizations, political parties, religious groups, and other organizations which play an important role in the local society." CI forces were to concentrate on "leaders of Dissident groups (minorities, religious sects, labor unions, political factions) who may be able to identify insurgent personnel, their methods of operation, and local agencies the insurgents hope to exploit." In fact, organized workers were a clear target of CI, since insurgents tend to work closely with union leaders to determine "the principal causes of discontent which can best be exploited to overthrow the established government [and] recruit loyal supporters."[41]

Again, this core theme continues in current doctrine. A recent manual, entitled *Doctrine for Joint Psychological Operations,* stated that US psyops forces can assist host nation (HN) security forces engaged in foreign internal defense by "improving popular support for the HN government . . . Projecting a favorable image of the HN government and the United States . . . Strengthening HN support of programs that provide positive populace control [and] . . . Passing instructions to the HN populace." Specifically, psyops is to be targeted at "the uncommitted," that is, "members of the general populace who are neutral, but may doubt the potential success of a resistance organization or friendly government supported by the United States and its allies." And, in clear parallel to the Cold War manuals that legitimated the manipulation of civilians to instill fear, the current doctrine outlines how psyops should be directed against enemy "sympathizers": "Hostile sympathizers can be categorized as willing collaborators, persons under duress, or passive hostile sympathizers. PSYOP are used to halt or prevent the sympathizers *by sowing doubt as to the validity of the hostile power's actions and instilling fear for collaborating.*"[42] In particular, population control continues to form a central strand of CI thinking, with the author of the Pentagon's recent CI training manual (Lieutenant Colonel Jan Horvath) arguing that it remains a good mechanism "to collect social and economic intelligence . . . The Nazi's Gestapo and the Eastern European communists were the best at this. Without becoming tainted or infected by their methods and attitudes, we have picked up some of their systems and processes."[43]

As a direct consequence of this view of civil society as a legitimate target for CI warfare, coupled with the kinds of insurgency often thrown up by foreign military occupation, CI doctrine has often emphasized the need to engage in a "dirty war" of assassination and torture against a wide range of armed and unarmed perceived threats to the regime. Pro-US militaries have consequently undergone training in precisely this. The coercive, force-based element of psyops is explicit. Indeed, the 1962 manual entitled *Psychological Operations,* specifically advocated the use of coercion to achieve this: "If these ['psychological'] programs fail, it may become necessary to take more aggressive action in the form of harsh treatment or even abductions. The abduction and harsh treatment of key enemy civilians can weaken the collaborators' belief in the strength and power of their military forces."[44]

The use of coercive techniques as part of the overall CI effort was openly advocated by US trainers as a legitimate part of the counterinsurgents' arsenal. For example, in the CIA's *Human Resource Exploitation Training Manual*, it was stated that although US trainers "do not stress the use of coercive techniques, we do want to make you aware of them and the proper way to use them." The manual outlined a number of coercive techniques, including sensory deprivation, solitary confinement, and different forms of physical torture, including bizarre forms of water torture whereby subjects were "suspended in water and wore black-out masks." The manual continued that the "stress and anxiety become unbearable for most subjects . . . how much they are able to stand depends upon the psychological characteristics of the individual . . . the 'questioner' can take advantage of this relationship by assuming a benevolent role."[45]

The use of dirty-war tactics was typically characterized by US trainers as a reactive form of "counter-terror" within US CI doctrine, necessitated by the terroristic enemy typically faced by CI troops. For example, a 1966 CI manual stated that CI forces "may not employ mass counter-terror (as opposed to selective counter-terror) against the civilian population, i.e., genocide is not an alternative."[46] US trainers were not unaware of the problematic nature of the use of harsh measures, especially in relation to the psychological effects on military recruits. A US Army manual called *Operations against Irregular Forces* outlined the fact that US-trained forces could potentially be subject to "moral and psychological pressures different from those normally present in regular combat operations." The manual highlights as problematic the "ingrained reluctance of the soldier to take repressive measures against women, children, and old men who usually are active in both overt and covert irregular activities or who must be resettled or concentrated for security reasons."[47]

As a result of the public outcry that accompanied the release of the Cold War manuals, more recent publications have refrained from advocating dirty-war tactics in such an explicit manner. However, the legitimation of such practices from within the CI framework remained during the Bush administration's war on terror, with "coercive interrogation techniques" being advocated as a legitimate tool in the arsenal of US-backed states. A number of torture techniques were recommended for use in 2003 by a working group headed by former US secretary of defense Donald Rumsfeld. These techniques are almost identical to those outlined above and included:

> hooding; dietary and environmental manipulation, including extremes of temperature or introducing unpleasant smells; the adjustment of sleeping times;

threat of transfer to a country that the detainee is likely to fear would subject them to torture or death; forced shaving of hair or beard; prolonged standing, but not for more than four hours in a 24 hour period; sleep deprivation, allowing individuals to rest briefly but repeatedly waking them, but not for longer than four days in succession; forced nudity, with no time limit placed on this; increasing anxiety through the presence of a dog without directly threatening action.[48]

Similarly, a memo prepared by Jay Bybee, of the US Justice Department's Office of Legal Counsel, and sent to Alberto Gonzales, counsel to the President in 2002, advised that "leading scholarly commentators believe that interrogation" of suspects employing methods that "might violate Section 2340A [of Title 18 of the US Code, which implements the UN's Convention against Torture] would be justified under the doctrine of self-defence."[49] The overt recognition of Washington's use of torture reached such levels that even former US vice president Dick Cheney argued for the efficacy of the water torture technique outlined above (now called "water-boarding"), whereby suspects are immobilized and subjected to mock drowning. When questioned about the use of water-boarding, Cheney argued that it had been "a very important tool that we've had to be able to secure the nation" and that its use was a "no-brainer."[50] Likewise, Cheney argued that Washington had to increasingly work on the "dark side," with the US needing to "have on the payroll some very unsavory characters" to win the "war on terrorism."[51] In a high-profile reversal of Bush policy, Barack Obama has outlawed such interrogation techniques by CIA employees and published memos from the Bush administration providing "legal justification."[52] However, given the wider framing by current CI doctrine and the demonstrable increase in global CI training for foreign security forces seen under the Obama administration, it is likely that civil society will continue to be targeted by proxy forces across the South (regardless of the president's declared commitment to the promotion of human rights).

The third central theme of CI doctrine, following from the identification of unarmed civil society as a threat and the view of this group as a legitimate target, has been the mobilization of pliant sections of civil society to meet this threat. Again, this aspect works to blur the boundaries between armed and unarmed groups within society and often provides a degree of "plausible deniability" in the face of the unsavory realities of counterinsurgency. Thus, members of the population are to be recruited as informants and positioned within insurgent groups. This use of civilian "employees" is considered vital to the CI effort with, as an early manual made clear, an informant's worth increasing through the number of "arrests, executions, or pacification[s]" the informants' information led to, all the while needing to take care "not to expose the employee as the information source."[53] This manual, entitled *Handling Sources*, advocated the harsh treatment of civilians in order to make certain that sufficient informants are recruited. It explicitly stated that good techniques to force people to inform were the targeting of family members and the use of physical violence. The "CI agent could cause the arrest of the employee's parents, imprison the employee or give him a beating as part of the placement plan of said employee in the guerrilla organization."[54]

CI doctrine has also explicitly advocated the development of a close relationship between state security forces and the widespread and pervasive use of paramilitary forces (or "death squads"). Paramilitary units were to form the vanguard for both monitoring and intelligence-gathering on alleged enemy civilians and civil society organizations. In training paramilitary forces, an early US CI field manual entitled *US Army Counterinsurgency Forces* explained that "paramilitary units can support the national army in the conduct of counterinsurgency operations when the latter are being conducted in their own province or political subdivision," with assistance "for organizing, equipping, and training paramilitary forces" being "provided through the [US] Military Assistance Program, the US AID Mission (for civil police), or other elements of the Country Team."[55] In a section entitled "Secure Population Centers," the manual outlined how "mobile reserves" that were "generally made up of paramilitary units" could be used to "move rapidly to the assistance" of villages under attack from insurgent forces. These paramilitaries were also to be involved in the establishment "of an intelligence network in the community for the purpose of developing information about guerrillas in the area and to insure the prompt exposure of any undercover insurgent sympathizers in the community."[56]

The centrality of paramilitary forces to the effort continues to be documented by CI doctrine. According to the 2004 Department of Defense publication entitled *Joint Tactics, Techniques, and Procedures for Foreign Internal Defense (FID)*, special operations forces "are an integral part of FID" and the "SOF role in FID is to train, advise, and support HN military and paramilitary forces." Further, the "US joint intelligence network must be tied into the country team, the local HN military, paramilitary and police intelligence capabilities."[57] The Pentagon was provided with explicit authorization and funding for supporting paramilitary groups, with the passage of the 2005 Defense Authorization Act. Section 1208 of this bill authorizes up to $25 million each year to "provide support to foreign forces, irregular forces, groups or individuals engaged in supporting or facilitating ongoing military operations by United States special operations forces to combat terrorism."[58]

We see, then, a very clear development of US strategy that has militarized the relationship between security forces and populations in the South. As part of this reorientation, US military aid and training has often advocated the deployment of military force against civil society as a legitimate part of the overall CI effort. On the ground, the militarization of state-society relations has led directly to the active targeting of both armed insurgents and civil society more broadly. Across the South, union leaders, student activists, intellectuals, teachers, and progressive religious clergy have been the principal targets of US-backed CI states. Torture has often been institutionalized and routinely practiced against perceived enemies. Although such abuses are not directed from Washington, they form part of a useful mechanism for the entrenchment of stability in important regions and the creation of a climate wherein foreign corporations have the confidence to invest. A clear line exists between specific abuses as they happen on the ground—where individual trade unionists, for example, are targeted by US-based CI forces—and the overarching grand strategy of the United States to preserve and extend its global hegemonic position.

## The Militarization of Energy Security

As we have seen, US interests in the oil-rich South revolve around the transnationalization of local political economies and their full integration into the wider global economy. In this way, it is hoped, major energy producers become productive circuits of global capital, embedding and deepening market relations. In many cases, however, achieving this objective has not been easy. Oil-rich zones are often highly unstable, with political elites that either rule without any form of democratic legitimacy or that otherwise experience significant political opposition from below. As one major report from the Center for Strategic and International Studies (CSIS) has declared: "Stability in petroleum exporting regions is tenuous at best . . . recent experience has shown that exporting countries in Africa, the Caspian Sea and South America are no more stable than the Gulf." According to the authors, this is due to a wide range of domestic threats to stability, including "pipeline sabotage in Nigeria, labor strikes in Venezuela . . . and civil unrest in Uzbekistan and other [Caspian] states."[59]

In a world that relies heavily on a smooth flow of oil to market, such sources of unrest present a threat to economic stability. Shutting down production at one site, destroying a large export pipeline, or closing a major route to shipping traffic are all potential political tools to be wielded by those who wish to alter the prevailing order. And as research sponsored by the US National Intelligence Council has concluded, it is "reasonable to ask who, among present-day occupants of the international stage, would like to see a great deal changed? To which the immediate answer would obviously be the ramshackle assemblage of rogue states and revolutionary movements whose machinations consume such a disproportionate share of time and attention from the defense establishments around the world . . . [M]ilitary planners and civilian strategists are [inclined] to point to the potential threat that terrorists and other disenfranchised groups pose to global energy markets; and indeed they have good reason to."[60]

In particular, "resource nationalism" has been identified as a challenge to US interests. For example, John Deutch (former director of Central Intelligence) stated to Congress in March 2007 that "a major shift in control of reserves and production is under way in international oil markets from international oil companies to national oil companies" with the NOCs having "both commercial *and political* objectives."[61] These political objectives often present Washington with a challenge, with the National Petroleum Council (NPC)— the most prominent oil industry advisory body to the US government—noting in a 2007 report to the secretary of energy that there is "a new generation of sovereign governments [beginning] to reassert greater control over natural resources in an effort to extract maximum commercial advantages—often by violating existing contracts." And crucially for the NPC, resource nationalism presents a threat to US interests, because it "undermines investor confidence in the long run and can lead to many undesirable results," as "investment capital, as well as the best industry technology and manpower, cannot be applied in the most economically effective manner to increase supplies of oil and gas for the world market."[62]

Whether "subversion from below" or "popular nationalism from above," there exists a range of immediate and serious threats to global energy security. As such, US planners have long identified the need to armor the processes of globalization that will achieve maximum levels of stable oil production. Opening up the oil-rich South needs to take place alongside "stabilization operations" to protect key infrastructure and to provide for a wider environment conducive to long-term investment. In this way, the emergent energy security paradigm is increasingly being defined against forms of social change that might potentially impact upon energy supplies to world markets. This fact was recognized in a report by the influential Council on Foreign Relations, *Strategic Energy Policy: Challenges for the 21st Century*. In it, the authors were clear that as "the 21st century opens, the energy sector is in critical condition. A crisis could erupt at any time from any number of factors, from an accident on the Alaskan pipeline to a revolution in a major oil-producing country." Social or political changes could affect "US national security and foreign policy in dramatic ways." Capturing the essential nature of US strategy, the report argued that the US should take the lead in policing the global energy regime, by promoting "market forces wherever and whenever possible, while *acting to ensure order* in case of market failures" such as "interference in trade flows by private or state-owned entities and actions by adversaries."[63]

In this context, Washington has deployed—and continues to deploy—coercive statecraft throughout the oil-rich South. American armed forces serve as an "invisible hand," and both the active use and implicit threat of overwhelming force are employed to safeguard the system within which international commerce operates.[64] As John Brodman, former deputy assistant secretary for international energy policy, testified before Congress, the existence of such a diverse range of challenges to global energy security means that the US must act to "minimize many of these new internal threats to stability, and to promote, protect and defend our security of supply, and our own security in commercial energy trade and development relationships."[65]

This "safeguarding" function has several interrelated components. As we shall see in later chapters, the Pentagon works to ensure that there exists a large direct American military presence—or the potential to rapidly establish one—in every key oil-rich region. In this way, US power is "concretized" at strategic points in the system. The US Navy, for example, has almost unchallenged command of the maritime environment around each oil-rich zone and directly polices strategic chokepoints and offshore fields. As the US *National Strategy for Maritime Security* states, "preserving the freedom of the seas is a top national priority. The right of vessels to travel freely in international waters, engage in innocent and transit passage, and have access to ports is an essential element of national security."[66] Under the banner of "maritime security," naval activity is geared toward building local capacity but is also a mechanism for embedding direct American presence without costly or politically sensitive land bases. And in regions where energy reserves play a crucial role in US strategic thinking, American naval operations are designed—in the words of Tom Rowden, commander of EUCOM Naval Surface Combatant Warships—to "ensure a more stable maritime environment to ensure their ability to get those resources to market."[67]

Should direct onshore intervention by American troops become necessary, the Pentagon has also been working to negotiate access to "forward operating locations" (FOLs). Rather than permanent "bases," FOLs are "strategic, cost-effective locations" that allow US forces to use existing facilities to carry out operations. Such agreements have been in place in Latin America since the late 1990s, with US counternarcotic and counterinsurgency operations ongoing in the region since that time.[68] The concept is also being expanded to West Africa and the Caspian Basin, although here the idea is to "mothball" facilities, providing latent capacity to serve as sites for American military insertion if necessary.[69]

In the Persian Gulf, of course, this military presence has been deployed directly against regional adversaries, most notably in Iraq since 2003. More often, however, American coercive strategy is firmly premised on "contracting out" stabilization operations, either to local security forces or private military companies (PMCs). Security assistance programs that are run through the US State Department and the Pentagon are often explicitly designed to enhance regional security and stability for the purposes of resource extraction. Time and again, American military commanders maintain that energy security is a primary objective for Washington and that security assistance programs play a central role.

In just one example, high-level military personnel in the US European Command (EUCOM)—the Combatant Command responsible for coordinating US military policy toward part of the Caspian Basin—state that their role includes working with regional security forces to further Washington's economic interests. In outlining EUCOM's 2008 posture statement, CINC General Bantz

J. Craddock stated that "security, economic interests, and shared political values provide the impetus for engagement with our international partners, and form the basis for our Strategy of Active Security." This strategy aims to "create and maintain an environment that advances US strategic and economic interests." In the context of the Caspian region, such interests are wrapped up with the provision of "access to Central Asian hydrocarbon reserves, which, together with Azerbaijan's own resources, provide an important alternative energy source for our European Allies." Craddock was clear that a high "strategic priority" of EUCOM is to "support improved energy security for Europe, Eurasia and the Black Sea region." In this context, security assistance to regional allies was motivated by the "economic difficulties, inter- and intrastate conflicts, insurgency [and] deteriorating infrastructure" that beset the region and the consequent need to improve the capabilities of regional militaries to impose internal and cross-border stability. Security cooperation is "the cornerstone of this strategy," with EUCOM focused on building "able partners" in this strategic region.[70] Details of these programs, and the ways in which they intersect with Washington's energy security agenda, will be examined in depth in the remaining chapters.

Alongside the provision of security assistance to oil-rich states, US planners can often rely on IOCs making their own arrangements to defend their investments. On the ground across the oil-rich South, multinational oil companies work in close cooperation with HN security forces and PMCs in order to protect specific installations, create localized "zones of stability" to allow operations to continue unimpeded, and even to influence wider dynamics of conflict. In this way, PMCs "act as 'investment enablers' [for IOCs], providing clients with robust security that make otherwise extremely risky investment options safe enough to be financially viable. In the midst of conflict, they create localized stability that reduces costs and increases investment values."[71] Private military companies also often work alongside host governments, and relations between the state, oil companies, and PMCs can be complex. Given that host governments tend to be economically underdeveloped, direct state contracts with PMCs are often paid for in part through the granting of concessions to commercially exploit the resource secured. Such concessions are then managed by a consortium of extractive companies supported by PMCs. Indeed, "it is not unusual for [PMCs] and extractive interests to be controlled by the same company (though the ownership and corporate affiliations of [PMCs] are typically obscure)."[72]

In stark illustration of the symbiosis between local governments, foreign capital, and the use of force, there have been cases of governments privatizing public assets that are under control of rebel forces and selling these to international consortia involving PMCs, which then establish control over the areas.[73] Companies in Nigeria (Shell, Chevron), Colombia (BP, Occidental Petroleum), and Georgia (BP again) all employ private military firms to protect critical infrastructure. Likewise, in countries where national oil companies (NOCs) predominate, a similar nexus between commercial operation and military force can be found. Literally tens of thousands of private security personnel are on the ground in Saudi Arabia, Iraq, and other Gulf states, deployed to provide frontline protection as well as advise state security forces. Formations such as the Saudi Petroleum Installation Security Force (PISF) and the Iraqi Facilities Protection Force (IFPF) are heavily armed and comprise thousands of soldiers alongside high-tech fighter jets.

Much of this effort is directed at what is known as critical infrastructure protection (CIP). US planners have become increasingly concerned with funding CIP programs as fears increase over instabilities in the energy supply network. As President Clinton found in May 1998, the fact that the US "possesses both the world's strongest military and its largest national economy" means that "future enemies, whether nations, groups or individuals, may seek to harm us in non-traditional ways . . . attacks on [key] infrastructure and information systems may be capable of significantly harming both our military power and our economy."[74] Although the resulting CIP strategy was initially designed to protect US-based infrastructure, it has increasingly contained a large international component, with the State Department chairing an International CIP Working Group since 1999 for the coordination of efforts "designed to encourage allied nations to enhance the security of those critical infrastructures and key resources on which the US military depends for its operations." Such efforts "directly enhance the security of the United States by reducing the risk to foreign infrastructures to which we are inextricably linked" and are located within the State Department's Bureau of Political-Military Affairs (the principal link to the Pentagon).[75]

In the aftermath of the foiled attack on the Abqaiq oil facilities in Saudi Arabia in February 2006,[76] the Bush administration further developed US efforts to secure oil facilities across the world, with the creation of a *Global Critical Energy Infrastructure Protection Strategy*. This strategy is based upon the premise that the "importance of assuring reliable supplies of energy for US national security and economy makes the security of critical energy infrastructure worldwide particularly important." As such, it focuses attention on "key foreign petroleum facilities located in host nations with similar interests and concerns" and on providing security assistance for them.[77]

US assistance programs have been supplemented by an increased interest in energy security by NATO. In 1997 Warren Christopher (former secretary of state) and William Perry (former secretary of defense) were urging the organization to "adapt its military strategy to today's reality" and move beyond its traditional collective defense posture to meet threats to members' "collective interests *beyond their territory*," including the prevention of any "disruption to the flow of oil."[78] This has fed into NATO's strategy formulation; a report to its Parliamentary Assembly in 2007 emphasizes that "protecting energy infrastructure *at home* only provides a partial response to the challenge posed by energy security" and that European and North American dependence on foreign energy supplies means that they have "an interest in enhancing protection of energy infrastructure *in producing and transit countries, and of energy routes worldwide.*" As a result, high-level NATO officials have suggested providing "security assistance to partners for the protection of their energy infrastructure." Such assistance would incorporate "military operations and rapid reaction capabilities," including "isolated patrolling and surveillance missions of specific sites."[79]

Whereas CIP has moved up Washington's energy security agenda, the militarization of the oil-rich South ranges far wider than static infrastructure protection. Indeed, security assistance is geared more around active counterinsurgency. Training and equipment programs are designed to build local capabilities for rapid reaction, troop mobility, intelligence networks, nightfighting, surveillance, and offensive tactics. This was confirmed by Brigadier General Galen Jackman, SOUTHCOM J-3 (Operations) chief, when discussing American assistance to pipeline protection units in Colombia. According to Jackman, "These brigades that we're talking about will be very offensively orientated. That is focused [on] the enemy, as opposed to static defense around the pipeline."[80] Elsewhere, the head of the US Army Special Forces mission to the country stated that the "advisors" were there to "train the Colombians to find, track down, and kill the terrorists before they attack the pipeline."[81] High-end CI training characterizes US assistance across the oil-rich South, as Washington works to stabilize strategic regions in the face of widespread unrest. We will see this play out on the ground in chapters 4, 5, and 6.

It is perhaps unsurprising that the confluence between American coercive statecraft, local security forces, PMCs, and oil companies has had a profound impact on human security across the oil-rich South. Both armed and peaceful opposition to the activities of oil companies—and to the wider political and economic contexts within which these activities take place—have been met by indiscriminate and unlawful uses of force. The record is, at times, truly shocking. Strategies include the widespread use of arbitrary detentions, "disappearances," and holding people incommunicado for long periods of time; beating, punching, and kicking opponents; electric shocks and asphyxiation as forms of torture; rape and other forms of sexual violence; dismemberment and summary executions; and reprisals against family members and wider communities. CI forces have used "scorched earth" tactics, destroying entire communities as part of "clearing" regions of "insurgents" and "subversives." There have been widespread forcible movements of populations, with many thousands of internally displaced persons created as a result. Villagers suspected of supporting the opposition to oil activities have been denied access to agricultural, fishing, and hunting land. Some leaked government orders have directed the coordination of "wasting operations," wherein vocal members of civil society have been targeted, alongside whole communities living close to vulnerable energy infrastructure. Other secret military papers and strategy documents—both from US intelligence and local military commanders—have ordered the formation of paramilitary intelligence networks, for the express purpose of surveillance of communities and civil society organizations, and the assassination of prominent members. At other points, such organizations have been branded by the authorities as subversive, their activities heavily circumscribed or outlawed altogether, and their leadership arrested or otherwise targeted.

Given the close relationship between IOCs and CI campaigns, it is perhaps also unsurprising that there exists evidence across the South of deep corporate involvement in human rights violations by PMCs and government CI troops. According to the UN special representative on business and human rights, John Ruggie, the extractive sector (oil, gas, and mining) "utterly dominates" the record of documented abuses by transnational corporations in the South. These companies account for most of the "allegations of the worst abuses, up to and including complicity in crimes against humanity, typically for acts committed by public and private security forces protecting company assets and property; large-scale corruption; violations of labour rights; and a broad array of abuses in relation to local communities, especially indigenous people."[82] In fact, the outsourcing of security requirements to private companies is used, in many cases, to give plausible deniability in the face of any abuses that result.[83] IOCs have deployed military force both for static defense and active counterinsurgency purposes, with evidence of involvement in paramilitary operations against local residents, intelligence-gathering, and targeting of vocal opponents to their activity. In just one example, Shell has admitted to arming and paying Nigerian security forces to protect its investments in the Niger Delta, and these forces have in turn been directly accused of widespread violations against the local Ogoni community, including arbitrary detentions, beatings, and harassment. Peaceful occupation by community members of Shell facilities, to protest the environmental destruction being caused, was met by the company calling in the notorious Mobile Police Force, and subsequent killing of scores of unarmed civilians.[84]

## Conclusion

Overall, we have seen an aspect of US hegemony in the South that looks decidedly different from that experienced by the core capitalist powers. Whilst the exercise of US power has appeared relatively benign to the developed core, its application to the often chronically unstable South has been a different matter entirely. Due to the often brittle social base of a number of peripheral state formations, coupled with instability that can (and often does) occur in the face of widespread economic inequality, US planners are often forced to fall back on a strategy of support for authoritarianism and repressive state control. CI has become the strategy par excellence for the containment and rollback of social forces considered inimical to US global interests. The human costs of these policies have often been shocking. Moreover, CI has become increasingly wedded to the policy of global energy security, with the US working through proxy local and private security forces to stabilize oil-rich zones. Ensuring domestic stability in oil-rich states, often through the use of US counterinsurgency training and equipment, has become the central means by which local elites maintain their rule and armor the ongoing process of economic liberalization. In turn, CI has become a primary mechanism for ensuring an environment wherein oil capital can confidently operate and, in this way, has become a central plank for ensuring maximum levels of global energy security. In the remaining chapters, we pick up on the themes outlined over the past two and develop our understanding of the nexus of American hegemony, economic transnationalization, coercive statecraft, and global energy security. We do this by tracing the ways in which US strategy has been deployed—and continues to be deployed—across specific oil-rich regions in the South: the Persian Gulf, the Caspian Basin, West Africa, and Latin America.

# CHAPTER THREE

# The Persian Gulf and Beyond

Because of the extent to which Washington's grand strategy in the postwar era has relied upon the control of the world's major oil supplies, establishing American hegemony in oil-rich zones has long been a central objective of the US state. And given where the largest reserves of oil lie, US power has been deployed continuously within the Persian Gulf region. This region sits on top of no less than 61 percent of all proven reserves in the world, making it absolutely crucial to the entire international system. Twenty-eight percent of global oil production is located in the Gulf, with predictions that this proportion will rise to 33 percent by 2030 as production is ramped up from 23 mbpd to 38 mbpd.[1] In considering oil reserves and production capacity, no other region has (or will) come close to the Persian Gulf in importance. This is a point not lost on US planners; the National Energy Policy Development (NEPD) report maintains that the region "will remain vital to US interests" and "a primary focus of US international energy policy" in coming years, with Saudi Arabia continuing as a "lynchpin of supply reliability."[2] Saudi Arabia holds more than 20 percent of the entire global stock of oil and—along with other regional producers—over 80 percent of the world's "excess production capacity." This capacity is crucial and establishes Saudi Arabia as the "swing state" in the system, able to make up for lost production elsewhere in the globe (whether as a result of natural disaster, corporate accident, or political instability).[3] Controlling this region, and Saudi Arabia in particular, is therefore a high priority for Washington, and this has been so throughout the postwar era. As Bradley Bowman, fellow of the Council on Foreign Relations and formerly professor at the US Military Academy at West Point, states: "The need for a reliable and uninterrupted flow of oil from the Persian Gulf region to the United States and other industrialized countries represents the first and longest-standing vital US interest in the Middle East . . . If the US or global economy were deprived of this oil or natural gas, the economic and political consequences would be devastating and far-reaching."[4]

Following the pattern of rule established elsewhere, ensuring US hegemony in the Persian Gulf has not involved territorial acquisition. Washington has instead preferred to exercise control through existing state forms and sovereign governments, with substantial effort put into pulling them firmly within a US orbit. Enabling American strategy has been the overwhelming military superiority of US forces in the region, primarily through a massive and uninterrupted naval presence since the 1940s.[5] Such forward deployment has combined with the firm political will by successive American administrations to actively intervene, through force of arms when necessary, in order to retain US hegemony. At times, such interventions have taken the form of direct deployment of American combat troops. More frequently, however, coercive power has been deployed through the provision of vast amounts of security assistance to "friendly" regional militaries. In line with Washington's broader counterinsurgency (CI) strategy, discussed in chapter 2, this assistance has been primarily designed to build local capacities to confront domestic challenges to the current order. CI equipment and doctrine has formed the basis for substantial training by US forces, specifically in order to reorientate militaries in the Persian Gulf toward an internal policing role. The first half of this chapter will chart this series of interventions and the ways in which US policy has worked to insulate pro-US elites in the postwar era. Most recently, of course, this strategy translated into the invasion and reorientation of Iraq. We will explore this episode in some depth in the second half of this chapter. Finally, we will briefly explore the increased focus by Washington in recent years on diversification of energy production away from the Persian Gulf, as a strategy to counteract continuing instability in the Middle East and to maximize production levels. This will set the context for the final three chapters of the book, which will explore US strategy toward the Caspian Basin, West Africa, and Latin America, respectively.

## Establishing US Hegemony in the Persian Gulf: Threats and Response

Since 1945, US planners have identified a wide range of threats to its dominant position in the Persian Gulf, and American strategy has focused on ensuring that these are contained or even—where necessary and possible—destroyed. In the immediate postwar years, such threats predominantly arose from other extraregional powers intent on exerting their own influence. Consequently, US planners focused on preventing competing imperial powers from pulling key states within their orbit. Initially, this strategy centered on usurping Great Britain from its hegemonic position in the Persian Gulf; a 1944 report by the Office of Strategic Services (the OSS, the forerunner of the CIA) suggested that the problem of security in the Middle East "means in particular security from our present allies, almost all of whom have fingers in the Moslem pie and who have shown themselves particularly anxious to keep us out."[6] As British power succumbed to US dominance, Washington's geostrategic concerns centered on ensuring that the USSR was excluded from the region. Moscow had a large military presence in Iran at the end of World War II, and US planners focused significant effort on rolling back this strategic position and carving out the entire oil-rich Middle East as a zone within which US hegemony was unchecked. Reporting in October 1946, the Joint Chiefs of Staff were clear that "as a source of supply (oil) Iran is an area of major strategic interest to the United States." This was compounded by the fact that "the area offers opportunities to conduct delaying operations and/or operations to protect United States–controlled oil resources in Saudi Arabia." Indeed, in any possible military conflict with the USSR, "the oil resources of Iran and the Near and Middle East are very important and may be vital to decisive counter-offensive action from any area." As a consequence, it was in "the strategic interest of the United States to keep Soviet influence and Soviet armed forces as far as possible from oil resources in Iran, Iraq and the Near and Middle East."[7]

In the post–Cold War era, of course, Washington's interests in the region are increasingly entwined with those of other core powers, with energy security for all achieved through the smooth flow of Persian Gulf oil onto international markets. Geopolitical moves by so-called peer competitors have remained a relatively distant concern for the United States, with its position in the region almost totally unchallenged from other core powers. Recent moves by Chinese and Indian and even Russian leaders to forge closer links with the oil-rich Gulf states may worry some of those who see a reemergence of geopolitical rivalry over energy.[8] However, the lack of any non-US strategic military presence in the region, and the likelihood that this will be the case for many years (if not decades) to come, means that American regional hegemony will almost certainly continue to reign unchecked from outside pressures.

In contrast, US hegemony in the Gulf has been repeatedly challenged by social and political forces from within the region. Throughout the postwar era, US planners have had to deal with the reality of powerful expressions of nationalism, pan-Arabism, and Islamism. This was embodied not least in the creation of the Gulf-dominated Organization of the Petroleum Exporting Countries (OPEC) in 1960, the subsequent transfer of substantial oil reserves to national oil companies (NOCs), and the ejection of Western-based international oil companies (IOCs) as major players in the region. In fact, the NOCs from Saudi Arabia, Iraq, Iran, and Kuwait together own 60 percent of the world's oil reserves.[9] Accommodation of many such nationalist forces by Washington has been a strategic and political necessity, especially where they control the region's states and not least because the vast oil wealth at their disposal leaves them impervious to the lever of the International Monetary Fund (since they need no economic assistance). In this regard, American strategy toward the Gulf has often contrasted with that in other oil-rich zones, where Washington has been able to support ruling elites more receptive to the adoption of free market political economies. As we shall see, it was only with the occupation of Iraq that neoliberalism finally found a firm hold in the region and IOCs began to have a greater control of the region's oil.

Despite the need to accommodate OPEC nationalism, US planners have remained alert to the dangers of overly populist expressions of independence in the region, in case these should challenge either American regional hegemony or the free flow of oil onto markets under relatively favorable conditions. In this light, Washington has worked to stabilize pro-US regimes in the Persian Gulf and to counter those social and political forces that challenge the wider economic order. This was acknowledged early on; the US National Security Council (NSC) identified in 1953 that "the current danger to the security of the free world [in the region] arises not so much from the threat of direct Soviet military attack as from a continuation of the present unfavorable trends." These trends were "inimical to Western interests" and included the determination of states in the region "to assert their independence." As a result, US objectives were to include the creation and maintenance of "stable, viable, friendly governments in the area, capable of withstanding communist-inspired subversion from within and will to resist communist aggression." And in working toward this objective, the NSC argued that the United States should "seek to guide the revolutionary and nationalistic pressures throughout the area into orderly channels not antagonistic to the West" and should "support leadership groups which offer the best prospect of orderly progress toward free world objectives."[10] By 1958, the NSC had further clarified its thinking in this regard and was declaring in secret that the United States needed to be prepared "when required, to come forward with formulas designed to reconcile vital Free World interests in the area's petroleum resources with the rising tide of nationalism in the area." Crucially, the NSC was clear on the need to use "force . . . as a last resort" to ensure that "the quantity of oil available from the Near East on reasonable terms is sufficient . . . to meet Western Europe's requirements."[11]

The primary challenge to US interests in the Gulf had always been the potential for domestic and regional political developments to disrupt the flow of oil. In the worst-case scenario for US planners, of course, such developments would lead to the seizure of power by "unfriendly" forces, who would then seek to orientate states away from the US-led system. As Bradley Bowman states, the main threat to the flow of Persian Gulf oil comes not from strategic positioning by the United Kingdom, France, Russia, or even China but by "a successful revolution or widespread instability in a major oil-producing country such as Saudi Arabia." It is this need to guard against overly populist and reformist forces—whilst accommodating the relatively conservative nationalism of current OPEC producers—that has driven the long history of US attempts to shore up pro-US regimes in the oil-rich Persian Gulf and to contain or unseat leaders who have proved unacceptably independent.

## The "Twin Pillar" Strategy

American planners understood the centrality of oil from the Persian Gulf as they worked to build a US-centric world order from the ashes of World War II. In 1944, as the war was drawing to a close, the US State Department published a report urging "a broad policy of conservation of Western Hemisphere petroleum reserves" in order to "assure the adequacy for military and civilian requirements of strategically available reserves." Instead of relying upon dwindling US reserves of oil, which had largely propelled the Allies to victory, the report suggested, Washington should promote the "substantial and orderly expansion of production in Eastern Hemisphere sources of supply, principally the Middle East."[12] Similarly, the 1944 OSS report discussed earlier had concluded that Washington's national interests in the Middle East were "oil, airbases and future markets."[13]

Given the strategic importance of Saudi oil reserves, the United States has long been committed to forging close relations with the Kingdom. The central role that Saudi oil was to play in sustaining US global power was increasingly understood during World War II and underscored in 1945 when the head of the US State Department's Division of Near Eastern Affairs, Gordon Merriam, argued that the country's oil riches were a "stupendous source of strategic power, and one of the greatest material prizes in human history."[14] The United States was quick to act. In 1945, President Roosevelt committed Washington to secure the Saudi monarchical dictatorship from significant threat, in return for an agreement to export oil cheaply onto international markets. This strategic posture was concretized with the 1951 deployment of the US Military Training Mission (USMTM): a large-scale, Pentagon-led advisory mission designed to funnel training and equipment to protect Washington's client state. Security assistance programs were explicitly designed not only to enhance local capacity to defend against external aggression; according to a 1961 USMTM publication, their function was also to "provide a small, modern well balanced Saudi Arabian Army, Navy, and Air Force *designed to maintain the internal stability of the Kingdom*."[15] This required a twin-track approach from Washington, with the Pentagon working to bolster the Kingdom's conventional forces whilst also taking over the training of the Saudi Arabian National Guard (SANG) from the British in 1973.

The SANG is a paramilitary force designed to consolidate the rule of the Saudi dictatorship and is highly trained in internal warfare and CI techniques. The American contract to train and equip the SANG is still in place and is largely subcontracted to private military companies (PMCs), which have been deployed en masse by Washington to transfer CI skills. Central to this assistance effort is the Vinnell Corporation, which has been paid hundreds of millions of dollars to coordinate the provision of CI doctrine, equipment, and operational training in small-unit tactics and advanced infantry maneuvers. As one Vinnell official told *Time:* "We are not mercenaries because we are not pulling triggers. We train people to pull triggers. Maybe that makes us executive mercenaries."[16] Overall, contracts between the Saudi elite and US-based PMCs—mediated by Washington—run into billions of dollars and have resulted in 35,000 to 40,000 private security personnel deploying to the country at any one time to buttress the military and internal security forces.[17] In turn, these forces have been deployed by the House of Saud to entrench its rule over Saudi society; any sign of unrest is met with harsh repressive measures.

Saudi Arabia remains one of the least free countries in the world, with political and economic power held by a very small ruling elite. Because this rule largely rests upon American military support and such support is contingent upon the free flow of oil, US and Saudi interests have remained deeply entwined throughout the postwar era.

This interest in securing unfettered access to Saudi oil was matched by a strategy to maintain dominance over Iran, as the second significant oil state of the region. Events on the ground, however, caused US policy choices to take very different path in relation to Tehran. Enormous levels of wealth inequality and mass deprivation in Iran in the immediate postwar years ran alongside clear exploitation by the UK-owned Anglo-Iranian Oil Corporation (AIOC). By 1950, the AIOC had made £200 million in profit through its oil extraction in Iran but had paid only £16 million to the Iranian government (a figure that was, in fact, less than that paid by the corporation to the UK government). Not lost on the Iranian people, this situation led to widespread political unrest across the country, which culminated in the democratic election of Mohammed Mossadegh in May 1951. Standing on a platform of fierce independence from the West, Mossadegh moved quickly to nationalize the AIOC, a turn of events that posed a direct threat to US interests. And crucially, this threat arose not just because of the ejection of Western oil companies and not just because of the new, less favorable terms upon which Iranian oil would be available to market (although both certainly played a part). US planners were also motivated by a fear that acquiescence in the face of Mossadegh would set an unacceptable precedent throughout the global South. US planners were concerned with the "threat of a good example": should the newly elected leader be left to act with the freedom that the Iranian population desired, it was feared, this might tempt independent forces across the South, leading to what Daniel Yergin has termed "an epidemic of nationalization and expropriation."[18]

The turn of events in Iran led first to the imposition of sanctions on the country, as the Eisenhower administration publicly declared Mossadegh a potential threat to US interests. Fears were deliberately stoked by Washington, with overstated claims that Iran and its oil were moving into Soviet orbit. In fact, despite Washington's public position, a US State Department report of 1953 concluded that Mossadegh was neither a communist nor communist-supporter and noted that he was despised by the pro-Soviet Tudeh Party, which considered his overthrow a high priority.[19] Regardless, Mossadegh posed a real threat to US interests, namely, the nationalization of oil production coupled with the symbolic power of his anticolonial stance. Ultimately, this fact moved Washington and London to foment a counterrevolutionary coup, organized by the British MI6 and the CIA. Conservative elements within Iran were supplied with training, arms, and tactical plans by the Western intelligence agencies, and with this assistance they overthrew Mossadegh, replaced him with a pro-Western dictator, Mohammad Reza Shah Pahlavi, and thus extinguished the short-lived democratic experience in Iran.[20]

Given the fragile social base of the Shah's dictatorship, US planners moved quickly to consolidate the pro-Western regime. To this end, the United States began to train and equip Iran's security forces. Between 1953 and 1960, Iran received $450 million in US military aid. By 1975 Iran was the largest single purchaser of American arms in the world, and between 1972 and 1977 US military sales to Iran topped a staggering $16 billion.[21] Throughout the Shah's reign, over 11,000 Iranian military personnel trained by the Pentagon—a figure that, thirty years after the military relationship was frozen, still represents the highest number of personnel trained by the US throughout the wider Middle East.[22] Primary amongst the objectives of this assistance program was the policing of Iranian society to suppress vocal elements, with the United States playing a key role in the formation of the Iranian internal paramilitary security force, SAVAK. The SAVAK was tasked with rooting out anti-Shah elements and ensuring the "stability" required for the continued flow of Iran's oil. Although US aid and training for Iran was provided under the pretext of containing the Soviet Union, Fred Halliday notes, the "Soviet Union had nothing to fear from the Iranian army, and the foes against which the Shah was being armed [by the United States] were those inside and not outside the country."[23]

Because of Mossadegh's popularity, it was perhaps unsurprising that the SAVAK had its work cut out for it and it became responsible for the torture and imprisonment of thousands of Iranians during the Shah's reign. According to James Bill, the force became a "police-state monster" that penetrated a wide section of Iranian society and that acquired an "unsavory reputation not only in Iran but throughout the world," with the "systematic use of the ugliest forms of torture [becoming] the order of the day" throughout the 1970s.[24]

Washington pursued a "twin pillar" strategy in the Persian Gulf during the 1950s, 1960s, and 1970s, with Saudi Arabia and Iran designated as vehicles through which the United States could exercise its hegemony across the region. Concrete levels of control were exercised by providing political, military, and economic support to suitably pliant local elites. As Nixon's deputy assistant secretary of defense, James H. Noyes, argued at the time, "We are willing to assist the Gulf states but we look to them to bear the main responsibility for their own defense and to cooperate among themselves to insure regional peace and stability," with "the leading states of the area, Iran and Saudi Arabia" central to that purpose.[25] Both of these states became bulwarks against reformist or revolutionary elements in the region, and suppression of social and political forces from below was the central means by which pro-US rule was consolidated. At the time, US senator Henry Jackson stated bluntly that intervention in the region was an absolute necessity and that the post-Mossadegh Iran was now a reliable friend of the United States who, along with Saudi Arabia, has "served to inhibit and contain those irresponsible and radical elements in certain Arab states . . . who, were they free to do so, would pose a grave threat indeed to our principal source of petroleum in the Persian Gulf."[26]

## "By Any Means Necessary"

Regardless of the vast sums of money poured into Saudi Arabia and Iran during the first decades of the Cold War, this twin pillar strategy suffered a calamitous setback in 1979. The Iranian Revolution and the Soviet invasion of Afghanistan, both occurring almost simultaneously, ensured that powerful forces deeply inimical to US interests were in control of, or in close proximity to, significant reserves of Persian Gulf oil. In the face of this new turn of events, Washington was presented with the first major challenge to its regional hegemony and was forced to act. The outgoing Carter administration swiftly announced a commitment to retain Washington's dominance in the Persian Gulf, although this time through a policy of direct US intervention in the face of any major threat to the flow of oil. This was a significant turning point in US declaratory policy and for the first time committed US combat forces themselves to protecting American oil interests. In this light, President Carter's 1980 State of the Union address outlined "the overwhelming dependence of the Western democracies on oil supplies from the Middle East" and stated bluntly that an "attempt by any outside force to gain control of the Persian Gulf region will be regarded as an assault on the vital interests of the United States of America," with any such assault to be "repelled by any means necessary, including military force."[27] As Carter's secretary of defense, Harold Brown, argued: the "particular manner in which our economy has expanded means that we have come to depend to no small degree on imports, exports and the earnings from overseas investments for our material well-being." Going on, Brown identified the core commitment of successive US administrations up until the present day: the "protection of the oil flow from the Middle East" is a vital interest of the United States, and as such Washington would need to "take any action that's appropriate, including the use of military force," to keep it flowing.[28]

To give teeth to his new doctrine, Carter ordered the formation of a Rapid Deployment Force (RDF) that could speedily assemble for forward power projection in the region. This force was later upgraded by Ronald Reagan to a full-scale regional command, US Central Command (CENTCOM), which has since been the main vehicle through which US power is exercised across the Persian Gulf. From the outset this force structure was designed at least in part to counter the potential spread of anti-US forces *within* the region, as embodied by the new regime in Tehran. Of course, hedging against Soviet geostrategic moves always factored into decision making in Washington; Carter, however, maintained that "the press of social and religious and economic and political change in the many nations of the developing world, exemplified by the revolution in Iran," posed a considerable threat to American interests.[29] Washington's response—the creation of the RDF and the declaration of vital US interest in the continued flow of oil—was designed to make sure that this "press of change" did not spread. Carter's national security advisor, Zbigniew Brzezinski, believed that a leading rationale for the creation of this force was to assist "a friendly government under a subversive attack."[30] Likewise, Defense Secretary Harold Brown was later clear that "one sensitive issue is whether the United States should plan to protect the oil fields against internal or regional threats" and urged Washington to prepare plans to guard against further success by other revolutionary movements.[31] These plans were confirmed by a US Senate report, which noted that the new RDF was designed, amongst other things, to train for and fight "regional wars or leftist or nationalist insurgencies that threatened US and allied access to the region's oil supplies."[32]

Throughout the 1980s, as Iran and Iraq waged a brutal war against each other, the security of oil flows from the Gulf remained the most important concern for Washington. In 1983, the Reagan administration passed National Security Decision Directive 114, declaring: "Because of the real and psychological impact of a curtailment in the flow of oil from the Persian Gulf on the international economic system, we must assure our readiness to deal promptly with actions aimed at disrupting that traffic." As a result, "US military forces will attempt to deter and, if that fails, to defeat any hostile efforts to close the

Strait [of Hormuz] to international shipping."[33] Alongside this military commit-ment to protect Gulf oil tankers, Reagan also supplemented the Carter Doc-trine through a program of increased military sales to the remaining pillar, Saudi Arabia, with an $8.5 billion package announced in 1981. This massive military commitment to the Saudi Kingdom continued throughout the 1980s and kept the key oil state in the region firmly within a US orbit. Throughout, the specter of Iranian nationalism was invoked by Reagan, who was clear that "there is no way we could stand by and see [the country] taken over by anyone that would shut off that oil."[34]

The commitment by Washington to check any overt counterhegemonic moves by regional powers was thrown into stark relief by the Iraqi invasion of Kuwait in August 1990. A stalwart ally against anti-US forces in Iran during the 1980s, Saddam had now proved himself dangerously out of Washington's sphere. With Saddam in direct control of twice the amount of oil that he had been, the most pressing concern for US planners became ensuring that Sad-dam did not invade Saudi Arabia: a move that would have invariably given him control of around 46 percent of the world's oil reserves.[35] This concern was confirmed by CIA director William Webster: if "Saddam stays [in Kuwait] he'll own twenty percent of the world's oil reserves. And a few miles away he can seize another twenty percent."[36] As President George H. W. Bush argued at the time, the American economy and that of "friendly countries around the world will suffer if control of the world's great oil reserves fell in the hands of that one man, Saddam Hussein."[37] In an address to the nation, Bush affirmed the longstanding importance attached to the free flow of oil from the Gulf: "My administration, as has been the case with every President from President Roosevelt to President Reagan, is committed to the security and stability of the Persian Gulf . . . Let me be clear, the sovereign independence of Saudi Arabia is of vital interest to the United States."[38]

The resulting US-led campaign against Iraq was designed to remove this new threat to US interests and to create the conditions necessary for contin-ued strategic dominance in the post–Cold War era. As the leaked draft of the 1992 *Defense Planning Guidance* stated, in the oil-rich Middle East "our overall objective is to remain the predominant outside power in the region and pre-serve US and Western access to the region's oil."[39] Likewise, Defense Secretary Cheney's 1993 *Defense Strategy for the 1990s* (DPG) declared: "We must be pre-pared to act decisively in the Middle East/Persian Gulf region as we did in Operations Desert Shield and Desert Storm if our vital interests are threatened anew." And specifically to "discourage the rise of a challenger hostile to our interests in the region, we must maintain a level of forward military presence adequate to reassure our friends and deter aggressors and present a credible crisis response capability."[40] And although this was expressed in the relatively bellicose language of the elder Bush's team, the *DPG* and subsequent defense strategy in fact reflected longstanding policy objectives in the region. These were again summed up in Clinton's 1998 *National Security Strategy:* "Over the longer term, US dependence on access to foreign oil sources may be increasingly important as domestic resources are depleted . . . Conservation and energy research notwithstanding, *the United States will continue to have a vital interest in ensuring access to foreign oil sources.* We must continue to be mindful of the need for regional stability and security in key producing areas to ensure our access to and the free flow of these resources."[41]

Such thinking underpinned the sanctions-based containment policy that drove US strategy toward the Persian Gulf during the 1990s, with both the Iraqi and Iranian regimes posing a challenge to US regional hegemony and therefore in need of containment. In the case of Iran, this led to regular denunciations of the Tehran regime by US planners, eager to ensure the greatest degree of international isolation possible. In the case of Iraq, this assessment translated to a continued low-level war throughout the decade, with the US Air Force controlling Iraqi airspace and engaging in countless airstrikes to keep Iraqi infrastructure degraded. As Brigadier General William Looney, head of CENTCOM's Airborne Expeditionary Force, argued: the Iraqi population "know we own their country. We own their airspace . . . We dictate the way they live and talk." Furthermore, this degree of US control was a "good thing," because "there's a lot of oil out there we need."[42] Since its formation, CENTCOM has provided the key instrument for ensuring access to Gulf oil: a function long acknowledged by its successive commanders-in-chief (CINC). Anthony Zinni (CINC, 1997–2000), for example, was clear that the command's military strategy toward the region is "basically energy driven," with the significant oil deposits in the region "one of the prime considerations in determining our interests."[43]

Right up until the election of President George W. Bush, therefore, successive US administrations had identified control over the Persian Gulf and its oil reserves as a vital national security priority for Washington and had worked to contain or destroy threats to this control. The sheer scale of the region's oil deposits, which simply dwarf all other reserves in both size and concentration, ensures that the area holds major strategic significance for any power wishing to establish regional, extraregional, or indeed global hegemony. It also means that the Persian Gulf necessarily plays a central part in any strategy designed to boost global levels of production, as these states have an unrivaled potential to increase their output. It was against this backdrop that the Bush administration took power in 2001, and the energy security agenda received a much greater focus with the formation of the high-level NEPD Group (discussed in chapter 1). In this sense, the Bush team's agenda did not represent a step-change in American strategy but rather an acceleration and sharpening of existing core themes.

## The Bush "Turn" and the Invasion of Iraq

With the election of Bush in 2000, US policy toward the Persian Gulf took a dramatic twist. Neoconservatives who had coalesced around the Project for the New American Century (PNAC) were at last able to enact their long-held desire to remove the challenge presented by Saddam Hussein. In fact, working under the PNAC, prominent figures in the Bush administration had spent the 1990s arguing for a more assertive policy toward Iraq. They published an open letter in 1998, urging President Clinton to remove Saddam's regime in order to "secure the interests of the United States and our friends and allies around the world" and "to protect our vital interests in the Gulf."[44] After years in the political wilderness, the Bush team finally had the opportunity—enhanced not least by the increased room for maneuver secured as a result of 9/11—to remake the region for the interests of the United States through the invasion, occupation, and reorientation of Iraq.

In the direct lead-up to the invasion, of course, US officials strenuously denied that oil factored in any way into the strategic planning. Secretary of Defense Donald Rumsfeld argued that it was "nonsense" to suggest that the US invasion of Iraq had anything to do with oil. He continued that "there are certain things like that, myths that are floating around . . . it has nothing to do with oil, literally nothing to do with oil."[45] Similarly, acting in support of US objectives in the region, British prime minister Tony Blair stated bluntly that the idea that access to, and control of, Iraqi oil lay behind the invasion was a "conspiracy theory idea" and that there "is no way whatever if oil were the issue that it would not be infinitely simpler to cut a deal with Saddam."[46] The invasion was officially justified by reference to a specific threat posed by Iraq's WMD program, by its supposed support for international terrorism, and by its repression of the Iraqi people.[47] However, there is ample evidence that the Bush administration was—in line with the wishes of PNAC members—planning the assault prior to 9/11, even if these attacks on the United States were used as the necessary pretext for invasion.[48] Several months before the invasion, Dick Cheney spoke of the "enormous" implications of Saddam acquiring WMD: "Armed with an arsenal of these weapons of terror and sitting atop ten percent of the world's oil reserves, Saddam Hussein could then be expected to seek domination of the entire Middle East [and to] take control of a great portion of the world's energy supplies."[49] After the war, it became increasingly apparent that the US administration had deliberately inflated the threat of WMD and had already made a decision to invade whilst public negotiations in the UN Security Council and detailed weapons inspections were ongoing.[50] In fact, US Air Force assets patrolling the no-fly zone over Iraq had, in secret, begun direct reconnaissance missions over the country in 2002, as the Pentagon prepared for outright invasion well before the diplomatic and weapons inspection process had exhausted itself.[51]

Speaking soon after the collapse of Saddam's regime, Deputy Defense Secretary Paul Wolfowitz stated quite brazenly that Washington had used the WMD pretext, as it was the one "issue that everyone could agree on."[52] As the chairman of the US Federal Reserve during the crisis, Alan Greenspan, later declared, it was "politically inconvenient to acknowledge what everyone knows: the Iraq war is largely about oil."[53] Although he was told by officials that "unfortunately, we can't talk about" this motivation, Greenspan's understanding of the threat posed by the Iraqi regime neatly surmises the logic that drove US policy: "If Saddam Hussein had been head of Iraq and there was no oil under those sands, our response to him would not have been as strong as it was in the first Gulf War. And the second gulf war is an extension of the first. My view is that Saddam, looking over his 30-year history, very clearly was giving evidence of moving towards controlling the Straits of Hormuz, where there are 17, 18, 19 million barrels a day [passing through.] I'm saying taking Saddam out was essential."[54]

In the long history of US energy interventions in the Persian Gulf, the invasion and occupation of Iraq represents the clearest embodiment of the intersection between Washington's pursuit of global hegemony and concerns over energy security. Perhaps unsurprisingly, this episode has led many to believe US strategy was motivated by a desire to secure Iraq's oil wealth for its own corporate and national interests. As James Paul has succinctly argued, "the war was primarily a 'war for oil' in which large, multinational oil companies and their host governments acted in secret concert to gain control of Iraq's fabulous oil reserves and to gain leverage over other national oil producers."[55] Similarly, both the Retort Collective and the editors of *Monthly Review* argued that the war in Iraq was driven by the close interrelationship between US oil corporations and those in power in Washington. Accordingly, both the American "government and the major media" have assiduously avoided any mention that the United States "had more crass imperialistic motives for the invasion, such as control of Iraqi oil." This was in contrast to major "US corporate interests," which have "never been shy about explaining—at least within business circles—their post-war economic goals for Iraq."[56] With the invasion of Iraq it was argued that this oil conspiracy reached right into the heart of the Bush administration; senior figures were said to be using American military might to open productive new markets for US oil corporations.[57] As Ian Rutledge argued, the decision to invade Iraq was largely driven by the close synergy between the vice president, Dick Cheney, and oil corporations. Cheney is a "single-minded representative of oil capitalism. Someone who, given the opportunity, would not hesitate to mould US foreign policy into a form conducive to the business opportunities and profit maximisation so earnestly sought after by the huge energy multinationals of which his own company was a leading representative."[58] Whereas some analysts hold that "there was little doubt that one of the principal objectives of the US occupation was to secure access to Iraq's oil for US companies,"[59] the wider argument set out in this book points us to a different conclusion.

## The Transnationalization of Iraq

In invading and occupying Iraq, US planners were concerned not only with removing a major challenge to American hegemony in the region and Bush administration officials in particular were not only (or even primarily) motivated by US corporate wealth. Washington has used the invasion to transnationalize the Iraqi economy, opening it up to investment by global capital and reinventing it as a showcase for neoliberal doctrine. In other words, Saddam was removed not only because he posed a continuing threat to US control of the region's oil reserves but because the act of removal provided the opportunity to replace him with a ruling strata more compliant to the interests of global capital. William Robinson has provided the most clear exposition of this logic to date: the intervention in Iraq was *not* a "US imperialist plan to gain the upper hand over French, German, and Russian competition" by monopolizing Iraq's crucial oil reserves. Instead, Washington has acted since the invasion to open Iraq's largely nationalized economy to the penetration of global capital, with the incorporation of its massive oil reserves as a productive circuit within the global economy remaining a crucial component of this strategy.[60] America's primary goal in Iraq has been to "cultivate transnationally orientated elites who share Washington's interest in integrating Iraq into the global capitalist system and who can administer the local state being constructed under the tutelage of the occupation force."[61]

In this way, Robinson's transnational argument correctly pinpoints the redundancy of conceptions of contemporary world order as characterized by overt rivalry and zero-sum competition between capitalist powers. The invasion was not an oil grab by the US state for US economic interests, to the exclusion of rival powers. Instead, the invasion was designed to allow Washington to install a more pliant regime for the purposes of further (re)incorporating the Iraqi political economy and its massive oil reserves within the US-led liberal international order. Colin Powell, then secretary of state, inadvertently confirmed this point when challenged about Washington's designs over Iraq's oil: "We have not taken one drop of oil for US purposes, or for coalition purposes. Quite the contrary. We put in place a management system to make sure that Iraqi oil is brought out of the ground and put onto the market."[62] For the first time in decades, there existed an opportunity for a major (re)insertion of IOCs into the region so as to establish the mechanism preferred by Washington for the extraction of oil and its delivery to market.

In this light, the US-installed occupying authority in charge after the invasion—the Coalition Provisional Authority (CPA)—used its relatively brief window of political sovereignty to restructure the Iraqi political economy along neoliberal lines. The CPA passed a number of executive orders in the months following the invasion, privatizing the Iraqi economy to an extent hitherto unseen and forcing Iraq wide open to foreign investment. Central to this process was CPA Order 39, entitled "Foreign Investment," which worked to manage Iraq's "transition from a non-transparent centrally planned economy to a market economy characterized by sustainable economic growth through the establishment of a dynamic private sector." In this way, the Order wrenched open Iraq for global capital, mandating that a "foreign investor shall be entitled to make foreign investments in Iraq on terms no less favorable than those applicable to an Iraqi investor," with the "amount of foreign participation in newly formed or existing business entities" unlimited. Any foreign investor was now free to invest in all parts of Iraq and to establish a *wholly* foreign-owned business entity in the country. And crucially, such investors were empowered to "transfer abroad without delay all funds associated with its foreign investment, including: shares or profits and dividends . . . [and] interest, royalty payments, management fees, other fees and payments made under a contract."[63] By this Order, and in likely contravention of international law pertaining to the duties of occupying powers, the CPA drastically altered Iraq's economy, allowing virtually unlimited and unrestricted foreign investment into Iraq and placing no limitations on the expatriation of profit.[64] Other executive orders were passed during these months, as the Iraqi economy was remade in the image of what the *Economist* termed a "capitalist's dream."[65] As Paul Bremer (head of the CPA) allegedly boasted as he left Iraq, the Authority's biggest accomplishments were "the lowering of Iraq's tax rate, the liberalization of foreign-investment laws and the reduction of import duties."[66]

In an economy as reliant on oil as Iraq's, these measures were clearly designed to facilitate transnational investment in this sector. Importantly, however, the orders left out Iraq's oil from the program of mass privatization. Sensitive to charges of direct imperialism, and conscious of the danger of inflaming the anti-American insurgency, US planners opted to preserve ostensible control of the sector by the Iraqi state and to allow it to remain within OPEC. Instead, underlying control was achieved through the use of production sharing agreements (PSAs) between oil transnationals and the Iraqi state. Through this system, the state retains nominal ownership of reserves but issues long-term exploration and extraction contracts to IOCs, which then receive the profits after transferring a set amount of revenue back to the state. PSAs primarily serve a political, rather than economic, function, with the host country able to maintain the principle of national sovereignty over its petroleum reserves whilst simultaneously placing effective control over oil production in the hands of oil transnationals. As Greg Muttitt states, "PSAs represent a radical redesign of Iraq's oil industry, wrenching it from public into private hands." Furthermore: "The debate over oil 'privatisation' in Iraq has often been misleading due to the technical nature of the term, which refers to legal ownership of oil reserves. This has allowed governments and companies to deny that 'privatisation' is taking place . . . Oil experts agree that [the purpose of PSAs] is largely political: technically they keep legal ownership of oil reserves in state hands, while practically delivering oil companies the same concession agreements they replaced."[67]

PSAs are, in effect, privatizing Iraq's oil whilst leaving nominal control in the hands of the Iraqi state. In the words of Ian Rutledge, PSAs "provide the ideological and political gloss that the oil *in situ* remains wholly the property of the state, while at the same time allowing the private sector oil company to extract and sell a proportion of it" that can often yield "massive profits."[68] This mechanism has allowed IOCs to play a full role in the new Iraq, with oil capital from around the world now beginning to compete for the ability to operate in the country (albeit cautiously, in the face of continuing instability). As a result, private capital has vital access to the country's oil reserves for the first time since nationalization in the early 1970s. As ExxonMobil corporate vice president Daniel Nelson argued, "Every international oil company in the world, knowing Iraq is blessed with terrific god-given natural resources, is interested in Iraq."[69] Thus, when the Iraqi government released details of the first round of bidding for exploration and production contracts, no less than 120 foreign companies submitted bids, with 35 *US and non-US* corporations selected to go through to the next round. In the event, the first oil company to sign a significant, multibillion-dollar deal in Washington's Iraq was not US-based: the China National Petroleum Corporation (CNPC) became the first foreign oil company in thirty-five years to do business in the newly opened Iraq. Likewise, when a further 40 billion barrels of Iraqi oil were put up for sale in October 2008—representing the largest sale of oil ever recorded—oil corporations from a number of states (including China) clamored to show their interest.[70]

Of course, as we discussed in chapter 1, we think that Robinson takes his transnational argument too far and underplays the extent to which American strategy in the region—transnationally orientated as it might be—in fact works to bolster American interests. In other words, US hegemony in the region is not just designed to provide benefits to global capital (especially transnational oil corporations); it is also designed to maintain US strategic primacy over other core powers, all of whom continue to be reliant upon Washington for their energy needs. Whether receptive to the presence of IOCs or not, states in the Persian Gulf have long received US support as long as they accept the fact of American hegemony in the region and promise to supply a smooth flow of oil onto market. And vital to its ability to provide this is a degree of political stability, both internal and throughout the region. Consequently, after the invasion of Iraq in 2003, the Bush administration moved to stabilize the country, as well as Saudi Arabia, against forces inimical to US interests. And such efforts seem to be underpinning Obama's strategy, even as he makes a sharp break with many of the policies enacted by his predecessor.

## Stabilizing Iraq and Saudi Arabia

In the years after the invasion of Iraq, US planners in Washington, and US forces on the ground in Iraq and Saudi Arabia (acting either directly or through proxy security forces), have been engaged in an ongoing struggle against movements that reject American hegemony and all that it entails. As a result, Washington is continuing to put significant effort into protecting the region's oil infrastructure and bolstering the capacities of pro-US elites to stabilize their respective territories and repress challenges to US interests. Under American tutelage, the Saudi regime now deploys a vast force, consisting of 25,000–30,000 troops and round-the-clock F-15 fighter-jet patrols, to protect the country's oil infrastructure. This effort is coordinated through the Petroleum Installation Security Force and supplemented by specialized brigades of the SANG, with training provided by the US defense company Lockheed Martin in close cooperation with the state oil corporation Aramco. Overall, according to the Middle East Economic Survey (MEES), the scale of the security initiative is "immense" and likely to cost over $5 billion in total.[71]

Likewise, as violence and political instability continue to rock Iraqi society, Washington has begun to transfer substantial levels of security assistance to Baghdad in a bid to reduce US troop commitments. This trend is set to accelerate under Obama, as the United States now moves to withdraw at a much faster rate. The Pentagon is increasingly acting in an advisory role for the Iraqi army and has supplemented this relationship with a reliance on PMCs, with an estimated 40,000 private security employees present in Iraq.[72] As in Saudi Arabia, a primary focus is on the immediate protection of the country's oil infrastructure, which has come under sustained attack by armed insurgents. The postinvasion regime in Iraq has put substantial effort into working with PMCs and state security forces to secure oil facilities and infrastructure from attack, with the CPA initially seeking to "enhance energy security through a complicated combination of security arrangements utilizing US military personnel, independent security contractors and local tribes living along the pipeline routes," and with thousands of armed guards now in place as part of the Iraqi Facilities Protection Force.[73]

In line with longstanding strategy toward the region, US efforts have also gone far beyond static infrastructure protection. Huge sums of security assistance have been provided to pro-US regimes for disciplining internal sources of unrest, continuing the support provided throughout the postwar era. In just one example of concrete US aid to an oil-rich ally, the Pentagon's Defense Security Cooperation Agency (DSCA) notified Congress in October 2005 of the possible provision of $918 million worth of equipment to support the modernization of the SANG. The package included 144 armored personnel carriers, water cannon vehicles, command, control, and communications equipment, and tens of thousands of assault rifles with grenade launchers, as well as scopes and sights for sniper weapons systems. The assistance—which came with training and advice—was designed to "make a key regional ally and partner in the Global War on Terror more capable of defeating those who would threaten regional stability, and less reliant on the deployment of US combat forces to maintain or restore stability in the Middle East." Specifically, the SANG "needs these defense articles," not for legitimate defense against external aggression, but so it can "effectively conduct security and counterterrorism operations."[74]

In parallel, indigenous units of special forces trained by the US military now provide the front line against a wide range of social and political forces in Iraq. Washington has openly deployed the paramilitary option, with US personnel overseeing the training programs of Iraq's Interior Ministry commandos. These commandos are heavily implicated in the disappearance, murder, and torture of large numbers of Iraqi civilians, and many are drawn from Saddam Hussein's notorious Directorate of General Security. The Center for Nonproliferation Studies (CNS) outlined the fact that the Directorate was responsible for "detecting dissent among the Iraqi general public" under Saddam's dictatorship by monitoring the "the day-to-day lives of the population, creating a pervasive local presence." The use of paramilitaries in Iraq fits clearly into longstanding CI doctrine and was drawn from earlier US-backed CI campaigns, especially in Central America during the 1980s when, as *Newsweek* notes, the "US government funded or supported nationalist [*sic*] forces that allegedly included so-called death squads directed to hunt down and kill rebel leaders and sympathizers" in El Salvador.[75] This so-called Salvador Option is clearly being deployed in Iraq, with "insurgent" kidnapping and assassination programs underway.

Asked whether the United States should establish a project to identify and target specific adversaries, along the lines of the infamous Operation Phoenix in Vietnam (where tens of thousands of Vietnamese were tortured and executed under the guidance of the CIA), General William Boykin, then deputy undersecretary of defense for intelligence, maintained that US Special Forces were "doing a pretty good job of that right now. We're going after these people. Killing or capturing these people is a legitimate mission for the department . . . I think we're doing what the Phoenix program was designed to do, without all the secrecy."[76] Likewise, the *Independent* reported that US forces were routinely releasing Iraqi kidnappers—who themselves had targeted and killed civilians—in order to spy on insurgents: "An Iraqi government source confirmed that criminal suspects were often released if they agreed to inform on insurgents, despite the danger to ordinary Iraqis," including specifically the Iraqi middle class, which "has been heavily targeted by kidnappers since the fall of Saddam Hussein."[77]

Importantly, the US, Iraqi, and Saudi authorities continue to view elements of unarmed civil society, alongside armed insurgents, as forming a legitimate target of their stabilization operations. Although increasingly wrapped up in the language of counterterrorism, assistance to the SANG has been designed to provide the means for the Saudi regime to suppress domestic challenge to its rule, with overt activity by unionized workers or political activists targeted through widespread imprisonment and torture. Given the immense importance of Saudi Arabia to US interests and the need for stability, ongoing US security missions have continued to require the policing of the Saudi population, with hundreds of people imprisoned, tortured, or killed for their opposition to the government. These include 700 people imprisoned by the authorities in 2006 who, according to the Saudi Ministry of the Interior, "were not involved in terrorist acts" but were suspected of "harbouring extremist thoughts."[78]

In Iraq, meanwhile, the imposition of neoliberal economic reforms and the reentry of private oil corporations into the country led to widespread protest amongst the Iraqi population, with Iraq's oil unions threatening workers' strikes and a public campaign against the sell-off of Iraqi oil.[79] In response, the Iraqi authorities issued arrest warrants for union leaders before issuing a directive (in contravention of the new Iraqi Constitution and reminiscent of Saddam Hussein's infamous Article 150) banning unions from participating in official negotiations around the future of Iraqi oil.[80] This targeting has involved the forcible transfer from Basra to Baghdad of trade union leaders who opposed the oil sell-off. Indeed, according to the NGO called War on Want: "The Iraqi Federation of Oil Unions has been leading the opposition to the sell-off of Iraq's oil and these members are clearly being targeted for their political actions."[81] Similarly, the use by Washington of PMCs has had severe consequences for the local population, as several have been accused of targeting the civilian population with force. As just one example, evidence exists that a key PMC contracted to provide pipeline protection—Erinys International—has been involved in the targeting of civilians throughout the oil-rich South, even whilst on operations alongside US Army units in Iraq.[82]

This targeting of active civilians as part of the wider CI effort has been extensive. Human Rights Watch reported that, by 2007, there were tens of thousands of Iraqi civilians in detention—many with dubious links to the armed insurgency. According to the Pentagon, the average length of detention for the more than 25,000 Iraqis in US custody was 300 days, with many held for years without charge or trial. As the Abu Ghraib scandal demonstrated, torture is common in detention facilities, with "reports of widespread torture and other abuse of detainees in detention facilities run by Iraq's defense and interior ministries and police continu[ing] to emerge. In October 2007, officials from the United Nations Assistance Mission for Iraq (UNAMI) reported that detainees had been hung by their limbs, subjected to electric shocks, forced to sit on sharp objects, and burned by their jailers."[83]

This fits within a wider pattern of abuses suffered by political and social activists in states receiving US counterinsurgency support. According to Amnesty International, the focus by Washington and local elites on "state security" and "public safety" has occurred to the significant detriment of the human rights cause, with "grievous human rights abuses continu[ing] to be both widespread and firmly entrenched" in the region: "Throughout the region, state power is maintained, and dissenting voices or debate repressed, by all-powerful security and intelligence services. Those who speak up risk arbitrary arrest and detention without trial, torture and other ill-treatment by security police whose political masters allow them to abuse human rights with impunity . . . [T]he USA and other Western states have made allies among the security and intelligence services of some of the most repressive regimes in the region . . . [helping to] entrench the abusive methods of the region's security apparatus."[84]

Although it is tempting to view this record as a product of the excesses of the Bush administration's war on terror and to look to Obama's commitment to revoking some of the harsher counterterrorist measures as a guide to future policy in the region, we would guard against any presumption of significant strategic discontinuity. Indeed, whilst Obama's policy toward Iraq represents a major shift from his predecessor, the underlying objectives of Washington's strategy are likely to remain in line with past administrations. Simply, the sheer importance of the region's oil constrains Obama's room for maneuver and will continue to do so even as he attempts to eliminate America's dependency on foreign oil. In this light, one of the objectives of the occupation has been—and continues to be—to provide a site for the continued presence of US military power in the region. Although the Obama team has moved quickly to withdraw the majority of combat troops from the country, there are obvious signs that a significant proportion of the troop pullout will in fact be a *pullback* behind the walls of large political and military compounds. The new American embassy in Baghdad—which will survive long after Obama's term(s) in office—is the largest diplomatic mission in the world, ten times larger than the new embassy in Beijing (the second-largest mission) and six times larger than the UN buildings in New York.[85]

Likewise, a number of massive American military bases now exist throughout the country and are likely to endure far beyond Obama's withdrawal. Advanced plans exist within the Pentagon to retain a US military presence in Iraq well into the future, and these are fully supported by the Obama administration; within weeks of taking office President Obama himself declared that the combat mission in Iraq—now scheduled under his leadership to end by August 2010—will be replaced by a massive "transitional force." Consisting of 35,000–50,000 troops, this force will be designed to perform three functions: "training, equipping and advising Iraqi security forces as long as they remain non-sectarian; conducting targeted counter-terrorism missions; and protecting our ongoing civilian and military efforts within Iraq."[86] In this way, Obama's strategy looks set to continue major themes of the Bush administration, which in turn drew upon a long history of training and equipping of local security forces to further US interests.

Regardless of the change in administration in the White House, therefore, Washington will continue to work toward retaining a permanent and abiding presence for forward power projection in the region, albeit with far fewer troops on the ground than at the end of the Bush years.[87] Ultimately, should

America manage to successfully install a pro-US protectorate in Iraq (by no means a foregone conclusion), it will be able to shore up its hegemony in the Persian Gulf well into the twenty-first century. Washington's ultimate logic in this regard has been captured well by conservative commentator Charles Krauthammer: Iraq is "one of the three principal Arab states, with untold oil wealth, and educated population [and] an advanced military and technological infrastructure that . . . could easily be revived if it falls into the right (i.e., wrong) hands. Add to that the fact that its strategic location *would give its rulers inordinate influence over the entire Persian Gulf region,* including Saudi Arabia, Kuwait and the Gulf states," and it is easy to understand the strategic imperative underlying the invasion.[88]

However, our identification of a fundamental continuity in Washington's grand strategy in the postwar era, and its translation into ensuring a certain form of control in the Persian Gulf, does not imply an undisputed ability on behalf of US planners to *enact* this strategy on the ground. American power in the years since 2003 has been singularly unsuccessful in pacifying the country and establishing a stable pro-US protectorate—despite the plaudits offered to Bush's "surge" strategy in 2007. Indeed, the inability of US forces to impose stability led to a considerable dip in oil production in Iraq for several years after the invasion, whereas the shrill cries among some hawks at the time to continue the drive to Tehran and Damascus are now a distant memory.[89] With Obama in power, the potential failure of Washington's core objectives have become common parlance; the president himself is clear that "we cannot rid Iraq of all who oppose America or sympathize with our adversaries. We cannot police Iraq's streets until they are completely safe, nor stay until Iraq's union is perfected."[90]

The continuing—indeed heightened—instability in the Persian Gulf and the increasing realization of the limits of American power, have translated directly to rising levels of concern amongst US planners as to the sheer vulnerability of an American economy and a wider global position, which are both ultimately reliant on the steady flow of oil from this region. This is especially the case given the physical concentration of oil production and transportation from the Persian Gulf, which ensures that high-profile targets exist for any group wishing to reduce export levels. This was brought home in dramatic style after the failed suicide bombing of the Abqaiq oil processing plant in Saudi Arabia in February 2006. Had this been successful, output from a site through which two-thirds of the country's oil passes would have been drastically affected, with overall exports from Saudi Arabia potentially halved for up to a year.[91] Likewise, almost all of this oil travels through the twenty-one-mile wide Strait of Hormuz, labeled by the US government "by far the world's most important chokepoint with an oil flow of 16.5–17 million barrels per day" and clearly vulnerable to closure or severe disruption through nonstate or state activity.[92] In this way, the beating heart of US global power rests upon an exceptionally fragile set of conditions, and this will continue to be the case regardless of Washington's various attempts to become ostensibly "energy independent."[93]

As a result of this vulnerability, US planners have increasingly pursued a dual approach to provide the highest possible degree of global energy security. On the one hand, the United States has sought to entrench its dominance over the Persian Gulf, with the primary goal of ensuring that it has the coercive means to prevent serious disruptions to oil production. This militarization of energy security has translated to the active use of counterinsurgency and repression to destroy those who would pull the region away from the US orbit, alongside more static defenses at key installations. On the other hand, Washington has increasingly pursued a policy of energy diversification away from the Persian Gulf. By this, US planners aim to supplant Persian Gulf oil supplies with those from other oil-rich regions within the South, with increasing efforts to cultivate new sets of relationships with alternative oil suppliers.

## Energy Diversification

Although instability in the Persian Gulf area has increased since 9/11 (and especially since 2003), US planners have long been aware of the need to diversify global production of oil. In response to the multitude of regional crises in the late 1970s and early 1980s, former Exxon and US government official Melvin Conant published a high-profile monograph in 1982 through the influential Council on Foreign Relations. In it, Conant argued that "the most fundamental [priority] is to reduce dependence on the Gulf" and that US strategy needs to be orientated around "maximizing supply from [other] countries to reduce dependence on the Gulf."[94] Conant's arguments gained increasing credence during the 1980s and as a result of the Iraqi invasion of Kuwait and the policy of dual containment of Iran and Iraq. By 1996, the Clinton administration had a stand-alone section in its 1996 *National Security Strategy* on "providing for energy security." Here it was stated that the "experiences of the two oil shocks and the Gulf War show that an interruption of oil supplies can have a significant impact on the economies of the United States and its allies."[95] And within two years, the White House had formulated a plan to reduce dependency on the Gulf, through "encouraging investments, especially by US companies, in energy resources [outside the Persian Gulf] and their export to world markets, thereby expanding and diversifying world energy supplies."[96] According to Clinton, this strategy was vital to ensuring that US interests were served "in a world of growing energy demand." Specifically, he stated that "our nation cannot afford to rely on any single region for our energy supplies" and that, by working with regions outside the Persian Gulf, the United States would "help diversify our energy supply and strengthen our nation's security."[97]

It was this long-running concern of successive US administrations regarding overreliance on Middle Eastern supplies that formed the backdrop for the increased exposure to the issue brought by the Bush administration. With the formation of the NEPD Group in 2001, the issue was given unprecedented attention at the cabinet level, and the Group was given a wide remit to examine all potential approaches to promoting stable and affordable future energy supply to meet America's growing needs. However, although it produced a final report that was wrapped up in the language of energy conservation and efficiency, the Group's underlying focus was clear. Because "energy use per person in the United States is expected to rise [in the future] as is overall demand for energy" and any "significant disruption in world oil supplies could adversely affect our economy and our ability to promote key foreign and economic policy objectives," the United States needs to "strengthen our own energy security . . . by working cooperatively with key countries and institutions *to expand the sources and types of global energy supplies*."[98] In this way, the strategy of opening up the Persian Gulf to investment and stabilizing this region through military force, was matched by a parallel strategy to find and exploit other oil reserves. As Bush made absolutely clear when discussing the Group's findings: "Oh, I think conservation has got to be an integral part of making sure we've got a reasonable energy policy. But what the Vice President was saying is that we can't conserve our way to energy independence; nor can we conserve our way to having enough energy available . . . [W]hat people need to hear, loud and clear, is that we're running out of energy in America. And so it's important for this nation to improve its infrastructure so that we can not only deliver supplies, *but we need to go find new supply*."[99]

And in seeking this new supply so crucial for US energy security, Bush declared, "Diversity is important not only for energy security, but also for national security. Over-dependence on any one source of energy, especially a foreign source, leaves us vulnerable to price shocks, supply interruptions, and, in the worst case, blackmail."[100] Unsurprisingly, the NEPD report came to the same conclusion, urging Washington to take the lead in seeking greater diversity of world oil supply. Whilst the report stated that the Persian Gulf will continue to be "a primary focus of US international energy policy"—a conclusion that would be impossible to avoid—it also stressed the need to identify and focus on "existing and emerging regions that will have a major impact on the global energy balance." In this light, the Group recommended a concerted effort to "strengthen our trade alliances, to deepen our dialogue with major oil producers, and to work for greater oil production" in three specific regions of the periphery: the Caspian Basin, West Africa, and the Western Hemisphere.[101] These three regions in particular are seen by US planners as "important factors that can lessen the impact of a supply disruption" and are therefore considered the most "high-priority regions" in the search for improved US energy security.[102]

Washington's interest in oil production from these regions significantly predates the Bush administration. However, in line with increased concerns over control of overall oil stocks from 2001, we have witnessed a parallel acceleration of attempts to secure control of oil in the Caspian Basin, West Africa, and the Western Hemisphere. This new focus has found its way into a range of strategy statements and documents. For example, the 2002 *National Security Strategy* declared, "We will strengthen our own energy security and the shared prosperity of the global economy by working with our allies, trading partners and energy producers to expand the sources and types of global energy supplied, especially in the Western Hemisphere, Africa, Central Asia and the Caspian region."[103] In his State of the Union address in January 2006, Bush laid down a marker for increasing diversity of oil supply, declaring that the United States was "addicted to oil" from "unstable parts of the world" and that it needed to replace over 75 percent of its imports from the Persian Gulf by 2025, so making "our dependence on Middle Eastern oil a thing of the past."[104]

And again, although Bush talked about more efficient technology to reduce dependency, the underlying thrust was clear. Later that year the 2006 *National Security Strategy* laid out a plan to reduce reliance on the Persian Gulf: "Only a small number of countries make major contributions to the world's oil supply. The world's dependence on these few suppliers is neither responsible nor sustainable over the long term. The key to ensuring our energy security is *diversity in the regions from which energy resources come.*"[105] Accordingly, Washington has worked to establish its hegemony over each of these three regions, with the purpose of drawing oil-rich states within its orbit and integrating them within the US-led order. And this is not for the sole national interests of the American state. As the NEPD report laid out: "Concentration of world oil production in any one region of the world is a potential contributor to market instability, benefiting neither oil producers nor consumers . . . Greater diversity of oil production remains important. Encouraging greater diversity of oil production and, as appropriate, transportation, within and among geographic regions has obvious benefits to all market participants."[106]

In an international regime where oil is traded on the open market, US planners have maintained that these regions are significant for Washington's interests regardless of the amount of oil physically transported to the United States itself. Indeed, less than 4 percent of Caspian oil is exported to the United States, where it makes up less than 1 percent of American imports.[107] It is the important contribution that the regions will make to *global* energy security over the coming decades that makes them of interest to Washington. As Barack Obama said during his April 2009 visit to Turkey, the United States "will continue to support [Turkey's] central role as an East-West corridor for oil and natural gas," not for delivery to US markets, but in order "to power markets in Turkey and Europe."[108]

By integrating these political economies within the wider US-led order, Washington attempts to facilitate the creation of an attractive and stable investment climate, specifically so that transnational oil capital (the IOCs) can operate with confidence. Unlike in the Persian Gulf, IOCs have key access to many of the oil reserves in these regions and are deeply involved in exploration, production, and exportation. In this light, through the continued development of market mechanisms that serve these corporations, it is hoped that production levels of oil will increase as the efficiencies of the market prevail, and overall supply will be stabilized. As the NEPD report stated: "Overall policies in each of these high-priority regions will focus on improving the investment climate and facilitating the flow of needed investment and technology."[109] And although there is a degree to which Washington seeks to provide US-based oil companies with advantages over their corporate rivals, this is mostly subsumed within a strategy to promote an environment for all international oil companies. It is through this strategy that the US hopes to contain (re)emergent geopolitical rivals as they search for oil supplies outside of the Persian Gulf. Although Russian and especially Chinese activity in the oil sector of these regions is growing, by promoting a market-orientated approach to sector development and encouraging capital from potential rivals to operate within this order, Washington hopes to pacify and integrate these states under US hegemony.

## Conclusion

US strategy in the Persian Gulf has not been solely about controlling the region's oil resources. As the Joint Chiefs of Staff stated in 1946, the region was "one of the few favorable areas for counteroffensive action" against any aggressive move by the Soviet Union, and "the proximity of important Soviet industries makes the importance of holding the Eastern Mediterranean–Middle Eastern area obvious."[110] Geopolitical positioning and the desire to secure a strategic bridgehead on the Eurasian landmass—designed in part to militate against the emergence of one dominant Eurasian power with the potential ability to threaten the continental United States—has continued to be at least one concern of US planners in the postwar era. As Zbigniew Brzezinski declared: "For America, the chief geopolitical prize is Eurasia . . . America's global primacy is directly dependent on how long and how effectively its preponderance on the Eurasian continent is sustained."[111]

However, it is undeniably the case that hegemony in the Persian Gulf has been sought primarily to assure control over the region's oil reserves. For the past sixty years, successive US administrations have understood the central role played by Persian Gulf oil to both stability and prosperity at home *and* to the projection of military power and the entrenchment of US global hegemony abroad. Consequently, US grand strategy in the region has sought to ensure that Washington's power—expressed most clearly through the Pentagon's forward presence in the region—goes unchallenged by any rival, whether perceived as "friendly" (the UK) or "hostile" (the USSR during the Cold War, Iran since 1979, or Iraq under Saddam Hussein). Washington has intervened time and again in the region to maintain control over the globe's largest reserves of oil and to contain threats to this control, ensuring that US energy security has—since World War II—been closely bound up with the deployment and utilization of military force. This logic has most obviously manifested itself with the invasion and occupation of Iraq in 2003, with the Bush administration exploiting the greater political maneuverability provided by the 9/11 attacks to remove a perceived threat to its interests, to secure Iraqi oil, and to position a US military presence at the heart of the region.

Simultaneously, US planners have increasingly worked to diversify production away from the Gulf and to establish American hegemony in other oil-rich zones in the South. The final three chapters of this book will look in detail at how US strategy vis-à-vis the oil-rich South is playing itself out in the Caspian Basin, in West Africa, and in Latin America.

# CHAPTER FOUR

# The Caspian Basin

## US Oil Hegemony in the Former Soviet Union

Located in the center of the Eurasian landmass, the states of the Caspian Basin are surrounded by a set of much larger powers: Russia to the north, China to the east, India and Pakistan to the southeast, Iran to the south, and Turkey to the west. At its heart lies the Caspian Sea, which sits on top of vast quantities of oil and forms the focus of interest in the region. Indeed, the political landscape of the Caspian Basin has experienced a seismic shift since the end of the Cold War. Newfound independence for the eight states of the region has been met with interest from several external powers and, in turn, their competing agendas have led many to proclaim the existence of a new "Great Game" being played across the Caspian Basin.[1] Those who analyze world affairs through the lens of interimperial rivalry or Great Power geopolitics have often made much of events and dynamics in Central Eurasia since the end of the Cold War, and in particular, the ongoing competition for control of the natural resources found therein.[2]

Washington has had to confront rival centers of power in the region to an extent unlike anywhere else in the world. Moscow, for instance, has continued to view the region as firmly within its sphere of influence.[3] The Kremlin has continued to station thousands of troops across its "near abroad" and uses these as a disciplinary force to modulate regional elites.[4] Significantly, around 3,000 Russian troops were stationed in the "geostrategic bridge" state of Georgia throughout the 1990s, ensuring a military presence was maintained between the Caspian and the West. These forces were used to support various secessionist groups in the country, in a deliberate attempt to undermine the power of the autonomous government in Tbilisi and retain Russian influence in the region. Although agreements on withdrawal were forced by the new, pro-Western Saakashvili administration in 2005, Russian troops were back in the summer of 2008, as Moscow invaded northern Georgia for the purposes of "defending" the semiautonomous regions of Abkhazia and South Ossetia. At the time of this writing, these troops are maintained within these regions in what Moscow calls "buffer zones" but which are in fact an overt attempt to retain a significant foothold in the region.[5]

Russia complements this strategic military presence with an effort to sustain those regional institutions and agreements through which its preponderance of power can be exercised. These include the Commonwealth of Independent States (CIS) and the Shanghai Cooperation Organisation (SCO), along with a host of bilateral arrangements. In turn, the SCO has been used as an instrument by Beijing to maximize its power in the region, but despite the hyperbole surrounding the emergence of China as a superpower, its influence throughout the Caspian remains relatively minimal. Historically, Moscow has been the imperial center of power in the region, and although its power and influence over incumbent ruling elites has waned considerably over the past two decades, it remains the most powerful external power with a direct interest in the Caspian.

In contrast to regions such as Latin America, where Washington's postwar hegemony has been almost complete, the Caspian Basin exists at the very farthest reaches of US power. This is compounded by the existence of ruling elites in the region that have, in some cases, proved resistant to US overtures. Overall, these dynamics have lent a unique flavor to Washington's relations with Caspian states, as US policy has had to reflect the abiding reality of significant Russian influence. In fact, US strategic relations with the Caspian region in the first years of the post–Cold War era were decidedly subservient to the goal of managing the decline of post-Soviet Russia. Washington's foreign policy elites focused upon deinstitutionalizing military competition with the Kremlin, pulling Moscow as far within America's orbit as possible and securing political cooperation for the restructuring of Russia's economy along capitalist lines. Washington pursued a clear "Russia-first" policy toward the former Soviet Union and consequently viewed the Caspian region through Moscow's lens.[6] This prioritization was evident in the 1996 *National Security Strategy,* which focused on tying Russia and Ukraine deeper into the global economy and to European security frameworks and which made only passing reference to the former Soviet states of Central Asia and the Caucasus.[7]

Notwithstanding the complex power dynamics at play in the region and the cautious approach adopted by Washington in the early 1990s, the broad logic that has driven US intervention throughout the South is also at play here. Indeed, the dissipation of Cold War rivalries, alongside the newfound sovereignty of numerous capitals throughout the former Soviet Union, presented Washington with an opportunity to extend its reach to a hitherto-closed region. For the first time, transnational capital could penetrate the region, whilst Washington could move to secure this access by the strategic employment of political, diplomatic, and military statecraft to stabilize nascent state formations. This has been the central objective of US policy toward the region since 1991, as US planners have sought to reorientate the post-Soviet states away from Moscow's orbit, integrate them into Western-led economic and security institutions, and minimize the influence of emerging powers (primarily China). Moreover, Washington has worked to insulate incumbent elites from a variety of internal and transnational pressures that threaten US interests. In this way, the dramatic rise in attention given to US relations in the region since 9/11, and the undoubted acceleration in assistance provided by Washington to cement its interests, is underpinned by a continuity in its strategic objective. Although refracted through the lens of the war on terror by the Bush administration, US intervention in the region has been—and continues to be—based on an agenda that stretches far wider than counterterrorism. As such, in its first months of power, the Obama administration has continued to develop many of the themes that have animated past strategy toward the region. Despite a high-profile shift in tone by the Obama team in early 2009, it appears that the underlying strategic push into the region remains largely unchanged, based as it is around the transnationalization and integration of local political economies into the wider global economy and the parallel militarization of state-society relations to bolster pro-US elites.

Central amongst American interests in the Caspian has been securing unfettered access to the region's substantial oil deposits. Although initial estimates of 200 billion barrels of oil or more in the region have since proven wildly inflated, current estimates still point to sizable reserves. Energy Information Administration (EIA) estimates have now stabilized at somewhere between 17–50 billion barrels, and the well-respected British Petroleum (BP) estimates at the high end of this (48 billion barrels), representing around 4 percent of the world total.[8] Motivated by the desire to diversify world production away from the Persian Gulf, the United States has increasingly turned to the Caspian Basin as a potential alternative source of oil for the global market. As insecurity in the Middle East continues to build, stabilizing the Caspian region and working to guarantee the smooth flow of oil to market has become a major US foreign policy objective, one that is pursued primarily by pushing for the creation of a stable and attractive investment climate throughout the region. Foreign investment in the Caspian Basin is largely in the oil sector, and whilst energy security does not determine every facet of US policy, it is fair to say that American interests in the Caspian Basin are primarily concerned with securing a stable flow of oil onto markets.

## The Strategic Importance of Caspian Oil

US interests in the resources of the Caspian Basin region were insignificant before 1991. With the collapse of the Soviet empire, however, the five states of Central Asia (Kazakhstan, Kyrgyzstan, Uzbekistan, Tajikistan, and Turkmenistan) and the three states of the southern Caucasus (Georgia, Armenia, and Azerbaijan) gained independence.[9] In the early years after the Cold War, US interests in the region remained relatively minimal and were subsumed within the overarching strategy toward the former Soviet Union as a whole. Naturally, this strategy was determined by managing relations with Moscow, and a distinctly regional focus was not prominent during the early 1990s. Overall there was little of real economic interest in the region, either for foreign corporations or for US planners concerned with managing the decline of the Russian hegemon.

From the very beginning of the post–Cold War era, the oil sector stood out as one area where investment by transnational corporations would possibly make a return sufficient to justify the bureaucratic difficulties encountered. The first major investment came in April 1993, as the Tengizchevroil consortium (75% owned by ChevronTexaco and ExxonMobil) agreed to invest $20 billion in the development of the Tengiz field in Kazakhstan.[10] This was followed quickly by major IOC investment in Azerbaijan, with corporations such as BP, ChevronTexaco, Lukoil, Statoil, ExxonMobil, and Amerada Hess signing the "contract of the century" with the government in 1994 and opening the way for the entry of foreign capital into the aging Azeri oil sector.[11] Despite these major advances by IOCs, and the vast sums of money that poured into the regional sectors as a result, it took longer for the potential of the region's energy reserves to filter through to US planners. This lack of interest was perhaps not surprising, since oil production in the region stagnated, and even fell, through the first half of the 1990s.[12]

However, there came a sharp break with existing US policy in the second half of the decade, as Washington's growing concerns over the need to diversify away from the Persian Gulf combined with a realization of the scale of untapped oil in the Caspian Basin. Whereas initial estimates of reserves in the region had been relatively modest, during the mid-1990s these were inflated to levels that placed the Basin alongside the Persian Gulf in importance. Figures of 150–200 billion barrels and more were circulated, and US government agencies were not immune to the excitement: according to the EIA in 1998, the Caspian was "an area of vast resource potential," with only the United States and Saudi Arabia "thought to have more ultimately recoverable conventional oil resources." As a result, the strategic importance assigned to the region rose rapidly.[13]

It was this newfound significance that prompted President Clinton to invite regional elites to Washington in 1997 and 1998. During these meetings, the importance of the region's oil resources for US interests were made clear to all, as the Clinton administration fundamentally reprioritized its commitments to the Caspian.[14] In the context of "a world of growing energy demand," the president declared that the Caspian Basin was "a vital region for new oil and gas development, and the decisions made in the years ahead on energy extraction and transportation will profoundly affect generations to come."[15] This new policy direction was formalized in the 1998 *National Security Strategy,* which, unlike the version two years previous, focused on a Caspian region that "promises to play an increasingly important role in meeting rising world energy demand in coming decades." The United States was working to bring the region's oil to market, "thereby expanding and diversifying world energy supplies and promoting prosperity" in the region.[16]

The Caspian's reserves are located almost wholly within the borders of two states in the region: Kazakhstan, which is thought to hold around 40 billion barrels (over 80% of the region's total), and Azerbaijan, thought to hold around 7 billion barrels (about 15% of the total).[17] Kazakhstan is by far the largest producer and exporter in the region, with activity traditionally centered on the Tengiz field.[18] However, Tengiz production is likely to be dwarfed by the offshore Kashagan field, discovered in 2000 and 2001. This is now the largest known field outside of the Middle East and the fifth largest in the world, representing the most significant find anywhere in the world since the 1960s.[19] Likewise, Azeri production and exports are centered on the "ACG fields"

(Azeri, Chirag, Guneshli), located offshore in the Caspian Sea, which account for around 80 percent of Azeri production.

Exports from the region are set to continue expanding rapidly, matching the substantial increases witnessed already as IOC activity ramps up the scale of exploration and production.[20] By 2030, the US government estimates further production increases will lead the region to contribute around 5 percent of global production.[21] Production levels only tell one aspect of the story, however. Given the low levels of domestic consumption in the Caspian region and the low projected rise of consumption in the forthcoming decades, the future development of the region's oil reserves will primarily serve wider international markets.[22]

Emergent understandings of the significance of the Caspian's oil reserves began to drive US policy to the region during the late 1990s and laid the groundwork for the Bush administration's strategic consideration of US energy security. Despite being hailed as a fundamental reassessment of US energy requirements in the first years of the twenty-first century, the NEPD report did little to alter the position that the Caspian held in planners' minds. The region had already been pegged as vital to US and global energy security, and it was simply confirmed as "a rapidly growing new area of supply" requiring close US attention in order to increase the flow of oil to world markets.[23] What did occur as a result of the new prioritization under the Bush administration was a greater effort to develop the region's resources in a manner beneficial to the United States. In the new political environment generated by 9/11, this led to accelerated bilateral agreements and activity. For example, an Energy Partnership was signed between the US and Kazakhstan, based on the fact that the country had "the potential within the next decade to become the second largest oil-exporting nation in the world. The new Kashagan field alone, for example, has oil reserves greater than those of the entire United States."[24]

The Obama administration—whilst stressing energy independence and a rapid switch to "clean" energy—has in fact been continuing this theme. Richard Morningstar, special advisor for Caspian Basin energy diplomacy during the Clinton administration and a key player in the construction of the Baku-Tbilisi-Ceyhan (BTC) pipeline during the 1990s (discussed later in the chapter), has been appointed as special envoy for Eurasian energy. Speaking at a conference on regional energy supplies in Baku in June 2009, Morningstar read out loud a letter from President Obama. The letter congratulated Azerbaijan on emerging as "an important and reliable supplier of energy to world markets" and declared the country "an example of how developing energy resources with the involvement of international companies can result in rapid progress." Washington under Obama, the letter continued, will continue to support efforts "to develop your hydrocarbon sector in a process that will increase regional prosperity and cooperation as well as global energy security . . . In your drive to continue developing your energy resources, Azerbaijan will find a strong friend and partner in the United States."[25]

The presence of large reserves of oil in the Caspian Basin has caused it to emerge from relative obscurity in the early 1990s to a key region today, wherein US planners are keen to exert Washington's hegemony. The rise in attention has been rapid, fueled fully by the realization of the energy resources under the Caspian Sea. As future vice president Dick Cheney stated in 1998, speaking to oil-industry executives as the CEO of Halliburton: "I can't think of a time when we've had a region emerge as suddenly to become as strategically significant as the Caspian."[26]

## Strategic Rivalry in the Caspian Basin

Because of the growing importance of Caspian oil to the stability of international energy markets, US planners have—since the scale of the region's reserves became apparent in the mid-1990s—sought to ensure that as much of it as possible reaches the open market without political interference.[27] However, given the historical and current balance of power in the region, where US influence is counterbalanced by Russian hegemony (and, to a lesser extent, increasing Chinese activity), there remain abiding concerns in Washington regarding the degree to which market forces will be allowed to dictate the flow of oil. Such concerns are unsurprising, since China and Russia have been working to maintain and deepen their relations with the states of the Caspian region, with an eye to countering the growing influence of Washington. For instance, the SCO draws together Russia, China, and four Central Asian states (minus Turkmenistan) to discuss regional security and economic cooperation. This has been matched by a significant number of bilateral deals and assistance as each state in the region attempts to balance its interests in relation to all others. Crucially, Russian and Chinese interests in the region have been increasingly refracted through the lens of energy security. Russian and Chinese desires to control the region's energy resources have been expressed through the SCO; during the organization's 2006 annual summit, Russian president Vladimir Putin proposed that it should establish an "energy club."[28] Substantial investments have been made by Russia and China in the Caspian's energy sector. Beijing has invested in oil fields in Kazakhstan and in a multibillion-dollar pipeline project to carry this oil across the border.[29] Meanwhile, Russia has secured access to substantial quantities of Turkmen and Kazakh oil and has used its control of most of the export pipelines from the region to exert pressure on oil-producing states (by example, in order to gain access to oil projects for Russian companies).[30]

As we argued in chapter 1, investments in energy production by strategic rivals do not pose a threat to US interests per se. To the extent that any oil produced is released onto global markets, the origin of the investment or the physical destination of the oil is not particularly relevant. US officials are well aware of this fact and have often appeared sanguine in the face of the increased flow of oil to China. According to Paul Simons (former deputy assistant secretary of state), such developments "should not pose a threat to US energy security. In a global context, additional [exports to China] would free up supplies elsewhere, from other producers, to meet market demand in the United States and other growth markets."[31] What concerns Washington is that China and Russia may actually be acting to secure direct access to the region's oil reserves for strategic rather than purely economic reasons. It would make more economic sense for China to ship its Kazakh oil to consumers in Europe via existing Russian pipelines and then import its required oil from the Persian Gulf.[32] Instead, most of the oil extracted from Kazakhstan does not in fact enter the market at all but instead goes directly to the Chinese government.[33] As we have already seen, officials in Beijing are acutely aware of the dominance—especially in military terms—that the United States has over global energy supplies, particularly from the Persian Gulf. In this light, securing direct access to Kazakh oil, whilst economically unsound, would help to free Beijing from Washington's grasp in the event of a severe disruption in Sino-US relations.[34] The relatively low levels of oil that are exported from Kazakhstan to China ensure that bypassing the market in this way does not pose an immediate threat to the United States, but the potential that such activity has to undermine the international economic order clearly challenges Washington's global hegemony.

In response, Washington has striven to alter the political orientation of the oil-rich Caspian states. By seeking to pull the region away from Russia's orbit and by remaining cognizant of future counterhegemonic moves by Moscow, Beijing, and even (to a lesser extent) Tehran, US planners have hoped to wield decisive influence amongst regional elites. This has primarily involved deepening economic and security ties so as to firmly integrate the oil-rich Caspian economies within the wider US-led system. Bilateral economic assistance to the region's states, channeled through the 1992 Freedom Support Act (FSA), reached well over $3 billion in the decade between 1997 and 2006.[35] In providing this assistance, Washington maintains that its interests lie in promoting states that are "stable, independent, democratic, market-orientated and prosperous," with "strong links to the West." Specifically, this is driven by a desire to develop the region's oil resources and provide "diversified routes for oil and gas exports to world markets" and integration "into the world trading system."[36]

Likewise, the Pentagon has been granted a key role in ensuring the region's states are pulled into the US orbit. Military commanders have identified oil reserves as a key US interest; Admiral William J. Fallon, of US Central Command, has been clear that the region is "playing an increased role in global energy markets" and that "restricted oil and gas export options" are a vital concern.[37] This prioritization has played itself out through substantial levels of security assistance to regional militaries. In comparison to the minimal engagement during the early 1990s, the ascendancy of energy considerations in the second half of the decade led to a huge acceleration of aid. As regional leaders were filing through Washington in the mid-1990s to agree to closer relations with the United States, they were universally offered increased security cooperation with the Pentagon.[38] These agreements led to massive changes on the ground, with a stark ramping up of military assistance to the region. In fact, of the roughly $93 million of military assistance supplied to the region in the decade between independence and 9/11, $84 million (over 90%) came during the last half-decade, as the region's strategic importance became clear.[39] Through such programs, Pentagon planners have hoped to reorientate regional militaries away from Soviet-era weaponry and doctrine and begin to enmesh them within Western security institutions such as NATO, wherein US influence is supreme.

This was the primary objective behind the September 1997 "peacekeeping" exercise involving Centrazbat (the NATO-created Central Asian Battalion), Russian and Turkish forces, and no fewer than 500 US paratroopers. Centered on the longest-distance parachute jump ever recorded by the US 101st Airborne Brigade, straight into the heart of a region where American military presence would have been unthinkable just years before, the purpose of this training exercise was clearly expressed at the time. Observing the exercise, Catherine Kelleher (then deputy assistant secretary of defense) declared that it was "a dramatic demonstration of US interests in [a] region" which included the "potential for conflict, plus the presence of enormous energy resources." These comments were echoed by then–US ambassador to Kazakhstan, Elizabeth Jones, who noted that the region's energy resources were to form "a backup or fill-in" to the Middle East in the event that Persian Gulf supplies should be interrupted. And crucially, the hypothetical crisis forming the backdrop of the exercise involved "quelling local opposition from renegade, separatist forces *that are assisted by a foreign power.*"[40]

Attempts by Washington to cement its influence in this way hugely accelerated with the declaration of the war on terror in 2001. In the years following the 9/11 attacks, US security relationships with states in the Caspian region underwent a qualitative shift, with embargos removed and funding levels multiplied.[41] Compared to the $84 million in military assistance channeled through major programs in the five years between 1997 and 2001, the five years since 9/11 saw a staggering $663 million provided in military assistance. This represents a near eightfold increase in pre-9/11 levels and almost 90 percent of the $756 million provided to the region in the fifteen years between independence and 2006. Moreover, this figure does not include an *additional* $220 million worth of "nonstandard" assistance, run through specific "counterterrorism" and "counternarcotic" programs in the Department of Defense. As we shall see later, this Pentagon funding has been used specifically to bypass the ream of human rights restrictions placed upon assistance run through the State Department. Overall, this massive increase in military aid— unprecedented in the region and unparalleled elsewhere in the world—was primarily justified by reference to the relatively short-term interests of Operation Enduring Freedom in neighboring Afghanistan.[42] However, although securing cooperation for the campaign against the Taliban was a major objective of US officials during the autumn of 2001, the levels and types of assistance provided since 2001 belied a wider set of objectives.[43] And given the eventual presence in the region established by the United States, it has become obvious that the initial agreements in October 2001 between Washington and the Caspian states were substantially different from those reported in the press.[44]

These agreements facilitated a US engagement in the region that, within a few years, was positioned far wider than the goal of countering Afghan-based terrorism would suggest. Not least, this was evident in the attempt to formalize the ad hoc agreements reached with the region's governments in autumn 2001 regarding direct US military presence, with plans for a semipermanent footprint pushed by high-level Pentagon officials.[45] Washington's long-term thinking in this regard was made most clear by Colin Powell, then secretary of state: "You know, you're plugging along, you're having meetings, things are moving slowly, there is wariness. And then you have something like the 11th of September come along, and it just breaks through a lot of barriers. We need military help, we need access to your base, to suddenly open up other opportunities for further dialogue. The key here is not to just say thank you for the use of your base and we're out of here, but to use that opening for other purposes of liberalization, democracy, putting their economies on a sounder basis."[46]

Contrary to the expectations of some, the Obama administration has continued to deepen this security relationship with the region, and is in fact increasing the military assistance provided to oil-rich and oil-transit states. Requested funds for the Foreign Military Financing (FMF) program for 2010 represent a more than 60 percent increase on the last budget of the Bush administration. Funds to Turkmenistan are increasing tenfold, as the United States "continues to support Turkmenistan's efforts to expand its oil and gas exports." Kazakhstan, Azerbaijan, and Georgia are also experiencing large rises in assistance.[47] Such increases have a definite geopolitical logic, as Washington under Obama, according to the State Department, "rejects the notion that any country has special privileges or a 'sphere of influence' in this region; instead, the United States is open to cooperating with all countries in the region and where appropriate providing assistance."[48]

Increased US presence and influence in the Caspian Basin since 9/11 has not been received without resistance from other powers. Russia and China have used the SCO as a vehicle to call for US withdrawal from the Manas airbase in Kyrgyzstan, a move that prompted an emergency trip to the region by former defense secretary Donald Rumsfeld to (successfully) secure a continued presence for US forces.[49] Balancing moves by Russia and China have continued to unsettle US planners and have been successful in pulling the Uzbek regime—an important US ally in the immediate post-9/11 era—away from Washington's influence.[50] Likewise, as Moscow reasserts its influence over the Caucasus, Russian president Dmitri Medvedev in November 2008 blamed its summer conflict with Georgia on Washington's attempts to pull the region closer within the US-led system. The "arrogant course of the US administration," he argued, was at fault, because it "hates criticism and prefers unilateral decisions."[51] The Obama administration may be able to adopt a more conciliatory tone with Moscow during its time in power. Its continued interest in accessing Caspian oil remains, though, and will likely ensure that US interests clash with those of Russia in the years ahead.

In this light, Washington's attempts to integrate the Caspian within the wider US-led order has translated into a deep concern over the means by which the region's oil reaches markets: namely, the routes taken by oil pipelines from the region. In 1991, the region's entire export infrastructure pointed northward, and was designed to service the needs of the Russian empire. This position was further cemented by the Russian-led upgrading or construction of new northbound routes during the early 1990s.[52] In response, US planners have increasingly worked to undermine this dominance by supporting the construction of new, westward-pointing pipelines. These strategic priorities for the region were outlined by Clinton's energy secretary Bill Richardson. In 1998, he stated: "This is about America's energy security, which depends on diversifying our sources of oil and gas worldwide. It's also about preventing strategic inroads by those who don't share our values. We're trying to move these newly independent countries toward the West. We would like to see them reliant on Western commercial and political interests rather than going the other way. We've made substantial political investment in the Caspian, and it's very important to us that both the pipeline map and the politics come out right."[53]

In promoting the independence of the oil-rich states of the Caspian, US officials have maintained that the strategy has been designed "in essence [to] break Russia's monopoly control over the transportation of oil from that region."[54] In practice, this has meant working to open up viable routes between the Caspian and the West that bypass both Iran and Russia. In isolation, commercial logic would lead to the development of export routes from the Caspian through Iran, in light of its relative political stability, the shorter distance to the open ocean, and the extensive facilities that already exist at a range of terminals on the Persian Gulf. However, given Washington's strategic concerns over containing Iran, embodied in the wide-ranging set of US sanctions discussed in chapter 1, this option has not been viable.[55]

As an alternative, the US threw its full support behind a plan to construct a pipeline from the Azeri capital Baku, via the Georgian capital of Tbilisi, and then southeast through Turkey to the Mediterranean port of Ceyhan. This plan was largely motivated by a desire to provide Turkey with an element of control over the region's resources and thus to secure the position of a NATO member as a regional power vis-à-vis Iran and Russia. Zbigniew Brzezinski succinctly outlined the thinking in this regard: "An independent, Turkic-speaking Azerbaijan, with pipelines running from it to the ethnically related and politically supportive Turkey, would prevent Russia from exercising a monopoly on access to the region and would thus also deprive Russia of decisive political leverage over the politics of the new Central Asian states."[56] Because a shorter route to the Georgian Black Sea port of Sup'sa made more commercial sense for the oil companies financing the plan, the Clinton administration had to embark upon a concerted lobbying effort to secure its preferred route. This intensified during 1998, when the message was unambiguous: Undersecretary of State Stuart Eizenstat insisted that, "overall, Baku-Ceyhan offers the best option from environmental, economic *and strategic* standpoints. No-one should underestimate our determination to make Baku-Ceyhan a reality."[57] In a clear example of Washington's relative autonomy from the interests of particular representatives of oil capital, US strategic logic designed to entrench the wider capitalist order trumped the narrow commercial interests of the oil companies, who understandably favored the shorter Sup'sa route.

With the BTC pipeline now operating to carry Azeri oil to market, US planners have turned their attention to rerouting Kazakh oil from the Caspian Pipeline Consortium (CPC) pipeline, which is privately operated but runs through Russian territory. With Moscow holding a potential block on the 50 percent of all Kazakh exports that travel through the CPC, US planners have begun to seriously push for the construction of a major pipeline from Aktau on the Caspian shore to the Azeri capital of Baku in order to feed into the BTC. Under the benign rubric of "diversifying export options," officials in Washington have sought the development of "multiple pipelines that will ensure delivery of Caspian energy to world markets, unfettered by monopolies or constrained by geographic chokepoints."[58] In particular, the ABTC option would service the expected huge increase in production as operations begin at the massive Kashagan field. According to Paul Simons, this would dramatically increase the value of Kazakh oil reserves by "bringing them closer to world markets" and would "greatly improve Kazakhstan's position in terms of investment potential and attractiveness—and return on investment."[59] Again, the Obama administration has continued to push for the ABTC option and other routes bypassing Russia. As the special envoy for Eurasian energy, Richard Morningstar declared in June 2009 in an address to the American Chamber of Commerce in Baku: "Given current global financial and economic conditions, it is more important than ever to have a reliable international energy supply . . . [pipelines bypassing Russia] *are extremely important from a diversification and strategic standpoint.*"[60]

Through the politics of pipeline routing, through economic assistance, and through closer military-to-military ties with states in the region, Washington has worked to counter Russian and Chinese influence in the Caspian Basin. And in parallel, officials in Moscow and Beijing have worked to counter growing US interest and activity. In this context, a form of zero-sum interimperial analysis captures much of the dynamic at play in the Caspian region. Indeed, such an analysis has become a dominant framework when examining the geopolitics of the region. As Michael Klare argues:

> Right now, the United States, Russia and China are competing for the energy riches of [the Caspian Sea]. All three powers have a vital stake in the global flow of oil, and all three seek some degree of control over the political dynamics of the most important oil-producing regions. All three have deployed combat forces in these areas or established military ties with friendly local governments. And, as the global demand for petroleum rises and more countries begin to rely on these regions for their energy, we can expect all three to bolster their strategic positions and to try to curb the influence of their rivals.[61]

For Klare, the region is "now the cockpit for a twenty-first-century energy version of the imperial 'Great Game' of the nineteenth century," resulting in nothing short of a "dangerous vortex of competitive pressures."[62] However, even here, an interimperial rivalry analysis is incomplete, since it does not take account of the full logic driving US strategy in the oil-rich South. The integration of the Caspian region into the international economic system remains of far more relevance for US planners than old-fashioned notions of imperial resource control.[63] In this light, the former US senior advisor on diplomacy to the region, Steven Mann, succinctly summarized the logic driving Washington's strategy: "A fundamental misconception is that the United States is engaged in a 'Great Game' and seeking to challenge Russia in the region. I must stress here that this is not an anti-Russia policy . . . Our policy is a policy of antimonopoly."[64] Furthermore, Richard Morningstar reiterated this viewpoint at the start of the Obama administration: "The US holds the view that energy security is not a zero-sum game. Indeed, no nation's energy security can be had at the expense of any other nations'—we're all in this together."[65]

## Integrating the Oil-Rich Region: Liberalization and US Energy Security in the Caspian Basin

In order to increase the flow of Caspian oil onto world markets and to stabilize this flow in the face of potential peer competition by rivals, US strategy has been geared around embedding an economic framework within which foreign capital can confidently operate. As one high-level official from the Department of Energy stated with regard to the Caspian region: "Our job in the government is to encourage the adoption of the best environment for commercial actors to do business."[66] High-level officials in successive US administrations have stressed transparency and respect for the rule of law because these are the prerequisites for increased foreign investment in the energy sector.[67]

The United States has used both bilateral foreign policy tools and support for the international financial institutions (IFIs) to fundamentally change the economies of the Caspian region. Aid has been provided to reform the previously closed economies along strict neoliberal lines. Bilateral assistance through the FSA program, and more recently through the 1999 Silk Road Strategy Act, has been designed to guide regional economies in their transition from communist central planning toward a free market model (so-called supporting transformational diplomacy). Specifically, it has the objective of making economies "more competitive and open [to] trade and investment" by designing "the structures and means necessary for the growth of private sector economies based upon market principles."[68] Likewise, under US direction the International Monetary Fund (IMF) has provided significant assistance in return for wholesale economic adjustment designed explicitly to maximize the benefits accrued by transnational capital investment in the region. In true neoliberal style, the desired end-state was—according to the IMF's managing director—nothing less than a "redefinition of the role of the State in the economy," where it was to be restricted to upholding the law and "establishing a fair and transparent regulatory framework for private sector activity." Government expenditure on public services was to be substantially reduced and intervention in the economy banished, with market forces left to set prices and allocate resources. Of central concern was the reduction and removal of

barriers to foreign trade and investment and the creation of "a suitable institutional framework that will give domestic and foreign entrepreneurs the
confidence to invest."[69]

In this light, the IMF took the lead role in forcing open the two major oil-
rich economies of the region: Kazakhstan and Azerbaijan. After an initially
slow start, the IMF was positive about the accelerated "pace of structural reform" in Kazakhstan and by 1998 was declaring that the country had "made
substantial progress in transforming its economy into a market-based system,"
with the domestic market "fairly liberalised and open to foreign competition."[70] True IMF satisfaction came in 1995, when large state enterprises were
released for sale to foreign companies and corporations from across the world
rushed to invest.[71] As a result, inward foreign direct investment (FDI) has shot
up, exceeding $1 billion each year since. The percentage of the country's GDP
located in the private sector also ballooned from 25 percent in 1995 to 60
percent in 1999 (it had been just 5% in 1991), as foreign companies snapped
up core Kazakh assets.[72] Similarly, IMF loans to Azerbaijan in the mid-1990s,
totaling around $400 million, came with instructions designed to "initiate
comprehensive structural reform," including the privatization of 70 percent
of state enterprises and the completion of a trade liberalization process by the
end of the 1990s, as well as a comprehensive reform of the social safety net to
make it "financially secure" and to "improve its efficiency." The IMF's central
objective in Azerbaijan was to "prepare the country for the prospective oil
boom as oil production is projected to double by the turn of the century and
to quadruple shortly thereafter."[73]

At the core of Washington's Caspian policy has been a drive to dismantle
existing monopolies on the extraction and transport of energy resources and
an opening up of the sector throughout the region to private investors. US
planners have stressed the need to provide a predictable investment regime
supported by investor-friendly legislation in order to attract global capital to
the energy sector.[74] The Clinton administration led the drive to open the oil-
rich economies of the region; as regional elites were summoned to Washington for the first time in 1997, they were informed in no uncertain terms of the
interests held in the region's oil reserves and of US plans to exploit them. As
a result, a myriad of agreements were signed to facilitate deeper liberalization,
the removal of barriers to trade, and greater partnership in energy extraction.[75] These were later consolidated by the Bush administration, which did not
break step with the policy direction of its predecessor and which used the

events of 9/11 as a mechanism to further accelerate the free marketization of the Caspian Basin. The 2001 NEDP report noted that "foreign investors and technology are critical to rapid development" of infrastructure and to "ensure that rising Caspian oil production is effectively integrated into world oil trade."[76] As a result, a raft of "strategic partnerships" were signed with states in the region, ostensibly as part of the war on terror, but in fact orientated to accelerate the existing program of economic liberalization and "creating an attractive investment climate to attract foreign capital."[77]

Just several months into the Obama administration, it appears as though the same strategy is being pursued by the new team in Washington. According to Richard Morningstar: "Openness to foreign investment and a welcoming investment climate, including transparency and respect for the rule of law, are hallmarks of a modern society . . . Free market forces and the private sector should be the primary means through which oil and gas are produced, transported and purchased. Transparency and respect for the rule of law are essential principles that must be demonstrated."[78]

Overall, and despite the fact that the transition from planned to market economies across the region has been far from smooth, the removal of substantial barriers to investment has resulted in the entry of significant levels of FDI into the region. As Caspian economies were restructured and large enterprises were privatized, FDI stocks in the region increased from $28 million at the point of independence to over $6 billion in 1996, over $20 billion in 2001, and over $56 billion in 2006. Integration into the world economy has clearly facilitated capital from throughout the world entering the region and benefits this over and above Caspian capital itself (with outward FDI from states in the region totaling less than $1 billion in 2006).[79]

The reforms carried out in the Kazakh and Azeri oil sectors, for example, have created two of the most investment-friendly regimes in the world. Indeed, the phenomenal growth in FDI across the Caspian has been concentrated overwhelmingly in the region's energy sector, with over 80 percent of the FDI stock in the region in 2006 held in Azerbaijan and Kazakhstan, and the proportion of this in the energy sector approaching 70 percent.[80] Moreover, well over 90 percent of all FDI in Azerbaijan in recent years has been in the oil sector.[81] And again, this stock originates from all over the world, as transnational oil capital has penetrated the region. Production sharing agreements (PSAs) exist with companies from, amongst other places, Russia, the United States, the United Kingdom, France, Italy, South Korea, Canada, Hungary, and

Oman, whilst the export infrastructure (such as the CPC and BTC pipelines) has received investment from corporations based in the United States, the United Kingdom, Norway, Turkey, Italy, France, and Japan. Of particular interest in this regard, Chinese state-owned companies have invested in multinational ventures in the region *alongside* Western IOCs, operating clearly within the free market model.[82]

Production and exportation has increased exponentially as a direct result of the foreign investment in regional infrastructure (both extractive and transportation), with overall exports multiplying more than five times between 1997 and 2007.[83] Thus oil has increasingly dominated the economies of these two countries. Kazakh oil exports are nothing less than "the foundation of the country's economy," with the sector now accounting for around 30 percent of GDP and over half of all Kazakh export revenues.[84] Similar figures characterize the Azeri economy, as a 2008 IMF assessment found that "over the last three years, rising oil production together with very high oil prices has boosted GDP and export growth to unprecedented levels." Oil revenue has grown hugely as a proportion of government revenue, from 38 percent in 2004 to 59 percent in 2007.[85] However, the economic reforms that have led to this concentration of investment in the oil sector, and the concentration of investment itself, has had a largely negative impact upon much of the Caspian population and has in turn worked to strengthen authoritarian forces in the region.

## Poverty, Dictatorships, and Oil in the Caspian Basin

In contrast to the benefits provided to foreign capital by neoliberal economic reforms, the free marketization of the Caspian Basin has been nothing short of disastrous for the majority of the population. An extensive report published by the World Bank in 2000 found that, after nearly a decade of free market reforms across Eastern Europe and the former Soviet Union, poverty levels across the region had increased "dramatically." Whereas only 4 percent of people in the "transition countries" lived on less than $2.15 per day whilst under Soviet rule (the World Bank's poverty line), this figure had exploded to 20 percent by 1998. Furthermore, the Bank found that levels of absolute income deprivation "vary considerably across the region, with the highest levels found in the Central Asia and Caucasus region." Overall, the authors concluded, the sheer "magnitude of the increase in poverty—and its persistence during the past decade—alone would probably suffice" to distinguish the region from all others in the world. And crucially, they were clear as to the reason behind this catastrophe: "On the economic front, transition to a market economy—in many countries not yet fully achieved—has brought new opportunities for many, while for others it has meant unaccustomed material hardship and loss of security. Successive economic shocks—the loss of jobs or prolonged nonpayment of salaries, hyperinflation and loss of savings, and the drastic erosion of accustomed supports (such as low-cost or free social services, subsidies, and discounts on goods and services)—have made people feel unusually vulnerable, powerless and unable to plan for the future."[86]

Although by 2005 the World Bank had found that the region had in many respects improved from the disaster at the end of the 1990s, poverty was still endemic across much of the Caspian Basin. Levels of those classed as "poor" had dropped from around 20 percent of the population in 1998 but still stood at more than 12 percent (three times higher than during Soviet times). Moreover, according to the authors, these figures told only part of the story: "Even where incomes have grown and absolute material deprivation at $2.15 per day is low, the standard of living is not high, and large shares of the population . . . have relatively low savings and [are] vulnerable to poverty in the event of shocks that affect earning potential."[87] Alongside measures of absolute poverty and economic vulnerability, the removal of extensive Soviet-era social services has led to a significant decline in health and education levels. Across the region, and particularly in rural areas, free health care is a distant memory and access to quality services is now reserved for the rich. As wealth and spending has become concentrated amongst ruling elites, similar trends have characterized education throughout the region, and costs have spiraled as subsidies have been eliminated.[88]

Oil-rich economies in particular were subjected to this form of shock. The Kazakh economy underwent a severe contraction throughout the 1990s (with GDP at the end of the decade less than two-thirds the size of that at the start), and government spending on social services went from 80 percent of overall expenditure in 1997 to 25 percent in 2002. As a result, Kazakhstan's rankings on the Human Development Index scale free-fell seventy-six places, from 53rd to 129th. The number of doctors decreased by 10 percent, and nurses by 25 percent, leading to a decline in the general health of the population and an increase in previously controlled diseases. Likewise, the education system was in decline throughout the country, with school closures becoming the norm.[89] Even with recent economic growth as a result of rising oil production, income inequality between socioeconomic groups, as well as between oil-producing regions and the rest of the country, have continued to grow.[90] According to the United Nations Development Programme, despite significant economic growth over recent years, no less than 24 percent of the population in 2002 lived in absolute poverty, with incomes below the subsistence minimum. Unemployment rates for women, youth, and rural residents were also large. Within the context of gradually falling unemployment figures, more than 44 percent of those in employment were receiving wages "which did not provide for an adequate standard of living."[91]

Similarly, poverty levels remain "the major challenge" for Azerbaijan, according to the Asian Development Bank, with rates approaching 45 percent and lack of access to affordable quality services "an increasing concern." When surveyed, many of those in poverty in Azerbaijan have noted a decline in employment opportunities, reduced access to health care, and limited clean water: factors that combine to produce "feelings of hopelessness and apathy and [skepticism] about the prospects for a visible improvement in their standards of living" in the future.[92]

The deleterious effects experienced by local populations across the region have been exacerbated by the emphasis of both international actors and local governments on expanding oil production and exportation. Those in power in the oil-rich Caspian states have spent significantly more energy on consolidating their rule and maximizing the revenue from the oil sector than they have on maximizing the welfare of their populations.[93] As in several other oil-rich regions in the South, such as the Persian Gulf and West Africa, oil wealth in the region tends to have centralizing and "democracy-dampening" tendencies, as the lack of transparency, absence of any real separation of powers, and significant levels of corruption leads to the emergence of "patronage politics" and the consolidation of existing power-holders. The oil-rich states of the Caspian are no exception to this pattern.[94]

On the ground, this has translated into a concerted effort to remove any challenge to incumbent rule. There is an almost complete absence of a vibrant civil society across the region and, in most cases, a lack of effective political opposition. In many of the states, ruling elites have little popular legitimacy, and regime transition is unheard of, with Soviet-era leaders or dynasties still in power. As the authors of the highly authoritative *Nations in Transit* report found, "the consolidated authoritarian regimes of the former Soviet Union have tilted an already dramatically uneven playing field more sharply by refocusing state power to restrict critical voices and institutions." Over the past five years, these states have "focused intently on controlling media infrastructure and content" and have instigated "a crackdown on freedom of association." In conclusion, the authors argue that "obstacles to the development of democratic standards and institutions in many countries have increased [over recent years] as authoritarian regimes seek to suppress local pressures for change and fend off external ones. [This trend] is explained in part by the emergence of a distinct set of authoritarian states, boosted in several key cases by extraordinary energy riches, which are playing an influential role in subverting democratic governance." This newfound oil wealth has functioned as an "authoritarian propellant," providing ruling elites with the means by which to consolidate power and destroy any real or potential opposition.[95]

This plays out in both Kazakhstan and Azerbaijan, where the massive increase in oil wealth caused by the privatization process has been "widely identified with burgeoning corruption and deteriorating standards of governance" and has consolidated the rule of incumbent elites, both sets of which are unchanged since independence.[96] Kazakhstan under the Nazarbayev regime is a one-party state, and exclusion from the political process by nonparty groups has effectively been legalized. Likewise, the vast oil wealth has been used to "disburse power and privileges to family, friends and clients," and "this concentration of wealth and power in a narrow social stratum of elites has marginalized a significant number of citizens."[97] Meanwhile, in Azerbaijan the Aliyev dynasty rules through an enormous concentration of power in the presidency, with opposition parties attempting to contest elections effectively silenced. Indeed, Human Rights Watch found that the Aliyev regime has "consistently exercised its overwhelming power to control and manipulate electoral processes," and harassment of parties, journalists, and activists is widespread.[98]

Throughout the region, statehood is designed primarily to serve the needs of the ruling elite, and widespread popular discontent has been shut down as leaders work to consolidate their power.[99] And overall, this concentration of wealth and power in a small elite group has impacted upon regional stability. Discontent amongst the population is widespread in many areas and—in a region where ethnic identity is strong and does not correlate well to state boundaries—separatist forces are also strong. Despite the high concentration of state power across the Caspian Basin, government authority often does not extend far outside the capital cities, and many regions remain outside of central control. In addition, most borders between states are exceptionally weak, which allows for the unregulated movement of people, groups, weapons, and drugs.

Regional instability threatens the Caspian in a myriad of ways and takes a wide variety of forms. Of special concern for both ruling elites and US planners is the presence of multiple forces in the region who seek to challenge the political and economic status quo. This has included separatist forces seeking greater autonomy from central government—and often taking up arms in the process—as well as national and transnational movements that cast themselves through the lens of political Islam. Such movements are fueled to an extent by the reduction of space for legitimate political opposition and the severe economic conditions in the region rather than by the dictates of extremist Islamist ideology.[100] Armed movements in conflict with incumbent regions have proliferated, from the activities of the Islamic Movement of Uzbekistan (IMU) throughout Central Asia to the many separatist forces challenging Georgian state authority. Resistance has also emerged in nonviolent forms, as groups such as Hizb ut-Tahrir work to overthrow incumbent regimes through peaceful means, with the goal of building a regionwide Islamic form of governance.[101]

As elsewhere, US planners would prefer stable liberal democracies in the region that would be open to penetration by global capital and responsive to the needs of their citizens. However, attempts to promote a greater voice for civil society in the region and to persuade incumbent regimes to make provisions for political transition, have fallen afoul of resistance from local regimes keen to remain in power. Since political space across the region remains closed, Washington has been unable to manage the rise of acceptable counter-elites who would remain pliant (or be even more so) in the face of Washington's interests. As a result, forces that the United States would consider to be "moderate" have little room for expression and the ruling strata are instead faced with an opposition that pursues an agenda largely inimical to that of the United States.

For example, in addition to positioning itself firmly against ruling elites across the region, Hizb ut-Tahrir has developed a critique of the relationship between these elites and the United States, as well as the economic framework within which this relationship is conducted: "As for the American campaign to make capitalism an ideology for all nations and peoples of the globe, it meets no resistance except in the Islamic world . . . This campaign has other motives such as capitalist greed, the ambitious desire of America and the West towards the resources of the Muslim lands, the geographic and strategic advantages of these lands, and the fact that they constitute a huge market for the products of the West and are a source for the raw materials necessary for its industries as well as its huge oil reserves vital for its life." The group urges Muslims to "reject market policies because they contradict Islam" and because they prevent local populations from "building their economies on a productive basis and will lead to enabling the Kuffar [unbelievers] to maintain their control on Muslims and their lands."[102] As a result, the presence of such forces throughout the region ensures that Washington has had to secure its interests by falling back upon policies that work to bolster the prevailing order against such challenges.

## Stabilizing the Silk Route: Militarization and Human Rights in the East-West Corridor

The precarious position of regional elites vis-à-vis the societies over which they rule has had profound implications for US policy toward the region, as Washington has been forced to rely heavily upon incumbent rulers in order to pursue its interests. These elites have not always embraced the necessary market reforms wholeheartedly, and there have been several points at which these changes have stagnated and even been reversed, but in the absence of any viable alternative set of elites for Washington to support, they have continued to provide the steadiest route to liberalization of their economies. It is in this light that the massive amounts of security assistance we outlined earlier must be considered. Washington *is* concerned with influencing the external orientation of Caspian states toward the West and has a distinct agenda to make sure that its military assistance works to pull the region away from Russian and Chinese power and toward the US orbit. And the oil reserves of the region are the obvious driver in this regard. However, since the threats to the stability required for the smooth transport of oil often stem from below, the *internal* stabilization of Caspian states has been elevated as a top US priority. This explains the deepening military ties with local security forces as much as, if not more than, concerns over containing Russian and Chinese influence. As Strobe Talbott, deputy secretary of state during the Clinton administration, stated: "The United States has a stake in [the region's] success . . . If economic and political reform in the countries of the Caucasus and Central

Asia does not succeed—if internal and cross-border conflicts simmer and flare—the region could become a breeding ground of terrorism, a hotbed of religious and political extremism, and a battleground for outright war. It would matter profoundly to the United States if that were to happen in an area that sits on as much as 200 billion barrels of oil."[103]

Planners in Washington have long been aware that "political uncertainty" is a potential barrier to the development of the region's energy resources and that the United States needs to actively stabilize the region in order to remove it.[104] And this strategy has relied primarily upon the provision of military assistance to local security forces in order to insulate pro-US elites and to protect a favorable regulatory and investment environment from a variety of armed and unarmed threats.

Examining the types of assistance provided under the massive injection of military aid into the region reveals that the imposition of internal stability provides the overriding rationale for the programs. Political and military control by governments in the region over their entire territory have tended to be exceptionally weak, and those posing an internal threat to the stability of incumbent regimes have often been at liberty to move across national borders at will.[105] Moreover, oil has to be transported hundreds of miles across vast expanses of lawless territory and across multiple national boundaries. Securing the stable environment required for investment in this infrastructure by foreign capital therefore requires ensuring that local security forces can project their power throughout the territory where political and military opposition finds refuge, as well as across the entire pipeline routes and around the oil installations themselves. In this context, US security assistance programs range far wider than static infrastructure protection and are plainly geared toward the provision of counterinsurgency training and equipment. Programs emphasize the necessity of building capacity for force mobility, rapid reaction, and border security in a bid to impose stability upon areas where government influence has traditionally been weak or nonexistent. This objective was evident in the newly minted "strategic partnerships" established between Washington and Caspian governments in the aftermath of 9/11.

Prominent amongst these have been the agreements between the United States and Uzbekistan and Kyrgyzstan. Although these latter two countries are not oil-rich themselves, the presence within them of radical forces that have the potential to destabilize the wider region has caused US planners to take a keen interest in ensuring domestic stability.[106] Alongside a mutual commitment to the deepening of economic reform, the United States sought to "establish qualitatively new and mutually beneficial relations" in the military sphere, including "training special units" in the Uzbek armed forces and reequipping them with weapons and military hardware in order to stabilize the increasingly weak state.[107]

Likewise, support for economic restructuring in Kyrgyzstan was accelerated alongside a redefinition of "joint activity to ensure security and stability in Central Asia."[108] This assistance has come as Washington has fully backed the regimes' response to internal unrest, with one top official claiming that "we need to support [Uzbek dictator] Karimov's efforts to crack down on terrorism, then move onto democracy."[109] According to J. D. Crouch, assistant secretary of defense for international security policy during the Bush administration, "Uzbekistan's own struggle against an indigenous terrorist group" has given the regime a "keen awareness of the threat facing the region and the world."[110]

A similar focus guides US assistance to the oil-rich states themselves, as Washington acts to secure both the oil infrastructure specifically and the wider investment environment more generally. Top US and Kazakh defense officials have stated that their relationship stretches far wider than the immediate needs of the war on terror in Afghanistan and is underpinned by a common interest in the stability of the Caspian region.[111] In order to guarantee this stability, both Kazakh defense spending and US military assistance to the country have risen substantially. Crucially, this has been designed to reconfigure security forces away from external defense and toward suppressing domestic unrest, with the publication of a new military doctrine focusing on combating sources of internal instability.[112] Aid from Washington has been geared toward this new mission and has included the delivery of Huey helicopters and C-130 Hercules aircraft for increased troop mobility across the vast Kazakh territory, alongside the overt and covert provision of counterterrorist and "antiguerrilla" training by US Special Forces for hundreds of troops. According to the US embassy in Kazakhstan, this training involved "individual soldiering techniques and soldiering in mountainous terrain."[113]

There is a clear energy security dimension within this broad reorientation toward internal defense. The United States has provided assistance to create command structures dedicated to energy security and, whilst on a visit to Kazakhstan in February 2004, then–defense secretary Rumsfeld pledged $12 million for "projects involving the Kazakhstani army as part of an ongoing five-year plan to address Caspian Sea security": a vital task, since "it is important for the world that the security be assured in that area."[114] Assistance to Kazakhstan has been provided explicitly with the goal of "equip[ing] and training [to] enable Kazakhstan's border authorities to protect Caspian energy infrastructure and key energy transport routes." FMF and IMET funds have been used to "support development of a rapid reaction brigade near the Caspian oil field in Atyrau," which will "enhance Kazakhstan's capability to respond to major terrorist threats to oil platforms or borders."[115] Furthermore, in the first budget request from the Obama administration, the State Department maintained that the 60 percent increase in FMF funds over the previous year was designed for the same strategic goals that have motivated assistance throughout the Bush years and before: "A major priority will continue to be the development of Kazakhstan's nascent Huey II helicopter fleet, intended to enhance military capability to protect significant energy infrastructure and respond to threats in Kazakhstan and in the Caspian Sea."[116]

Similarly, security assistance to Azerbaijan has been orientated so as to stabilize the Aliyev regime and guarantee the steady flow of oil onto market. Requests by both the Bush administration (in FY 2009) *and* the Obama administration (in FY 2010) highlighted the need to strengthen Azerbaijani security institutions in order to combat terrorism and "the struggle against other transnational threats." In particular, both administrations believed that assistance will "continue to help develop Azerbaijani maritime capabilities and contribute to the overall security of the resource-rich Caspian Sea."[117] Assistance over the past several years has been designed to support US national interests in the country, which include "the provision of a significant and growing supply of hydrocarbon resources to global markets . . . With large estimates of oil and gas reserves in the Caspian, Azerbaijan has the potential to play a significant role in the diversification of American and global energy supplies."[118]

Former secretary of state Colin Powell stated that aid to Azerbaijan was geared toward crucial US national security interests, including the uninterrupted extraction and transportation of oil: "The Administration believes that building up the capacity of Azerbaijan and other Caspian littoral states is important in order to prevent the transit of destabilizing items and to secure the oil flow that is critical to U.S. national security interests."[119] On the ground, this assistance has been geared toward complementing the vast increases in Azeri military expenditure in recent years and further integrating the state into the Euro-Atlantic security architecture via closer ties with NATO. But specifically, it has facilitated US forces to train Azeri counterparts in oil security, alongside employees from the private military company Blackwater.[120]

As part of its increasing concern over securing the supply of oil to international markets, NATO has accelerated its involvement in the region. Azerbaijan has expressed interest in cooperation with the organization over critical infrastructure protection, and a NATO seminar in Baku in March 2008 on Caspian and Central Asian security "stressed the paramount importance of the physical security of [the region's] energy infrastructure, and that NATO's expertise could be utilised in this area," with the BTC pipeline "an extremely important asset for the Euro-Atlantic region in terms of energy security."[121] Recent interest in energy security by the alliance appears to move beyond simple expressions of interest: in a trip to the region following the seminar, NATO's special representative for the Caucasus and Central Asia, Robert Simmons, told journalists that the alliance "intended to include the joint protection of Kazakhstan's energy infrastructure in its program of collaboration with Kazakhstan."[122]

Of special note is the *coordinated* package of military aid to Azerbaijan and Kazakhstan under the rubric of the $100 million Caspian Guard initiative, designed to improve the capabilities of the oil-rich states to protect oil installations—both exploration and transportation. As Mike Anderson, the chief of the Europe Plans and Policies Division at EUCOM, said: "We've been equipping and training Azeri special forces with the ability to go out and take down one of their own gas and oil platforms if it was seized by terrorists." And this is directly focused on meeting US strategic objectives in the region: "It's good old US interests, it's rather selfish. Certainly we've chosen to help two littoral states, Azerbaijan and Kazakhstan, but always underlying that is our own self-interest."[123] As Anderson's senior at EUCOM, General Charles Wald has also stated that "British Petroleum has a consortium of 20 different countries and agencies that are developing the oil in the Caspian Sea, $20 billion over the next 5 years, which is the diversification issue . . . very important. We think that's an important area. As a matter of fact, we have a lot of initiatives going on in the Caucasus Region [such as the Caspian Guard] . . . It's one of the most brilliant strategic issues that the United States has pulled off in the last 20 years, a brilliant program. We're well behind it."[124]

Because the Azeri parliament passed a "no foreign troops" law in 2005, the Pentagon has had to operate through Blackwater. Hired in early 2004, the company was tasked with deploying to Azerbaijan under a $2.5 million contract.

Chris Taylor, Blackwater's vice president, has outlined the purpose of the mission: "We've been asked to help create, for lack of a more educated term, a SEAL team for Azerbaijan, both to help them with their oil interests in the Caspian but also to kind of monitor what goes on in the Caspian during the wee hours of the night. These are very, very politically . . . sensitive issues."[125]

As well as stabilizing the two oil-rich states themselves, the United States has moved to ensure that the transit state of Georgia, through which the BTC pipeline travels, is secured against internal instability. In support of the exponential rise in Georgian defense spending over recent years, this has required programs designed to protect the BTC pipeline itself from attack as armed groups across the region identify it as a target.[126] In January 2003 it was revealed that US instructors would be providing military training to the 400-strong pipeline-protection battalion within the Georgian Special Protection Service (GSPS), which is dedicated to guarding the Georgian section of the BTC. The United States would allocate $11 million to the project, with US Special Forces working alongside employees of private military companies.[127] Assistance for the pipeline protection program was eventually privatized, as Washington contracted the services of the company Cubic for a three-year, $15 million deal to support all aspects of the Georgian military, including pipeline protection.[128] This now runs alongside the training provided to the GSPS by Bowman Risk Management, in subjects such as planning skills, patrols, and the use of firearms. These guards are heavily armed and—according to a monitoring team paid for by British Petroleum—display AK-47s openly in villages and checkpoints along the pipeline route.[129] This support from the United States and PMCs is designed to complement regional coordination efforts at improving pipeline protection, which have included joint military exercises involving Azerbaijan, Georgia, and Turkey, to make sure that host militaries were "trained to prevent terror attacks, acts of sabotage, and environmental catastrophes along the pipeline route."[130]

As elsewhere in the region, this US assistance is not orientated solely around the provision of static defense capabilities. The BP-led consortium does not simply concern itself with reactive security forces; according to risk assessments seen by the monitoring team, the companies "examine the patterns and causes of regional violence so that steps can be taken to diminish the possibility of violence related to the Projects."[131] This wider understanding of the stability required to maintain investor confidence is matched by US assistance, which is geared toward active counterinsurgency training. Since

9/11, Washington has deployed to Georgia one of the largest in-country train-ing programs in the world, with initial funding of $64 million provided for US Special Forces to conduct a wide range of on-the-ground training for local security forces. Through this program—initially called the Georgia Train and Equip Program (GTEP)—over 2,000 troops have received high-end training in order to improve their combat effectiveness. The delivery of US counterinsur-gency expertise, with the explicit aim of creating counterterrorist forces within the Georgian Ministry of Defense, revolved around instruction in small-unit infantry and airmobile tactics (including platoon-level offensive operations, rifle marksmanship, and individual movement techniques), backed up by the supply of a plethora of combat weapons (including assault rifles, light and heavy machine guns, mortars, and hand grenades). This has been com-plemented by a $2.8 million Special Forces training program, run through the Turkish military, as Georgian forces improve their combat abilities.[132]

In order to get domestic approval in the United States, the rationale pro-vided by officials for this extensive assistance program was initially couched in terms of the wider war on terror, with repeated references to the presence of al Qaeda–related fighters in the Pankisi Gorge.[133] However, this claim was quickly revealed to be based on nonexistent intelligence conjured up for po-litical purposes in Washington. This became obvious during an extraordi-nary, if little-noted, press conference with General Peter Pace (vice chair, Joint Chiefs of Staff) and Victoria Clarke (assistant secretary of defense, public af-fairs) as GTEP was getting off the ground in February 2002. Coming under sustained questioning regarding the evidence held by the administration of al Qaeda–related terrorists in Georgia, both Pace and Clarke struggled to pro-vide a coherent account of Washington's narrative and exposed the absence of any concrete intelligence.[134] This lack of evidence of al Qaeda presence in Georgia became clearer once GTEP was fully underway and was confirmed by both US defense officials in Tbilisi and Georgian officials.[135]

In contrast to public justifications orientated around counterterrorism, GTEP and its successor, the Georgia Security and Stability Operations Program (GSSOP), have been designed to improve internal stability against a wide range of threats (of which Islamist forces has been relatively minor). And the objective of imposing this stability is clear. According to a senior government advisor in Georgia: "There are some problems in Pankisi, but I think it is mostly a social issue. I am not so worried about it. Antiterrorism is not the only reason for the relationship between the United States and Georgia. Georgia is also the shortest route between the [oil reserves] of the Caspian Sea and Turkey."[136] This rationale was confirmed by the US ambassador to Georgia, Richard Miles: "The primary purpose [of GTEP] is to modernize the Georgian army. And it does have a back up role I would say in with regards to pipeline security. The pipeline is a strategic asset for Georgia and all of the countries that are involved."[137]

Indeed, efforts to stabilize Georgia for oil transportation preceded 9/11 by some years. Clinton's defense secretary, William Cohen, visited Georgia in 1999 to "personally extend the hand of defense cooperation" by providing six helicopters to Georgia to help with border security and wider stability (a gift which Georgian premier Shevardnadze declared was "very serious assistance to us in military development"). These assets were seen as a potential solution to the "problems pertaining to the transport of energy resources from Central Asia and the Caspian region to the West," which would risk an increased "terrorist" threat should internal security fail to be maintained.[138] Likewise, the Obama administration has ramped up security assistance funding during its first year in office, with a 45 percent increase in FMF funds and a 75 percent increase in military training through IMET.[139]

Security assistance to the region has been provided by Washington since the mid-1990s in a bid to stabilize pro-US state forms and so maximize the flow of oil to markets. However, in a region where security forces are deeply abusive, this strategy has had profound implications for state formation and human rights in the Caspian Basin. US-trained forces in the region have engaged in egregious abuses against a wide section of civil society. Police forces often act with impunity, engaging in arbitrary arrest and detention, beating pretrial detainees, and imposing restrictions on freedom of the press and assembly. There are frequent reports of torture, abuse, and intimidation within detention facilities—verified by the US State Department itself—with documented methods including beating with table legs, asphyxiation with plastic bags, rape, and specific tactics to maximize pain and "break" detainees (such as the insertion of needles under finger nails).[140]

Overall, Amnesty International noted in 2007, "despite professed efforts by governments in Central Asia to fulfil their human rights obligations . . . grave human rights violations routinely continued to be committed with virtual impunity [as] thousands of people routinely alleged that they had been arbitrarily detained and tortured or ill-treated in custody in order to extract a confession." And crucially, this was not the result of "bad apples" within the security forces; Amnesty found that systemic violations are often used as a deliberate means of consolidating rule: "The fight against terrorism and issues of national security were frequently quoted as crucial in securing stability, but only too frequently used as a cloak to clamp down on dissent, consolidate power and target vulnerable groups or groups perceived as a threat to national or regional security, such as banned Islamic groups and opposition political movements . . . Although the presumption of innocence was enshrined in law, it was violated on a regular basis, especially in the context of national security and 'the war on terror,' with suspects branded guilty in public before the start of their trials."[141]

Attempts by opposition parties and movements to mobilize against incumbent elites are often met with violence, with security forces employing little discrimination in order to suppress challenges to the status quo. This has often been applied by regimes at "election" time to maintain stability. According to Human Rights Watch, violence and arbitrary arrests were used in the 2004 Azeri presidential election to intimidate the opposition; the result was a sham. When violence broke out from frustrated opposition supporters, "the government responded with brutal and excessive force, unleashing its security forces to beat hundreds of demonstrators unconscious." Nearly one thousand people were arrested after the election, many of whom were subjected to beatings and torture (including electric shocks). More than one hundred remained in custody several months later, and many others were fired from their jobs in retaliation for their political affiliation.[142]

In response to the use of force against civilians by ruling elites, Washington has proved relatively unconcerned. In visits to the region, US officials have often sidestepped concerns over abuses and instead prioritized the importance of ruling elites in stabilization efforts. Continued repression in Azerbaijan, for example, has been met with limited high-level criticism from the US government. When President Aliyev visited the White House in April 2006, Bush thanked him for Azerbaijan's leadership as a "modern Muslim country that is able to provide for its citizens and understands that democracy is the wave of the future."[143] Similar support has been provided to Kazakh president Nazarbayev.[144]

In parallel, US planners have worked to bypass standing congressional restrictions on the provision of military aid to abusive security forces. This has been achieved by running assistance through Pentagon channels, which are removed from the oversight afforded State Department aid. Programs such as the Military Assistance Program (MAP), the Coalition Support Fund (CSF), and a new Global War on Terror Partners Fund have been used to channel millions of dollars to the Caspian states.[145] Likewise, the Counterterrorism Fellowship Program (CTFP) has provided lethal military training across the region, with oil-rich and -transit states receiving 70 percent of the funding.[146] Similarly, the Pentagon's Counterdrug Program has provided more than $30 million to the Caspian states, with the list of eligible countries in the region expanded in 2007 to include Azerbaijan, Armenia, Kazakhstan, and Kyrgyzstan for the first time.[147] This funding is significant, because it has been used to bolster the capabilities of states' special forces units and other security forces responsible for guaranteeing regime survival. Although such efforts are justified publicly according to the need to staunch the flow of drugs through the region, the assistance provided allows for enhanced performance across the entire range of internal "stabilization" operations, including those targeted at "subversives," "terrorists," and other opponents of the incumbent elites.

US assistance to the region's security forces has bolstered those repressive institutions used to consolidate the power of ruling elites. This is a deliberate strategy of Washington, which has required bypassing congressional restrictions on aid to abusive militaries. Such a strategy has been deemed necessary, if unfortunate, in order to stabilize the oil-rich region. Infuriated by the Pentagon's actions in regard to supporting abusive forces in the region, Senator John McCain was clear about what was motivating Washington: "There's a great game going on in that part of the world. The oil supplies and how the oil is transported have had an impact on some of the administration's policies. I think that's well known with some of these countries whose names end with -stan."[148]

## Conclusion

US strategy toward the Caspian Basin has been driven primarily by concerns over the region's oil resources and the desire to see these extracted by foreign corporations and exported to market without political interference. This objective has necessitated an active strategy to minimize Russian and Chinese influence in the region and to pull Caspian states firmly toward the West. Although this has not been totally successful—perhaps unsurprising, given the relative distances between the region and Washington, Moscow, and Beijing—the privately led construction of multiple pipelines westward, bypassing Russia and Iran, has been welcomed by US planners. As we have seen, however, Washington's energy security agenda in the region has not simply required engaging in Great Power competition over resources.

To the extent that the Caspian states now welcome foreign capital, US planners hope to integrate Chinese and Russian influence within an open door framework under US hegemony. And considering the political reality on the ground, where authoritarian regimes hold power over a highly unstable region, extending this liberal economic order to the post-Soviet space has required the provision of substantial levels of military aid to local security forces in order to stabilize the region in a way conducive to Washington's interests. Security assistance has been designed to orientate these forces toward internal stability tasks: an agenda that has been enthusiastically adopted by pro-US elites, with significant consequences for the human rights of those in the region. The first signs of US strategy toward the region under the Obama administration reveal significant continuities with its predecessors. Transnationalization of local political economies, integration into the global economy, and stabilization in the face of unrest continue to form the bedrock of American strategy. In many ways, this runs parallel to US strategy toward West Africa and Latin America, despite the fact that the three regions are different from one another on almost every count.

# CHAPTER FIVE

# West Africa

## Stabilizing the Gulf of Guinea

Due to a number of related factors, sub-Saharan Africa has historically been accorded low priority in Washington's strategic thinking. This can be explained not least by the legacy of European empire; the absence of any potential rival to US global hegemony; and the low levels of economic development and high levels of political instability, both of which make penetration by foreign capital difficult.[1] The relative uninterest of US planners is most clearly evidenced by the historical absences of a permanent military presence in Africa. Whereas a network of US military bases has been positioned throughout the world since 1945 in order to undergird Washington's primacy in vital strategic regions, US troops have rarely set foot in Africa. Indeed, until 2007, the Pentagon's system of Unified Combatant Commands divided responsibility for Africa between European, Pacific, and Central Commands, which in turn considered the continent a distant second priority in relation to their primary zones of responsibility.[2]

As a result of this low prioritization, combined with the endemic instability of the major oil-rich states in West Africa—notably Nigeria and Angola—the region's oil has often not received huge attention from US planners. Throughout the Cold War, Washington did work to pull the newly independent states away from the old colonial order, and the region's energy resources were a factor driving this, but US strategic planning was largely focused elsewhere. However, this began to change during the 1990s, as concerns over instability in the Persian Gulf began to mount and US planners became increasingly focused on the need to diversify production to other regions. In an early statement of intent, Clinton's secretary of state Madeleine Albright flew to a Chevron oil platform off the coast of Angola in 1997, where she declared for the world's media that she stood in "one place where Africa's economic promise is coming a reality" and that the United States "had important national interests in helping" this along, with "our economic interests . . . directly connected to the prospects for long-term stability" in the region. This declaration accompanied a US loan for $90 million to develop new oil fields, with a further $350 million package under negotiation.[3] This newfound interest in the region informed the 1998 *National Security Strategy*, which made absolutely clear that a key US interest in the region was "unhampered access to oil and other vital natural resources."[4] As such, Washington moved to deepen ties with the region's main oil producers.

Oil released onto international markets from West Africa forms an important element of global supply. Several states in the region hold significant reserves of oil, all of which are orientated around the Gulf of Guinea. Starting in the north, these states include Nigeria, (landlocked) Chad, Equatorial Guinea, Gabon, the Republic of Congo, and in the south, Angola. Together, these states are thought to hold over 51 billion barrels: a figure comparable to reserves in the Caspian Basin, only slightly less than the large North American deposits, and significantly more than the entire stock of Western Europe or the Asia Pacific.[5] Of these states, two—Nigeria and Angola—dominate the region's oil sector. Together, they hold 87 percent of the proven oil reserves in the region, are responsible for over 80 percent of production, and contribute over three-quarters of the regional oil that is exported to international markets.[6]

Together, the extraction of oil from these six states contributes to around 6 percent of world production.[7] However, the true significance of West African oil for global markets derives from the exceedingly small proportion of West African production consumed domestically, with no less than 96 percent of the oil that is extracted being exported to market. This contrasts extremely favorably with other major producers in the South, which tend to export only between 70 and 80 percent of their production; West African oil contributes more like 10 percent of all oil released onto the market.[8] In addition, the location of West African oil on the Atlantic coast, or in the open oceanic water of the Gulf of Guinea, ensures that, once loaded onto tankers, it can be swiftly and securely transported to the major consumers. This is in stark contrast to reserves in many other regions of the world, which must pass through various strategic chokepoints in order to reach their destination. Together, low domestic consumption and the unproblematic transport of exports to their destinations make the region important in stabilizing world oil markets. Although West Africa contributes relatively little in absolute terms when compared to the Middle East, both factors make it a potential "swing producer," allowing oil companies to leverage export levels in response to changes in world demand, export levels from other regions, and the security of transport routes along which the majority of oil passes. By increasing production at relatively short notice, and with the liberty of exporting the entirety of this excess to world markets, oil companies operating in West Africa can, in theory at least, act quickly and securely to alleviate pressures in the market arising elsewhere in the system.

However, despite the vast potential of the oil reserves in the region, lack of investment combined with significant instability has meant that oil-rich states have not been able to maximize their output. Consequently, the potential exists to increase production dramatically in coming years. Indeed, this has been forecast by the US government, with Nigeria and Angola's production set to double by 2020 as new projects come online and oil companies begin to fully exploit the "stunning" exploration success rate that has occurred in the Gulf of Guinea and led to the recent discovery of fields of "astonishing" size.[9] In addition, the landlocked producer Chad is considered by experts to be underexplored, with significant chances of finding new reserves in the future to pipe through the newly opened Chad-Cameroon pipeline to the Gulf coast.[10] Overall, the region's production rates are set to rise faster than any other OPEC region and rivaled only by the Caspian Sea region.[11] And given the forecast lack of future industrialization, domestic consumption is likely to grow far less than production. This would mean that almost all additional oil will be released onto world markets: a trend not expected in some other exporting regions, where rises in local consumption is projected to match or outstrip additional future production (leading either to a net small increase, or even reduction, in exported oil).[12]

These characteristics fascinate US planners and drive American strategy toward West Africa. This chapter will examine how Washington has increasingly attempted to secure the necessary conditions on the ground for the stable flow of investment by foreign corporations *into* the region and the stable flow of oil *out* onto international markets. As elsewhere, US interests in West Africa do not revolve solely around the region's oil resources, and there remains a myriad of objectives sought by US planners. However, in a similar fashion to the Caspian Basin, securing the region's oil reserves forms a primary goal of US statecraft and goes some way to determining overall policy toward the region.

## Securing West African Oil

Because of the neocolonial connotations of Western interest in resource extraction, particularly in a continent with long experience of imperial exploitation, leading US officials have often been challenged on the nature of Washington's objectives in the region. In turn, they have had to deny any interest in securing access to West Africa's oil reserves. Thus, whilst accompanying President Bush on a high-profile trip to Africa in July 2003, then–secretary of state Colin Powell was adamant that "we did not come to Africa—the President did not come to Africa on this trip for the purpose of taking anyone's oil or imposing our will on anybody. We are here to visit friends. We are here by invitation." Throughout the visit, he claimed, "we have not participated in one single discussion with any leader about oil in any way, shape, manner, fashion or form."[13] Likewise, when questioned over claims that the United States was primarily interested in African oil, President Bush's response was unequivocal: "Well, conspiracy theorists about everywhere, I guess [sic]. That's one of the most amazing conspiracies I've heard. Heck, no one has ever made that connection."[14]

Regardless of such explicit denials when confronted directly, in other contexts US planners are absolutely clear on the importance of African oil to global energy security. Despite previous policy declarations from the Clinton administration during the 1990s, US interests in the region's oil accelerated substantially with the election of the Bush administration and the release of the final report of the National Energy Policy Development (NEDP) Group. West Africa was identified as "one of the fastest-growing sources of oil," which was "of high quality and low in sulfur, making it suitable for stringent refined product requirements" and guaranteeing that it was highly prized by the industrialized core. As a result, US planners increasingly highlighted the strategic importance of the region's oil, with Walter Kansteiner (then assistant secretary of state for African affairs) claiming in 2002 that "African oil is of national strategic interest to us, and it will increase and become more important as we go forward."[15] According to Kansteiner: "As we all start looking at the facts and figures of how many barrels per day are coming in from Africa, it's undeniable that this has become a national strategic interest for us."[16]

This view was reinforced by senior congressmen with an influential role in policymaking toward Africa; prominent figures were clear that the region's growing strategic importance was directly linked to its substantial oil reserves.[17]

Indeed, the final report from the African Oil Policy Initiative Group—influential planners who included congressional, State Department, and Pentagon officials—recommended that the United States "declare the expanded Gulf of Guinea region of western and southern Africa as an area of 'vital interest' to the United States": a phrase redolent of the Carter Doctrine's declaration of the intention to use US military power to directly secure access to Persian Gulf oil. In this light, the Group argued for an increased force presence in the region, in order to "safeguard increasing volumes of petroleum shipments from producing states" and so "produce significant dividends in the protection of US investments."[18]

For its part, the Pentagon has long been aware of the region's importance as a swing producer and the security that comes from having so much oil offshore. Securing these resources is a major objective of US military planners. This is reflected in Pentagon planning documents, which often explicitly discuss the subject of West African oil and the desirability of ensuring its continued release onto markets. According to one declassified document, the Pentagon stressed that this oil is "of high quality, is easily accessed offshore and well positioned to supply the North American market."[19] Similarly, EUCOM strategy papers have stated that Africa's oil wealth is "of increasing importance" for the United States and "directly impacts" upon American national security.[20] In this light, General Charles Wald (deputy commander, EUCOM) has emphasized the importance of West African oil, since corporations can "dig right now through the seabed and pump the oil right straight into a ship that's sitting off the coast. You don't have to put it into a refinery. You don't have to put it into a pumping station. You pump it right to the ship." And crucially, this has a huge impact on the stability afforded to markets by the region's oil: "And what else do you do [in West Africa]? You go like this 'pffft.' There's no Straits of Hormuz, there's no Red Sea, there's no Suez Canal, there's no Tunisia, Sicily, there's no Straits of Gibraltar. There's just this [the open ocean]. You go that way [straight to the United States and Europe]. That's a good thing because it's easier and more secure."[21]

To the extent that West African oil is located offshore, it remains attractive to US officials because it is insulated from any onshore instability. As a State Department official explained to Jon Lee Anderson of the *New Yorker*: "Folks have finally figured out that we don't need to rely on the Middle East for oil . . . much of [African oil] is in deep water far offshore, so the natives don't notice it being taken, whereas in the Middle East it's pumped out of the ground under the noses of Wahhabi fundamentalists . . . It's perfect."[22] This dynamic has continued under the Obama administration. According to the State Department's first budget request for foreign assistance to the region, submitted in early 2009, the Gulf of Guinea off the coast of West Africa is "oil-rich" and "strategically significant," thus continuing to require increased attention by US planners.[23] Speaking to more than fifty African military leaders in February 2009, Obama's acting assistant secretary of state Phillip Carter stated: "For too long Africa has been an afterthought in US foreign policy interests. In World War II, Africa was a strategic stepping stone to the places that mattered in Europe. In the Cold War, Africa was a pawn in East-West struggles." According to Carter, this had now changed, with US strategy focused on developing "a network of well-governed states capable through responsible sovereignty of protecting themselves and contributing to regional security. By so doing, they also protect the international system."[24]

The increased interest by Washington during both the Bush and Obama administrations has translated into accelerated levels of assistance to West Africa. Substantial levels of economic and security assistance now flow into the region, and these are increasingly defined in terms of the energy resources that West Africa holds. For example, the Bush administration justified its assistance to Nigeria by reference to attempts to build "a strategic relationship" with the country, with assistance focused on "economic progress and democratic consolidation" in order to "make it a reliable and increasingly important trading partner." Specifically, programs were directed toward US interests in the country, which included its "large oil and gas reserves" and, crucially, the avoidance of any "disruption of supply from Nigeria [which] would represent a major blow to the oil security strategy of the United States."[25]

Likewise, assistance toward Angola was geared toward the fact that the country's oil production "is expected to reach to two million barrels per day by 2008," with foreign investment in the sector an important element driving policy.[26] To secure these interests, Washington ramped up the levels of security assistance provided to crucial oil-rich states. Millions of dollars' worth of military equipment was sold or granted to Nigeria and Angola during the Bush administration through key security assistance programs such as Foreign Military Financing (FMF) and Foreign Military Sales (FMS), as well as through the licensing of direct sales from US defense companies.[27] In addition President Bush used emergency legislative mechanisms to authorize the drawdown of $4 million worth of military hardware from the Pentagon's stock, specifically to bolster Nigeria's military capacity.[28] Military training programs were also accelerated, as Nigeria became the second largest African recipient of IMET funds in 2006 (with nearly $800 million allocated), and Angola received another $400 million. As Pentagon officials noted, despite the fact that IMET relationships with the region have been sketchy in the past, the situation is "improving."[29] In fact, under the Obama administration, funds for this training program for oil-rich African states have increased by over 30 percent, as the United States works to pull the region more fully within its orbit. As Senator James Inhofe declared in March 2009 during testimony by AFRICOM's commander-in-chief General Ward: "You know, once there was a time when we thought we were doing them a favor in this program [IMET]. But quickly we learned that once they are tied into us, that kind of relationship remains."[30]

According to the interimperial rivalry analysis, this increased assistance is a sign of Washington asserting its economic and military power in order to secure the region's oil for its own purposes. For some, US strategy is part of a Great Power "scramble," with the world's largest oil consumers showing "extraordinary interest in the development of African oil reserves, [and] making huge bids for whatever exploration blocks become available." In this reading, the pursuit of African oil has "taken on the character of a gold rush," and the United States is positioning itself in order to—at some point in the future—use "military force to make sure that African oil continues to flow *to the United States*."[31] Those adopting this viewpoint stress the fact that Nigeria and Angola provide large amounts of oil directly to the US economy. Nigeria is the fifth largest oil importer to the United States, and Angola the eighth, whilst the US National Intelligence Council has forecast that the proportion of US imports originating in West Africa will grow from 14 percent in 2006 to 25 percent in 2025.[32]

This analysis successfully captures one element of US strategy vis-à-vis other core states with interests in West Africa, and it grasps the substantial concerns held by some over China's increasing relations with West African states. Beijing is now a major trading partner with the continent; two-way trade mushroomed from less than $1 billion in 2000 to over $50 billion by 2006, motivated by a "singular focus on resource acquisition and commercial opportunism" as part of a "global search for untapped resources, new markets and reliable diplomatic partners."[33] Investment in the African energy sector is the focus of Beijing's strategy, as it seeks out sources for its increasing oil needs outside of the US-dominated Persian Gulf. US planners worry that some of this activity is designed to bypass global markets, as Chinese state-owned companies practice old-fashioned, direct acquisition. By undercutting tenders from Western-based IOCs (international oil companies) through economically unviable bids tied to political promises of associated economic aid and investment, Beijing is buying itself direct access to African oil. In 2004, for instance, the Chinese state oil corporation Sinopec signed an agreement with Gabon's Bongo administration that would allow the company to explore for oil and build a refinery, in order to supply Beijing *directly* with 20,000 bpd. Similarly, China reached an agreement with Angola for the direct provision of 10,000 bpd of oil in exchange for $2 billion in economic aid. Agreements have also been reached with the regime in oil-rich Chad. Most significantly, Chinese oil companies have struck large deals in Nigeria, buying major stakes in offshore and onshore fields and gaining the go-ahead to build refineries and pipelines. Much of this has come alongside promises to invest in the country's infrastructure as well as the provision of military assistance to the government.[34] To the extent that these activities bypass the US-led liberal order and are reminiscent of an earlier interimperial era of resource scramble, they do present a challenge to US hegemony in the region and therefore a threat to core US interests. In turn, there is some validity in viewing Washington's increased activity in the region as an attempt to counter growing Chinese influence and to ensure that West African oil does not become "locked up" by Beijing.

Certainly, there has been a step-change in military focus toward the region and, as a supplement to increased funding for security assistance programs, there has been a noticeable increase in the direct presence of US forces. There is a clear desire by Pentagon planners to establish an enlarged presence in the region, leading to an explicit focus on "the utility of forward-operating bases and locations" from which to project power.[35] Such facilities would represent a "family" of military bases across the continent that would be mothballed until needed, whereupon they could serve either small units of special forces or larger, brigade-sized units.[36] Such a network of facilities can provide substantial benefits over permanent bases, because it allows for an increased strategic footprint in the region and enhanced relationships with local militaries without the need to invest in, and then protect, a significant physical presence.[37]

On the back of this vision of future US military presence in Africa, numerous reports have circulated of specific bilateral access agreements between the Pentagon and various countries in the region.[38] And chief amongst these plans, considering its position at the center of the Gulf of Guinea and within easy striking distance of the oil fields of West Africa, has been the development of a forward operating location in Sao Tome and Principe (STP). The islands were visited on several occasions by high-ranking commanders in EUCOM throughout 2002 and 2003, and further discussions occurred between President Fradique De Menezes and the Pentagon, National Security Council, and State Department.[39] This interest has resulted in more than discussion, however; the US Trade and Development Agency announced in 2004 that it was financing a feasibility study for the development of a deepwater port and expanded airfield facilities on the islands.[40] President De Menezes, for one, has been clear regarding the purpose of any such facility on the islands: "It is not really a military base on our territory," he claimed, but rather a "support port for aircraft, warships and patrol ships so that they can come to this port and stay for some time." Further, this would be beneficial to the islands for "those that are ambitious and are looking to come to the country when oil is extracted from our waters."[41] American interest in STP has accelerated under Obama, with increased military training provided to professionalize security forces, improve maritime security capabilities, and address port security in the strategically located islands.[42]

This evolving strategic presence in Africa is designed primarily to serve increased contact between US military personnel and local security forces. As Phillip Carter stated in February 2009, "Our first priority is providing security assistance programs that are critical to securing" our objectives.[43] The Pentagon nearly doubled the number of defense attachés on the continent between 2000 and 2002, whilst US naval presence and operational activity in the region has accelerated significantly in recent years.[44] High-level defense officials have declared that US carrier groups are likely to spend significant time "going down the west coast of Africa," in a move designed to provide "a sure sign of this commitment" from the United States to securing its interests in the region.[45] Significantly, heightened Pentagon activity in the region has been consolidated with the creation of a new Combatant Command—Africa Command (AFRICOM)—in February 2007.[46] For the first time, US military posture toward the region is coordinated within one command structure, allowing for a greater focus on maximizing Washington's interests. This was considered vital by military planners, because—in 2006, when the region fell within EUCOM's remit—staff were finding that they were spending more than half of their time on African issues, up from almost none three years previous.[47]

Pentagon strategy is clearly intended to extend and entrench US hegemony in the region and to maximize the flow of oil onto world markets. As the commander-in-chief of EUCOM James Jones stated in 2006, "Africa's vast potential makes African stability a near-term global strategic imperative."[48] Likewise, according to General Wald, the United States has a "huge interest in Africa from a security standpoint, from a strategic standpoint and from the standpoint of protecting our security interests and investment interests."[49] Elsewhere, the general has declared that the Gulf of Guinea is "a region where stability is needed, especially for economic reasons," and has maintained that Pentagon objectives in the region are designed to maximize "governed domestic space" in West African states in ways that "promote increased globalization of their economies." Stabilization of the region is considered necessary for US interests, for the interests of private enterprise, and for the interests of "our global society."[50] In a clear example of the managerial role played by Washington, Wald is concerned not only with securing oil for the United States: "All of these mineral reserves, by the way, [are] important to not just the United States, but the rest of the world. So there's a security issue there as well."[51]

To the extent that this engagement is designed to pull the region firmly within the US-led order, it can be read as a direct move against rival powers attempting to exert influence outside of Washington's control. However, as we have argued throughout this book, viewing this activity as simply an attempt to counter Chinese (and other rival) influence in the region does not capture the full logic of US statecraft. US planners *are* concerned with Chinese attempts to bypass and undermine the US-led order, but the primary response has been to push Beijing to work within the current system and therefore remain subservient to US hegemony. In this light, US officials have stated that Beijing's objectives in the continent "are not necessarily incompatible with US priorities and, in fact, may offer important opportunities . . . In general, we see China's growing activity on the continent as a potentially positive force, [given that] we see [no] evidence that China's commercial or diplomatic activities in Africa are aimed at diminishing US influence on the continent . . . Our goal, *as with other areas of the world,* is to engage Chinese officials to try to define and expand a common agenda for Africa that ultimately will serve both our national interests."[52]

As top US officials have stated, none of the expanding Chinese interests in Africa "is inherently threatening to US interests. We do not see China's involvement, economic or diplomatic, in Africa as a zero-sum game." Consequently, "the important thing from the US perspective is to encourage China to become involved in Africa in a way that supports international norms." Indeed, "Our overarching goal remains to see China become a responsible stakeholder in the global system," and "we see China's involvement in Africa [as] a test case of its willingness to work toward the broader interests of the international system."[53]

Despite the hype surrounding Chinese activity in Africa, and especially in its oil sector, Washington's priority remains the incorporation of its potential strategic rival within the current order, wherein the United States has hegemonic status. And—as elsewhere—US strategy is focused on the integration of oil-rich African political economies into the wider global economy to facilitate investment and operations from IOCs. As Pentagon official Theresa Whelan stated in testimony in July 2008: "Natural resources such as oil represent Africa's current and future wealth, but all we seek is a fair market environment where all can fairly compete and benefit along with others in the global market."[54] In this sense, US strategy toward West Africa needs to be read largely as an attempt to reconfigure local political economies in order to enhance the ability of transnational oil capital to operate without hindrance.

## Liberalization for Oil

Through both bilateral economic assistance programs and the work of the IFIs (in particular the IMF), Washington has long pushed for the restructuring of key economies in West Africa.[55] Substantial funds have been channeled through the State Department with the express purpose of stabilizing regional economies and ensuring their seamless integration into the wider global economy. Just one of many US government programs, the State Department's Africa Regional Fund, is provided with millions of dollars each year to open up local economies by enhancing regional efforts to "promote trade and investment, and encourage the development of capital markets" as well as to "strengthen Africa's private sector [and] increase productivity."[56] Likewise, the Bush administration's highly trumpeted Millennium Challenge Account (MCA), continued by the Obama team, specifically links extensive new bilateral development aid funds to the removal of barriers to investment and trade.[57] Indeed, for countries to become eligible for MCA funding, they must prove "demonstrated commitment to economic policies that encourage individuals and firms to participate in global trade and international capital markets, promote private sector growth and the sustainable management of natural resources, protect private property rights [and] strengthen market forces in the economy." In determining whether a country should receive funding, Washington evaluates the government's record on enacting the core agenda of the neoliberal project.[58] MCA funds are limited to those countries adopting radical neoliberal reforms, by ensuring that "state intervention in the goods and land market is generally limited to regulation and/or legislation to smooth out market imperfections."[59]

US efforts to embed neoliberal, free market capitalism in Africa accelerated with the passage of the African Growth and Opportunity Act (AGOA) in 2000. Introduced by the Clinton administration, and so far maintained by the Obama team, this legislation is "a fascinating compound of professed philanthropy and raw self-interest," specifically targeted toward the elimination of barriers to trade and capital flows in sub-Saharan Africa and the widespread privatization of key state-owned industries.[60] By restricting the considerable preferential trade deals on offer to those states that move forward with a neoliberal reform agenda, AGOA forces African states to establish and extend a market-based economy; to minimize any government interference through price controls, subsidies, and state-ownership; to take significant steps to protect private and intellectual property rights; and to guarantee a return for international investors through engagement with a rules-based trading system. An annual eligibility review process ensures that the United States can pressure individual states to maintain or extend the pace of economic reform.[61] Such "free market" provisions, however, are not reflected in relation to the American economy, which retains significant protectionist measures to shield US producers from "import surges" of "sensitive" articles.[62]

As a consequence of this sustained effort to open up local economies in West Africa, met with enthusiasm by many ruling elites, foreign corporations have made substantial investments, a large proportion of which are in the oil sector. Whilst Washington's broader economic strategy toward West Africa is not totally reducible to oil interests, policy is largely driven by a wish to maximize and stabilize the global supply of oil. The fundamental linkage between broader economic reform and energy security in particular has been clearly stated by US planners. For instance, Matthew McManus from the State Department declared in 2003 that "encouraging the reforms needed to improve the investment climate" in West Africa is a priority, since countries with sound economic policies and market-based regulation will "make better hosts to the huge investments needed to develop energy resources, and they make more reliable contributors to our own energy security."[63] This linkage is reflected in the location of most of the new foreign direct investment (FDI) into the region, which doubled between 2004 and 2006 to a record $36 billion and was "spurred by the search for primary resources and increased profits and by a generally improved business climate."[64] No less than 11 percent of all US exports to the region were oil and gas field machinery and equipment, sent to support American FDI in the sector (which, in turn, is more than half of all US FDI in sub-Saharan Africa).[65] Trade between the United States and sub-Saharan Africa is highly concentrated, with the oil-rich states of West Africa (alongside the large, non-oil-rich South Africa) accounting for an overwhelming share of the total for both imports and exports.[66] Oil accounted for 80 percent of all US imports from sub-Saharan Africa in 2006 (with platinum second-placed at less than 5%).[67]

Foreign direct investment in the region's oil sector has been truly global, with corporations from around the world establishing a presence in West Africa. Companies operating in Nigeria include the Dutch company Shell (the largest and longest-standing operator in the country), alongside US companies ExxonMobil, Chevron, and ConocoPhillips, the French company Total, and the Italian company Agip. IOCs operating in Angola include BP (UK), Chevron, ExxonMobil, and Occidental Petroleum (US), Eni (Italy), Total (France), Maersk (Denmark), and Statoil (Norway). Similarly, the Chad-Cameroon pipeline is operated by an international consortium led by ExxonMobil, with major involvement by Chevron and Petronas of Malaysia, whilst the Canadian Energem Petroleum Corporation has exploration rights in Chad. Oil dominates the export earnings and overall wealth of the producing states in the region, whose economies are extremely concentrated in this sector. Oil accounts for well over 90 percent of total export revenues for the oil-rich states in the region, and rising production levels are due to the increased investment by IOCs.[68]

Overall, then, US strategy toward West Africa has been orientated around the restructuring of local economies and their integration into the global economy for the primary purpose of creating an attractive environment for oil companies. The consequences of this strategy for the populations of West Africa have often been disastrous, as economies geared toward the favorable treatment of global capital have failed to meet the most basic needs of their own societies.

## The Disaster of Restructuring in West Africa: Poverty, Inequality, and the "Oil Curse"

Sub-Saharan Africa has long been the poorest and least-developed region in the world. Since the process of decolonization brought independence to the continent during the 1960s and 1970s, and largely as a result of this earlier imperial domination by the European powers, African states and societies have been plagued by a host of deep structural problems. Alongside exceptionally weak state forms the region is the site of "some of the most disheartening examples of political stagnation, democratic backsliding and state failure."[69] Armed conflict is endemic across Africa, causing massive economic and social turmoil and impacting hugely upon development levels.[70] On the UN's Human Development Index—a combined metric of several indicators of quality of life—Africa lags far behind the developing world in almost every indicator of well-being, from life expectancy and infant mortality to the prevalence of mass killers such as HIV, malaria, and TB, and from school enrollment and teacher-pupil ratios to measures of individual income and overall economic growth.[71]

The deep structural problems facing Africa are caused by a complex set of factors, but there exists a large body of evidence to suggest that the US-led economic restructuring of Africa has been disastrous for the continent's people. Rather than making any real positive change, such policies have in fact worked to entrench preexisting problems. Thus, whilst trade has ballooned as a result of the lowering of barriers and African exports have massively increased, this has not translated into economic growth, debt reduction, or decreases in poverty and inequality. And given the generous repatriation allowances built into the newly liberalized African economies, much of the proceeds from expanding economic activity in the continent in effect remain in the home countries of those corporations making investment. Per capita GDP for sub-Saharan Africa fell by 15 percent between 1980 and 2000. Africans living below the poverty line of $1 per day increased to 65 percent by the end of the 1990s, "accompanied by regressive changes in income distribution," as decline in income for the poorest 20 percent has been twice that of the population as a whole.[72] This has translated to lower life expectancy across the continent, which has dropped dramatically as spending on health fell by 50 percent throughout the 1980s.[73] Crucially, according to a report by the UN Commission on Trade and Development (no enemy of FDI in Africa): "Adjustment policies, including trade and financial liberalization, privatization and retrenchment of the public sector, have played a significant role in the hollowing out of the middle class that has become a prominent feature of income distribution in many developing countries." Recent "poverty reduction" programs run through the IMF continue to prescribe adjustment that is virtually identical to that espoused by the Washington Consensus, based on the premise that liberalization and rapid integration into the global economy hold the key to fast and sustained growth.[74]

This has especially been the case in the oil-rich states of West Africa, where economic reform and foreign investment have led to the exacerbation of existing problems. In Nigeria, for instance, the poorest 20 percent of the population own just 5 percent of the overall wealth, with the richest 20 percent owning 49 percent.[75] These inequalities have deepened as economic reform has gone ahead; according to the World Bank, 66 percent of Nigerians living in absolute poverty (less than $1 per day) in 2004, compared with only 43 percent in 1986.[76] Likewise, as oil wealth has accelerated in Angola, with vast sums pouring into state coffers, the living standards for ordinary people remain extraordinarily low. The UN ranks Angola as the seventeenth least-developed country in the world; two-thirds of the population live in poverty, beset by "appalling living conditions, sky-high infant mortality rates, dirty water, illiteracy and a host of other ills."[77] In parallel with oil-rich states in the Caspian Basin, political elites in West Africa tend to pocket large proportions of the revenue from oil exports and use them for personal satisfaction or to further increase their power over society. Literally billions of dollars of oil-generated revenue has disappeared from public accounts across the region, as poverty levels have remained endemic and those questioning the division of wealth have been exposed to the force of the state.[78] The role that oil has played in widening existing wealth disparities has been spelled out by Human Rights Watch:

> With world oil prices closing in on $150 a barrel, Nigeria's coffers are filling at record pace. Nowhere is the oil bonanza more evident than in the state governments of the region. In Rivers State, the volatile heart of the oil industry, the state government's $3bn annual budget far exceeds the entire central budget of most West African nations. However, while government coffers collect windfall oil revenues, ordinary Nigerians derive precious little benefit from this tremendous wealth. Abject poverty in Rivers State ranks amongst the worst in the world. Oil revenues . . . [have been] squandered and embezzled by the political elite.[79]

The corrupting effects of oil wealth are felt throughout the region, as the vast sums of money are used not only to line individual pockets but to further consolidate the power of the military within society. According to Human Rights Watch in 2007—and in a pattern repeated across the region—President Déby of Chad "has used much of the oil revenue that was supposed to help the poor on military hardware in a bid to bolster his regime against the threat of armed opposition groups."[80] Soon after the Chad-Cameroon project was given the go-ahead, with initial support from the IFIs, the *Guardian* reported that "embarrassed World Bank officials have already admitted that the notoriously corrupt Chad government has spent the first £10m of grant money it received from the consortium on arms for its security forces rather than on the educational and development projects for which the money was intended."[81] The government "admitted in 2000 using some associated funding to purchase military equipment," and it was claimed to have spent $4.5 million, received as a "bonus" from the oil companies before the project was approved, "to buy arms to fight the rebel movement in the northern Tibesti region," including the purchase of two helicopters.[82]

Socioeconomic and political problems tend to be even more stark in the immediate oil-producing regions within each oil-rich state. Whereas corruption and inequalities beset much of Nigeria, the oil-rich Niger Delta is the scene of particularly pressing problems. According to one study by the US Institute of Peace (USIP), the lack of political legitimacy felt across the country is "more pronounced in the Niger Delta, which suffers from . . . a 'striking lack of democracy.'" Elections in the region are often rigged, and ruling elites have little popular basis from which to govern. The people of the Delta "experience terrible poverty despite living in the region that produces the vast majority of Nigeria's wealth," whilst "equally importantly, neither the government nor the oil companies have adequately addressed environmental problems such as gas flaring and oil spills."[83] The environmental impact of IOC activity in the Delta is nothing short of catastrophic; one panel of independent experts who visited the region in 2006 concluded that the Delta was one of the world's five most polluted areas. Around 1.5 million tons of oil have been spilled into the Delta over the past 50 years—the equivalent of a major oil spill every twelve months.[84]

Although perhaps not as stark as in the Niger Delta, similar conditions exist in the oil-rich Angolan province of Cabinda, where visitors report that the sand on the beach is black from oil spills and the gas flares from the offshore rigs light up the night. Foreign oil workers live in a heavily guarded complex onshore, flown in and out by helicopter, whilst people in surrounding villages experience high levels of poverty as the oil wealth bypasses local communities.[85]

## Resistance in West Africa

The extraction and exportation of oil in West Africa has generated significant internal instability within the key oil-rich states, as local groups work for fundamental economic and political reform. Extreme poverty within the Niger Delta, combined with widespread environmental degradation as a direct result of oil operations, has given rise to substantial unrest within the region. Much of this has been directed against local, state, and central governments, alongside IOCs operating in the area. Groups have demanded a greater level of autonomy from central government, compensation for the environmental destruction wrought by oil company activities, and protection from unrestricted pipeline and facility construction on their land. A wide range of movements in the delta, often organized along ethnic lines, have fought for such rights for many years. In so doing, they have utilized a myriad of strategies. Particularly high-profile has been the peaceful campaign by key elements of the Ogoni community in the region, which coalesced in the early 1990s around the Movement for the Survival of the Ogoni People (MOSOP). Consisting of a collection of trade unions, church bodies, women's associations, and student unions, MOSOP adopted a constitution declaring that "over 30 years of oil mining have led to the complete degradation of the Ogoni environment" and that "we as a people must through all lawful and non-violent means fight for social justice and fair play for ourselves and our progeny."[86] The group has been vital in organizing mass protests against oil operations on Ogoni land, including demonstrations of more than 200,000 in January 1993 (close to half of the Ogoni population), 10,000 in April 1993, and 20,000 in 1998. Since the mid-1990s, such mass-participation events have taken place on the anniversary of the execution of nine Ogoni activists by the Nigerian state, including MOSOP's president, Kenule Saro-Wiwa.

As well as pursuing social justice through the courts and via peaceful demonstrations, groups of protesters have taken to direct action to protest the exploitation resulting from local oil production. Protestors have occupied oil facilities and platforms throughout the region. In May 1998, for example, over a hundred unarmed Ijaw Youth Council members occupied Chevron's Parabe oil platform in order to demand more employment for local workers and a greater effort to clear up the pollution that resulted from the company's operations.[87] This was followed by the release of the Kaiama Declaration in December 1998, authored by the Youth Council, which declared an intent to "cease to recognise all undemocratic decrees that rob our peoples/communities of the right to ownership and control of our lives and resources" and demanded "the immediate withdrawal from Ijawland of all military forces of occupation and repression by the Nigerian state."[88] This tactic was repeated by 600 Itsekiri women in 2002, who peacefully occupied ChevronTexaco's Escravos export terminal for ten days, shutting down around 25 percent of the country's production.[89]

Increasingly, though, such protests have been matched by armed campaigns in the Delta designed to forcefully change the status quo. Many of the militant groups emerging in the region in recent years have predominantly criminal agendas, with "oil bunkering" (where pipelines are tapped by groups who load oil directly onto barges) estimated to result in the loss of a staggering 200,000 barrels per day (bpd). Because the practice cumulatively nets millions of dollars *each day* for those involved, many groups (including elements within the military and other security forces) are deeply implicated in the trade.[90] Bunkering has a detrimental effect on the stability required for international investment in the oil sector, as well as on the ability of this sector to bring the Delta's oil wealth onto the legitimate global market. However, a far more profound threat to political and economic stability arises from a different set of armed groups: those with political agendas concerning the ultimate control of the oil in the region. Two groups in particular—the Movement for the Emancipation of the Niger Delta (MEND) and the Niger Delta People's Volunteer Force (NDPVF)—have emerged in recent years, and both use armed force explicitly as part of a campaign to seize "total control" of the Niger Delta's oil wealth.[91] Frustrated that prior peaceful protests have yielded nothing but greater repression from the state, an increasing number of locals within the Delta support armed struggle designed to wrest control from central government and the oil companies.[92]

MEND, for example, is explicitly fighting for 25–30 percent of oil revenues to be returned to local communities in the Delta (as opposed to the local governments mired in corruption).[93] It aims to achieve this by halting the current activities of the oil sector. On January 11, 2006, four oil workers were taken hostage when three speedboats attacked a Nigerian naval vessel and a Shell-leased boat. This was quickly followed by an attack on a Shell facility wherein seventeen were killed, mainly security personnel. In an email statement released to the media, MEND stated: "It must be clear that the Nigerian government cannot protect your workers or assets. Leave our land while you can, or die in it. Our aim is to totally destroy the capacity of the Nigerian government to export oil."[94] Further hostage-taking and attacks on oil installations and pipelines have continued since. In May and June 2009 MEND attacked several of Chevron's pipelines and pumping stations, as the group's campaign accelerated and they declared an "all out war" against the Nigerian military.[95] Such attacks have proved very effective in shutting down oil production in the region: many sources indicate that 20 percent of Nigeria's oil production has been lost due to armed insurgency, whilst some estimates suggest that up to 800,000 bpd have been lost.[96]

A similarly wide range of armed and unarmed opposition to the activities of oil companies and to the particular form of economic stability within which these activities take place has existed in Angola for many years. This is especially so in the enclave of Cabinda: the Angolan region wherein 60 percent of the country's oil deposits are located and which has been militarily dominated by Angolan troops in response to longstanding calls for autonomy or independence.[97] Many civil society figures and groups have played a vocal role in Cabinda and are dedicated to highlighting the injustices, poverty, and abuses suffered by the population. This movement is personified to a great extent by the Roman Catholic priest Father Jorge Casimiro Congo, who has remained a vocal critic of the status quo. For instance, in an interview in October 2003, Congo stated that the current form of stability was deeply unjust and cried out for fundamental reform: "The amount of wealth the oil companies receive doesn't compare to the small financial investment they have made in the development of the province. Cabindans resent the fact that they live in abject poverty while there are oil companies making huge amounts of money out of what belongs to Cabindans. Something has to be done to correct this situation."[98]

Alongside the broad-based movement within Cabindan civil society exists the Front for the Liberation of the Enclave of Cabinda (FLEC), a group that has fought an armed insurgency for several decades. Motivated by the poverty suffered by the population in Cabinda, which reinforces collective calls for independence, the group has targeted not only Angolan security forces (the

FAA), but the extensive infrastructure associated with the oil industry. This has included numerous attacks on oil workers themselves, many of whom have been kidnapped by FLEC.[99] Such targeting forms part of an overall campaign to force the redistribution of the region's oil wealth, estimated to be worth around $100,000 per year, per Cabindan.[100]

Faced with this instability in the region, and in particular the presence of social forces that directly challenge the basis upon which foreign oil companies operate in West Africa, US planners have fallen back on traditional forms of coercive statecraft. Accordingly, Washington has moved to increase the process of militarization in order to stabilize the ground for oil production and exportation.

## Insulating Order in West Africa

As the strategic importance of the region's oil has become clear, US planners have increasingly worked to secure the ground in West Africa for IOCs. There is an understanding in Washington of the importance of ensuring political stability in the region to facilitate the continued IOC investments that are so crucial to global energy security. As Jendayi Frazer (former assistant secretary of state for African affairs) noted at a 2006 Pentagon-hosted conference: "Private companies are the vast majority of operations in the Gulf of Guinea. If kidnapping of their workers and attacks on their facilities continue, they are unlikely to make the necessary investments to increase production, or even maintain current levels."[101] This instability has a huge impact upon investor confidence and greatly reduces the amounts of FDI required to speed up oil production in the region. In this way, planners maintain that stability is a prerequisite for ensuring energy security. As laid out by John Brodman of the Bush administration's Department of Energy, although "we don't tell our companies where to invest or where to buy oil and gas" and it is "up to them to weigh all the factors involved and to make their own decisions," there are "a considerable number of obstacles to realizing successful development of commercial trade and investment flows, directly related to economic, political, and security risks." Such risks—derived from "internal sources of conflict such as corruption, the lack of 'rule of law,' political instability, ethnic and religious conflicts and other so-called governance issues"—produce an "unfavorable business climate [which] may keep needed resources locked away from development for a long time."[102]

Increased Pentagon activities in the region may have a geostrategic purpose, insofar as Washington wishes to counter growing Chinese influence in the region; they are, however, also designed to impose stability on a region where *local forces* are attempting to overturn the current order. According to Theresa Whelan, the United States has "legitimate security interests in ensuring that the offshore oil is protected and that the states that own those offshore rigs are able to protect them."[103] A key modality for this stabilization has been the provision of security assistance to local pro-US elites that have proved pliant to American interests. Washington has operated through proxy forces on the ground by bolstering military capabilities and reconfiguring local militaries toward internal security missions. This can most clearly be seen in the rationale underpinning the 2007 creation of AFRICOM. This new body is designed not as a precursor to the direct deployment of US troops to the continent but, as President Bush stated at the time, as a tool to "strengthen our security cooperation with Africa and create new opportunities to bolster the capabilities of our partners in Africa."[104] AFRICOM was envisaged from its outset as a vehicle to provide a more sustained training and equipping mission to local forces, tailored to meet threats to US interests.[105] Indeed, in his keynote speech to a conference hosted by the American Enterprise Institute, Wald explicitly declared that realizing US energy security interests in the region is "going to take security. We're going to try to help with that from the standpoint of advice . . . And so what we're going to do is recommend to them—intellectual capital is free—how to set up a better security capability for themselves in the Gulf of Guinea."[106] Given the threats to oil investment and production in the region, US planners argue for the need to develop "a strategy to protect this production from terrorism, and [that] this raises critical concerns about the role of the US military in the region and its relations with African militaries."[107]

Networking with local security forces is geared toward building local capacities to conduct broad-based counterinsurgency campaigns. High-ranking military figures have been clear on this; General Wald, for example, stated explicitly that African militaries are "never going to be like the United States military, and they shouldn't be . . . they don't need all of the high-tech capacity." However, they can certainly "learn from our ethos from the standpoint of *how we do operations.* And I can tell you right now, at the low end of the spectrum, the United States military is *as good as they come fighting those kind of wars.* We're going to help Africans with that."[108] This was confirmed by Ryan Henry, former principal deputy undersecretary of defense for policy, in a press conference in 2007. Asked whether AFRICOM would have a significant coun-terinsurgency element to it, Henry replied that, whilst such training would not be focused through AFRICOM per se, centers already exist for that purpose. Important in this regard is the Africa Center for Security Studies (ACSS)—a regional equivalent to WHINSEC (formerly the School of the Americas)—which is based at the National Defense University in the United States. Run by private military companies on behalf of the Pentagon, the Center provides high-level training on a wide range of counterterrorism, counterinsurgency, and energy security matters.[109]

For instance, senior African defense officials met in Nigeria in March 2005 under the auspices of the ACSS, specifically to discuss how "a combination of increased global demand and apparent supply rigidities/uncertainties in other petroleum-producing regions has necessitated a closer look at Africa's petro-leum." Trainers emphasized "the urgent need for the continent's producing nations to adopt development and security policies that optimize returns." Moreover, because of the "frequent violent domestic conflict over the control of these resources [which] continues to undermine socio-political stability," one module examined "the main challenges African countries face in secur-ing petroleum production, storage and transportation facilities" (including "the urgent need to review maritime security arrangements"). These modules were capped by an exercise wherein participants were given the opportunity to "conduct a risk assessment of key internal and external threats facing the energy sector of a notional developing sub-region."[110]

High-level training has been matched by specific assistance programs to local militaries, designed explicitly to provide "domestic and regional stabil-ity," by improving capacity "to secure . . . oil resources" in the region. In par-ticular, Angolan assistance is directed to securing oil investments in Cabinda, whereas Nigerian assistance is geared toward tackling the absence of "security and stability in the vulnerable oil-producing Niger Delta region" through, for instance, the provision of "C130 technical support to enhance air mobility" and the development of "a small boat unit to enhance energy security in the Niger Delta." Likewise, military programs to Chad are designed to create se-curity forces that are designed as a counterbalance to "anti-US forces in the region." As such, they have provided "improved communication, mobility for its troops and troop support equipment" to support the "US national security interests of waging war on terrorism" and "countering the small-scale insur-gency in the north."[111]

Much of this assistance is run through "peacekeeping" programs, which assume a dual function, since the transfer of capacity-building for peacekeeping looks very similar to the transfer of highly needed skills for counterinsurgency. As William Hartung and Frida Berrigan point out: "Arms supplied to Nigeria, for example, may be applied to regional peacekeeping, but they could also be used in support of efforts (some directly supported by Western oil companies), to suppress dissent in the oil-rich Niger Delta."[112] That this is possible is not hard to envisage, given the focus of certain regional peacekeeping programs. For instance, the African Crisis Response Initiative (ACRI), run during the Clinton administration, was designed to provide in-country training of regular military tactics by sixty-man units of US Special Forces, skills that could be readily transferred to internal defense. ACRI was replaced by the Bush administration in FY 2003, with the Africa Contingency Operations Training Assistance (ACOTA) program. This new initiative is designed to provide "more robust training and assistance relative to the likely threat environment" by providing training for offensive military operations and supplying offensive military weaponry to be used in combat.[113] The domestic function of this program has been made clear by US officials. Theresa Whelan stated that although the ACOTA program primarily focuses on peacekeeping missions, "some of the tasks that would need to be carried out in the [Niger] delta in order to assist in providing security are not unsimilar [*sic*] to the types of tasks you might have to carry out in a peacekeeping mission. So to a certain extent that does get at the problem [of instability in the oil-producing region] a bit."[114] Likewise, Ed Royce stated that the "framework of the Africa Crisis Response Initiative (ACRI) is a starting point for exporting security arrangements to protect offshore energy resources in selected [West African] countries."[115]

Although provision of such assistance serves a range of US interests, there is a definite energy security focus underpinning them. A primary mission for proxy forces in the region is to secure the vital oil fields.[116] In his 2004 visit to Nigeria, Wald discussed US military involvement in securing the Gulf of Guinea and its resources and "offered to help Nigeria protect the flow of oil" in the region and "combat terrorist attacks on the oil industry." After the meeting, the Nigerian Defense Minister announced that cooperation with the United States was to include securing the oil sector: "Where you have wealth, if you don't protect it, you are vulnerable to terrorism and illegal arms dealers and so you are not safe . . . all countries which believe in global peace and stability must at one point come together and say no to evil."[117] This was confirmed by Wald himself, who, when asked whether cooperation would extend to the protection of Nigerian oil infrastructure, replied: "Wherever there's evil, we want to get there and fight it."[118] Similarly, Theresa Whelan has stated that the United States views the military as "the primary internal crises response unit within Nigeria," needing significant support from US security assistance programs in order to "help with aspects of the problem in the [oil-rich] delta."[119] In this light, specific programs to Nigeria have been justified in order to protect oil facilities against "terrorists," and there have been reports of US instructors training Nigerian counterinsurgency (CI) troops in the Niger Delta.[120]

## Human Rights and Counterinsurgency in West Africa

The attempt by US planners to stabilize existing hierarchies in the region has had severe consequences for the process of state formation in West Africa as well as for the protection of human rights. The local security architecture bolstered by Washington, and refocused against domestic threats to stability, is made up of institutions that are—almost without fail—deeply abusive and corrupt. As such, counterinsurgency and internal policing assistance helps local forces to target both armed insurgents *and* vocal elements of unarmed civil society. The confluence between oil extraction, US support for local military forces, and systematic human rights abuses directed against wide sections of the population is evident throughout West Africa. By focusing operations against domestic civil society, incumbent elites work to remove any real threat to their rule. The State Department, along with eminent human rights NGOs, has documented in some detail the use to which force is put in West Africa. According to Amnesty International, across the region "it continued to be dangerous to express critical or independent views. Political opposition groups, human rights defenders, independent journalists and wider civil society all faced state repression." Security personnel "harassed, arrested or ordered the arrest of, and briefly detained political opponents," whilst torture, incommunicado detention, and deaths in custody or due to "semi-clandestine" executions remained widespread.[121]

Chadian security forces have a long history of using CI warfare to suppress dissent in oil-rich regions of the country. Confronted by both armed and unarmed opposition to central government and to the plans for extracting oil from the south, Chad's president Déby has responded by instigating a particularly brutal counterinsurgency campaign in order to pacify the south of the country. This often involved severe reprisals by government forces against whole communities, triggered by the activities of armed political groups. Real and suspected members of both organizations, as well as the communities in the areas in which they operated, were subjected to systematic human rights violations, whilst the counterinsurgency forces involved in such attacks enjoyed complete impunity.[122] Throughout the 1990s, thousands of civilians were tortured, raped, and killed by CI forces in "reprisals" against the armed campaign undertaken by two groups in the region: the Committee of National Revival for Peace and Democracy (CSNPD) and a breakaway faction, the Armed Forces for a Federal Republic (FARF). Time and again, ostensibly in response to insurgent activity, security forces conducted house-to-house searches, identifying community leaders and "rebel sympathisers," who were often those who had spoken out against the activities of the oil sector in the region. Those rounded up were often either executed on the spot or removed for lengthy torture sessions before being "disappeared."[123]

The human rights situation in the south "worsened again shortly before the [pipeline] project was approved [by the World Bank], when government officials went to harass, intimidate, arrest and torture inhabitants of the Doba region." Although the World Bank lauded the Chadian government for "having conducted a public information campaign" regarding the route of the pipeline, in fact this "consisted of brutal intimidation. Local organizations reported that critical NGOs were threatened via the national radio. People were reportedly forced to sign statements in favour of the oil project and to participate in government sponsored mass demonstrations to promote 'unconditional immediate support' for the oil development." Shortly after the World Bank approved the project, residents from the project region reported new killings by government forces as well as ongoing threats to local organizations. Open discussion about the oil project is still not possible, and even the exchange of information remains risky.[124] Indeed, freedom of expression is "constantly undermined by harassment, and arrests and intimidation of activists critical of the pipeline have raised fears that force may be used to stifle peaceful protests about the project by local communities in the south." Violence and human rights abuses in the area of oil exploration during its "pacification" in 1997 and 1998 "forced the issue into the open, and led to international non-governmental organisations linking with civil society groups in Chad in a public campaign. The independent media have also been attacked on several occasions in relation to their work on issues around the pipeline project." Prison sentences, fines, torture, and closure of media outlets have been used against critics of the project.[125]

Similarly, the Angolan military has long engaged in counterinsurgency operations within Cabinda, with the objective of defeating secessionist forces and repressing those calling for a radical redistribution of oil ownership and profits. Such operations have treated the entire population in the enclave as a legitimate target for counterinsurgency and have attempted to police and discipline both the armed insurgency and the wider civil society. Fighting escalated in early 1993 and then again during 1997 and 1998, as the government of Angola deployed vast numbers of troops (estimated at around 15,000) to Cabinda.[126] FAA operations in Cabinda increased during these years, where villages suspected of supporting the separatists were targeted, causing large-scale displacement of the civilian population. In September 1998, the UN's special rapporteur on torture, Sir Nigel Rodley, reported that the situation had deteriorated over the prior eighteen months. Rodley noted that both government forces and the paramilitary group of the Polícia da Intervencão Rápida (Rapid Intervention Police, or PIR) had committed widespread acts of torture and ill treatment. Rather than an unfortunate consequence of a focused campaign against FLEC, such acts were *systematically* targeted at "persons from whom the government soldiers were trying to obtain information, or against the civilian population in reprisal for armed attacks by separatist groups." They were also believed to be "aimed at punishing or intimidating political opponents," including those who were "suspected of supporting FLEC policies or disobeying Government orders." Methods used to target activist civil society in this way are standard CI techniques: "punching and kicking, as well as beatings with a truncheon or a machete, bullets fired into the limbs, or electric shocks and bayonets pointed at the throat."[127]

Fighting intensified exponentially in 2002, as US interests in the region's oil began to accelerate and the government in Luanda deployed 30,000 troops in a major escalation of its counterinsurgency campaign. Such a large deployment was facilitated by the ceasefire with the National Union for the Total Independence of Angola (UNITA) in the main part of the country, allowing troops to be freed up for the operation. Reports even suggested the integration of ex-UNITA fighters within this newly deployed force.[128] These forces engaged in a "systematic counterinsurgency campaign that swept through the province" in 2002 and had virtually destroyed FLEC's military forces by mid-

2003.[129] Indeed, the Angolan defense minister stated at the end of 2003 that Cabinda was no longer a military problem: "It is not correct to say that we enjoy relative peace. I would go as far as to say that there is absolute peace in Angola. Although there is much talk about it, Cabinda is no longer a problem. [It has been] practically resolved."[130]

As with the campaign in the late 1990s, security forces targeted not only armed insurgents but sections of the wider population. Cabinda's "year of war" resulted in "the displacement and indiscriminate abuse of thousands of civilians, in summary executions, rape and torture, in the destruction of property and in the pillage of villages."[131] Human Rights Watch noted that the military operations of 2002 and 2003 were accompanied by "an increase in violations of international humanitarian law and human rights abuses against the civilian population by the Angolan Armed Forces (FAA)."[132] Again, evidence is strong that such abuses were not the unintended consequences of operations directed against armed groups; rather, they formed a central part of the counterinsurgency effort. Security forces adopted "scorched earth tactics and forced movements of rural populations as part of its counterinsurgency operations," and they stand accused of a systematic and deliberate campaign of murder, rape, and detentions in Cabinda in an effort to quell the insurgency.[133] According to one local leader: "It is no secret that the majority of Cabinda people support the FLEC's call for self-determination, but it seemed that during the October [2002] raids government soldiers were targeting civilians instead of soldiers, because of this tacit support."[134] There are multiple, credible reports of summary executions, arbitrary detentions, sexual violence, and torture committed by security forces on civilians, specifically because of their alleged links with the insurgents. As just one example, a group of women married to FLEC fighters were detained for over three months at a military base, interrogated, and denied freedom of movement.[135]

Despite the apparent military victory over insurgent forces by 2003, over 30,000 FAA troops continued to be stationed in the province in the years that followed (providing a staggeringly high ratio of 1:10 with the population) and continued to target the population in order to suppress political calls for independence and a redistribution of oil wealth. In 2004, the FAA continued "to commit violations against the civilian population, including killing, arbitrary detention, torture, sexual violence, and the denial of access to agricultural areas, rivers, and hunting grounds through restrictions on civilians' freedom of movement."[136] A UN High Commissioner for Human Rights working group found in 2007 "credible allegations that civilians are held incommunicado at military facilities in [Cabinda]."[137]

The targeting of civil society groups by Angolan counterinsurgency forces has led to the representation of such groups as inextricably entwined with the violent insurgency. Thus, the Angolan army chief of staff, Agostinho Nelumba "Sanjar," blamed the Catholic Church for "banditry" in Cabinda and followed this up with an attempt to arrest the high-profile church leader, and proindependence voice, Father Jorge Casimiro Congo.[138] Likewise, the Angolan government initially refused to register the Cabindan human rights organization, and prosecessionist group, Mpalabanda, citing it as a "subversive" entity with leaders who were "countering the efforts of President [dos Santos] to pacify the oil-rich country." In February 2004, troops used force to break up a crowd that had gathered, despite the ban, to launch the group.[139] Eventually, the organization was registered with the authorities and began to play a vocal role in pushing for reconciliation between fighters in Cabinda and security forces.[140] However, the group has also been outspoken about abuses committed by security forces in the region. For example, its leader confirmed the claims made by the bishop of Cabinda that entire villages had been "decimated" by counterinsurgency forces and that additional military units had been introduced into the region.[141] As a result of these statements, and for its explicit objective of securing a more just settlement for the people of Cabinda vis-à-vis relations with Luanda and the oil companies, Mpalabanda was banned in June 2006; the government alleged that it "incited violence and hatred."[142] In September 2006, Mpalabanda's spokesman Raul Danda was arrested and charged with "instigating crimes against the security of the state" for carrying proindependence literature.[143]

It is perhaps in the Niger Delta that counterinsurgency warfare has been most pronounced, most destructive, and most bound up with the protection of oil production activities.[144] The oil companies themselves are deeply implicated in the militarized response to unrest in the region. Human Rights Watch has reported in some depth on existing evidence that Shell and its contractors have been involved in state-directed repression, by arming, paying, and calling out security forces whenever its facilities appear to be threatened.[145] This came to somewhat of a head in June 2009, as Shell decided to settle out of court with a group of Ogoni who sued the company for complicity in violations.[146] This was a pattern mirrored by other IOCs, with Chevron admitting to having security forces on its payroll and transporting them in company helicopters to retake the Parabe platform from the peaceful protest in 1998. The security forces opened fire, killing two protesters. Eight months later, Chevron again transported forces in an attack against two Ijaw villages after compensation demands were made, and more than sixty villagers were killed. Both "supernumerary police" *and* armed militants are often paid covert protection money by the oil companies (often through "surveillance contracts" dressed up as community development contracts).[147]

In response to the peaceful MOSOP movement, the Nigerian state has undertaken a campaign of massive military repression, with countless instances where military and police forces have fired on unarmed civilians protesting against oil pipeline construction. As the Ogoni movement took off in the early 1990s, "approximately 1000 Ogonis were killed in attacks believed to be sanctioned by governmental authorities. Villages were destroyed, and thousands of Ogonis were displaced."[148] In May 1994, after Shell suspended drilling operations in the face of civil unrest, Lieutenant Colonel Paul Okuntimo (head of the Rivers State Internal Security Task Force) signed a memo to the regional governor declaring: "Shell operations [are] still impossible unless ruthless military operations are undertaken for smooth economic activities to commence." The strategies proposed include "wasting operations during MOSOP and other gatherings, making constant military presence justifiable"; "wasting targets cutting across communities and leadership cadres, especially vocal individuals in various groups," and "restriction of unauthorized visitors, especially those from Europe, to Ogoni."[149]

According to a 1994 internal memo from the Rivers State commissioner of police—entitled Operation Order No. 4/94: "Restoration of Law and Order in Ogoni Land"—forces were directed to engage in an operation involving "the Nigerian Army, the Nigerian Air force, the Nigerian Navy and the Nigerian Police" to "restore and maintain law and order in Ogoni-land" and "to apprehend intruders who may wish to use the period to ferment further disturbances." And in particular, the order stated that "the purpose of this operation order is to ensure that ordinary law abiding citizens of the area [and] non-indigenous residents carrying out business ventures or schooling within Ogoniland are not molested."[150] MOSOP's leader Ken Saro-Wiwa responded to this memo by declaring that "the drafting of such a large force into the small Ogoni area is meant to intimidate and terrorize the Ogoni people in order to allow Shell to recommence its operations in the area without carrying out the environmental, health, and social impact studies which the Ogoni people have demanded since 1992."[151] As a consequence of Saro-Wiwa's high-profile opposition activities, he was arrested repeatedly throughout 1993 and 1994. He was finally arrested, tried, and executed on trumped-up charges of murder, in a trial that international observers agreed was fundamentally corrupt.

As peaceful movements have been met with severe repression from the Nigerian authorities and dissent within the Niger Delta has become increasingly militant, security forces have continued to target wide sections of civil society. The end of military rule in 1999 has changed little on the ground in the Delta, and protestors occupying oil installations have been repeatedly fired upon by Nigerian special forces. In February 2005, for instance, soldiers from the Nigerian Joint Task Force violently retook Chevron's Escravos oil terminal from a group of demonstrators, killing one and beating several others.[152] Similarly, the release of the Kaiama Declaration by the Ijaw community saw the Nigerian military enter the region in vast numbers, using what one author has described as "pre-emptive militarisation, hunting, arrests, and incarceration of the youth leaders, crackdown on protests, and a conquest of Ijawland."[153] Across the region, Nigerian security forces are deployed in an overt attempt to quash any resistance against oil operations in the Delta, with severe consequences for human rights. In May 2009, the counterinsurgency campaign accelerated as the Obama administration continued its practical support for the Nigerian military. The Joint Task Force deployed helicopter gunships, air strikes, and ground troops across the Delta region in May and June; Amnesty International reported hundreds of civilian deaths as the population at large was targeted.[154]

Whether in Nigeria, Angola, Chad, or other repressive states in the region, US planners are well aware of the brutality with which security forces work to provide the requisite stability. Indeed, Congressman Ed Royce—influential in American policy-making circles for Africa—is on record that "oil is where you find it. Oil companies cannot always invest in democratically governed countries. It would be ideal if it could be guaranteed that the head of an African country where a US oil company invested was, in fact, an advocate of democracy and always respected human rights. Unfortunately, that is not a realistic expectation in today's Africa."[155]

As a result, despite the existence of such an abusive relationship between ruling elites and the general population, it is imperative that Washington is "able to take the baby with the bathwater" and continue to support the incumbent regimes against domestic unrest.[156] This recommendation has been wholeheartedly enacted by the United States, which granted to AGOA accession to five out of the six oil-rich states of West Africa in spite of ostensible human rights criteria written into the trade legislation. Eligibility was granted to countries even where the compulsory AGOA review acknowledged poor human rights conditions, leading Human Rights Watch to declare that although the law "clearly links human rights to AGOA benefits, the US government has not used human rights criteria effectively to improve human rights performance in the beneficiary countries."[157]

For instance, Angola was granted eligibility in December 2003, even as it was intensifying its counterinsurgency campaign in the Cabinda province. This prioritization of US strategic interests over concerns about human rights violations runs throughout the assistance provided to security forces in the region. Speaking at a conference held at the Center for Strategic and International Studies (CSIS), Theresa Whelan stated that despite security forces in Nigeria which "would respond in the past . . . incredibly brutal[ly], and that was essentially the way they accomplished their mission," the provision of assistance to these forces was a priority; "the ability to provide security, or some semblance of security, is an *enabling factor* in terms of achieving some of the socioeconomic reforms that really are the key to resolving the problems in the delta." Of vital concern for Whelan and other defense planners was the fact that poor training and equipping within the Nigerian military meant that it was now "even questionable whether they could respond effectively even with their brutal tactics and still accomplish the mission."[158]

## Conclusion

With due regard to the specificities of the region, we see in West Africa a similar pattern of relations as found in the Caspian Basin. US strategic planners have increasingly focused on the region's oil supplies as an alternative to those from the Persian Gulf—not to replace Middle Eastern oil but to act as a "fill in" should core supplies become disrupted. The strategy of maximizing and stabilizing the flow of oil onto world markets has necessitated the creation of conditions on the ground in West Africa that are conducive to long-term and substantial investment by foreign oil corporations. As elsewhere, Washington is not attempting to carve out an exclusive zone for American economic profit. IOCs in the region come from a variety of core states, and although US planners are concerned to some extent with securing contracts for US-based corporations, overall it is the successful creation of a stable investment climate that is of priority.

In a region where wealth inequalities are stark, this objective has required imposing a particular form of political and economic order throughout West Africa. Acting through the preexisting ruling strata, US planners have increasingly worked to militarize state-society relations in the region in order to destroy any vocal opposition to the activities of the IOCs (whether armed or otherwise). In the Niger Delta, in Cabinda, and in southern Chad, US-trained forces—explicitly reorientated toward the provision of internal security—have been engaged in CI campaigns to secure the ground for international investment. And in so doing, they have strengthened the rule of authoritarian leaders, even where these leaders have taken power through "democratic" elections. As in the Caspian Basin and the Persian Gulf, this implementation of US strategy has had huge consequences for the people and has generated severe insecurities amongst wide sections of the civilian population.

# CHAPTER SIX

# Latin America

## Capital, Crude, and Counterinsurgency in America's "Backyard"

Throughout the postwar era—indeed, ever since US president James Monroe formulated the Monroe Doctrine in 1823—Washington has viewed Latin America as its "backyard." Consequently, it has long reserved the right to intervene throughout the region to preserve a stability considered conducive to its national interests. In a continent where overwhelming US military superiority has ensured an almost total absence of direct threat to American national security, regional hegemony has been assured throughout the postwar era. The sheer supremacy of US power in Latin America has not granted Washington carte blanche to act as it wishes at all points; the history of US–Latin American relations is one of struggle rather than simply domination and submission. However, it has allowed the United States to pursue its agenda without needing to take significant note of peer competitors, and this has lent a unique flavor to US regional strategy. Washington has had unprecedented freedom to force open regional economies for foreign capital and to increasingly integrate them into the wider global economy. And in parallel, Washington has acted to remove a wide range of political and military threats to its regional hegemony: threats that have never had the capacity to disrupt core US national security (despite some of the more hysterical rhetoric at times) but that have nevertheless posed significant challenges to Washington's interests. As with the other regions we have explored in this book, these two aspects of US policy do not exist in isolation from each other, and America's efforts to promote economic integration within a neoliberal framework are intimately bound up with efforts to remove political and military challenges to its hegemony.

US policy toward Latin America has long been orientated to achieve these twin goals. Throughout the Cold War, Washington worked to open up local economies in the region, with Latin America the test-bed for the application of neoliberal adjustment. Conducted first in Chile under Augusto Pinochet, and then across the continent in the world's "first wave of forced neoliberalisation," this strategy provoked what has been termed a "'lost decade' of economic stagnation and political turmoil."[1] Although commonly refracted through the lens of global communism by Washington in order to justify intervention, political instability during the Cold War was in fact—more often than not—the result of a struggle between ruling elites and local forces advocating economic and political reform. As a result, the United States often fell back upon coercive statecraft to insulate the form of order conducive to its interests. Massive amounts of security assistance flowed to regional militaries throughout the Cold War, and by reorientating Latin American militaries away from an external defense posture and toward the provision of internal security, this aid was often a key driver in the acceleration of local campaigns against elements of civil society.

US strategy toward Latin America has, in many senses, remained constant in the post–Cold War era. Although the geopolitical, regional, and local contexts have changed considerably since 1991, and again since 9/11, US policy continues to be characterized by twin concerns: ensuring that the process of neoliberal reforms have been driven forward and working to destroy any potential or real challenges to this process (and to Washington's regional hegemony). Of course, the military and civilian dictatorships that characterized the region during the Cold War have long gone. However, the ability of elected governments to forge independent policies in the political, economic, and military spheres often remain severely circumscribed; Washington continues to ensure the responsiveness of elites to American needs. As local economies have undergone US-led restructuring and are increasingly integrated into the global economy, transnational capital has acquired the ability to move in and out of the region at will. The phenomenon of "capital flight" and the implicit threat of this occurring should elected governments pursue overly populist policies, ensures that elites are closely disciplined. Moreover, the legacy of US policy toward the region continues to influence many in power. Memories of the severe repression experienced throughout the continent during the Cold War, and a fear of the return of the generals, limits the degree of freedom in the spheres of political and economic policy and provides a ceiling beyond which governments dare not push reforms.[2] As we will see, such fears are not unfounded, given the continued linkages between Washington's economic and security agendas in the region. The United States may no longer sponsor dictatorships in Latin America; it does, however, continue to insulate processes of economic liberalization from challenge by the provision of substantial support to regional militaries.

This objective has driven US policy toward Latin America's oil-rich states. As concerns over global energy security have moved up the foreign policy agenda in Washington, focus has increasingly turned toward accessing the region's substantial energy deposits. Latin American stocks total more than 120 billion barrels, representing 10 percent of global supplies: larger than the reserves found in the Caspian Basin and West Africa and larger than stocks in North America, Europe, Russia, and the Asia Pacific. Only the Middle East has more oil than Latin America.[3] Unlike the two regions already explored, however, US objectives in Latin America range substantially wider than oil. In the Caspian Basin and West Africa, maximizing and stabilizing oil flow plays a significant role in ordering US regional strategy overall. In Latin America, by contrast, Washington's goal of controlling the region's oil reserves does not overbear the entire strategy. Even in some of the oil-rich states, US interests are broader than oil, although a significant energy security dimension runs throughout Washington's policies. In the Caspian Basin and West Africa, then, US interests in oil can be seen to act as a primary driver for the embedding of free market capitalist social relations and for destroying threats to this process. In Latin America, interests in oil need to be cast within these wider strategic objectives, which would continue to be pursued even if there were no oil (and are pursued in the many countries of the region where there is none). As a consequence, this chapter will differ slightly from the previous two by starting with an examination of how Washington has worked to liberalize and stabilize the region in the post–Cold War era, before coming on to look at its energy security agenda in particular.

With over 80 percent of the oil reserves known to exist in the region, and the source for over 80 percent of the region's total oil exports, three states in particular have the potential to ameliorate US concerns over global energy security: Colombia, Venezuela, and Mexico.[4] This is in contrast to some other major producers in the region, such as Argentina, Brazil, and Peru, which do not export a substantial proportion of their oil. The key position of these states was acknowledged in the *National Energy Policy* report in 2001. According to the authors, Mexico is "a leading and reliable source of imported oil, and its large reserve base, approximately 25 percent larger than our own proven reserves, makes [the country] a likely source of increased oil production over the next decade." Likewise, Venezuela is singled out as the world's fifth largest exporter and third largest supplier to the United States, with its energy sector "increasingly integrated into the US marketplace," whilst Colombia has "also become an important supplier of oil to the United States."[5] US military planners are keenly aware of the value of Latin American oil, the "vital interest" that the United States has in maintaining supplies, and the consequent need to allow these resources to reach the market.[6] This focus has only increased in recent years, as concerns over global energy diversification have taken center stage in Washington. As the former US ambassador to Colombia, Anne Patterson, explained: "After September 11, the issue of oil security has become a priority for the United States," especially as the "traditional oil sources" in the Middle East have become even "less secure." By sourcing oil from Latin America, the United States would have "a small margin to work with" in the face of a crisis and could "avoid price speculation."[7]

Venezuela and Colombia, along with Ecuador and Bolivia, form what might be called the Andean region. Although Bolivia and Ecuador produce smaller amounts of oil, events there have huge symbolic importance for the success (or otherwise) of US-led attempts to gain deeper access to regional oil supplies. As such, they are of primary concern for US planners. Indeed, political dynamics in the Andean region—where all these oil-rich states (bar Mexico) are located—are intimately interlinked. This means that US strategy toward one state has to be cognizant of the implications this has for neighboring oil-rich states. Despite the fact that Colombian oil production is in decline, and the country is forecast to become a net importer in coming years, its location close to the significant oil fields of Venezuela makes political instability a major concern for Washington. US strategy toward oil-rich Latin America has two major objectives: stabilizing and integrating the Andean region, and further integrating the oil-rich Mexican economy into the wider global order.

## Liberalization and Stability in Latin America

Throughout the post–Cold War era, Washington has worked tirelessly to open up markets throughout Latin America for the benefit of global capital. As early as 1989, George H. W. Bush authorized a trade package specifically for this purpose. Culminating with the passage of the Andean Trade Preference Act (ATPA) in December 1991, the deal aimed to "encourage and support fundamental economic reform in the countries of the region on the basis of market-driven policies," explicitly for the benefit of investments by foreign capital. Bush was unambiguous: "Our goal must be to help create an environment where entrepreneurship can flourish and comparative advantages can be successfully pursued in competitive world markets."[8] This was followed in 1993 by the North American Free Trade Agreement (NAFTA), a parallel agreement binding the United States, Canada, and Mexico. Designed to create the largest and richest market in the world, NAFTA was sold as an arrangement that would "demonstrate American leadership in opening markets and promoting democracy here in our hemisphere" and was designed to force open the Mexican economy for the benefit of its neighbors to the north. Intricate tariffs and other barriers to investments and exports, which had long been in place in Mexico to protect its own economy from this fate, were either removed instantly or rapidly dismantled, thus immediately creating "substantial market access for key export sectors" and "extraordinary new opportunities for US companies and workers."[9]

Regardless of the disastrous effects this had for the Mexican economy, Washington did not break step as it began attempts to expand the free trade zone to include the entire continent. Negotiations for a Free Trade of the Americas Act (FTAA) continued throughout the 1990s, based on a corporate-led model of development that would allow capital to move freely and invest across a raft of newly privatized industries. Such provisions were designed to benefit transnational capital over local capital, and, in a similar fashion to NAFTA, US capital was especially privileged. The preponderance of the US economy within the Western Hemisphere is overwhelming. The cumulative GDP of states on the continent was $17.4 billion in 2006; of this, the United States had a share of no less than 76 percent, with the next largest economies holding significantly smaller shares (Canada's was 7%, Brazil's 6%, Mexico's 5%, and all other economies the remaining 6%). By opening up the Colombian economy, for example, the United States is working to maintain unlimited access for capital based in an economy over eighty times its size.[10] Although at the time of this writing the FTAA has yet to be agreed upon, the United States along with Costa Rica, the Dominican Republic, El Salvador, Guatemala, Honduras, and Nicaragua signed the Central America Free Trade Agreement (CAFTA) in 2004.[11] As the agreement came into force, tariffs on the majority of goods were eliminated, and trade has since expanded. Increases in trade have been largely one-way, however, as US-based corporations take advantage of their newfound freedom to enter the markets of Central America unimpeded.[12]

The destruction of local industry and farming sectors as a result of the increased freedom of movement by large foreign corporations under "free trade" has led to an increase in malnutrition and unemployment and a decline in living standards. The World Bank found in 2003 that inequality in Latin America was "extensive," with even the most equal country in the region still more unequal than any OECD country. Along with some countries in Africa and the former Soviet Union, income is concentrated at the very top of society, with the wealthiest 10 percent of individuals receiving between 40 and 47 percent of total income in most Latin American societies. In contrast, the poorest 20 percent receive only 2–4 percent of wealth. Inequality has also been incredibly pervasive, "characterising every aspect of life, including access to education, health and public services; access to land and other assets; the functioning of credit and formal labour markets; and attainment of political voice and influence." And following the "lost decade" of the 1980s, continuing trade liberalization and economic reforms throughout the region were implemented alongside a deepening of inequality, with "more countries experiencing a worsening than an improving trend."[13] Land tenure patterns remain "medieval" throughout the continent, and land possession is often concentrated in the hands of a tiny minority and consequently with a continuing agricultural elite retaining "deep levels of political and social power."[14]

Unsurprisingly, the region has been the site for sustained and wide-ranging resistance to this model of development. Free trade in Latin America has proved deeply unpopular in the region, and anti-US feeling pervades local politics in many states. This has led in several cases to the election of administrations on platforms that emphasize political and economic autonomy from the United States, but even here the actual pace of populist reform has often been slow and relatively marginal. In Brazil, for instance, President Lula da Silva has been careful not to rock the boat with Washington and has continued to follow economic reform measures led by the International Monetary Fund (IMF).[15] In a similar fashion to left-of-center parties in Europe, these administrations have not presented a real threat to US interests. Although not true for those who have gained power in three of the oil-rich states in the region—Hugo Chavez in Venezuela, Evo Morales in Bolivia, and Rafael Correa in Ecuador, all of whom will be discussed later—most of the region's governments have been largely receptive to both US hegemony and the neoliberalization of their economies. This has meant that opposition to US policy has more often emerged from below, amongst elements of civil society that have arranged themselves against ruling elites. And in turn, this has had profound consequences for the ways in which the United States has responded to such opposition. Primarily, and in clear parallel to the thrust of Cold War policy toward the region, Washington has worked to insulate ruling elites by accelerating the militarization of state-society relations and supporting the reconfiguration of local militaries toward a focus on internal security.

The intricate ways in which regional economic liberalization continues to be underpinned by US coercive statecraft are revealed by the explicit role designated to the US military in creating the conditions on the ground necessary for capital investment in Latin America. This is acknowledged by military personnel at the very top of the regional command, including successive commanders-in-chief (CINC) of US Southern Command (SOUTHCOM).[16] For example, in confirmation hearings for the job of CINC-SOUTHCOM in 2000, General Peter Pace stated that the national interests of the United States, which he defined as "those of broad, over-riding importance to the survival, safety and vitality of our nation," included, first, "continued unhindered access to strategic natural resources in the USSOUTHCOM AOR [area of responsibility]," alongside a "continued stability required for access to markets in the USSOUTHCOM AOR, which is critical to the continued economic expansion and prosperity of the United States." Pace went on to explain that "our trade within the Americas represents approximately 46 percent of all US exports, and we expect this percentage to increase in the future."[17]

Similar statements were made by Pace's successor as CINC-SOUTHCOM, General James T. Hill, who stressed the need to make US defense policy responsive to the economic interests Washington has in a region where it "conducts more than 360 billion dollars of annual trade": trade links that would increase through the continued integration of Latin America with US capital as "we progress toward the President's vision of a Free Trade Agreement of the Americas."[18] The identified need to guarantee that US military policy in the region underpins economic integration and the opening up of Latin American economies to foreign capital translated to SOUTHCOM's 2007 posture statement. A military document, this statement nevertheless emphasized Washington's "strategic objective" in strengthening economic links between the United States and Latin America through the embedding of free trade agreements. SOUTHCOM's activities were designed specifically to equip regional militaries in order to deal with sources of instability that threaten to undermine this investment, with the Command employing a "theater cooperation security strategy" (i.e., close military-to-military engagement) in order to build host-nation military capacity, so as to "help achieve the security conditions necessary to create the enduring basis for prosperity."[19]

The security programs run through SOUTHCOM's command, designed to build capacity amongst regional militaries, have ballooned in recent years. US aid to Latin American military and police forces tripled from the mid-1990s to the early 2000s, and now runs between $800 million and $900 million each year. Overall, Washington provided an estimated $7.3 billion in security assistance to the region in the ten years between 1997 and 2007, and total funding now equals the entire provision of economic and social assistance. Latin American militaries have been locked into US training programs to an extent not found elsewhere in the world, with over 15,000 students each year from a wide range of military and police agencies sent on US-led courses.[20] Much of this training and other security assistance has been passed through programs explicitly designated as counternarcotic, but this assistance has served a far wider set of regional objectives for Washington. This was apparent from the speed with which it was ditched as a primary rationale in the post-9/11 era. With the declaration of a global war on terror, SOUTHCOM recast almost all of its activities through the prism of counterterrorism. As CINC James T. Hill stated in front of Congress in March 2003: "Narcoterrorism is most pervasive in Colombia, where citizens suffer daily from murder, bombings, kidnappings, and lawlessness. However, narcoterrorism is spreading increasingly throughout the region. Narcoterrorist groups are involved in kidnappings in Panama, Venezuela, Ecuador and Paraguay. They smuggle weapons and drugs in Brazil, Suriname, Guyana, Mexico, and Peru, are making inroads in Bolivia, and use the same routes and infrastructure for drugs, arms, illegal aliens and other illicit activities."[21]

Crucially, this "new" threat did not result in any significant change in the focus of assistance to the region. The upward trend in aid had little to do with the war on terror, and the content of the training and equipment programs largely resembled that which has been offered for decades.[22] This continues to be the case with Obama in office. Whether labeled counternarcotics (CN) or counterterrorism (CT), assistance to the region's militaries has largely remained the same and has been built around the need to combat internal sources of instability and domestic unrest through the application of military force. For example, of the nearly 23,000 Latin American personnel trained by the United States in 2003, the most heavily subscribed course (with over 5,500 students) was on generalized "light infantry skills" rather than CN- or CT-specific subjects. This has been matched by large, US-coordinated joint exercises designed to combat a wide range of threats to the internal security and investment environment throughout Latin America. For example, the annual Fuerzas Comando (Commando Forces) exercise draws together over 300 military personnel from across the region as a "unique opportunity for participating nations to improve their special operations capabilities," including a focus on skills such as close-quarters combat, marksmanship, "shoot and move," and "stalk and shoot," with high-level seminars designed to "develop, refine and improve political and military relations and multinational cooperation" in the provision of regional stability.[23]

Prominent amongst the challenges to this stability, according to SOUTH-COM, is "an emerging threat best described as radical populism, in which the democratic process is undermined to decrease rather than protect individual rights."[24] US planners have identified political forces in the region as threats to the security of Latin America and US interests, where these are pushing for alternative paths of economic and social development. The entrenchment of internal security in the face of threats to "free political systems and free economic systems" is a primary objective of US security assistance to Latin America, in order specifically to "achieve the security conditions necessary to create the enduring basis for prosperity."[25] Direct internal policing by militarized forces is now routine across the region. Internal operations by the military itself against noncombatants have occurred in recent years in Guatemala, El Salvador, Honduras, and Brazil, as security forces utilize the training to police their population.[26] This continued in early 2009, as Peruvian security forces opened fire on indigenous demonstrators protesting the implementation of the US-Peru Free Trade Agreement and the increased access to the country's natural resources it will provide for multinational corporations.[27]

## Stabilizing the Andes: US Strategy toward Colombia

As elsewhere throughout Latin America, the United States has long acted in Colombia to open up the economy for investment by transnational capital and to stabilize existing, favorable state-society relations. The fate of this country has consistently been considered of vital strategic importance for US planners, largely due to a combination of its significant natural resource base (including oil); its geographical position close to areas of major strategic importance such as the Panama Canal and the vast oil fields of Venezuela; and the chronic instability throughout the country. As CINC-SOUTHCOM Admiral James Stavridis stated in 2009, "Colombia is a strategic ally, an important friend, and a crucial anchor for security and stability in this hemisphere."[28] As a result, the sheer scale of the coercive statecraft deployed in Colombia is unparalleled anywhere else on the continent, as Washington has provided vast amounts of assistance to the Colombian military. Indeed, of the $7.3 billion in security assistance provided by the United States to countries in Latin America in the ten years between 1997 and 2007, fully two-thirds ($4.9 billion) has been for Colombia. Likewise, of the more than 82,000 security personnel trained by Washington in the five years between 1999 and 2004, no fewer than 45 percent (around 37,000) were Colombian.[29]

Concerns regarding energy security have been increasingly entwined through Washington's policy objectives in Colombia, and the United States has explicit interests in securing the country's oil. Oil accounts for more than one-third of all Colombian exports to the United States, and "the bulk" of the rapidly increasing US-based foreign direct investment into Colombia ($10.5 billion in 2008) is "in the manufacturing, mining and energy sectors."[30] This FDI has been enabled by a drastic restructuring of the sector, in line with a wider "adjustment" strategy pursued by Washington and the IMF. Starting with the Gaviria administration (1990–1994), in what became known as *la apertura* (the opening), industries and public services have been privatized, the complex system of subsidies and tariffs eliminated, and social spending drastically cut. Central to this program was the removal of barriers to foreign imports and investment and the systematic dismantlement of longstanding protectionist measures. The consequences have been sweeping across the economy, as foreign capital has moved in to dominate and overtake domestic business. The Colombian agricultural sector has retracted, with the country now a net importer of food dumped by larger economies (primarily the United States).[31]

Notwithstanding this fact, the Pastrana administration accelerated the process of embedding neoliberal reforms throughout the country with the publication of Plan Colombia. Released in 1999, the strategy proposed that efforts should be stepped up to remove the "distrust among foreign investors, [which places] a major roadblock in the path of modernizing the way things work, which is essential for generating employment and securing a stable and prosperous place for Colombia in a newly globalized world." A raft of measures were introduced to create a more favorable environment for the penetration of transnational capital, and efforts were closely coordinated with the international financial institutions (IFIs).[32] The election of the far-right Uribe administration in 2002 has led to an even greater acceleration of this process, with the conclusion of negotiations for a free trade agreement with the United States in February 2006 (the US-Colombia Trade Promotion Agreement, or TPA). Again, the benefits of this agreement will be felt most keenly by US-based capital. This was explicitly designed into the framework and was acknowledged as such by the US International Trade Commission, which reported that "the primary effects of the TPA will be improved US access to the Colombian market and an increase in US exports to Colombia." Upon implementation, over three-quarters of industrial and agricultural goods will be tariff-free, leading to a forecast increase in meat, grain, and soybeans as well as oil and gas equipment and other machinery.[33]

A central objective of this restructuring program has been the revamping of Colombia's oil sector in order to make it more attractive for foreign investment. Existing "50–50" contracts between the state oil company Ecopetrol and IOCs (where each took half of the oil extracted from Colombia's fields) have been replaced by a new 70–30 split in favor of foreign companies, whilst royalties owed to the Colombian government have been slashed from 20 percent to 8 percent for most fields. Similarly, the Uribe administration has acquiesced to IMF demands by restructuring and partially privatizing Ecopetrol by removing its guaranteed involvement in all oil exploration and production as well as forcing it to compete in the market against IOCs. Time limits on production rights have been removed, allowing companies to keep their now-100 percent share of the oil for as long as the field remains productive.[34] These reforms have been hailed as "creating one of the most attractive oil investment regimes in the world," with an estimated $2 billion investment by foreign companies in 2006, and eleven new exploration and production contracts signed in the first half of 2007.[35]

US-based firms are by no means the exclusive source of foreign capital in the Colombian oil sector, which attracts investment from oil companies headquartered throughout the world. The largest oil field in Colombia—the Cusiana/Cupiagua complex in the northeastern Casanare department—is operated by UK-based British Petroleum (BP), which is also a major shareholder in the consortium operating the 500-mile Ocensa pipeline (along with Canadian firms TransCanada and IPL Enterprises and French oil company Total).

This pipeline takes oil from the field to the major coastal export terminal at Covenas. Likewise, the US-based Occidental Petroleum (OP) runs the second-largest field—the Caño Limón, in the northeastern Arauca department—along with the 460-mile Caño Limón export pipeline to Covenas. The Canadian firm Petrobank, operating through a subsidiary (Petrominerales), is also present in smaller fields located in the southern Putumayo department. And in a clear sign that oil-rich economies under American guidance are geared toward welcoming capital from anywhere, China and Colombia have concluded major bilateral trade deals, especially in the area of oil exploration and extraction. In 2005 Colombian president Alvaro Uribe went so far as to declare that the "economic prospect of the two countries will be vast if there is an effective partnership."[36]

In stark contrast to the "success" of structural adjustment for foreign-based corporations, including oil capital, this process has had disastrous effects for the majority of Colombian citizens. During the 1990s, unemployment nearly doubled from 10.5 percent to 19.7 percent, the percentage of Colombians living in poverty grew to 60 percent, and income ratios between the poorest and richest 10 percent grew from 40:1 to 80:1.[37] And although the Colombian economy has recovered from the severe recession of the 1990s, the continuing process of liberalization under Uribe has failed to alleviate the grinding socioeconomic conditions experienced by the majority of the population. The US government's primary development agency (the US Agency for International Development, or USAID) has stated that recent economic growth is a result of "improved investor confidence" as liberalization began to provide an ideal site for global capital. However, alongside this rosy picture, USAID noted that the country "faces severe income disparities, poverty and inadequate social services," with the World Bank estimating that 65 percent of the population lived below the poverty line: a figure rising to a staggering 80 percent in rural areas.[38]

The ongoing process of economic neoliberalization in Colombia has occurred alongside—and has in turn exacerbated—severe political violence throughout the country. Civil war in Colombia has been a major part of the country's social, political, and economic history, as severe dislocation has given rise to numerous forces pushing for radical change. These include a significant armed resistance to the state, conducted specifically to roll back the process of neoliberalization.[39] However, the resistance is much broader than armed insurgency, and large sections of the Colombian population are deeply and vocally opposed to Washington's agenda.[40] This resistance has organized around many struggles within Colombia. A core ongoing theme, however, has been opposition to the opening up of the country's oil sector and the parallel exploitation by transnational oil capital. Throughout the oil-rich regions of Colombia, oil unions, church leaders, and community-based organizations have coalesced to halt the privatization of Ecopetrol, the repression of unionized oil workers, and the activities of large foreign corporations.[41] As the president of the Barrancabermeja branch of the Central Workers Union (CUT), Juan Carlos Galvis, declared in 2004: Uribe's restructuring of the oil sector is "setting the groundwork for privatization and is paving the way for the FTAA. It is savage capitalism, without a human face."[42]

Although most of the opposition to this exploitation has been peaceful, armed groups have also targeted operations by foreign oil corporations. Pipelines have come under sustained attack from the Revolutionary Armed Forces of Colombia (known by its Spanish acronym, the FARC) and National Liberation Army (ELN), with no fewer than 263 attacks recorded by the Ministry of Defense in 2001. The majority of these targeted the OP-owned Caño Limón pipeline in the north of the country, which cost around $500 million for the company and the government.[43] This came on the back of over 700 attacks on the pipeline between 1983 and 2000.[44] Likewise, in the southern department of Putumayo, the FARC attacked oil facilities on well over one hundred separate occasions in both 2000 and 2003.[45]

In turn, these forms of resistance have been countered by the Colombian state and closely related paramilitary groups, which have engaged for decades in catastrophic levels of violence in order to suppress any movement for change. Working alongside the Colombian military and paramilitary forces, several oil corporations have moved to secure their investments against this opposition.[46] These ties are not limited to static pipeline defense but incorporate much wider stabilization (CI) efforts. Confidential files leaked from the country's largest oil investor, British Petroleum, proved that the company had contracted the services of private military companies (PMCs) to provide the security for its operations. This included the use of Defence Systems Limited (DSL) to protect its major oil fields and a deal with the Israeli PMC, Silver Shadow, to provide armored attack helicopters, night-vision goggles, secure communications equipment, and the "direct supply of anti-guerrilla special weaponry and ammo" to the notorious 14th Brigade of the Colombian Army. This unit has extensive ties with paramilitary groups in the region and is responsible for multiple and widespread atrocities against civilians in the oil-rich region. According to BP's representative in the country, this close relationship with the Brigade, including the provision of military equipment, was "unavoidable" and justified by the "terrible security situation at the time." However, the security operations of the oil company were focused not only on countering the threat from insurgents. The papers show that Silver Shadow was to provide BP top management with "a state-of-the-art investigation-intelligence and psychological warfare 18-day seminar," tailored to "suit Ocensa/BP special requirements" along the pipeline. This focus correlated with other BP activities in intelligence-gathering on "subversives" in local communities, alongside the support provided to paramilitaries to neutralize these civilian "threats."[47]

A similar tight-knit relationship between oil companies, PMCs, and the Colombian military-paramilitary nexus exists along the Caño Limón pipeline. Here, OP has routinely provided extensive support to local military units, including one notorious military offensive during which a US-supplied cluster bomb was dropped on the hamlet of Santo Domingo, killing eleven adults and seven children. Between them, OP and the PMC Airscan provided troop transportation, planning facilities, fuel, surveillance, and target coordinates for the offensive. In addition, OP officials openly admit to supporting the 18th Brigade in order to reduce insurgent attacks against the Caño Limón. The 18th Brigade receives significant US support for pipeline protection, despite being deeply implicated in many human rights violations and collusion with paramilitaries.

In parallel to the oil companies' security activities, US planners have fully accepted the need to secure the local environment for transnational investment and resource extraction in the oil-rich regions of the country. Speaking to Congress in 1998, then–CINC of SOUTHCOM Charles Wilhelm—the man in charge of coordinating the vast amount of security assistance to Colombia— was clear that oil discoveries in the country had increased its "strategic importance."[48] What this meant for US policy was subsequently laid out by the US energy secretary Bill Richardson, on a visit to Colombia in 1999: "The United States and its allies will invest millions of dollars in two areas of the Colombian economy, in the areas of mining and energy, and to secure these investments we are tripling military aid to Colombia."[49]

The provision of security assistance to Colombia to stabilize the region for oil production fits into a much wider pattern (and longer history) of securing the ground for global capital. Throughout the Cold War, the United States provided substantial political, financial, and military support for a decades-long counterinsurgency campaign in Colombia designed to destroy all significant challenges to the economic and political status quo.[50] Meanwhile, throughout the post–Cold War era, Washington has continued to insulate pro-US elites from sources of internal "instability" (whether armed or otherwise). During the 1990s, military assistance to Colombian security forces accelerated massively, ostensibly as part of a "war on drugs."[51] On the ground, though, there was little separation between US support provided to the CN campaign and the broader CI effort prosecuted by the Colombian government. Washington simply identified the main target of the war on drugs as the "narcoguerrillas" and virtually ignored the paramilitary forces deeply implicated in the drugs trade and with close connections to top government officials (such as the current president Uribe).[52] Counternarcotic units trained and equipped by the United States (such as the two 950-man CN divisions created under Plan Colombia) have been used for a far wider set of operations, whilst many members of the new CN units have since rotated to other formations that are not even in theory focused on counterdrug operations.[53] Moreover, the transfer of offensive Black-hawk helicopters to these units was clearly (if covertly) designed to target insurgents.[54]

That US-sponsored CN training and operations overlaid upon the existing CI campaign were confirmed in an interview with Stan Goff, a former US Special Forces trainer who had worked in Colombia: "You were told, and the American public were being told, if they were told anything at all, that this was counternarcotics training. The training I conducted was anything but that. It was pretty much updated Vietnam-style counterinsurgency doctrine. We were advised that this is what we would do, and we were further advised to refer to it as counternarcotics training should anyone ask. It was extremely clear to us that the counternarcotics thing was an official cover story. The only thing we talked with the actual leaders of the training units about was the guerrillas."[55]

In any case, the official distinction between CN and CI operations has been removed since 9/11, and the US Congress has sanctioned a "unified campaign against narcotics trafficking [and] against activities by organizations designated as terrorist."[56] US interests in Colombia are now argued to require "a broad, comprehensive approach," because "the challenges facing Colombia cannot be addressed in isolation."[57] Alongside this official widening of the war, funding has increased massively; total military and police aid to Colombia in the first five years of the war on terror reached more than $2.8 billion.[58]

The longstanding US-backed CI campaign in Colombia has been designed to target both antigovernment insurgents *and* elements of civil society opposed to neoliberalization. Violence against civilians by state forces is widespread and directed in particular against any vocal expression of opposition to Washington's economic agenda.[59] Much of this has been carried out by paramilitary groups, which the US State Department has acknowledged have carried out a war against reform-minded sections of society. Prominent state-backed groups have "killed, tortured, and threatened civilians suspected of sympathizing with guerrillas in an orchestrated campaign to terrorize them into fleeing their homes, thereby depriving guerrillas of civilian support." These groups—many of which come under the banner of the United Self-Defense Forces of Colombia (Autodefensas Unidas de Colombia in Spanish, or AUC)—initially arose as a response by wealthy landowners to unrest amongst the population and have in recent years been responsible for the vast majority (70–80%) of all recorded human rights abuses in Colombia.[60] Paramilitaries are closely linked to the state, with a vast amount of evidence pointing toward extensive collusion. Indeed, in areas of longstanding paramilitary activity, Amnesty International has documented "reliable and abundant information show[ing] that the security forces continued to allow paramilitary operations with little or no evidence of actions taken to curtail such activity."[61] Likewise, Human Rights Watch has compiled compelling evidence that "certain Colombian army brigades and police detachments continue to promote, work with, support, profit from, and tolerate paramilitary groups, treating them as a force allied to and compatible with their own."[62]

Military-paramilitary networks have long served US interests in the region and have been designed to insulate the incumbent elites from popular pressures as they undertake US-led structural reforms. Indeed, the United States has played a prominent role in promoting these structures; the Pentagon and CIA were crucial in reorganizing Colombian military intelligence apparatus during the early 1990s in order to create what Human Rights Watch has labeled a "secret network that relied on paramilitaries not only for intelligence, but to carry out murder."[63] Collusion is widespread throughout many of the units created and trained by Washington: a fact known by US officials. In just one of several examples, a 180-strong company from the First Counternarcotics Battalion, established under Plan Colombia, has worked extensively with the 24th Brigade of the Colombian Army, a notorious formation that has been implicated in human rights abuses and paramilitary collusion to such an extent that the US State Department suspended all assistance to it in October 1999.[64] Even so, then–secretary of state Albright viewed the 24th Brigade as "critical for counternarcotics operations and the success of Plan Colombia" and emphasized that "we very much want to be able to provide support to it."[65]

As a result, several thousand civilians were killed when Plan Colombia was put into effect, as state-backed paramilitaries accelerated their war against Colombian society.[66] Moreover, whilst the election of Uribe has led to the appearance of a reduced reliance on paramilitary violence by the state, many of the government's high-profile "demobilization" efforts have been exposed as propaganda, with a recycling of illegal paramilitary networks into more formal (and overt) Colombian military units, coupled with blanket amnesties, large-scale impunity, and the closing down of investigations of collusion.[67] In fact, the UN concluded that extensive and corroborated evidence exists that significant and sustained paramilitary violence has continued throughout the "ceasefire."[68]

The ongoing, US-backed war against reformist forces in Colombia is deeply entwined with securing the ground for foreign investment in the oil sector and with stabilizing the flow of Colombian oil onto international markets. The southern push into Putumayo under Plan Colombia, fully sponsored by Washington, included a definite oil-protection objective. Lieutenant Colonel Francisco Javier Cruz, head of an elite CI unit and the Colombian army commander responsible for protecting Putumayo's oil operations, stated in an interview that his units were able to use "helicopters, troops and training provided in large part by Plan Colombia . . . Security is the most important thing to me. Oil companies need to work without worrying and international investors need to feel calm." In a sign of the intricate links between the CI role and the mission to secure the region for oil operations, Cruz's Ninth Special Battalion operates two helicopters to transport troops on CI missions around Putumayo: helicopters that are owned by Ecopetrol, the state oil company, and Canada's Petrobank.[69]

This relationship is most stark in the northern region of Arauca, where the OP-owned field and pipeline has come under constant physical and political attack from both guerrillas and unarmed civilians demanding a redistribution of Colombia's oil wealth. In response, and in the context of the post-9/11 environment where the counternarcotics rationale is no longer required in

Washington, the United States has provided significant military assistance to troops in the region for pipeline protection. Specifically, it secured $98 million for a specially trained Colombian military CI brigade as part of its military aid package to Colombia in 2002–2003. Unlike the more generic Colombian CI brigades, this brigade was devoted solely to protecting OP's Caño Limón pipeline.[70] At the time, Secretary of State Colin Powell explained that the money was used to "train and equip two brigades of the Colombian armed forces to protect the pipeline" to prevent rebel attacks that are "depriving us of a source of petroleum."[71] Former US ambassador Anne Patterson went on to explain that "it is something that we must do" because it is "important for the future of the country, for our oil sources and for the confidence of our investors."[72] In more recent US funding the brigade has continued to receive large amounts of aid and has received additional equipment and training.[73]

This assistance represents an explicit attempt by Washington to increase the CI capability of Colombian troops throughout oil-rich regions, in order to actively destroy resistance to oil operations. In this light, US Special Forces have been deployed to Arauca in order to train members of the Colombian army's 18th Brigade in high-end counterinsurgency and infrastructure protection tactics. US units involved include specialized CI, psyops, and foreign internal defense (FID) forces, and training has included helicopter-borne operations, night-fighting, and intelligence-gathering as well as light infantry skills, which includes marksmanship, weapons familiarization, and ambush techniques.[74] This training has been used specifically to bolster the military-paramilitary network in Arauca, with direct collusion between members of the 18th Brigade and the AUC. Together, US-trained soldiers and paramilitaries are responsible for the majority of human rights violations in the region and have targeted not only guerrillas who have attacked the pipeline but also that section of civil society that has proved critical of the way oil resources have been exploited. Examples of repression abound and include the roundup of trade unionists as part of "Operation Heroic" in November 2002. And in an August 2003 operation, soldiers from the 18th Brigade, operating out of the base that housed the US trainers, arrested forty-two trade unionists, social activists, and human rights defenders under claims of "subversion." According to Amnesty International, these attacks form "part of an ongoing coordinated campaign to undermine the work of trade unionists and human rights activists [in the region] and expose these sectors to increased attack from army-backed paramilitaries."[75]

Throughout Colombia, therefore, we see the prosecution of an intensive counterinsurgency campaign by Washington. Acting through local elites, state security forces, and allied paramilitary groups, US planners have deployed extensive forms of coercive statecraft in the region to stabilize Colombian society and insulate ongoing economic structural reforms from challenge. The intricate linkage between US-led coercive statecraft and Washington's pursuit of wider political and economic interests was most clearly expressed by CINC-SOUTHCOM James Stavridis when testifying to Congress in March 2008. Asked about the security impact of a possible US free trade agreement with Colombia, Stavridis made the link explicit: "As your national security advisor in that region, I will tell you that it is very important that the free trade agreement be passed from a national security perspective."[76]

There has been a clear energy security element to US strategy, as Washington has worked to stabilize the region for the benefit of transnational oil capital. Given the distinct continuity in US interests in Colombia, we would expect the themes elaborated here to be extended during the Obama administration. Indeed, CINC Stavridis has shown no major change of military strategy toward the country during 2009 and has in fact argued that "this is the moment for Colombia. This is the time for Colombia and its friends to make the final push . . . Over the next two years, support for the Colombian armed forces' campaign to defeat the FARC" is essential.[77] As such, the huge military aid levels to Colombia have been largely kept in place during Obama's first budget, with some programs (such as the main non-drug-related vehicle, Foreign Military Financing) in fact receiving a boost. Buried in the Pentagon's request for 2010 was another $46 million for investment in an airbase in the country, sparking debate over the future of direct US operations in Colombia.[78]

As we will see in the next section, US strategy toward three other oil-rich states in the Andean region has looked very different from that deployed in Colombia: not because the objectives of the American state are different, but because the primary threat to US interests—"radical populism"—has manifested itself over recent years in very different ways.

## Containing the Andean Threat: Popular Nationalism in Venezuela, Bolivia, and Ecuador

Washington has long acted in the Andean region to insulate the prevailing political and economic order, since this serves wider US interests. In contrast,

US strategic posture toward three other major oil-exporting states in the Andes—Venezuela, Bolivia, and Ecuador—has taken a different trajectory in recent years. The election in each country of leaders dedicated to the rolling back of neoliberal economics, and the popular support they have received from large portions of their electorate, has posed a unique set of challenges to US planners. In turn, Washington has had to rethink its approach to these governments and has adopted a more confrontational stance.

Those in power in Venezuela, Bolivia, and Ecuador have not always posed a threat to US interests. Before the election of each of the incumbent governments, these countries were largely receptive to Washington's economic agenda, and received significant military assistance to insulate the ongoing reforms from instability. Throughout the 1990s, for example, successive administrations in Venezuela withstood popular unrest and attempted coups (including one by future president Hugo Chavez in 1992) as they accepted large loans from the IMF along with attached conditions on structural reform. In return for multi-billion-dollar payouts from the Fund, the Venezuelan economy was opened to foreign investment. Together, these reforms were met with deep pleasure at the IMF. The managing director, Michael Camdessus, claimed at the height of the program in 1996: "[Venezuela] is for us an extremely encouraging story, when one sees where we were one year ago and when one sees the giant leap of Venezuela in normalizing the working of its economy and . . . in adopting an important range of structural measures. When one sees the results [of these reforms, in terms of growth and inflation], one can really be satisfied and have even more admiration for the way in which things have been handled in Venezuela, and the fact that something that was seen as absolutely impossible . . . has been done smoothly, and has been accepted."[79]

Such superlatives were matched by Washington, where officials were keen to emphasize the positive direction taken by Venezuelan elites. In a trip to the country in October 1997, President Clinton spoke of a "quiet revolution" taking place, with a command economy giving way to free markets, and praised Venezuela for making the necessary reforms "in the wake of real sacrifice."[80] In particular, the oil sector, nationalized since 1976 and a major component of the Venezuelan economy, was reformed in order to encourage major transnational companies to invest. Thirty-two agreements were promptly signed with twenty-two separate oil companies. Royalties were lowered, and foreign companies were allowed to operate alongside the state oil company (Petroleos de Venezuela, Sociedad Anónima, or PDVSA). Similar moves were made by governments in Bolivia and Ecuador, with a restructuring of the large oil sectors forming a central part of the broader IFI-led adjustment. Existing legislation was amended to facilitate this investment, regardless of local opposition, which stressed the impacts that oil company activities had on indigenous movements.[81] As a result, foreign capital owned significant assets throughout these three sectors. Substantive investments were made from French Total, British BG Group, Spanish Repsol-YPF, Dutch Agip, and Brazilian Petrobas as well as American firms Occidental Petroleum, ExxonMobil, and ConocoPhillips.

However, as IMF-directed reforms were enacted in Venezuela, the sacrifice paid by the poor across the region increased substantially. As elsewhere throughout the continent, inequalities mushroomed across the board as neoliberal policies took effect. One study found that, despite $329 billion of fuel exports between 1963 and 1996, GDP per capita in Venezuela had fallen by 8 percent during this time. Inequality had "significantly worsened" since 1970, particularly between "those who own and those who do not own capital." In fact, the average worker in 1997 was approximately half as well-off as an average worker in 1970. All together, it was clear that "the macroeconomic, political, and distributive failures make Venezuela one of the great economic and social disasters of the post-war period."[82]

Similar patterns became evident after more than a decade of neoliberal economic reform in Bolivia. As "drastic measures were taken to stabilise the macro-economy, liberalise markets, privatise public enterprises, reform pensions, education, [and] the civil service," the standard of living for the majority of the population collapsed.[83] According to a World Bank study, poverty levels increased between 1997 and 2002, with "an overwhelming portion of the rural population" now living in poverty and the proportion of those in "extreme poverty" rising from 37 percent to 41 percent (and, in rural areas, from 59% to 67%). In addition, "income inequality increased significantly during 1997–2002," accompanied by "significant disparities in assets (e.g., education and land), household size, and earnings gaps." At the time of the report's release, in May 2006, standards of welfare continued to be exceedingly low throughout Bolivia, which "still ranks amongst the worst in the region in malnutrition, maternal and infant mortality rates." Fully 30 percent of the population did not have access to safe water and adequate sanitation.[84] Similar effects were noted in the World Bank's most recent assessment of poverty in Ecuador, which established that poverty rates across the country had climbed from 40 to 45 percent during the 1990s, with staggering 80 percent rises in urban poverty, as liberalization contributed to the collapse of the agricultural sector and led to mass migration to the cities.[85]

Given the significant unrest generated by the institutionalization of free market economics, this process was bolstered by the provision of substantial amounts of military assistance from Washington, as the armed forces were reconfigured to provide internal security. Venezuela formed the largest market in Latin America for US commercial defense sales throughout the 1990s and was a major recipient of US military training with, for instance, SOUTH-COM deploying to the country to train local security forces no fewer than thirty-five times in the year before Chavez won power. This activity eclipsed even the number of deployments to Colombia that year.[86] Likewise, during 2004 and 2005, when it looked as though domestic unrest may lead to a change in political leadership in Bolivia, the Pentagon moved to bolster security forces in the country, in an (ultimately unsuccessful) bid to repress radical social forces. According to CINC-SOUTHCOM General James Hill, in testimony to Congress in March 2004, the emerging "radical populist" threat in Bolivia was complementing the existing drug threat, and cocoa growers opposed to the US-led aggressive eradication program had "found leaders who have tapped into indigenous and other social tensions." In a reference to future president Evo Morales, who at the time was rising in popularity as a cocoa-growers' leader, Hill stated that "if radicals continue to hijack the indigenous movement, we could find ourselves faced with a narco-state that supports the uncontrolled cultivation of cocoa."[87]

Moreover, Pentagon officials repeatedly claimed that internal insecurity in Bolivia was driven by external support from the "radical" governments of Cuba and, by that point (under Chavez), Venezuela. In July 2005, Roger Pardo-Maurer, the most senior civilian defense official in charge of Latin America, argued that significant forces in Bolivia were controlled by Cuba and Venezuela and that the country was "the set piece battle in what's truly going on right now, which is the battle for the future of Latin America." According to Pardo-Maurer: "You have a revolution going on in Bolivia, a revolution that potentially could have consequences as far reaching as the Cuban revolution of 1959" and that "could have an impact on the way [we] deal with foreign policy for the rest of [our] lives."[88] In response, and as unrest began to grow, Washington rushed to provide increased funding for the armed forces and military police specifically to "increase their effectiveness in their traditional national security role and ensure effective control of crowd disturbances in urban settings."[89]

Notwithstanding efforts by Washington to shield existing pro-US elites from the widespread discontent, popular movements for reform have been voted into power in each of these three oil-rich states. Moreover, these new governments have acted to roll back the process of free marketization championed by Washington, including reform of the oil sector. In this way, the existing challenges to US regional hegemony from below in Colombia are complemented, for the first time on the Latin American mainland since the Cold War, by governments that openly reject US leadership.

The first of the three states to "turn red" was Venezuela, where Hugo Chavez won power in a landslide election in December 1998, winning 56 percent of the vote. Chavez moved quickly to enact his program of reversing the sell-offs of previous years and vastly increasing social spending in a bid to redistribute wealth to the poor. A hugely popular redrafted constitution, accepted by over 70 percent of the electorate in a December 1999 referendum, explicitly prohibited the privatization of the state oil company, PDVSA. This was followed up in 2001 by legislation that doubled the royalties to be paid by foreign oil companies to around 30 percent and that dictated that PDVSA must hold a stake of at least 51 percent in any future joint-venture projects. Speaking at the time, Chavez stated that "this is a liberating law because it breaks the chains that have bound us for so many years."[90] Given the huge stake in the Venezuelan oil industry held by foreign oil companies, they ultimately had little option but to accept Chavez's reorganization, and further moves to nationalize operations took place in May 2007.[91] As a result, Total and Statoil reduced their holdings, Chevron and BP continued to operate under the new conditions, and ConocoPhillips and ExxonMobil have left the country and sought compensation through Western courts.

Similar moves to renationalize significant sectors of the Bolivian economy have been made by Morales since his victory in the January 2006 presidential election, where he won 54 percent of the vote.[92] In his inaugural speech, Morales invoked his successful marriage during the election between the promotion of indigenous rights and the rejection of US-led neoliberalism:

> We are here and we say that we have achieved power to end the injustice, the inequality and oppression that we have lived under . . . When we talk about recovering the territory we are talking about recovering the natural resources, and

these need to be in the hands of the Bolivian people and the Bolivian state. We were told 10, 15, 20 years ago that the private sector was going to solve the country's corruption problems and unemployment, then years go by and there is more unemployment, more corruption, that economic model is not the solution for our country, maybe it is a solution for an European [sic] country or African but in Bolivia the neoliberal model does not work.[93]

This rejection of the US-led international economic order was translated into the rapid establishment of state control over Bolivia's energy sector, at a pace much faster than in Venezuela. Morales signed a decree in May 2006, just four months after his election, which placed the entire sector under state management. Giving foreign companies six months to renegotiate contracts or leave the country, Morales sent in the military to take control of the oil fields. According to Morales: "The time has come, the awaited day, a historic day in which Bolivia takes absolute control of our natural resources. The looting by foreign companies has ended."[94]

This tide of oil nationalism in Latin America gained further ground in November 2006, when presidential elections in Ecuador led to a runoff between the two main contenders: Alvaro Noboa, the richest man in the country, who campaigned on a ticket of increasing foreign investment to alleviate poverty; and Rafael Correa, who opposed a free trade deal with the United States and signaled that contracts with foreign oil companies would be renegotiated. Having won power with over 60 percent of the vote, Correa subsequently moved to enact his promised reform agenda. In October 2007, the new president signed a decree establishing a 99 percent windfall tax on oil company profits at any point when prices exceed $24 per barrel, and increasing the 50 percent rate established by his predecessor in 2006.[95] He has also seized several oil fields from Occidental Petroleum.

Washington has now found its influence to be much reduced. The IMF, so long an extremely powerful actor in the region and one of the strongest policy instruments for the United States, has been bypassed by these governments. Leaders such as Correa have used newfound oil wealth to pay off the IMF and have threatened to default on outstanding loans considered unfair.[96] The threat of retaliatory measures from the IFIs, which have long worked to discipline overly nationalist governments in the South, has become relatively ineffectual. This is primarily due to the willingness of Venezuela to provide both an alternative source of credit for these governments alongside heavily subsidized flows of oil, and the April 2006 signing of a People's Trade Agreement (TCP) by Bolivia, Venezuela, and Cuba. This agreement was promoted to "achieve a true integration among peoples that transcends the commercial and economic arenas," in response to "the collapse of the neoliberal model which is based on the core principles of deregulation, privatization and the indiscriminate opening of markets."[97]

In response to this lack of economic leverage, Washington has adopted a confrontational stance toward these governments in general and toward Chavez in particular. US officials now repeatedly represent Venezuela as a threat to American interests, often expressed in terms of the collision between Washington's "democracy promotion" agenda and the supposedly antidemocratic nature of the new governments. President Bush himself called on the region to choose between competing futures: a US-led "vision of hope" based upon "representative government [and] integration into the world economy" and a countervision that seeks to "roll back the democratic progress of the past two decades . . . blaming others for their own failures to provide for their people."[98] US officials have also continued to voice concerns regarding unsubstantiated reports of Chavez's support for Colombian guerrillas. This is a claim repeated ad nauseam by US officials, who focus on the ease with which Colombian "narcoterrorists" move across the Venezuelan border, and claim that "it is difficult to believe that the Chavez Administration is oblivious to this ongoing encroachment on its national territory."[99] In the 2006 *National Security Strategy,* the Bush administration maintained that Venezuela was run by "a demagogue awash in oil money . . . undermining democracy and seeking to destabilize the region."[100] But despite this framing of the threat, it is clear that the central challenge stems from the determination by the three leaders to reject US economic and political hegemony.

In turn, this impacts upon the degree to which Washington can ensure unfettered access to the region's oil. This deeper concern became clear as CIA director George Tenet was grilled by Congress on his assessment of the threat to the United States in its own hemisphere. In response, Tenet was adamant that Venezuela was vital to US interests specifically "because they're the third-largest supplier of petroleum" and that Chavez represented a threat since he "probably doesn't have the interests of the United States at heart."[101] Whilst relations have warmed slightly with the election of Barack Obama, the new president has stated that "the strategic interests" of the US in the region remain the same and will not be endangered by any policy switch.[102]

The rejection of the Washington Consensus by Chavez, along with Bolivia and Ecuador, remains a primary threat to American interests. This is acknowledged by the US military, with a SOUTHCOM report (leaked to the media in June 2006) cautioning that the extension of state control over energy production in these countries was deterring investment and therefore threatened "efforts to increase long-term supplies and production."[103] US military concerns over developments in the region were confirmed by SOUTHCOM's CINC, James T. Hill, who testified that "some leaders in the region are tapping into deep-seated frustrations of the failure of democratic reforms to deliver expected goods and services. By tapping into these frustrations . . . the leaders are at the same time able to reinforce their radical positions by inflaming anti-US sentiment."[104] As a result of this threat from "populist" leaders seeking an alternative path of development, the United States has moved to cut the support it has traditionally provided to political elites in these countries. There has been a complete squeeze on military cooperation with Venezuela, which has historically been close but which is now essentially nonexistent.[105] Indeed, in order to halt all commercial arms sales and so punish Venezuela for exercising its independence, Washington certified the country as "not fully cooperating" in the war on terror.[106] The Obama administration has thus far continued this isolationist strategy, refusing to reinstate security assistance programs with the country.[107]

Further, and in what seemed like an eerie return to Cold War strategy, there is evidence that this identification by Washington of a threat to its interests has led to direct complicity in fomenting unrest throughout the region. Evo Morales accused the US ambassador of "conspiring against democracy" in September 2008, as violence flared amongst the traditionally conservative regions of the country in protest at Morales's renationalization of energy reserves.[108] Likewise, there is evidence of involvement in the planning and execution of an attempted coup in Venezuela in April 2002. Street demonstrations by sections of the country's business elite led to clashes with pro-Chavez supporters outside the PVDSA, and the resulting violence was used to justify seizure of the presidential palace by coup plotters. Chavez was promptly removed from power and replaced by Pedro Carmona, a man the *New York Times* described as "a respected business leader," in contrast to the "would-be dictator" and "ruinous demagogue" Chavez.[109]

Although the coup ultimately failed—not least due to the mobilization of hundreds of thousands of Venezuelans to demand the restoration of their elected leader—and Chavez was soon back in power, it rapidly became apparent that Washington had influenced events. A State Department report released in July 2002 outlined that "it is clear that [National Endowment for Democracy, or NED], Department of Defense (DOD), and other US assistance programs provided training, institution building, and other support to individuals and organizations understood to be actively involved in the brief ouster of the Chavez government."[110] Although there is no evidence that this assistance was actively directed at supporting the coup, declassified CIA documents show that Washington knew that a coup was in the pipeline, despite denials of any such knowledge in the immediate aftermath.[111] Furthermore, Otto Reich, then assistant secretary of state for Western Hemisphere affairs and a man with a history of involvement in death squad activities in 1980s Central America, had met with the coup plotters (including Carmona) several times in the weeks leading up to the events. According to officials at the Organization of American States (OAS), he had sanctioned the overthrow, discussing details right down to the exact timings.[112] Claims by a former US intelligence officer also pointed to US military involvement in the coup, including the provision of signals intelligence from US Navy ships in the region as events unfolded.[113]

The extent of US active involvement in the events of April 2002, and in Bolivia in September 2008, is still unclear. What is evident is that Washington views the threat from radical populism in oil-rich states to be serious enough to work to isolate these regimes in all spheres of international politics. And as a consequence, Chavez, Morales, and Correa have been pushed to deepen ties with Washington's potential strategic rivals, Russia and China. Chavez has visited Beijing repeatedly whilst in power, and the China National Petroleum Corporation (CNPC) is operating in Venezuela. As a result, increasing amounts of oil are being shipped to China in a deal considered mutually beneficial: China increases its imports of oil and bolsters a counterweight to Washington in its backyard; Venezuela reduces its dependency on the US market for its oil.[114]

In addition, Chavez has moved to sign arms and energy deals with Russia that he claimed, during a visit to Moscow in July 2008, represented a "strategic alliance" designed to "guarantee the sovereignty of Venezuela, which is being threatened by the United States." Russian oil companies are now being granted access to the country's oil-rich Orinoco belt, and Venezuela has contracts for military equipment worth over $4 billion. Indeed, since the United

States cut off military assistance to the country, Russia supplies a staggering 92 percent of Venezuelan arms imports. Similar ties are being forged by Morales and Correa. These moves make China one of the largest investors in Latin America.[115] However, US planners maintain that increased Chinese and Russian interests are not necessarily a threat to Washington and in many cases less so than the local regimes they are forging relations with.[116] The main threat to US hegemony across the Andes (Colombia included) has been clearly and repeatedly articulated as radical populism, not Great Power rivalry, and it is the nature of this challenge—manifested as we have seen in two very different ways—which determines US strategy in the region.

## Counterinsurgency Again: Stabilizing Mexico

US strategy for securing Mexico's oil reserves has necessarily been quite different from other states in Latin America, considering the longstanding refusal of local elites to open the sector to foreign capital. Oil plays a central role in the Mexican economy, where it forms over 10 percent of the country's export earnings and one-third of total government revenues. Almost all Mexican exports are transported by tanker to the US Gulf Coast, where they form the second largest source of US imports (1.7 mbpd).[117] Maximizing and stabilizing this flow of oil has been a key US objective, especially as supplies from other regions have become less secure. However, unlike Colombia, where successive administrations have proved enthusiastic in the face of the US-led economic model, and even unlike the three states considered in the previous section, where strong nationalist forces have come to power relatively recently, the Mexican oil sector has been fully nationalized for over seventy years. The Mexican Constitution itself forbids any foreign direct investment (FDI) in, or foreign ownership of, this sector, and the state-owned oil company (Petroleos Mexicanos, or Pemex) remains the sole operator in the country. Perhaps unsurprisingly, this has not been considered an ideal state of affairs by US planners. As one pro-Washington analysis put it, Mexican government officials "view natural resources as a political expression of their sovereignty" and "are not capable of understanding that being the monopolistic providers of energy does not intrinsically lead to the maximization of natural resources wealth."[118] In the event, however, there has been little to be done in the face of strong Mexican nationalism; US strategies have been limited to relatively low-level attempts to undermine Pemex's position.[119]

Resistance by the Mexican government to opening the oil sector has not been replicated in other areas of the economy, and the government fully embraced IMF- and US-led programs of neoliberal adjustment. And in this context, US strategy toward Mexico—where economic reforms have been matched with substantial support for the security forces in order to suppress opposition—has obvious parallels with US strategy toward Colombia. Furthermore, this wider process of integration has been used by Washington to progressively undermine the sanctity of the state-owned oil sector: a strategy that US planners are eagerly adopting as they survey the prize that such dismantling would bring.

Throughout the past twenty-five years, Mexico has undertaken what has been described as a "radical experiment in economic liberalisation" outside of the oil sector.[120] The hitherto-closed economy has been progressively opened to foreign investment, and the country has become a favored site for commercial operations by foreign companies eager to exploit the lower wages and weaker regulatory environment that persists. The increasing domination of the Mexican economy by transnational capital continued through the 1980s and has been massively accelerated as a result of its successful post–Cold War integration into a North American trading bloc. The passage of NAFTA in 1993 marked the creation of the single largest market in the world and irrevocably changed relations between the United States and its southern neighbor. NAFTA is designed to force open the Mexican economy for the benefit of foreign capital, with the imposition of free trade and the continued removal of barriers to investment leading to an accelerated retraction of the public sector.[121] This trend was supported throughout the decade by IMF loan agreements that provided "a reinforcement of the Government's strategy for privatization and the granting of concessions to the private sector in areas previously reserved for the public sector."[122]

The results of economic adjustment, and of significantly freer trade between the United States, Canada, and Mexico, have been disastrous for the majority of the Mexican population. In fact, whilst liberalization has allowed larger Mexican companies to thrive and has provided distinct benefits to large foreign corporations, it economically destroyed many other individuals and firms by removing significant state protection against the open market.[123] Wealth inequality has widened throughout Mexico, with the absolute income of the wealthiest 10 percent increasing by 21 percent between 1984 and 1994, alongside a *drop* of 23 percent in the income of the poorest 10 percent across the same time period.[124] The lowering of tariffs under NAFTA has allowed US companies to flood Mexico with cheaper, subsidized agricultural produce, destroying the livelihoods of many small-scale farmers who, with no land ownership anymore, have been forced to migrate to large urban areas. Large-scale internal displacement has resulted in mass rises in unemployment, crime, and family breakdown as well as a sharp drop in wages.[125] According to an extensive study by the Carnegie Endowment for International Peace, NAFTA led to a loss of no fewer than 1.3 million jobs in the agricultural sector (where almost one-fifth of Mexicans still work) in its first ten years, and parallel increases in the manufacturing sector as a result of increased foreign direct investment failed to make up for this shortfall. The authors of the report are unambiguous about the consequences of NAFTA on the Mexican people: "While NAFTA's overall impact may be muddled, for Mexico's rural households the picture is clear—and bleak. NAFTA has accelerated Mexico's transition to a liberalized economy without creating the necessary conditions for the public and private sectors to respond to the economic, social and environmental shocks of trading with two of the biggest economies in the world."[126]

These consequences for the Mexican people have had little impact upon the restructuring process driven by Washington. US planners have not broken step as they have sought deeper integration with the Mexican economy, and the Bush administration pushed what has been labeled the "NAFTA-Plus" agenda. As with the original NAFTA framework, this is designed primarily to improve the investment environment for transnational corporations operating throughout the bloc, and especially in Mexico. Remaining barriers to the flow of capital are targeted by the process, thus facilitating foreign direct investment across the board.[127] And to an extent not seen before, a primary rationale driving further integration is to provide an improved investment climate in the energy sector. According to an influential Council on Foreign Relations task force, Mexico needed to "reorient its economic policies to encourage more investment," including "dramatically expanding investment and productivity in the energy sector." Specifically, Mexico "has major oil and gas reserves, but these are relatively untapped. Development has been hampered by constitutional restrictions on ownership, which are driven by an understandable desire to see this strategic asset used for the benefit of Mexicans. This restriction on investment, coupled with the inefficient management of the state monopoly, Pemex, has contributed to low productivity . . . Reforms in this area are needed urgently."[128]

These recommendations have been taken on board by the US, Mexican, and Canadian governments, and they form a clear part of the NAFTA-Plus agenda. The three countries have established an Energy Working Group, which acts to "strengthen North America's energy markets by working together . . . to increase reliable energy supplies for the region's needs and development, by facilitating investment in energy infrastructure . . . production and reliable delivery of energy."[129] In Mexico, this has translated into the boldest move yet to reform the nationalized oil sector. Under the NAFTA-Plus agenda, President Felipe Calderon has called for a modernization program that would allow private firms to enter into partnership with the state-owned body, thereby investing their capital into the sector for the first time. Whilst insisting that privatization is not in the cards, Calderon has stated that "time and our oil are running out" and that therefore the government needs to "act now" to revitalize the industry.[130] For Calderon, the "real question we should be asking ourselves is how to take better advantage of our petroleum resources to bring prosperity to Mexico in the future."[131] As a result, the Mexican Congress passed a bill in October 2008 opening Pemex to foreign investment for the first time in decades.[132]

Given the devastating consequences of structural adjustment for the majority of Mexicans, resistance from below to the process of continued neoliberalism has been substantial. Significant unrest throughout the country at various points since NAFTA was signed has shattered the illusion of stability constructed by Mexican political elites. The removal of the longstanding *ejido* rights for indigenous peasants to use extensive communal tracts of land—a precondition by Washington before the original NAFTA process got underway—has caused widespread unrest across the country. Initially, this manifested itself in dramatic style, sparking the Zapatista uprising on January 1, 1994 (the day that NAFTA came into effect). Declaring the agreement a "death certificate for the Indian peoples of Mexico," Subcomandante Marcos—the spokesman for the newly formed Zapatista National Liberation Army (EZLN)—signaled the launch of a short-lived armed struggle demanding land reform, economic justice, and the fundamental reordering of Mexican politics from representative to participatory, "radical" democracy. Although the period of active Zapatista insurgency was short (a number of weeks), social resistance to NAFTA has continued since, and it finds broad support from sections of the population suffering under the process of economic integration.[133] Farmers', teachers', and workers' unions have all demonstrated against the effects of economic liberalization and reductions in social spending, as popular resistance throughout communities grows.[134] Moreover, the partial privatization of Pemex has led to large-scale protest, culminating in opposition politicians storming both houses of Congress and remaining barricaded in the building for days.[135]

The Mexican state has responded to this opposition in a time-honored fashion: by continuing, to some degree, the "dirty war" carried out during the Cold War, in which security forces employed a policy of sustained violence against armed insurgents and student protesters, resulting in widespread massacres, forced disappearance, systematic torture, and genocide.[136] Popular movements for reform have been brutally suppressed by the Mexican state during the period of US-led economic integration. According to Human Rights Watch, the army responded to the initial Zapatista uprising in 1994 with serious human rights violations, including extrajudicial executions and torture.[137] But crucially, this was not just the result of an overly excessive response to armed challenge; instead, it fit within a longstanding pattern of repressing those sections of civil society pushing for reform. Indeed, according to Human Rights Watch in 1993—the year *before* the uprising—"Despite the Mexican government's efforts, in connection with the North American Free Trade Agreement (NAFTA) debate, to portray its human rights problems in the best possible light, Americas Watch's concerns in 1993 were virtually unchanged from prior years. Torture and police abuse; election-related abuses; and interference with freedom of expression and association of human rights monitors, independent trade unionists, peasant and indigenous rights activists, election observers, and journalists were still pervasive problems."[138]

The repression of reform-minded sections of civil society accelerated throughout the 1990s as the negative consequences of economic integration bit. Political assassinations continued throughout the decade and were used to silence members of "left-wing opposition parties, rural organizers, and social activists" as well as "prominent reformists within the ranks of the ruling PRI [Party of the Democratic Revolution]."[139] And, as with the situation in Colombia, antiopposition violence in the country has often been carried out by the military, as opposed to the police, and in close cooperation with an extensive network of paramilitary forces. As a secret 1993 US Army Intelligence assessment of the Mexican armed forces (since declassified) stated, the military was "organized and equipped primarily for internal defense. The mission of the armed forces includes the security and support of the administration, control against civil unrest, and suppression of drug trafficking." With this in mind, the "primary concentration of combat and service support units" was located in and around Mexico City, in order to "ensure that the army provides rapid internal support to the administration."[140] This objective continues to dominate the mission of the armed forces, which, as the US State Department acknowledged in 2007, "has significant domestic security responsibilities, particularly in combating drug trafficking and maintaining order."[141]

Although the maintenance of internal security in Mexico is largely refracted through the lens of a war on drugs, CN operations have served a wider set of objectives, as they have elsewhere in Latin America. Military units, alongside "civilian" paramilitary groups operating with the tacit (and even, on occasions, explicit) support of the military and ruling party, have been armed and directed against a broad section of vocal civil society. Groups such as Paz y Justicia (Peace and Justice) operate throughout Chiapas and are responsible for numerous and widespread violations of human rights against communities considered sympathetic to insurgents. Mirroring attacks seen in Colombia, these groups have been responsible for large-scale massacres, such as that in Acteal in December 1997, in which forty-five indigenous men, women, and children were killed. A large-scale armed campaign by the military and its paramilitary allies has taken place against peasant occupiers of previously communal, but now private, land. Throughout, there is strong evidence that paramilitaries are armed by Mexican security forces, which fail to intervene during attacks.[142] Published excerpts from a 1994 Mexican army planning document advocated "a strategy that included the training and arming of paramilitary groups, surveillance and harassment of civilian communities and organizations sympathetic to the Zapatistas; 'civic action' campaigns on the part of the military; and the financial and political support of local officials loyal to the government."[143]

Despite a traditionally cool relationship during the Cold War, the US and Mexican militaries enhanced their cooperation as a result of the Chiapas uprising and the ensuing CI campaign. Military sales from the United States jumped as NAFTA came into effect and the Zapatista uprising was suppressed, with the value of approved exports from the commercial sector rising from $9 million in 1993 to $96 million a year later. Likewise, the US Foreign Military Sales (FMS) program grew from $6 million in 1993 to $15 million in 1994. As in Colombia, aid throughout the 1990s was justified under the rubric of "counternarcotics," and the war on drugs was the apparent rationale behind the accelerated military relationship. For these purposes, the Clinton administration authorized the transfer of more than fifty UH-1 helicopters along with four C-130 troop transport planes. However, as unrest grew in southern Mexico throughout the decade, the underlying rationale for US assistance became clearer, with Washington offering CI aid for the first time. The US ambassador to Mexico, James Jones, offered intelligence and military training to combat what he referred to as the "terrorist" group, the Popular Revolutionary Army (EPR). Questioned about the extent of the aid on offer, Jones stated that "all the [Mexican Government] needs to do is ask. Whatever they need, we will certainly support."[144]

The twin-track process of integrating North American economies through NAFTA and working to destroy any significant resistance to it, accelerated under the Bush administration. And wider concerns over energy security have been increasingly entwined within this. Deeper economic integration between the United States and Mexico has been backed up by an enhanced capability to provide internal security. Launching the Security and Prosperity Partnership (SPP) in March 2005 as a central element of NAFTA-Plus, presidents George Bush and Vicente Fox (along with Canadian prime minister Paul Martin) stated that the new initiative was "based on the principle that our security and prosperity are mutually dependent and complementary" and was designed explicitly to "help consolidate our action into a North American framework to confront security and economic challenges."[145]

In this light, the United States has moved to substantially increase levels of assistance provided to Mexican security forces. In October 2007, the Bush administration submitted a request to Congress for an exponential rise in funding for the Mexican military and police forces. Buried as part of the $46 billion war supplemental for Iraq and Afghanistan, the $1.4 billion, three-year "Merida Initiative" included a staggering $500 million for Mexico in 2008 and $450 million in 2009.[146] According to the Congressional Research Service, this funding represents "a dramatic increase in aid to Mexico," with the proportion of aid to Latin America destined for this country increasing from 15 percent in 2007 to nearly 40 percent in 2008. This would match Mexico's own dramatic rise in security spending, where funding rose 24 percent in 2007 as the Calderon administration continued to militarize domestic politics.[147]

This massive increase in US assistance has continued during the Obama administration. During his first trip to the country in April 2009, the new president restated "the United States' commitment to work with Mexico on a broad range of issues, in particular on meeting our shared security challenges," and he reiterated Washington's support for the $1.4 billion Merida Initiative. The 2010 budget includes the next tranche of funding—to the tune of $450 million—and this is now supplemented by a further request for $66 million to "procure urgently needed Blackhawk helicopters to transport Mexican soldiers combating cartel activities." Should this request go through, Mexico will become the number one recipient of military aid in the Western Hemisphere (replacing Colombia).[148]

US assistance through the Merida Initiative, which has been christened "Plan Mexico" by critics who see parallels with Clinton's aid program to Colombia, is similarly justified in public as a CN package.[149] Just weeks after the president took office in December 2006, Calderon declared a war on drugs, appearing in public in full military uniform (the first time a Mexican president has done so for a century) as he deployed more than 20,000 troops and police into nine states across the country.[150] However, and again with parallels to Colombia, in funding the Mexican military Washington is in fact proposing to send assistance to an institution deeply implicated in the drug business. A 2008 report by the State Department noted that many members of the security forces "were involved in kidnapping, extortion, or providing protection for, or acting directly on behalf of organized crime and drug traffickers."[151] Although these links have tended to be strongest throughout the police force, where corruption is endemic, the increasing use of the military in a CN role does not spell an end to clandestine cooperation between official agencies and drug cartels. Mexican army general Jose de Jesus Gutierrez Rebollo, appointed as the top CN officer during the 1990s, has been convicted on charges that he aided the head of the Juarez Cartel, whilst five members of the army were indicted in January 2008 for leaking information on military movements to the Sinaloa Cartel.[152] Such collusion has not simply been the result of occasional "bad apples" in the security forces. Demonstrating the extent to which the lines between the military and drug cartels have become blurred, an entire unit of the US-trained army special forces deserted en masse in the late 1990s, forming a paramilitary group called the Zetas, which has since worked with the Gulf Cartel.[153]

Either way, assistance is now being provided across the board for Mexican security forces—military and civilian—as part of the Merida Initiative. And whilst the drug war is an obvious concern for US and Mexican officials, this aid can be, and is designed to be, used for more than simple CN missions. The eight Bell BH-412 and three Blackhawk UH-60 helicopters requested by the Bush administration (costing more than $200 million), along with night-vision equipment, were justified to Congress in order to support "counternarcotics and counterterrorism missions" by providing "mobility to rapid reaction forces." Likewise, the more than $16 million requested for the infamous Mexican intelligence service (CISEN) is designed to "bolster its capabilities to counter terrorism threats."[154] The package is designed to ensure a level of security cooperation that moves far beyond a war on drugs and the organized crime associated with trafficking. Instead, it can be understood as a much wider program to further militarize state-society relations in Mexico and to provide the armed forces with a greater capacity to guarantee internal stability across the board. In fact, the origins of Plan Mexico lie less in an escalated sense of threat regarding drugs than in the creation of the SPP as part of the NAFTA-Plus agenda and a desire to protect the free trade model in Mexico. In April 2008, Thomas Shannon, former assistant secretary of state for Western Hemisphere affairs, stated the goal of security assistance to Mexico: the SPP "understands North America as a shared economic space and that as a shared economic space we need to protect it, and that we need to understand that we don't protect this shared economic space only at our frontiers, that it has to be protected more broadly throughout North America . . . *To a certain extent [through the SPP], we're armoring NAFTA.*"[155]

With this objective in mind, Mexican security forces have targeted not just drug traffickers but broad social movements pushing for political and economic reform and for a rejection of deeper neoliberalization.[156] Thus, the Chiapas-based Center for Political Analysis and Socio-Economic Research (CAPISE) has documented "recent changes in military deployment, paramilitary activity, and highway projects that combine to form a counterinsurgency strategy to displace Zapatista communities," as the army reinforces "military bases near Zapatista communities with Special Forces, including airborne elite troops and special elite units from Mexico City."[157] Likewise, paramilitary forces opened fire and killed twenty people at a 2006 protest in Oaxaca, organized by a teachers' union and the umbrella organization, the Popular Assembly of the Peoples of Oaxaca (APPO).[158] Mexican police forces are specifically geared toward the violent suppression of protest and "routinely employ excessive force when carrying out crowd-control operations." Similarly, the military's involvement in internal security operations results in "egregious abuses," including, for instance, an operation in May 2007 where "soldiers ar-

bitrarily detained 65 people in Michoacán state, holding some incommunicado at a military base, beating many of the detainees, and raping four mi-
nors. That same month soldiers in Michoacán arbitrarily detained eight
people, keeping them incommunicado at a military base where they beat and
covered the heads of four of them with plastic bags."[159]

Torture is widespread throughout the Mexican security infrastructure and
is used as a means of repressing opposition. In a large-scale survey of forensic
physicians in Mexico in 2002, over half reported that torture was a "severe
problem for detainees in Mexico," with no fewer than half having documented
forensic evidence of torture in the past year.[160] US private security personnel
have been involved in the training of Mexican units in torture techniques.
In a video released to the Mexican media, a US advisor was filmed instructing
security officials in aggressive "interrogation" techniques, which include squirt-
ing water up the nose of detainees to simulate drowning, pulling them through
pools of vomit, and dunking their heads into holes filled with excrement and
rats. Although the police spokesman described the training as "counter-torture,"
for elite units that must face "real-life, high-stress situations" such as kidnapping by drug cartels, the methods used are remarkably similar to those used
by Mexican security forces themselves.[161] General José Francisco Gallardo, a
high-ranking officer in the Mexican army who has been arbitrarily imprisoned for proposing the creation of a human rights ombudsman for the military, has indicated a striking parallel between recent events and Cold War
repression. Speaking to Laura Carlsen of the Americas Policy Program, Gallardo stated that "we are already experiencing a return to the Dirty War."[162]

Overall, then, we see in Mexico a pattern emerging that replicates at many
levels the direction of US policy toward Colombia. Large-scale military assistance programs have been granted by Congress and continue to be granted
during the Obama administration, ostensibly to help combat the narcotraf-
fickers and narcoterrorists who pose a threat to the health of US citizens. However, this assistance is also directed against a far wider set of forces that
threaten the stability required for investment by transnational corporations
and is used to armor the process of neoliberalization and economic integration. With this policy, energy security is becoming an increasingly prominent
concern, as Washington acts to increase the productivity and reliability of the
Mexican oil sector by pushing for increased involvement of private capital.

## Conclusion

We have shown in this chapter the existence of substantive continuities in US strategy toward key oil-rich Latin American states. Regardless of how this strategy has played out on the ground, Washington has identified popular forces pushing for reform as the main threat to US interests in the region. These interests stretch far wider than energy resources, and the US is concerned with cementing a free market model of development in Latin America for a broad set of foreign corporations. However, concerns over energy security have played a distinct and significant role in US strategy. In this light, the drive to secure foreign access to the exploration and production of Latin American oil helps explain the ways in which the US has provided economic, political, and—crucially—military support to pro-US elites in the region in order to counter those forces with agendas inimical to US interests. Such concerns also help explain increasing attempts by Washington to contain or even overthrow such forces as and when they attain power.

# The Futures
# of American Hegemony?

In this book we have examined the nature of US power in the postwar system and the ways in which that power has been used to forge and defend a liberal order. In this regard, one observation has come through perhaps more than any other: whilst there have often been US policy changes in response to events in a chaotic world, the fact remains that Washington's *objectives* have remained remarkably consistent. These have been a commitment to maintaining the liberal open door capitalist global economy under US political hegemony and the containment and destruction of social forces that present a significant challenge to it.

Oil and the conditions that allow for its steady flow onto international markets has been an intimate part of this story. Not only was it strategically necessary to have stable sources of oil during the Cold War; these sources have also allowed for the rapid industrialization of the capitalist core economies throughout the postwar order. Oil has been the lifeblood for the successful consolidation of capitalism and the building up of a western "rump" upon which accumulation could proceed and globalization eventually springboard. As part of this relationship, US military power has been used to insulate specific kinds of globalized political economies. US coercive interventions have helped to shape, and provide the conditions for, specific kinds of state formation and class consolidation on the periphery of the world system. This is not to say that the United States is an omnipotent power nor that local, national, and regional dynamics have been irrelevant to the processes considered within this book. Rather, because of the central role that localized militaries have played in insulating specific kinds of rule, and the almost global reach of US-sponsored counterinsurgency (CI) and military aid programmes, American power has been a deep and abiding constitutive presence in state formation in the South.

These programs, coupled with an ideology of "internal warfare," have helped to concretize the view that civil society, especially restive sections that challenge a status quo geared toward perceived US core interests, are legitimate targets for security crackdowns and the imposition of stability. In this sense, forces dedicated to majoritarian reforms—often relatively mild in scope—have been refracted through a CI lens and labeled subversive. This broad designation, coupled with the dirty-war tactics and the brittle social base of a number of states in the South, has often led to a deadly mix. Adding to this concoction has been the fact that the requirement for stable supplies of energy by the core capitalist powers has meant that instability in the oil-rich regions of the global economy have been linked to the capacity of the United States both to project military power and to underwrite the industrial viability of rivals and allies alike. These needs have made the desire to combat the "threat" ever more urgent. Energy security thus became fundamentally hard-wired into US foreign policy in the postwar order, and the defense of the conditions that allows oil onto international markets has been a paramount concern for US planners, leading in turn to often devastating social consequences. Quite simply, energy security for the West has often meant insecurity for the rest.

Although the end of the Cold War and the advent of a global war on terror have seen a reconfiguration of the central threats to US power, the need for energy security has in fact become more intense. As part of the ever-increasing demands on global energy supplies, especially as formerly peripheral economies like China rapidly industrialize, we are seeing an increased push for greater diversification. The logic underpinning this move is that a greater diversity of suppliers eases bottlenecks within global markets whilst also providing a fallback should instability increase in core oil-producing regions such as the Middle East. As we have shown, this process of diversification has led to increased flows of military aid and training to states in the Caspian Basin, West Africa, and Latin America. In turn, this aid has been used to insulate pro-US elite structures that have proved suitably pliant to the needs of an open door, globalized economy. Through a process of unabashed neoliberalization, oil-rich political economies in the South have been restructured and reorientated toward the interests of global capital, which has generated an investment climate conducive to operations by the major international oil companies and often served the interests of elites within the countries concerned. These processes have, for the most part, been nothing short of disastrous for the majority of the population, as poverty reduction has stagnated and wealth inequalities have soared. Likewise, the overt militarization occurring as a result of security assistance has often led to the institutionalization of a corrupt and abusive posture toward civil society, with suspected subversive elements often disciplined through the application of CI. Whilst US CI is most effectively fought as a political war focused on hearts and minds, the contradictions inherent within foreign occupation and client states, coupled with the stakes involved when dealing with questions of energy security, means US military strategy has frequently translated into severe consequences for civil society across the oil-rich South.

Of course, many of the regimes now in receipt of US military assistance were highly abusive prior to the onset of US aid, and US planners could simply state, "We have to work with what is there!" This is, of course, correct. It is important for analysts of US intervention to always bear in mind the ways in which US policy must interact and work with local states, which themselves have their own histories, interests, and agendas. The central question is whether US security assistance leads to fewer human rights abuses, greater accountability, and the strengthening of genuine democracy or whether US military aid serves to consolidate authoritarian regimes and overlay (and reinforce) a preexisting culture of abuse and impunity. There is a very clear line between working with what you find and seeking to move toward ending human rights abuses and consolidating what you find so as to guarantee concrete economic and political interests. Sadly, there is a profound gulf between the protection of human rights and social justice and the need for stability and a favorable climate for foreign direct investment. This gulf is largely based upon the often highly brittle nature of the regimes that the United States has to work with, the extreme concentrations of wealth in these states, and the fear of change lest it lead to a political or economic climate less favorable for US interests. As we have shown, these fears crop up time and again in the planning documents and speeches given by key personnel.

Aside from tracing this history of US energy security, as well as documenting its current consequences on key oil-rich regions within the global economy, we have also sought to relate these sets of empirical questions to a wider set of debates as to the nature of US power and the ways in which its military primacy has served to undergird US hegemony in the postwar order. Specifically, we have argued that a dual logic exists at the heart of these processes, with US power working to transnationalize the global economy whilst simultaneously seeking to ensure that this momentum develops into a structural outcome that underpins US hegemony. The "public goods" that Washington has delivered via the liberal order have fostered the kinds of political economies that are conducive to US capitalism and have also maintained a derivative structural power for the American state, with other core powers coming to depend on US power projection. Whilst there have been a number of challenges to this liberal order, as well as a proliferation of analyses that seek to chart the emergence of new rivalries over ever-diminishing resources, we have argued that the liberal core remains remarkably durable. A return to a form of mercantilism on the part of Washington would undermine the very order upon which US power has come to depend. The momentum toward the internationalization of capitalism and the kinds of geopolitical and strategic relationships thrown up by this process is simply, in our opinion, too durable. The fracturing of the liberal order would hurt the interests of its core powers—and the United States in particular—far more than the relative gains that may accrue as a result of a more unilateral push.

Perhaps this was the biggest failing of the Bush administration. That is, as a particular set of imperial managers it misinterpreted the utility of military power whilst simultaneously mismanaging the liberal order itself. Given Washington's military preponderance, the unilateral temptation that was opened up by the ending of the Cold War has always been very strong. The events of 9/11 hastened a desire to attain a degree of strategic maneuverability in America's war on terror that was unencumbered by the often-burdensome requirements of multilateral forms of governance. Perhaps the crucial mistake that the Bush administration made was forgetting that US military power is constrained by two important factors. First, it is limited by the capacity of the American public to absorb losses. As Iraq has illustrated, the so-called Vietnam Syndrome is still alive in the public consciousness, and it continues to impose severe domestic political costs on any administration seeking to launch wars that rely on significant territorial control by US troops themselves. Because global conflict is increasingly characterized by "low intensity" insurgencies and thus requires "boots on the ground," this quandary will continue to bedevil US strategic planners.

Second, US military power has generally been effective only when used to attain goals that are agreed upon by the rest of the liberal core. Whilst Cold War anticommunism was an "easy sell," the war on terror and the commitment of post–Cold War administrations to maintain US military primacy has begun to worry other Great Powers. The high moment of this was the overtly imperial posture of the Bush administration that sought to work outside of the liberal core and thus undermine the legitimacy that the US derived through its managing role within the liberal order. Alongside this loss of legitimacy is the very real potential for other states to balance against US power when it is so obviously pursuing its own interests to the detriment of important allies. This is multiplied by the fact that other core states need to conjugate the needs of the imperial center with their own domestic requirements of consensual rule; the task of legitimation becomes even harder in the face of local popular pressures to resist the vagaries of American power. Bush's doctrine of preemptive war proved a much harder sell than previous interventions justified under the pretext of containment or humanitarian intervention. In many ways, the Iraq intervention represented the most naked national moment of the American empire, whilst also rendering that moment stillborn. Its lack of strategic restraint has not only worried other centers of power about the exercise of US military might but has also (and rather obviously) rendered a crucial region within the global economy even more unstable. Given the forms of global interdependency that we have sketched in this book, especially in international oil markets, the move into Iraq was a particularly high-stakes gamble that has, in many respects, failed.

Will an Obama presidency see a radical shift in US foreign policy? We would clearly answer "no"; indicators suggest that despite popular perception, under the Obama administration US troops will in fact remain in Iraq (albeit in reduced numbers) whilst there will be an increase in CI assistance in Afghanistan. Like his predecessors, Obama has committed to maintaining US military primacy and has in fact increased the military budget from the earlier Bush administration, with accelerated levels of CI training to security forces across the South. On a similar note, there are currently no viable sources of energy that can replace a carbon-based global economy, even though its use continues to threaten potentially devastating forms of climate change. As such, we cannot as yet see an alternative strategy that could be pursued, given the continued logic of strategic necessity adopted by US planners. Our bet is that, for the foreseeable future at least, US strategy vis-à-vis the oil-rich South will continue to develop along the lines outlined in this book and be characterized by a drive to transnationalize crucial oil-rich political economies for the operations of private oil capital, alongside an overt attempt to armor such globalizing processes against social and political challenge. Furthermore, we would not be surprised if this continuity of strategic objectives by Washington continued, in turn, to have profound effects on the promotion of human rights and genuine forms of democratic rule in the oil-rich South.

More optimistically, the fact remains that there is a massive disconnect between the actions of the American state and the wishes of the American people. America is a remarkably open and tolerant society, with domestic norms based around the respect of human rights and similar to other majorities across the world, a large majority of Americans reject the role of the United States as a global hegemon and favor a more altruistic foreign policy that is independent of US national interests. A strong majority "also feel that US foreign policy should be oriented to the global interest not just the national interest," with most in favor of "putting diplomatic and public pressure on governments to respect human rights."[1] This gives us cause for hope, and as we move further into the twenty-first century we hope this disconnect will shorten, that the decency and humanity of the American people is allowed expression in the foreign policy of the state, and that the logic of necessity is rejected in favor of a logic of humanity.

# Notes

INTRODUCTION: Global Oil Supplies and US Intervention

1. William I. Robinson, *A Theory of Global Capitalism: Production, Class and State in a Transnational World* (Baltimore, MD: Johns Hopkins University Press, 2004).

2. See, for example, George J. Tenet, Director of Central Intelligence, "Worldwide Threat 2001: National Security in a Changing World," testimony delivered to the Senate Select Committee on Intelligence, 7 February 2001. Reprinted at: "Usama bin Ladin as America's 'Most Serious Threat,'" *Middle East Quarterly* 8, no. 2 (Spring 2001), www.meforum.org/.

3. Office of the Press Secretary, "Dr. Condoleezza Rice Discusses President's National Security Strategy," 1 October 2002, http://georgewbush-whitehouse.archives.gov/, emphasis added; Nicholas Lemann, "The Next World Order," *New Yorker,* 1 April 2002. For a detailed analysis of the way in which the Bush administration constructed the "terrorist" threat and "counterterrorist" response in the months and years after 9/11, see Richard Jackson, *Writing the War on Terror* (Manchester: Manchester University Press, 2005).

4. President George W. Bush, "Address to a Joint Session of Congress and the American People," 20 September 2001, http://georgewbush-whitehouse.archives.gov/.

5. Josh White and Ann Scott Tyson, "Rumsfeld Offers Strategies for Current War: Pentagon to Release 20-Year Plan Today," *Washington Post,* 3 February 2006.

6. Troop levels as of October 2008. See "New Bid to Seal Iraq Troops Deal," *BBC News,* 20 October 2008, and "US Unable to Spare Afghan Troops," *BBC News,* 23 September 2008, both at news.bbc.co.uk/. As is often the case, there is significant controversy over the figures of civilian deaths in Iraq and Afghanistan, not least due to the fact that the Pentagon assiduously has avoided all discussion of the issue. Sabrina Tavernise, "US Quietly Issues Estimate of Iraqi Civilian Casualties," *New York Times,* 30 October 2005. For a respected and ongoing count of casualties in Iraq—which documented between 88,000 and 97,000 civilian deaths from violence by October 2008— see the database compiled by Iraq Body Count: www.iraqbodycount.org/.

7. Thom Shanker, "Proposed Military Spending Is Highest since WWII," *New York Times,* 4 February 2008.

8. Dana Priest, "CIA Holds Terror Suspects in Secret Prisons: Debate Is Growing within Agency about Legality and Morality of Overseas System Set Up after 9/11,"

*Washington Post,* 2 November 2005. For an excellent study of the CIA's global internment and "extraordinary rendition" program, see Stephen Grey, *Ghost Plane: The True Story of the CIA Rendition and Torture Program* (London: Macmillan, 2007).

9. Simon Tisdall and Ewen MacAskill, "America's Long War," *The Guardian,* 15 February 2006.

10. See, for example: Eric Schmitt and Mark Mazzetti, "Secret Order Lets US Raid al Qaeda," *New York Times,* 9 November 2008; Brooke Anderson, "Anti-US Sentiment Grows in Syria after Raid," *San Francisco Chronicle,* 10 November 2008.

11. "Iraq War Illegal, Says Annan," *BBC News,* 16 September 2004, http://news.bbc .co.uk/.

12. Michael Ignatieff, "Nation-Building Lite," *New York Times,* 28 July 2002. For a similar argument, see Chalmers Johnson, *The Sorrow of Empire: Militarism, Secrecy, and the End of the Republic* (New York: Metropolitan Books, 2004).

13. William Appleman Williams, "The Frontier Thesis and American Foreign Policy," *Pacific Historic Review* 24, no. 4 (November 1955): p. 379.

14. For a selection, see Wesley K. Clark, *Winning Modern Wars: Iraq, Terrorism and the American Empire* (New York: Public Affairs, 2003); Ivan Eland, "The Empire Strikes Out: The 'New Imperialism' and Its Fatal Flaws," *Policy Analysis* 459 (2002): 1–27; Niall Ferguson, *Empire: How Britain Made the World* (London: Allen Lane, 2003); Victor Davis Hanson, "A Funny Sort of Empire," *National Review Online,* November 27, 2002; G. John Ikenberry, "The Illusions of Empire," *Foreign Affairs* 83, no. 2 (March/April 2004): pp. 144–54; Charles S. Maier, "An American Empire," *Harvard Magazine* 105, no. 2 (2002): pp. 28–31; Max Boot, *The Savage Wars of Peace: Small Wars and the Rise of American Power* (New York: Basic Books, 2002); Michael Cox, "Empire, Imperialism, and the Bush Doctrine," *Review of International Studies* 30, no. 4 (2004): pp. 585–608.

15. Further members of the PNAC who formed part of the Bush team included Elliot Abrams (appointed by Bush as special assistant to the president at the National Security Council), Eliot Cohen (later counselor of the State Department), Paula Dobriansky (State Department), and Zalmay Khalilzad (later serving as ambassador to Afghanistan, Iraq, and the UN).

16. Project for the New American Century, "Statement of Principles," 3 June 1997, www.newamericancentury.org/.

17. Michael Cox, "The Empire's Back in Town: Or America's Imperial Temptation— Again," *Millennium* 32, no. 1 (2003): p. 8.

18. Thomas Freidman, "Peking Duct Tape," *New York Times,* 17 February 2003.

19. Michael Ignatieff, "The Burden," *New York Times Magazine,* 5 January 2003.

20. Emily Eakin, "It Takes an Empire Say Several US Thinkers," *New York Times,* 2 April 2002.

21. Sebastian Mallaby, "The Reluctant Imperialist: Terrorism, Failed States and the Case for American Empire," *Foreign Affairs* 81, no. 2 (March/April 2002).

22. See, for example, Niall Ferguson, *Colossus: The Price of America's Empire* (London: Penguin Press, 2004).

23. G. John Ikenberry, "America's Imperial Ambition," *Foreign Affairs* 81, no. 5 (September/October 2002).

24. "The Perils of Empire," Statement of Principles by the Coalition for a Realistic Foreign Policy, www.realisticforeignpolicy.org/.

25. Jay Solomon, "US Drops 'War on Terror' Phrase, Clinton Says," *Wall Street Journal*, 31 March 2009.

26. For an early enunciation of Obama's vision of the US role in the world, see Barack Obama, "Renewing American leadership," *Foreign Affairs* 86, no. 4 (July/August 2007).

27. G. John Ikenberry and Stephen Walt, "Offshore Balancing or International Institutions? The Way Forward for US Foreign Policy," *Brown Journal of World Affairs* 14, no. 1 (Winter 2007).

28. Christopher Layne, *The Peace of Illusions: American Grand Strategy from 1940 to the Present* (Ithaca, NY: Cornell University Press, 2006), pp. 8, 25.

29. G. John Ikenberry, "Liberalism and Empire: Logics of Order in the American Unipolar Age," *Review of International Studies* 30, no. 4 (2004): p. 615. Emphasis added.

30. Rather than a nonimperialist understanding of US aggression in the case of Iraq, which could be explained solely as a result of the unilateral impulses of the Bush administration in the context of controlling weapons of mass destruction in the hands of "rogue" leaders.

31. For clear examples of this periodization, see Ikenberry, "America's Imperial Ambition"; Mallaby, "The Reluctant Imperialist."

32. Simon Bromley, "The Logic of American Power in the International Capitalist Order," in Alejandro Colás and Richard Saull, eds., *The War on Terrorism and the American "Empire" after the Cold War* (London: Routledge, 2006), p. 45.

33. Cox, "The Empire's Back in Town," pp. 16–17.

34. For an excellent account of the often-informal, indirect nature of the British empire, see John Gallagher and Ronald Robinson, "The Imperialism of Free Trade," *Economic History Review* 6, no. 1 (1953): pp. 1–25.

35. Alejandro Colás and Richard Saull, "Introduction: The War on Terror and the American Empire after the Cold War," in Colás and Saull, eds., *The War on Terrorism*, p. 2.

36. See, for example, Alexander J. Motyl, "Empire Falls," *Foreign Affairs* 85, no. 4 (July/August 2006).

37. For the clearest account in these terms, discussed later, see Robinson, *A Theory of Global Capitalism*.

CHAPTER ONE: US Hegemony and Global Energy Security

1. For an earlier formulation of this argument, see Doug Stokes, "The Heart of Empire?: Theorizing US Empire in an Era of Transnational Capitalism," *Third World Quarterly* 26, no. 2 (2005): pp. 227–46.

2. David Painter, "Explaining US Relations with the Third World," in *Diplomatic History* 19, no. 3 (1995): pp. 530–31.

3. George Kennan, *Foreign Relations of the United States, 1948,* report by the Policy Planning Staff (Washington, DC: General Printing Office, 1976), pp. 524–25.

4. For a good argument in this regard, see Andrew J. Bacevich, *American Empire: The Realities and Consequences of US Diplomacy* (Cambridge, MA: Harvard University Press, 2002), p. 4. For an interesting critical overview of international history during the Cold War, see Allen Hunter, ed., *Rethinking the Cold War* (Philadelphia, PA: Temple University Press, 1998).

5. NSC 68, "United States Objectives and Programs for National Security," A Report to the President Pursuant to the President's Directive of January 31, 1950, top secret, dated 14 April 1950, www.fas.org/. Emphasis added.

6. White House, *US National Security Strategy*, National Security Decision Directive 32, 20 May 1982, http://fas.org/.

7. See Gabriel Kolko, *The Politics of War: The World and United States Foreign Policy, 1943–1945* (New York: Pantheon, 1990). See also Walter LaFeber, *America, Russia and the Cold War, 1945–1980* (New York: Wiley & Sons, 1980); William Appleman Williams, *History as a Way of Learning* (New York: Norton, 1988).

8. Hull quote from R. T. Robertson, *The Making of the Modern World: An Introductory History* (London: Zed Books, 1986), p. 113.

9. The most extensive study of the Council on Foreign Relations and the Grand Area concept is Laurence H. Shoup and William Minter, *Imperial Brain Trust: The Council on Foreign Relations and United States Foreign Policy* (London: Monthly Review Press, 1977). See also Stephen Gill, *American Hegemony and the Trilateral Commission* (Cambridge: Cambridge University Press, 1990), and Jonathan Marshall, *To Have and Have Not: Southeast Asian Raw Materials and the Origins of the Pacific War* (Berkeley: University of California Press, 1995). For a more liberal analysis of the Grand Area strategy, see G. John Ikenberry, "The Myth of Post-Cold War Chaos," *Foreign Affairs* 75, no. 3 (1996): pp. 79–91.

10. For the classic account of the development of the open door system, see William Appleman Williams, *The Tragedy of American Diplomacy* (New York: Norton, 1988); Shoup and Minter, *Imperial Brain Trust*, pp. 117–77. See also Stephen Gill, "Pax Americana: Multilateralism and the Global Economic Order," in Anthony McGrew, *Empire* (Milton Keynes: Open University Press, 1994); Alejandro Colás, "Open Doors and Closed Frontiers: The Limits of American Empire," *European Journal of International Relations* 14, no. 4 (2008): pp. 619–43.

11. See Laurence H. Shoup and William Minter, "Shaping a New World Order: The Council on Foreign Relations; Blueprint for World Hegemony," in Holly Sklar, *Trilateralism: The Trilateral Commission and Elite Planning for World Management* (Boston: South End Press, 1980), pp. 135–56. See also William Robinson, *Promoting Polyarchy: Globalization, US Intervention and Hegemony* (Cambridge: Cambridge University Press, 1996), p. 15.

12. See Thomas G. Paterson, *Meeting the Communist Threat* (Oxford: Oxford University Press, 1999), pp.20–21, for more on this; on the role that the United States played in *politically* supporting the European empires, see William Roger Louis and Ronald Robinson, "The Imperialism of Decolonization," *Journal of Imperial and Commonwealth History* 22, no. 3 (1994): pp. 462–511.

13. G. John Ikenberry, "The Myth of Post–Cold War Chaos," in *American Foreign Policy: Theoretical Essays* (New York: Longman, 1999), p. 618. Ikenberry's is a curious take on the postwar order, insofar as it posits an equality of power amongst western states in constructing the postwar system. See George Monbiot's *Manifesto for a New World Order* (New York: New Press, 2004) for an excellent history of the Bretton Woods negotiations and the disparities of power between Britain and the United States, the principal architects of the liberal postwar order.

14. "Current Issues of European Security," National Security Study Memorandum 83, 12 August 1970. Cited in Christopher Layne, *The Peace of Illusions: American Grand Strategy from 1940 to the Present* (London: Cornell University Press, 2006), p. 107.

15. David Harvey, *A Brief History of Neoliberalism* (Oxford: Oxford University Press, 2005).

16. Kissinger quoted in Seymour M. Hersh, *The Price of Power: Kissinger in the Nixon White House* (London: Simon & Schuster, 1983), p. 636.

17. Joseph E. Stiglitz, *Globalization and Its Discontents* (London: Penguin, 2002), p. 9.

18. Alongside this process of integration, most academic studies tended to uncritically trumpet globalization as freeing humanity from material want. See, for example, Thomas Friedman, *The Lexus and the Olive Tree: Understanding Globalization* (New York: Farrar, Straus & Giroux, 2000). However, a number of more critically inclined scholars instead began to question the presumed normative value in the extension of capitalist social relations. Many of these authors sought to examine globalization as part of the longer-term process of the steady spread of capitalism throughout the globe. For an excellent, critical overview on the long history of capitalist internationalization and the role of American power, see Immanuel Wallerstein, *The Decline of American Power: The US in a Chaotic World* (London: Norton, 2003). For a good introduction to current world systems analysis and its relevance to future world conflict, see Volker Bornschier and Chris Chase-Dunn, eds., *The Future of Global Conflict* (London: Sage, 1999).

19. Principal Deputy Undersecretary of Defense, "FY 94–99 Defense Planning Guidance Sections for Comment," 18 February 1992, www.gwu.edu/.

20. William Burr, "'Prevent the Reemergence of a New Rival': The Making of the Cheney Regional Defense Strategy, 1991–1992," National Security Archive, George Washington University, 26 February 2008, www.gwu.edu/.

21. James Mann, "The True Rationale? It's a Decade Old," *Washington Post,* 7 March 2004. Emphasis added.

22. Dick Cheney, *Defense Strategy for the 1990s: The Regional Defense Strategy,* January 1993, pp. 1–3, www.gwu.edu/.

23. See, for instance, Samuel P. Huntington, "Why International Primacy Matters," *International Security* 17, no. 4 (Spring 1993): p. 83; Zbigniew Brzezinski, *The Grand Chessboard: American Primacy and Its Geostrategic Imperatives* (New York: Basic Books, 1997), p. 40.

24. Office of the Press Secretary, White House, "President Delivers State of the Union Address," 29 January 2002, http://georgewbush-whitehouse.archives.gov/.

25. Peter Gowan, "The Bush Turn and the Drive for Primacy," in Alejandro Colás and Richard Saull, eds., *The War on Terrorism and the American "Empire" after the Cold War* (London: Routledge, 2006), pp. 132–33. Emphasis added.

26. See, notably, the spurious connection made by US planners between Saddam Hussein and al Qaeda, repeated by President Bush himself at numerous occasions in the buildup to the invasion. This, of course, ensured that Saddam's regime was indelibly linked to 9/11 in the minds of most Americans, thus building substantial support for the invasion. See, for example, White House, "President Bush Outlines Iraqi Threat," Remarks by the President on Iraq, Cincinnati Museum Center—Cincinnati Union Terminal, 7 October 2002, and White House, "President Discusses Beginning of Operation Iraqi Freedom," 22 March 2003, both at http://georgewbush-whitehouse.archives.gov/.

27. Rice cited in Nicholas Lemann, "The Next World Order," *New Yorker,* 1 April 2002.

28. On this aspect of the *NSS*, see Jeffrey Record, "The Bush Doctrine and Iraq," *Parameters* (Spring 2003): pp. 4–21; Philip H. Gordon, "The Bush Doctrine," *Commentary Magazine* 1 December 2006, www.brookings.edu/.

29. Accordingly, the *NSS* stated that: "For centuries international law recognized that nations need not suffer an attack before they can lawfully take action to defend themselves . . . Legal scholars and international jurists often conditioned the legitimacy of pre-emption on the existence of an imminent threat—most often a visible mobilization of . . . forces preparing to attack. *We must adapt the concept of imminent threat* to the capabilities and objectives of today's adversaries." White House, *National Security Strategy of the United States*, 2002, p. 15, http://georgewbush-whitehouse .archives.gov/. Emphasis added.

30. Ibid., p. 30. Emphasis added.

31. US Department of Defense, *Quadrennial Defense Review Report*, 6 February 2006, p. 30, www.defenselink.mil/.

32. US Department of Defense, *National Defense Strategy*, June 2008, pp. 2–3, www .defenselink.mil/. Emphasis added.

33. Data from Petter Stålenheim, Catalina Perdomo, and Elisabeth Sköns, "Military Expenditure," *SIPRI Yearbook 2008: Armaments, Disarmament and International Security*, http://yearbook2008.sipri.org/.

34. US Department of Defense, *Quadrennial Defense Review Report*, 6 February 2006, p. 9.

35. Paul Reynolds, "US Deploying for Quicker Action," *BBC News*, 16 August 2004, http://news.bbc.co.uk/.

36. Admiral Vern Clark, US Navy, "Sea Power 21: Projecting Decisive Joint Capabilities," *Proceedings*, October 2002, and US Navy, *Naval Power 21 . . . A Naval Vision*, October 2002, pp. 1, 6, both at www.navy.mil/.

37. Jim Garamone, "Joint Vision 2020 Emphasizes Full Spectrum Dominance," *American Forces Press Service*, 2 June 2000, and Navy Warfare Development Command, US Navy, *Sea Power 21*, both at www.nwdc.navy.mil/. Emphasis added.

38. "Remarks of Senator Barack Obama to the Chicago Council on Global Affairs," 23 April 2007, www.cfr.org/.

39. "Gates Optimistic on 2010 US Defense Budget Success," *Reuters*, 3 May 2009. For comparison, see Office of the Assistant Secretary of Defense (Public Affairs), US Department of Defense, "Fiscal Year 2009 Department of Defense Budget Released," 4 February 2008, www.defenselink.mil/.

40. US Department of Defense, *Fiscal Year 2010 Budget Request: Summary Justification*, May 2009, p. 1–1, www.defenselink.mil/.

41. Geir Lundestad, "Empire by Invitation in the American Century," in Michael J. Hogan, ed., *The Ambiguous Legacy: US Foreign Relations in the "American Century"* (Cambridge: Cambridge University Press, 1999), pp. 52–91. See also his more recent *The United States and Western Europe since 1945* (Oxford: Oxford University Press, 2005).

42. Leo Panitch and Sam Gindin, *Global Capitalism and American Empire* (London: Merlin Press, 2003), p. 21.

43. Susanne Soederberg, "The War on Terrorism and American Empire: Emerging Development Agendas," in Colás and Saull, eds., *The War on Terrorism*, p. 157.

44. David Harvey, *The New Imperialism* (Oxford: Oxford University Press, 2003), pp. 38–39.

45. Dani Rodrick, "One Economics, Many Recipes: Globalization, Institutions and Economy Growth," Transcript of a Book Forum, International Monetary Fund, 29 November 2007, www.imf.org/.

46. John Williamson, "The Washington Consensus as Policy Prescription for Development," World Bank, 13 January 2004, www.iie.com/.

47. Even at the moment of greatest crisis in the neoliberal system during the end of 2008, the outgoing President Bush was clear that "this is a decisive moment for the global economy. In the wake of the financial crisis, voices from the left and right are equating the free enterprise system with greed and exploitation and failure. It's true this crisis included failures . . . But the crisis was not a failure of the free market system. And the answer is not to try to reinvent that system. It is to fix the problems we face, make the reforms we need, and move forward with the free market principles that have delivered prosperity and hope to people all across the globe." Office of the Press Secretary, White House, "President Bush Discusses Financial Markets and World Economy," 13 November 2008, http://georgewbush-whitehouse.archives.gov/.

48. Harvey, *The New Imperialism*, p. 145.

49. United Nations Conference on Trade and Development, *Trade and Development Report, 1997* (New York: United Nations, 1997), pp. 65–66.

50. Oxfam International, "Signing Away the Future: How Trade and Investment Agreements between Rich and Poor Countries Undermine Development," Oxfam Briefing Paper 101, March 2007, www.oxfam.org/.

51. United Nations Economic and Social Council, *The Right to Food: Mission to Guatemala*, E/CN.4/2006/44/Add.1, 18 January 2006, Para. 55, p. 20, www.righttofood .org/.

52. Structural Adjustment Participatory Review International Network, *The Policy Roots of Economic Crisis and Poverty: A Multi-Country Study Participatory Assessment of Structural Adjustment* (Washington, DC: SAPRIN, 2002), p. 188.

53. Colin L. Powell, "Remarks to African Growth and Opportunity Act Forum," 29 October 2001, www.state.gov/.

54. John Bellamy Foster, "The New Age of Imperialism," *Monthly Review* 55, no. 3 (2003): p. 13. For a good summary of various different Marxist theories of imperialism, see Anthony Brewer, *Marxist Theories of Imperialism: A Critical Survey* (London: Routledge, 1980).

55. William Robinson, *A Theory of Global Capitalism: Production, Class and State in a Transnational World* (Baltimore, MD: Johns Hopkins University Press, 2004), p. 140.

56. For a selection, see Leslie Sklair, *The Transnational Capitalist Class* (Oxford: Blackwell, 2001); Kees van der Pijl, *Transnational Classes and International Relations* (London: Routledge 1998); Stephen Gill, *Power and Resistance in the New World Order* (London: Palgrave Macmillan, 2003); Richard P. AppelBaum and William I. Robinson, eds., *Critical Globalization Studies* (New York: Routledge, 2005).

57. Michael Hardt and Antonio Negri, *Empire* (Cambridge, MA: Harvard University Press, 2001), pp. 9–10. For a series of penetrating critiques of Hardt and Negri's *Empire*, see Gopal Balakrishnan, ed., *Debating Empire* (London: Verso, 2003).

58. Sklair, *The Transnational Capitalist Class*, pp. 3, 31.

59. William Robinson, "Capitalist Globalization and the Transnationalization of the State," in Mark Rupert and Hazel Smith, *Historical Materialism and Globalization* (London: Routledge, 2002), pp. 215–25.

60. For a similar formulation of the two distinct logics driving US imperialism, see Harvey, *The New Imperialism*, p. 30.

61. *Annual Report to the President and the Congress*, www.dod.mil/.

62. US Department of Defense, *National Defense Strategy*, June 2008.

63. Robinson, *A Theory of Global Capitalism*, p. 140. Emphasis added.

64. Both quotes cited in Bacevich, *American Empire*, pp. 38–40.

65. "Trade Agreements Work for America," Office of the United States Trade Representative, July 2006; "Opening Markets for Growth: The US FTA Agenda," Office of the United States Trade Representative, June 2006; "Trade Delivers Growth, Jobs, Prosperity and Security at Home," Office of the United States Trade Representative, February 2008. All found at: www.ustr.gov/.

66. US Code, Title 19, Section 2411 (19 U.S.C. 2411), "Actions by the United States Trade Representative," www4.law.cornell.edu/.

67. Peter Gowan, "Contemporary Intra-Core Relations and World Systems Theory," *Journal of World System Research* 10, no. 2 (2004): p. 477, http://jwsr.ucr.edu/.

68. Philippa Thomas, "Will US Stimulus Trigger a Trade War?" *BBC News*, 4 February 2009, http://news.bbc.co.uk/.

69. Perry Anderson, "Force and Consent," *New Left Review* 17 (September/October 2002), www.newleftreview.net/. See also Peter Gowan, "Triumphing toward International Disaster: The Impasse in American Grand Strategy," *Critical Asian Studies* 36, no. 1 (2004), www.bcasnet.org/.

70. Simon Bromley, "The Logic of American Power in the International Capitalist Order," in Colás and Saull, eds., *The War on Terrorism*, p. 49.

71. Energy Information Administration (EIA), *Annual Energy Outlook 2008, with Projections for 2030*, June 2008, Table A2, pp. 118–19, www.eia.doe.gov/; EIA, *International Energy Outlook 2008*, September 2008, p. 7, www.eia.doe.gov/; EIA, *World Petroleum Consumption, Most Recent Annual Estimates, 1980–2007*, 7 October 2008 update, www.eia.doe.gov/.

72. In 2006, net imports were 12.4 mbpd out of total consumption of 20.7 mbpd. For forecasts over increased levels of imports, see National Energy Policy Development Group, *National Energy Policy*, May 2001, p. 8-3, www.whitehouse.gov/; US Department of Energy, *Strategic Plan*, 2006, p. 9, www.energy.gov/.

73. "California Declares State of Emergency," *BBC News*, 18 January 2001, http://news.bbc.co.uk/.

74. National Energy Policy Development Group, *National Energy Policy*, May 2001, p. viii.

75. Office of the Press Secretary, White House, "Remarks by the President and Energy Secretary Spencer Abraham in Swearing-in Ceremony," 2 March 2001, www.whitehouse.gov/.

76. National Energy Policy Development Group, *National Energy Policy*, May 2001, p. viii.

77. "Remarks by US Secretary of Energy Spencer Abraham, US Chamber of Commerce, National Energy Summit," 19 March 2001, www.usembassy.it/.

78. "The Energy Plan: Excerpts from Bush's Speech Outlining a New Energy Policy," *New York Times*, 18 May 2001.

79. Michael Klare, "Bush-Cheney Energy Strategy: Procuring the Rest of the World's Oil," *FPIF-PetroPolitics Special Report*, January 2004, www.fpif.org/; National Energy Policy Development Group, *National Energy Policy*, May 2001, pp. 8-3.

80. Barack Obama, "Remarks by the President on National Fuel Efficiency Standards," Office of the Press Secretary, White House, 19 May 2009, www.whitehouse.gov/.

81. "Obama Announces Plans to Achieve Energy Independence," *Washington Post*, 26 January 2009.

82. Office of the Press Secretary, White House, "President Obama Announces Steps to Support Sustainable Energy Options," 5 May 2009, www.whitehouse.gov/.

83. US Department of Defense, *Transforming the Way DoD Looks at Energy: An Approach to Establishing an Energy Strategy*, Report FT602T1 (Washington, DC: NDCF, April 2007).

84. Milton R. Copulos, president, National Defense Council Foundation, "The Hidden Cost of Oil," testimony before the Senate Committee on Foreign Relations, 30 March 2006, http://foreign.senate.gov/; Bryan Bender, "Pentagon Study Says Oil Reliance Strains Military, Urges Development of Alternative Fuels," *Boston Globe*, 1 May 2007. See also National Defense Council Foundation, *America's Achilles Heel: The Hidden Costs of Imported Oil* (Washington, DC: NDCF, October 2003).

85. In this light, the defense secretary established an Energy Security Task Force in May 2006, tasked with defining "an actionable investment roadmap for lowering DoD's fossil fuel requirements," with this objective written into subsequent strategy documents as the Pentagon seeks to reduce its reliance on oil. US Department of Defense, "DoD Energy Security Task Force," undated, www.dod.mil/; US Department of Defense, *National Defense Strategy*, June 2008, p. 16.

86. Schlesinger cited in Michael T. Klare, *Rising Powers, Shrinking Planet: The New Geopolitics of Energy* (New York: Metropolitan Books, 2008), p. 29. Emphasis added.

87. Zbigniew Brzezinski, "Hegemonic Quicksand," *National Interest* 74 (Winter 2003/04): p. 8. For an extended discussion, see his *The Choice: Global Domination or Global Leadership* (New York: Basic Books, 2004). For further arguments of the geopolitical dimension of US control over the Persian Gulf, see Harvey, *The New Imperialism*, pp. 77, 198–99; Simon Bromley, "The United States and the Control of World Oil," *Government and Opposition* 40, no. 2 (Spring 2005): pp. 226–28.

88. National Energy Policy Development Group, *National Energy Policy*, May 2001, p. 8-4.

89. David S. Painter, *Oil and the American Century* (Baltimore, MD: Johns Hopkins University Press, 1986), p. 1.

90. National Energy Policy Development Group, *National Energy Policy*, May 2001, pp. 8-5–8-6.

91. General Charles Wald, Deputy Commander, EUCOM, April 2004, www.aei.org/.

92. National Petroleum Council, *Hard Truths: Facing the Hard Truths about Energy* (Washington, DC: National Petroleum Council: Washington, 2007), p. 6.

93. John Deutch and James R. Schlesinger, *National Security Consequences of US Oil Dependency*, Council on Foreign Relations, Independent Task Force Report No. 58, 2006, p. 5, www.cfr.org/.

94. National Energy Policy Development Group, *National Energy Policy*, May 2001, p. 8-3. Emphasis added.

95. International Monetary Fund, *World Economic Outlook: Financial Systems and Economic Cycles*, September 2006, p. 38, www.imf.org/.

96. James A. Baker III Institute for Public Policy, *The Changing Role of National Oil Companies in International Energy Markets*, Baker Institute Policy Report No. 35, April 2007, p. 17, www.rice.edu/.

97. See, for example, Pratap Chatterjee, *Halliburton's Army: How a Well-Connected Texas Oil Company Revolutionized the Way America Makes War* (New York: Nation Books, 2009). For a more detailed exposition of this analysis in relation to Iraq, see chapter 3.

98. Which are, respectively, the third and ninth most oil-rich countries in the world and which together are known to own around 180 billion barrels, or 15% of total world reserves. BP, *BP Statistical Review of World Energy,* June 2008, p. 6, www.bp .com/.

99. For background, see Kenneth Katzman, *The Iran-Libya Sanctions Act (ILSA),* CRS Report RS20871, 3 April 2006 update, http://fpc.state.gov/.

100. Unless otherwise stated, all data in this section are drawn from the authoritative Energy Information Administration, *International Energy Outlook 2008.*

101. Klare, *Rising Powers, Shrinking Planet.*

102. George Monbiot, "At Last, a Date," *The Guardian,* 15 December 2008.

103. Klare, *Rising Powers, Shrinking Planet,* p. 30.

104. Michael T. Klare, *Blood and Oil: How America's Thirst for Petrol Is Killing Us* (London: Penguin, 2004), p. 7.

105. Erica Downs, *China's Quest for Energy Security* (Santa Monica, CA: RAND, 2000), p. 45.

106. US Department of Defense, *National Defense Strategy,* June 2008, p. 3.

107. White House, *The National Security Strategy of the United States of America,* March 2006, p. 41, http://georgewbush-whitehouse.archives.gov/.

108. David E. Sanger, "China's Oil Needs Are High on US Agenda," *New York Times,* 19 April 2006. Emphasis added.

109. Office of the Press Secretary, White House, "Statement on Bilateral Meeting with President Hu of China," 1 April 2009, www.whitehouse.gov/.

CHAPTER TWO: Counterinsurgency and the Stabilization of Order

1. Simon Bromley, "The United States and the Control of World Oil," *Government and Opposition* 40, no. 2 (Spring 2005): pp. 226–28.

2. Joseph Stiglitz, "Foreword," in Svetlana Tsalik, *Caspian Oil Windfalls: Who Will Benefit?* Caspian Revenue Watch, Open Society Institute, 2003, http://archive.revenue watch.org/.

3. "Secretary Rumsfeld Remarks at Roundtable during the Central American Ministerial in Miami, Fl.," 12 October 2005, www.defenselink.mil/. Emphasis added.

4. Admiral James G. Stavridis, *The Posture Statement of United States Southern Command before the 110th Congress,* 21–22 March 2007, www.southcom.mil/.

5. US Department of Defense, *Fiscal Year 2010 Budget Request: Summary Justification,* May 2009, p. 1-2, www.defenselink.mil/.

6. "Political Implications of Afro-Asian Military Takeovers," May 1959, Policy Subseries, NSC series, Box 19, quoted in David F. Schmitz, *Thank God They're On Our Side: The United States and Right-Wing Dictatorships, 1921–1965* (Chapel Hill: University of North Carolina Press, 1999), p. 15.

7. George Kennan, quoted in Schmitz, *Thank God They're On Our Side,* p. 149.

8. Jeane J. Kirkpatrick, "Dictatorship and Double Standards," *Commentary,* November 1979, p. 44. Emphasis added.

9. Office of the Press Secretary, White House, "President Bush and President Mush-arraf of Pakistan Discuss Strengthened Relationship," 4 March 2006, http://georgewbush -whitehouse.archives.gov/.

10. William I. Robinson, *Promoting Polyarchy: Globalization, US Intervention and Hegemony* (Cambridge: Cambridge University Press, 1996).

11. Patterson quote from Michael McClintock, *The American Connection: State Terror and Popular Resistance in El Salvador* (London: Zed Books, 1985), pp. 8–9.

12. US State Department, *Congressional Budget Justification for Foreign Operations*, FY 2004, p. 151, 161, www.state.gov/.

13. Indeed, pursuing interoperability is one of the stated "strategic principles" for US military assistance and runs throughout most programs to the South. See Director of US Foreign Assistance, *Congressional Budget Justification for Foreign Operations*, FY 2008, p. 3, www.state.gov/.

14. US Department of Defense, "Transformation and Security Cooperation," remarks by Undersecretary of Defense for Policy Douglas J. Feith, ComDef 2004 Conference National Press Club, Washington, DC, 8 September 2004.

15. "Statement by General Charles R. Holland, Commander in Chief, United States Special Operations Command, before the Senate Armed Services Committee, Emerging Threats and Capabilities Subcommittee," 12 March 2002, www.globalsecurity.org/. Emphasis added.

16. Amnesty International, "Unmatched Power, Unmet Principles: The Human Rights Dimensions of US Training of Foreign Military and Police Forces," www.amnes tyusa.org/.

17. Rachel Stohl, "Questionable Reward: Arms Sales and the War on Terrorism," *Arms Control Today* 38, no. 1 (January/February 2008). For further data on recent arms deliveries, see Richard F. Grimmett, *Conventional Arms Transfers to Developing Nations, 1999–2006*, CRS Report for Congress, RL34187, 26 September 2007, www.fas .org/.

18. US Department of Defense, Security Cooperation Agency, *Foreign Military Sales, Foreign Military Construction Sales and Other Security Cooperation Historical Facts*, 30 September 2007 update, www.dsca.mil/.

19. See, for instance, George Withers, Adam Isacson, Lisa Haugaard, Joy Olson, and Joel Fyke, *Ready, Aim, Foreign Policy: How the Pentagon's Role in Foreign Policy Is Growing, and Why Congress—and the American Public—Should Be Worried*, March 2008, http:// justf.org/. For more on the unaccountable nature of much of the US training effort, see Ruth Blakeley, "Still Training to Torture?: US Training of Military Forces from Latin America," *Third World Quarterly* 27, no. 8 (2006).

20. US Department of Defense, *Fiscal Year 2009 Budget Request: Summary Justification*, 4 February 2008, pp. 102–3, www.defenselink.mil.

21. Robert Gates, remarks delivered at the Association of the United States Army, 10 October 2007, www.defenselink.mil/.

22. US Department of State, *Congressional Budget Justification for Foreign Operations*, FY 2010, p. 89.

23. For the declassified record on the Guatemalan coup, see Kate Doyle and Peter Kornbluh, "CIA and Assassinations: The Guatemala 1954 Documents," National Security Archive Electronic Briefing Book No. 4, www.gwu.edu/. On Chile, see Peter Kornbluh, "Chile and the United States: Declassified Documents Relating to the Military

Coup, September 11, 1973," National Security Archive Electronic Briefing Book No. 8, www.gwu.edu/. On Nicaragua, see Dianna Melrose, *Nicaragua: The Threat of a Good Example?* (Oxford: Oxfam Public Affairs Unit, 1985); Holly Sklar, *Washington's War on Nicaragua* (Cambridge, MA: South End Press, 1988). For a reading of the extensive record of US intervention in the South through coups by pro-Washington elements of the military, see Stephen Kinzer, *Overthrow: America's Century of Regime Change from Hawaii to Iraq* (New York: Times Books, 2006); Schmitz, *Thank God They're On Our Side;* Gabriel Kolko, *The Politics of War: The World and United States Foreign Policy, 1943–1945* (New York: Pantheon, 1990); Conn Hallinan, "Backyard Bully?" Americas Program (Silver City, NM: Interhemispheric Resource Center, September 12, 2002). On recent alleged US-backed coups, see "Aristide Says US Deposed Him in 'Coup d'Etat,'" *CNN News*, 1 March 2004, www.cnn.com/; Duncan Campbell, "American Navy 'Helped Venezuelan Coup," *The Guardian*, 29 April 2002.

24. National Security Action Memorandum No. 124, 18 January 1962, found in *Foreign Relations of the United States, 1961–1963*, vol. 2: *Vietnam, 1962*, document number 26, www.state.gov/.

25. *Foreign Assistance Act*, 1961, Chapter 22, Title 32, Section 501. Emphasis added.

26. Cited in Michael T. Klare and Peter Kornbluh, "The New Interventionism: Low-Intensity Warfare in the 1980s and Beyond," in Michael T. Klare and Peter Kornbluh, eds., *Low-Intensity Warfare: How the USA Fights Wars without Declaring Them* (London: Methuen, 1989), pp. 11–12.

27. Cited in Blakeley, "Still Training to Torture?" p. 1440.

28. On the development of US counterinsurgency and its use more generally in the Cold War, see D. Michael Shafer, *Deadly Paradigms: The Failure of US Counterinsurgency Policy* (New Jersey: Princeton University Press, 1988).

29. Dana Priest, "US Military Trains Foreign Troops," *Washington Post*, 12 July 1998.

30. Lora Lumpe, "Foreign Military Training: Global Reach, Global Power, and Oversight Issues," *Foreign Policy in Focus*, May 2002, p. 16. Emphasis added.

31. US Special Operations Command, *Posture Statement 2007*, USSOCOM, www.fas.org.

32. US Department of Defense, *National Defense Strategy*, June 2008, www.defenselink.mil/. See also US Department of the Army, *Stability Operations*, FM 3-07, October 2008, pp. 6–14, http://usacac.army.mil.

33. US Department of Defense, "Secretary of Defense Gates Interview with Judy Woodruff, The News Hour with Jim Lehrer," news transcript, 7 April 2009, www.defenselink.mil/.

34. US Department of the Army, "Foreword," *Counterinsurgency*, FM 3-24, December 2006, http://usacac.army.mil/.

35. US Government, *Counterinsurgency Guide*, Bureau of Political-Military Affairs, US Department of State, January 2009, www.state.gov/. Emphasis in original.

36. US Department of the Army, *Stability Operations—Intelligence*, FM 30-21, 1970, pp. 43, 73–74, http://usacac.army.mil.

37. Ibid., p. 78 and Appendix E.

38. US Department of the Army, *Counterinsurgency Operations*, FMI 3-07.22, October 2004, pp. E1–E5, http://usacac.army.mil.

39. US Department of the Army, *Psychological Operations*, FM33-5, 1962, pp. 115–16, 125, http://usacac.army.mil.

40. US Department of the Army, *US Army Counterinsurgency Forces*. FM31-22, 1963, pp. 106–7, http://usacac.army.mil.

41. US Department of the Army, *Stability Operations—Intelligence*, FM 30-21, 1970, p. 77.

42. US Department of Defense, *Doctrine for Joint Psychological Operations*, JP 3-53, pp. VI-8–VI-10, www.fas.org/. Emphasis added.

43. "Army's Insurgent Manual Author Speaks," November 17. 2004, www .defensetech.org/.

44. US Department of the Army, *Psychological Operations*, FM33-5, 1962, pp. 115–16.

45. Central Intelligence Agency, *Human Resource Exploitation Training Manual*, 1983, www.gwu.edu/. For background, see Dana Priest, "U.S. Instructed Latins on Executions, Torture," *Washington Post*, September 21, 1996.

46. US Department of the Army, *US Army Handbook of Counterinsurgency Guidelines for Area Commanders: An Analysis of Criteria*, No. 550-100, 1966, p.225. Although "genocide" was not "an alternative" to "selective counter-terror," genocide was indeed practiced by the Guatemalan military during the early 1980s.

47. FM 31-15, *US Army Field Manual: Operations against Irregular Forces*, May 1961, p.47, http://handle.dtic.mil/100.2/ADA310713.

48. Ruth Blakeley, "Why Torture?" *Review of International Studies* 33, no. 3 (2007): pp. 373–94.

49. Jay Bybee, "Memorandum for Alberto R. Gonzales, Counsel to the President. Re: Standards of Conduct for Interrogation under 18 USC 2340-2340A (US Department of Justice, Office of Legal Counsel)," in Karen Greenberg and Joshua Dratel, eds., *The Torture Papers: The Road to Abu Ghraib* (Cambridge: Cambridge University Press, 2002), pp.172–214.

50. Office of the Vice President, White House, "Interview of the Vice President by Scott Hennen, WDAY at Radio Day at the White House," 24 October 2006, www .whitehouse.gov/.

51. Richard Cheney, "The Vice President Appears on Meet the Press with Tim Russert," 16 September 2001, www.whitehouse.gov/.

52. "Obama Publishes 'Torture' Memos," *BBC News*, 16 April 2009, http://news.bbc .co.uk/1/.

53. US Department of Defense, US Army School of the Americas, *Manejo de Fuente*, p.66, translated by the National Security Archive and accessed at www.gwu.edu/.

54. Ibid., p.65.

55. US Department of the Army, *US Army Counterinsurgency Forces*, FM31-22, 1963, p. 84.

56. Ibid., p.99.

57. US Department of Defense, *Joint Tactics, Techniques, and Procedures for Foreign Internal Defense (FID)*, JP 3-07.1, 30 April 2004, pp. V-4, V-31, www.fas.org/.

58. Sec. 1208(a), *Ronald W. Reagan National Defense Authorization Act for Fiscal Year 2005*, P.L. 108-375, 28 October 2004, www.dod.mil/.

59. Anthony H. Cordesman and Khalid R. Al-Rodhan, *The Changing Risks in Global Oil Supply and Demand: Crisis or Evolving Solutions?* (Washington, DC: CSIS, 2005), p. 8, www.csis.org/.

60. Daniel Moran and James A. Russell, "The Militarization of Energy Security," *Strategic Insights* 7, no. 1 (February 2008).

61. Mark Trumbull, "Risks of Rising Oil Nationalism: Governments May Focus Much of Their Oil Wealth on Other Priorities, Causing Oil-Field Efficiency and Investment to Suffer," *Christian Science Monitor,* 3 April 2007. Emphasis added.

62. National Petroleum Council, *Hard Truths: Facing the Hard Truths about Energy* (Washington, DC: National Petroleum Council, 2007), pp. 219–20.

63. Council on Foreign Relations, *Strategic Energy Policy: Challenges for the 21st Century,* April 2001, www.bakerinstitute.org/. Emphasis added.

64. Edward L. Morse and Amy Myers Jaffe, "OPEC in Confrontation with Globalization," in Jan H. Kalicki and David L. Goldwyn, *Energy Security: Toward a New Foreign Policy* (Washington: Woodrow Wilson Center Press, 2005), p. 65.

65. Statement of John R. Brodman, Deputy Assistant Secretary for International Energy Policy, Office of Policy and International Affairs, US Department of Energy, before the Subcommittee on International Economic Policy, Export and Trade Promotion, Senate Committee on Foreign Relations, 15 July 2004, www.senate.gov/. For a similar argument of the need to intervene to guarantee stability, see the comments by David Gordon (senior CIA official) at a meeting organized by the Corporate Council on Africa. Julian Borger, "Oil and Terrorism Drive the US Presidential Tour," *The Guardian,* 7 July 2003.

66. White House, *National Strategy for Maritime Security,* September 2005, p. 11, http://georgewbush-whitehouse.archives.gov.

67. Donna Miles, "US Increasing Operations in Gulf of Guinea," *American Forces Press Service,* 5 July 2006, www.news.navy.mil/.

68. US Southern Command, "Fact Sheet: Forward Operating Locations," 8 June 2009, www.southcom.mil/; Sandra Edwards, "The US Forward Operating Location in Manta: The Ecuadorian Perspective," Washington Office on Latin America, 30 March 2007, p. 6, www.wola.org/.

69. See, for example, Eric Schmitt, "Threats and Responses: Expanding US Presence; Pentagon Seeking New Access Pacts for Africa Bases," *New York Times,* 5 July 2003; Svante E. Cornell, "The United States and Central Asia: In the Steppes to Stay?" *Cambridge Review of International Affairs* 17, no. 2 (July 2004): pp. 239–40.

70. Statement of General Bantz J. Craddock, Commander, United States European Command, before the House Armed Services Committee, 13 March 2008, www.eucom.mil/; Donna Miles, "Craddock: Security Cooperation Critical to Promoting Stability, Countering Terror," *Armed Forces Press Service,* 17 May 2007, www.defenselink.mil/.

71. P. W. Singer, *Corporate Warriors: The Rise of the Privatized Military Industry* (Ithaca: Cornell University Press, 2003), pp. 80–81.

72. Joanna Spear, "Market Forces: The Political Economy of Private Military Companies," Fafo Report 531, p. 8, www.fafo.no/; War on Want, "Corporate Mercenaries: The Threat of Private Military and Security Companies," p. 5, www.waronwant.org/; "The Impact of Mercenary Activities on the Right of Peoples to Self-Determination," Human Rights Fact Sheet No. 28, Office of the United Nations High Commissioner for Human Rights (Geneva: UNHCHR, 2002), p. 10,www.unhcr.org/.

73. For example, Angola has sold mining concessions in areas controlled by UNITA, thus bringing PMCs directly into the counterinsurgency campaign. Singer, *Corporate Warriors,* pp. 167–68.

74. "Critical Infrastructure Protection," Presidential Decision Directive 63, 22 May 1998, www.fas.org/. This was superseded after 9/11 by "Critical Infrastructure Identification, Prioritization and Protection," Homeland Security Presidential Directive 7, 17 December 2003, http://georgewbush-whitehouse.archives.gov/.

75. "International Critical Infrastructure Protection (CIP) Team," US Department of State, www.state.gov/.

76. "Saudis 'Foil Oil Facility Attack,'" *BBC News*, 24 February 2006, http://news.bbc.co.uk/.

77. US Department of State, *Global Critical Energy Infrastructure Protection Strategy*, US Department of State (Washington DC, 2006), www.state.gov/. Understandably, the initial focus of this strategy is on the largest of the Persian Gulf facilities, processing more than 1 mbpd and of crucial importance to the stability of global oil markets. See Alex Schindelar, "US Offers Data, Expertise to Protect Mideast Oil Facilities," *Oil Daily*, 15 November 2006.

78. Warren Christopher and William J. Perry, "NATO's True Mission," *New York Times*, 21 October 1997. Emphasis added.

79. "The Protection of Critical Infrastructures," Committee Report, 162 CDS 07 E rev 1, NATO Parliamentary Assembly, 2007, www.nato-pa.int/. Emphasis added. See also Ian Traynor, "Climate Change May Spark Conflict with Russia, EU Told: Alert over Scramble for Control of Energy Resources in the Arctic," *The Guardian*, 10 March 2008.

80. Center for International Policy's Colombia Program, Media Roundtable, 29 September 2002, http://ciponline.org/.

81. Quoted in Michael Walker, "Oil and US policy toward Colombia," *Colombia Journal*, 7 January 2008, www.colombiajournal.org/.

82. John Ruggie, *Interim Report of the Special Representative of the Secretary-General on the Issue of Human Rights and Transnational Corporations and Other Business Enterprises*, U.N. Doc. E/CN.4/2006/97 (2006), February 2006, www1.umn.edu/.

83. "Privatisation of Security and Warfare and Impacts on Human Rights," seminar co-hosted by the Business and Human Rights Resource Centre and the United Nations Working Group on the use of mercenaries as a means of violating human rights and impeding the exercise of the rights of peoples to self-determination, Geneva, 21 March 2007.

84. See, for instance, Human Rights Watch, *The Price of Oil: Corporate Responsibility and Human Rights Violations in Nigeria's Oil Producing Communities*, January 1999, www.hrw.org/.

CHAPTER THREE: The Persian Gulf and Beyond

1. Current Middle Eastern proven reserves stand at 755 billion barrels, out of total proven world reserves of 1,238 billion barrels. See British Petroleum, *BP Statistical Review of World Energy*, June 2008, p. 6, www.bp.com/. Current and forecast production figures and proportions from Energy Information Administration, *Country Analysis Briefs: Persian Gulf Region*, June 2007 update, www.eia.doe.gov/.

2. National Energy Policy Development Group, *National Energy Policy*, May 2001, pp. 8-4–8-5, http://georgewbush-whitehouse.archives.gov/.

3. Saudi reserves are currently calculated to be 264 billion barrels, or 21% of total world reserves. BP, *BP Statistical Review of World Energy*, June 2008, p. 6.

4. Bradley L. Bowman, "After Iraq: Future US Military Posture in the Middle East," *Washington Quarterly* 31, no. 2 (Spring 2008): pp. 78–79.

5. See, for instance, Edward J. Marolda, "The United States Navy and the Persian Gulf," Naval Historical Center, 15 May 1991, www.history.navy.mil/.

6. Cited in Christopher Layne, *The Peace of Illusions: American Grand Strategy from 1940 to the Present* (Ithaca, NY: Cornell University Press, 2006), pp. 47–48.

7. Cited in Geoffrey Warner, "The Truman Doctrine and the Marshall Plan," *International Affairs* 50, no. 1 (January 1974): p. 85.

8. Stephen Eke, "Putin in First Saudi State Visit," *BBC News*, 11 February 2007, and " 'New Era' for Saudi-Indian Ties," *BBC News*, 27 January 2006, both at http://news.bbc .co.uk/.

9. International Monetary Fund, *World Economic Outlook: Financial Systems and Economic Cycles*, September 2006, p. 38, www.imf.org/.

10. National Security Council, "United States Objectives and Policies with Respect to the Near East," statement of policy, top secret, NSC 155/1, 14 July 1953. Reprinted as document no. 145 in US Department of State, *Foreign Relations of the United States*, vol. 9 (Washington, DC: US Department of State, 1952–54), pp. 399–401.

11. National Security Council report, quoted in Micah L. Sifry, "US Intervention in the Middle East: A Case Study," in Micah L. Sifry and Christopher Cerf, *The Gulf War Reader: History, Documents, Opinions* (New York: Random House, 1991), p. 32.

12. US Department of State, Inter-Divisional Petroleum Committee, Foreign Petroleum Policy of the United States, April 11, 1944, as cited in Michael Klare, *Blood and Oil: How America's Thirst for Petrol Is Killing Us* (London: Penguin, 2004), p. 30.

13. Cited in Layne, *The Peace of Illusions*, pp. 47–48.

14. Merriam quote from Klare, *Blood and Oil*, p. 32.

15. *United States Military Training Mission Saudi Arabia*, descriptive booklet (Washington, DC: USMTM, 1961), no author. Cited in Thomas W. Lippman, *Inside the Mirage: America's Fragile Partnership with Saudi Arabia* (Boulder: Westview, 2004), p. 278. Emphasis added.

16. "The Executive Mercenaries," *Time*, 24 February 1975.

17. Jonathan Wells, Jack Meyers, and Maggie Mulvihill, "US Ties to Saudi Elite May Be Hurting War on Terrorism," *Boston Herald*, 10 December 2001.

18. Daniel Yergin, *The Prize* (London: Simon & Schuster, 1993), p. 465.

19. James A. Bill, *The Eagle and the Lion: The Tragedy of American-Iranian Relations* (London: Yale University Press, 1988), p. 93.

20. The best account of the joint US-UK operation is Stephen Kinzer, *All the Shah's Men: An American Coup and the Roots of Middle East Terror* (New Jersey: Wiley & Sons, 2003).

21. Fred Halliday, *Iran: Dictatorship and Development* (London: Penguin, 1979), p. 94; Bill, *The Eagle and the Lion*, pp. 114, 202.

22. US Department of Defense, Security Cooperation Agency, *Foreign Military Sales, Foreign Military Construction Sales and Other Security Cooperation Historical Facts*, 30 September 2007 update, pp. 31–36, www.dsca.mil/.

23. Halliday, *Iran*, p. 92.

24. Bill, *The Eagle and the Lion*, pp. 98, 186.

25. James H. Noyes, US Congress, House Committee on Foreign Affairs, Subcommittee on Near East and South Asia, *New Perspectives on the Persian Gulf*, 93rd Congress, 1st Session, 1973, p. 39.

26. Mark Curtis, *The Great Deception: Anglo-American Power and World Order* (London: Pluto Press, 1998), p. 133.

27. Jimmy Carter, State of the Union Address 1980, 23 January 1980, www.jimmy carterlibrary.org/.

28. Brown cited in Stephen R. Shalom, "The United States and Iran-Iraq War 1980–1988," www.iranchamber.com/.

29. Jimmy Carter, State of the Union Address 1980, 23 January 1980.

30. Zbigniew Brzezinski, *Power and Principle* (New York: Farrar, Straus & Giroux, 1987), p. 450.

31. Harold Brown, *Thinking about National Security* (Boulder: Westview, 1983), p. 157.

32. Cited in Shalom, "The United States and Iran-Iraq War 1980–1988."

33. National Security Decision Directive 114, US Policy toward the Iran-Iraq War, November 26, 1983, www.gwu.edu/.

34. Charles William Maynes, "Relearning Intervention," *Foreign Policy* 98 (Spring 1995): p. 105.

35. In 1990, Iraq, Kuwait, and Saudi Arabia were together known to be sitting on 450 billion barrels of oil, out of a global total of proven reserves at the time of 1,003 billion barrels. See BP, *BP Statistical Review of World Energy 2008: Historical Data* for more details.

36. Webster quote from Douglas Little, *American Orientalism: The United States and the Middle East since 1945* (Chapel Hill: University of North Carolina Press, 2004), p. 255.

37. Theodore Draper, "The True History of the Gulf War," *New York Review of Books,* 30 January 1992, p. 41.

38. "Confrontation in the Gulf: Excerpts from Bush's Statement on US Defense of Saudis," *New York Times,* 9 August 1990.

39. For full background, see " 'Prevent the Reemergence of a New Rival': The Making of the Cheney Regional Defense Strategy, 1991–1992," National Security Archive, George Washington University, 26 February 2008, www.gwu.edu/.

40. Dick Cheney, *Defense Strategy for the 1990s: The Regional Defense Strategy,* January 1993, pp. 23–24, www.gwu.edu/.

41. White House, *A National Security Strategy for a New Century,* October 1998, pp. 32–33, www.fas.org/. Emphasis added.

42. US Brigadier General William Looney, *Washington Post,* 30 August 1999, from Stephen Zunes, *Tinderbox* (Maine: Common Courage Press, 2002), p. 102.

43. "Anthony Zinni: 'Avoid a Military Showdown with Iraq,' " *Middle East Quarterly* 5, no. 3 (September 1998), www.meforum.org/.

44. Project for the New American Century, letter to President Clinton, 26 January 1998, www.newamericancentury.org/.

45. John Esterbrook, "Rumsfeld: It Would Be a Short War," *CBS News,* 15 November 2002, www.cbsnews.com/.

46. "Blair Denies Oil 'Conspiracy Theory' over Iraq," *The Times,* 15 January 2003. Stefan Halper and Jonathan Clarke also deny that oil factored into American decision making. See their *America Alone: The Neo-Conservatives and the Global Order* (Cambridge: Cambridge University Press, 2004).

47. White House, "President Discusses Beginning of Operation Iraqi Freedom," 22 March 2003, http://georgewbush-whitehouse.archives.gov/.

48. Bob Woodward, *Plan of Attack* (New York: Simon & Schuster, 2004); "O'Neill: Bush Planned Iraq Invasion before 9/11," *CNN News,* 14 January 2004, www.cnn.com/.

49. Office of the Press Secretary, White House, "Vice President Honors Veterans of the Korean War," 29 August 2002, http://georgewbush-whitehouse.archives.gov/.

50. Philippe Sands, *Lawless World: Making and Breaking Global Rules* (London: Penguin, 2005).

51. Gerry J. Gilmore, "No-Fly Zone Duty Prepared Pilots for OIF Missions," *American Forces Press Service,* US Department of Defense, 12 April 2006, www.news.navy.mil/; Michael R. Gordon, "US Air Raids in '02 Prepared for War in Iraq," *New York Times,* 20 July 2003.

52. "Wolfowitz Comments Revive Doubts over Iraq's WMD," USA Today, 30 May 2003.

53. Graham Paterson, "Alan Greenspan Claims Iraq War Was Really for Oil," *Sunday Times,* 16 September 2007.

54. Bob Woodward, "Greenspan: Ouster of Hussein Crucial for Oil Security," *Washington Post,* 17 September 2007.

55. James Paul, "Oil Companies in Iraq: A Century of Rivalry and War," *Global Policy Forum,* November 2003, www.globalpolicy.org/.

56. Editors, "Invasion Motives," *Monthly Review,* 10 January 2005, http://www.zmag .org/.

57. Dilip Hiro, "Oil, Iraq and America," *The Nation,* 16 December 2002.

58. Ian Rutledge, *Addicted to Oil: America's Relentless Drive for Energy Security* (London: I. B. Tauris, 2006), p.65.

59. Garry Leech, *Crude Interventions: The United States, Oil and the New World (Dis) Order* (London: Zed Books, 2006), p. 46.

60. William Robinson, *A Theory of Global Capitalism: Production, Class and State in a Transnational World* (Baltimore, MD: Johns Hopkins University Press, 2004), p. 140.

61. William I. Robinson, "What to Expect from US 'Democracy Promotion' in Iraq," *Focus on the Global South,* 1 July 2004, www.globalpolicy.org/.

62. Office of the Press Secretary, "Secretary of State Powell Discusses President's Trip to Africa," 10 July 2003, http://georgewbush-whitehouse.archives.gov/.

63. Coalition Provisional Authority, "Coalition Provisional Authority Order Number 39: Foreign Investment," 19 September 2003, www.cpa-iraq.org/.

64. Naomi Klein, "Iraq Is Not America's to Sell: International Law Is Unequivocal—Paul Bremer's Economic Reforms Are Illegal," *The Guardian,* 7 November 2003.

65. The *Economist* cited in Naomi Klein, "Baghdad Year Zero: Pillaging Iraq in Pursuit of a Neocon Utopia," *Harper's Magazine,* September 2004. Other executive decrees included Order 37, passed in September 2003, which suspended all income tax for the year and stipulated that the "highest individual and corporate income tax rates for 2004 and subsequent years *shall not exceed 15 percent.*" Coalition Provisional Authority, "Coalition Provisional Authority Order Number 37: Tax Strategy for 2003," 19 September 2003, www.cpa-iraq.org/. Likewise, Order 54, passed in February 2004, suspended "all customs tariffs, duties, import taxes . . . and similar surcharges for goods entering or leaving Iraq," ensuring that "there was no restriction as to the kind, origin or source of goods that may be imported into or exported from Iraq." Coalition Provisional Authority, "Coalition Provisional Authority Order Number 54: Trade Liberalization Policy 2004," 24 February 2004, www.cpa-iraq.org/.

66. Cited in Rajiv Chandrasekaran, "Mistakes Loom Large as Handover Nears: Missed Opportunities Turned High Ideals to Harsh Realities," *Washington Post,* 20 June 2004.

67. Greg Muttitt, "Crude Designs: The Rip-Off of Iraq's Oil Wealth," 2006, pp. 4–5, www.crudedesigns.org/.

68. Rutledge, *Addicted to Oil,* p. 192.

69. Andrew E. Kramer, "Deals with Iraq Are Set to Bring Oil Giants Back," *International Herald Tribune,* 19 June 2008.

70. "Iraq Invites 35 Companies to Bid for Oil Contracts," *International Herald Tribune,* 14 April 2008; "Iraq Signs $3 Billion Oil Deal with China," *CNN International,* 30 August 2008, http://edition.cnn.com/; Terry Macalister and Nicholas Watt, "Iraqi Government Fuels 'War for Oil' Theories by Putting Reserves Up for Biggest Ever Sale," *The Guardian,* 13 October 2008.

71. Ian Black, "Huge Saudi Force to Defend Oilfields from al-Qaeda," *The Guardian,* 28 August 2007; Anthony H. Cordesman and Nawaf Obiad, *National Security in Saudi Arabia: Threats, Responses and Challenges* (Westport: Praeger Security International, 2005), pp. 320–23.

72. Andrew Johnson, Marie Woolf, and Raymond Whitaker, "The Security Industry: Britain's Private Army in Iraq," *The Independent,* 3 June 2007.

73. Gordon Fellers, "Coalition Works to Make Iraqi Pipeline Protection a Top Priority," *Pipeline and Gas Journal,* March 2004.

74. Defense Security Cooperation Agency, "Saudi Arabia—Continued Assistance in the Modernization of the SANG," news release, transmittal no. 06-05, 3 October 2005, www.dsca.osd.mil/.

75. Michael Hirsh and John Barry, "The Salvador Option," *Newsweek,* January 8, 2005. See also Anthony Shadid and Steve Fainaru, "Militias on the Rise across Iraq: Shiite and Kurdish Groups Seizing Control, Instilling Fear in North and South," *Washington Post,* 21 August 2005. For an excellent review of the evidence concerning the deployment of the Salvador Option in Iraq, see Stephen Shalom, "Phoenix Rising in Iraq?" *ZNet,* 11 February 2005, www.zmag.org/. For more on the rise of US-sponsored paramilitaries in Iraq, see A. K. Gupta, "Let a Thousand Militias Bloom," *CommonDreams,* 22 April 2005, www.commondreams.org/.

76. Douglas Jehl and Thom Shanker, "Congress Is Reviewing Pentagon on Intelligence Activities," *New York Times,* 4 February 2005.

77. Patrick Cockburn, "US Frees Iraqi Kidnappers So They Can Spy on Insurgents: Americans Undermining Local Police Attempts to Crack Down on Waves of Abductions," *The Independent,* 20 March 2005.

78. For the disastrous human rights situation in Saudi Arabia, including information on the 700 prisoners, see Human Rights Watch, "Saudi Arabia: Events of 2006," *World Report 2007,* http://hrw.org/; US State Department, "Saudi Arabia," *Country Reports on Human Rights Practices 2006,* 6 March 2007, www.state.gov/. On the wider role of the SANG in suppressing dissent, see Lippman, *Inside the Mirage,* p. 294; Cordesman and Obiad, *National Security in Saudi Arabia,* p. 265.

79. Marcus George, "The Challenge of Exploiting Iraq's Oil," *BBC News,* 19 June 2008, http://news.bbc.co.uk/.

80. Heather Stewart, "Iraq Imposes 'Saddam Style' Ban on Oil Union," *The Observer,* 5 August 2007.

81. Richard Norton-Taylor, "Iraq: Alarm at Forced Transfer of Basra Union Activists," *The Guardian*, 25 July 2008.

82. Andrew E. Kramer, "Security Contractors Shoot at Taxi, Wounding 3 Iraqis," *New York Times*, 19 October 2007; Antony Barnett and Patrick Smith, "British Guard Firm 'Abused Scared Iraqi Shepherd Boy,'" *The Observer*, 14 November 2004.

83. Human Rights Watch, "Iraq: Events of 2007," *World Report 2008*, http://hrw.org/.

84. Amnesty International, "Middle East and North Africa," *World Report 2008*, http://thereport.amnesty.org/.

85. Jane C. Loeffler, "Fortress America," *Foreign Policy*, September/October 2007.

86. Barack Obama, "Responsibly Ending the War in Iraq," Camp Lejeune, North Carolina, 27 February 2009, www.whitehouse.gov/.

87. Thom Shanker and Eric Schmitt, "Pentagon Expects Long-Term Access to Four Key Bases in Iraq," *New York Times*, 19 April 2003; Christine Spolar, "14 'Enduring Bases' Set for Iraq," *Chicago Tribune*, 23 March 2004. On the abiding presence of US troops, see Patrick Cockburn, "Revealed: Secret Plan to Keep Iraq under US Control," *The Independent*, 5 June 2008.

88. Charles Krauthammer, "Which Is the 'Real War'?" *Washington Post*, 30 March 2007. Emphasis added.

89. "Iraq Exports Hit Post-War Low," *BBC News*, 2 January 2006, http://news.bbc.co.uk/.

90. Obama, "Responsibly Ending the War in Iraq."

91. "Saudis 'Foil Oil Facility Attack,'" *BBC News*, 24 February 2006, http://news.bbc.co.uk/.

92. Energy Information Administration, *World Oil Transit Chokepoints: Strait of Hormuz*, January 2008, www.eia.doe.gov/.

93. See, for instance, "Obama Aims for Oil Independence," *BBC News*, 26 January 2009, http://news.bbc.co.uk/.

94. Melvin A. Conant, *The Oil Factor in US Foreign Policy, 1980–1990* (Lexington, MA: Lexington Books, 1982), p. 107.

95. White House, *A National Security Strategy for Engagement and Enlargement*, February 1996, www.fas.org/.

96. White House, *A National Security Strategy for a New Century*, p. 40.

97. White House, "Visit of President Heydar Aliyev of Azerbaijan," Statement by the Press Secretary, 1 August 1997, http://clinton6.nara.gov/.

98. National Energy Policy Development Group, *National Energy Policy*, May 2001, pp. 8-1–8-3. Emphasis added.

99. White House, "Remarks by the President, Secretary of Energy Abraham and Deputy Secretary of Defense Wolfowitz, after Energy Advisors Meeting," 3 May 2001, http://georgewbush-whitehouse.archives.gov/. Emphasis added.

100. White House, "Remarks by the President to Capital City Partnership," 17 May 2001, http://georgewbush-whitehouse.archives.gov/.

101. National Energy Policy Development Group, *National Energy Policy*, May 2001, pp. 8-3–8-6.

102. Ibid., p. 8-7.

103. White House, *The National Security Strategy of the United States of America*, September 2002, pp. 19–20, http://georgewbush-whitehouse.archives.gov/.

104. George Bush, "State of the Union Address," 31 January 2006, http://georgewbush -whitehouse.archives.gov/.

105. White House, *The National Security Strategy of the United States of America,* March 2006, p. 28, http://georgewbush-whitehouse.archives.gov/. Emphasis added.

106. National Energy Policy Development Group, *National Energy Policy,* May 2001, p. 8-6.

107. 2007 figures, Energy Information Administration, *US Imports by Country of Origin,* http://tonto.eia.doe.gov/; Energy Information Administration, *World Production of Crude Oil, NGPL, and Other Liquids, and Refinery Processing Gain, Most Recent Annual Estimates, 1980–2006,* 21 April 2008 update, www.eia.doe.gov/.

108. White House, "Remarks by President Obama to the Turkish Parliament," Turkish Grand National Assembly Complex, Ankara, Turkey, 6 April 2009, www.whitehouse .gov/.

109. National Energy Policy Development Group, *National Energy Policy,* May 2001, p. 8-7.

110. Cited in Warner, "The Truman Doctrine and the Marshall Plan," p. 85.

111. Zbigniew Brzezinski, *The Grand Chessboard: American Primacy and Its Geostrategic Imperatives* (New York: Basic Books, 1997), p. 30.

CHAPTER FOUR: The Caspian Basin

1. Lutz Kleveman, *The New Great Game: Blood and Oil in Central Asia* (London: Atlantic Monthly Press, 2003); Ahmed Rashid, *Taliban: Islam, Oil and the New Great Game in Central Asia* (New York: I. B. Tauris, 2002).

2. Zbigniew Brzezinski, *The Grand Chessboard: American Primacy and Its Geostrategic Imperatives* (New York: Perseus Books, 1997); Michael T. Klare, "The New Geopolitics," *Monthly Review* 55, no. 3 (July–August 2003).

3. See Robert Kagan, "New Europe, Old Russia," *Washington Post,* 6 February 2008.

4. For example, Russian attempts to maintain primacy across Central Asia in the post–Cold War era have revolved in part around a 1993 agreement with Tajikistan to provide border security troops, which has seen no less than 14,000 Russian soldiers deployed to the country. Vladimir Socor, "Tajikistan Expands Effort to Take Over Protection of Its Borders," *Eurasia Daily Monitor* 1, no. 12 (18 May 2004), www.jamestown .org.

5. "Russian Troops 'to Leave Georgia,'" *BBC News,* 25 April 2005, http://news.bbc .co.uk/, and "Russian Tanks Enter South Ossetia," *BBC News,* 8 August 2008, both at http://news.bbc.co.uk/.

6. Michael Cox, "The Necessary Partnership?: The Clinton Presidency and Post-Soviet Russia," *International Affairs* 70, no. 4 (October 1994): pp. 647–48; Paul D. Wolfowitz, "Clinton's First Year," *Foreign Affairs* 73 (January/February 1994): pp. 41–42; Kenneth Weisbrode, *Central Eurasia: Prize or Quicksand?* Adelphi Paper 338 (London: IISS, 2001), p. 23.

7. White House, *A National Security Strategy of Engagement and Enlargement,* February 1996, www.fas.org/.

8. Energy Information Administration, *Caspian Sea Region: Survey of Key Oil and Gas Statistics and Forecasts,* July 2006, www.eia.doe.gov/; BP, *BP Statistical Review of World Energy: June 2008,* p. 6, www.bp.com/.

9. For the purposes of this chapter, these eight states are considered to form the Caspian region.

10. Gawdat Bahgat, "Pipeline Diplomacy: The Geopolitics of the Caspian Sea Region," *International Studies Perspectives* 3 (2002): p. 311.

11. Primarily for the development of the offshore Azeri-Chirag-Guneshli (ACG) field, working through the Azerbaijani International Oil Consortium (AIOC).

12. Energy Information Administration, *World Production of Crude Oil, NGPL, and Other Liquids, and Refinery Processing Gain, Most Recent Annual Estimates, 1980–2007,* 23 October 2008 update, www.eia.doe.gov/.

13. Energy Information Administration, *International Energy Outlook 1998,* p. 34, http://tonto.eia.doe.gov/; Stephen Blank, *US Military Engagement with Transcaucasia and Central Asia,* Strategic Studies Institute, US Army War College, June 2000, p. 1, www.strategicstudiesinstitute.army.mil/.

14. See, for instance, the visit of Kazakh premier Nazarbayev to the United States in November 1997. White House, "Joint Statement on US-Kazakhstan Relations," Press Release, 18 November 1997, http://clinton6.nara.gov/. Also, see Turkmen president Niyazov's first visit to Washington in April 1998, where the US vice president Al Gore oversaw the signing of a feasibility study for a trans-Caspian pipeline, under the auspices of the US Trade and Development Agency. White House, "Background on the Official Working Visit of President Saparmurat Niyazov of Turkmenistan," Press Release, 23 April 1998, http://clinton6.nara.gov.

15. White House, "Visit of President Heydar Aliyev of Azerbaijan," Statement by the Press Secretary, 1 August 1997, http://clinton6.nara.gov/.

16. White House, *A National Security Strategy for a New Century,* October 1998, pp. 32, 40, http://clinton2.nara.gov/.

17. BP, *BP Statistical Review of World Energy: June 2008,* p. 6.

18. In 2006, Kazakhstan produced 60% of the region's oil and made up over two-thirds of all exports. The Tengiz field is likely to be producing around 0.7 mbpd by the end of 2010. Energy Information Administration, *World Production of Crude Oil, NGPL, and Other Liquids,* 21 April 2008 update; Energy Information Administration, *World Petroleum Consumption: Most Recent Annual Estimates, 1980–2007,* 30 June 2008 update, www.eia.doe.gov/.

19. James Schofield, "Boom Time in Kazakhstan," *BBC News,* 15 May 2002, http://news.bbc.co.uk/. Multinational companies dominate the consortium developing the oil field, including, amongst others, ExxonMobil, Agip, British Gas, and Shell. See Justin Burke, "OKIOC to Complete First Well on Caspian Shelf by Month-End," *Eurasianet,* 10 March 2000, www.eurasianet.org/. However, in a sign of resurgent national claims to a greater share of the profits derived from oil, recent moves by the Kazakh government have led to an increased share of the consortium owned by the state. Joanna Lillis, "Kazakhstan: Officials Jubilant over Oil-Field Renegotiation Deal," *Eurasianet,* 23 January 2008, www.eurasianet.org/.

20. From 0.8 mbpd in 1992 to 2.6 mbpd in 2007. Energy Information Administration, *World Production of Crude Oil, NGPL, and Other Liquids,* 22 October 2008 update.

21. Based on forecasts of production levels of 5.7 mbpd by 2030. These figures have been calculated from data presented at Energy Information Administration, *International Energy Outlook 2007,* www.eia.doe.gov/.

22. As increases in production continue to significantly outstrip those in consumption, the oil available for export from the region has been growing hugely, from 0.8 mbpd in 2000 (58% of production), to over 1.9 mbpd in 2007 (over 83% of production). Energy Information Administration, *World Petroleum Consumption: Most Recent Annual Estimates, 1980–2006,* 11 February 2008 update. Figures for 2007 compiled from Energy Information Administration, *Country Analysis Briefs: Kazakhstan,* updated February 2008, and *Country Analysis Briefs: Azerbaijan,* updated November 2007, both available at www.eia.doe.gov/. Figures do not include production, consumption, and export data for the lesser producers of Turkmenistan and Uzbekistan.

23. National Energy Policy Development Group, *National Energy Policy,* May 2001, 8-7, 8-13.

24. Office of the Spokesman, US State Department, "The Energy Partnership between the Republic of Kazakhstan and the United States of America," 21 December 2001, www.state.gov/.

25. Barack Obama, letter to Ilham Aliyev, 22 May 2009. Reproduced at US Embassy, Azerbaijan, http://azerbaijan.usembassy.gov/.

26. "The Great Gas Game: Who Will Run Caspian Natural Gas through Afghanistan?" *Christian Science Monitor,* 25 October 2001.

27. Richard Morningstar, Special Advisor to President and Secretary of State for Caspian Energy Diplomacy, "The Caspian Sea: Where Foreign Policy and Business Interests Interact," Berkeley Program in Soviet and Post-Soviet Studies, *Contemporary Caucasus Newsletter* 8 (Summer 1999): p. 22.

28. Dilip Hiro, "Shanghai Surprise: The Summit of the Shanghai Cooperation Organisation Reveals How Power Is Shifting in the World," *The Guardian,* 16 June 2006.

29. See the investment made by the China National Petroleum Company in the Kazakh fields at Aktobe and Kumkol, and the pipeline from these with an ultimate capacity of 400,000 bpd. "Kazakhs Agree to China Pipeline," *BBC News,* 18 May 2004, http://news.bbc.co.uk/.

30. Sergei Blagov, "Russia Celebrates Its Central Asian Energy Coup," *Eurasianet,* 16 May 2007, www.eurasianet.org/; Jim Nichol, *Central Asia's New States: Political Developments and Implications for US Interests* (Washington, DC: Congressional Research Service, 2003), p. 14.

31. Testimony of Paul E. Simons, Deputy Assistant Secretary of State for Energy, Sanctions and Commodities, Bureau of Economic and Business Affairs, Department of State, at hearing "Energy Supplies in Eurasia and Implications for US Energy Security," Senate Committee on Foreign Relations, 27 September 2005, p. 6, www.senate.gov/.

32. Michael Klare, *Blood and Oil: How America's Thirst for Petrol Is Killing Us* (London: Penguin, 2004), p. 170.

33. Natalia Antelava, "China's Increasing Hold over Kazakh Oil," *BBC News,* 20 August 2007, http://news.bbc.co.uk.

34. Erica Downs, *China's Quest for Energy Security* (Santa Monica, CA: RAND, 2000), MR-1244-AF, p. 47, www.rand.org/.

35. White House, "Freedom Support Act of 1992 Fact Sheet," 1 April 1992, www.fas .org/. For funding levels, see the US State Department, *Congressional Budget Justification for Foreign Operations* for successive years since FY 1996.

36. US State Department, "Kazakhstan," *Congressional Budget Justification for Foreign Operations,* FY 2007, p. 501, www.state.gov/.

37. Statement of Admiral William J. Fallon, CINC-CENTCOM, before the Senate Armed Services Committee, 3 May 2007, www.centcom.mil/.

38. See, for instance, the agreement during Aliyev's visit to "explore the expansion of security cooperation [between the United States and Azerbaijan], including through the bilateral security dialogue inaugurated in March 1997"; the renewal by Clinton and Kazakh president Nazarbayev of "their commitment to regional security cooperation, including enhanced bilateral military-to-military cooperation, as reflected in the Defense Cooperation and Military Contact Plans for 1998"; and the joint statement between Washington and the archdictator of Turkmenistan on security issues. See White House, "Visit of President Heydar Aliyev of Azerbaijan"; White House, "Joint Statement on US-Kazakhstan Relations"; White House, "Background on the Official Working Visit of President Saparmurat Niyazov of Turkmenistan," Press Release, 23 April 1998.

39. Figures in this section have been calculated through the accumulation of data from various sources, including US State Department, annual *Congressional Budget Justification for Foreign Operations,* www.state.gov/; US Department of Defense, Defense Security Cooperation Agency, *Foreign Military Sales, Foreign Military Construction Sales, and Military Assistance Facts,* as of 30 September 2004; Center for Public Integrity, *Collateral Damage: Human Rights and US Military Aid after 9/11,* www.publicintegrity.org/; Center for Defense Information, *US Arms Exports and Military Assistance in the "Global War on Terror": 25 Country Profiles,* 2007, www.cdi.org/.

40. R. Jeffrey Smith, "US Leads Peacekeeping Drill in Kazakhstan; Multilateral Exercises Aimed at Promoting Stability in Resource-Rich Central Asia," *Washington Post,* 15 September 1997; Jim Drinkard, "US Paratroopers Fly around the World to Make Historic Jump," *Associated Press,* 15 September 1997. Emphasis added.

41. For instance, restrictions on military assistance to Tajikistan, in place since 1993, were removed shortly after 9/11: an action "taken in the interests of foreign policy and national security" in the context of the war on terror. See US State Department, "Amendment to the List of Proscribed Destinations," 22 CFR Part 126, Public Notice 3864, *Federal Register* 67, no. 6 (9 January 2002), www.fas.org/.

42. See, for example, various testimonies as part of "Contributions of Central Asian Nations to the Campaign against Terrorism," hearing before the Subcommittee on Central Asia and the South Caucasus, Senate Committee on Foreign Relations, 13 December 2001, http://frwebgate.access.gpo.gov/.

43. Visits to the region were common during the autumn of 2001, as officials sought to facilitate the deployment of US troops for Operation Enduring Freedom. Thus, Donald Rumsfeld toured the region in early October 2001, which resulted in an agreement for US forces to use Uzbek airspace and the Karshi-Khanabad (K2) airbase for operations in Afghanistan. Likewise, the US secured the use of the Manas airbase in Kyrgyzstan, and either landing rights, refueling facilities, or overflight rights in Tajikistan, Turkmenistan, Kazakhstan, Georgia, and Azerbaijan. See Kathleen T. Rhem, "Uzbekistan Grants US Flyovers, Limited Basing," *American Forces Press Service,* 5 October 2001, www.news.navy.mil/; "US and Uzbekistan Agree Pact," *BBC News,* 13 October 2001, http://news.bbc.co.uk/.

44. Tamara Makarenko, "The Dangers of Playing the Central Asia Game," *Jane's Intelligence Review,* June 2002, p. 14.

45. Svante E. Cornell, "The United States and Central Asia: In the Steppes to Stay?" *Cambridge Review of International Affairs* 17, no. 2 (July 2004): pp. 239–40. See also the text of Rumsfeld's press conference whilst in Uzbekistan during February 2004: "We have no plans to put permanent bases in this part of the world. We have been discussing with various friends and allies the issue of—I guess you call them 'operating sites'— that would not be permanent as a base would be permanent but would be a place where the United States and coalition countries could periodically and intermittently have access and support." US Department of Defense, "Secretary Rumsfeld and Ambassador Jon Purnell Press Conference in Uzbekistan," 25 February 2004, www.defenselink.mil/.

46. Colin Powell, "Press Briefing on Board Plane En Route Tashkent, Uzbekistan," State Department, 7 December 2001, www.state.gov/.

47. 2010 figures from US State Department, *Congressional Budget Justification for Foreign Operations*, FY 2010, pp. 311–562.

48. Cited in Joshua Kucera, "Central Asia: Washington Boosts Aid to Region to Bolster Afghan War Effort," *Eurasia Insight*, 12 May 2009, www.eurasianet.org/.

49. "US Urged to Give Bases Deadline," *BBC News*, 5 July 2005, and Damien Grammaticas, "Rumsfeld in Talks on US Air Bases," *BBC News*, 26 July 2005, both at http:// news.bbc.co.uk/; "US Gains Indefinite Continued Use of Air Base in Kyrgyzstan," *International Herald Tribune*, 26 July 2005.

50. Nick Paton Walsh, "Uzbekistan Kicks US Out of Military Base," *The Guardian*, 1 August 2005.

51. Ellen Barry and Sophia Kishkovsky, "Russian Leader Warns of Possible Missile Deployment to Counter US Shield," *International Herald Tribune*, 5 October 2008.

52. In particular, see the construction of the "Northern" and "Western" Early oil pipelines from Baku and the upgrading of the Atyrau-Samara pipeline from northern Kazakhstan. See Energy Information Administration, *Country Analysis Briefs: Caspian Sea*, January 2007 update, www.eia.doe.gov/.

53. Stephen Kinzer, "On Piping Out Caspian Oil, US Insists the Cheaper, Shorter Way Isn't Better," *New York Times*, 8 November 1998.

54. Dan Morgan and David Ottoway, "Drilling for Influence in Russia's Backyard: US Woos Oil-Rich Former Soviet Republics," *Washington Post*, 22 September 1997.

55. For a discussion of how the sanctions regime was used specifically to deter a pipeline from the Caspian through Iran, see Kenneth Katzman, *The Iran-Libya Sanctions Act (ILSA)*, CRS Report RS20871, 3 April 2006 update, http://fpc.state.gov/.

56. Brzezinski, *The Grand Chessboard*, p. 129. See also Weisbrode, *Central Eurasia*, pp. 24–25.

57. Steven Erlanger, "Caspian Sea: White House Presses Pipeline Plan," *New York Times*, 14 October 1998; Steven Kinzer, "US Pushing Its Route for Pipeline, Aids Turkey," *New York Times*, 22 October 1998. Emphasis added.

58. White House, "Joint Statement by President Bush and Kazakhstan President," 21 December 2001, http://georgewbush-whitehouse.archives.gov/. The NEPD report also recommended that Washington "continue working with relevant companies and countries to establish the commercial conditions that will allow oil companies operating in Kazakhstan the option of exporting their oil via the BTC pipeline." See National Energy Policy Development Group, *National Energy Policy*, May 2001, p. 8-13.

59. Testimony of Paul E. Simons, at hearing "Energy Supplies in Eurasia and Implications for US Energy Security," p. 9.

60. Ambassador Richard Morningstar, Special Envoy for Eurasian Energy, Speech at the American Chamber of Commerce, Baku, Azerbaijan, 1 June 2009. http://azerbaijan.usembassy.gov/. Emphasis added.

61. Klare, *Blood and Oil*, p. 147.

62. Michael T. Klare, *Rising Powers, Shrinking Planet: The New Geopolitics of Energy* (New York: Metropolitan Books, 2008), p. 115.

63. Jan H. Kalicki, responsible for coordinating energy and trade policy with the former Soviet Union, cited in Dan Morgan and David Ottoway, "Drilling for Influence in Russia's Backyard: US Woos Oil-Rich Former Soviet Republics," *Washington Post*, 22 September 1997.

64. "Remarks by US Senior Advisor for Caspian Basin Energy Diplomacy, Ambassador Steven R. Mann, at the Turkmenistan International Oil and Gas Exhibition," 20 October 2001, http://turkmenistan.usembassy.gov/.

65. Ambassador Richard Morningstar, Special Envoy for Eurasian Energy, Speech at the American Chamber of Commerce, Baku, Azerbaijan, 1 June 2009.

66. Testimony of Karen Harbert, Assistant Secretary for Policy and International Affairs, Department of Energy, at hearing "Energy Supplies in Eurasia and Implications for US Energy Security," Senate Committee on Foreign Relations, 27 September 2005, p. 9, www.senate.gov.

67. "Azerbaijan and Energy Cooperation," *Voice of America*, 9 June 2009, www.voanews.com/.

68. *Silk Road Strategy Act of 1999*, enacted as Section 596 of FY 2000 *Foreign Operations, Export Financing and Related Programs Appropriations Act*, Public Law 106–113, 29 November 1999; US State Department, "Freedom Support Act," *Congressional Budget Justification for Foreign Operations*, FY 2007, pp. 59–60.

69. Michael Camdessus, Managing Director, International Monetary Fund, "Challenges Facing the Transition Economies of Central Asia," address to conference on *Challenges to Economies in Transition*, Bishkek, 27 May 1998, www.imf.org/.

70. International Monetary Fund, "IMF Approves Stand-By Credit for Kazakhstan," Press Release No. 95/34, 5 June 1995, www.imf.org/; International Monetary Fund, "IMF Concludes Article IV Consultation with Kazakhstan," Press Information Notice No. 98/47, 1 July 1998, www.imf.org/.

71. Richard Pomfret, *The Central Asian Economies since Independence* (Princeton: Princeton University Press, 2006), pp. 40–60.

72. European Bank for Reconstruction and Development, *Transition Report 2003: Integration and Regional Cooperation* (London: EBRD, November 2003).

73. International Monetary Fund, "IMF Approves STF Drawing for the Republic of Azerbaijan," Press Release No. 95/24, 19 April 1995, www.imf.org/; International Monetary Fund, "IMF Approves Combined ESAF/EFF Financing for Azerbaijan," Press Release No. 96/64, 20 December 1996, www.imf.org/.

74. Testimony of Paul E. Simons, at hearing "Energy Supplies in Eurasia and Implications for US Energy Security," p. 2.

75. Amongst many initiatives and statements, see White House, "Visit of President Heydar Aliyev of Azerbaijan"; White House, "Joint Statement on US-Kazakhstan Relations."

76. National Energy Policy Development Group, *National Energy Policy*, May 2001, pp. 8-12, 8-13.

77. "Declaration on the Strategic Partnership and Cooperation Framework between the United States of America and the Republic of Uzbekistan," 12 March 2002, www.fas.org/. Almost identical language was employed in the joint statement from Bush and Kazakh president Nazarbayev in December 2001 and in the joint statement from President Bush and Kyrgyz president Akayev during his visit to the White House in September 2002. White House, "Joint Statement by President Bush and Kazakhstan President"; White House, "Joint Statement by President George W. Bush and President Askar Akayev on the Relationship between the United States of America and the Kyrgyz Republic," 23 September 2002, http://georgewbush-whitehouse.archives .gov/.

78. Ambassador Richard Morningstar, Special Envoy for Eurasian Energy, Speech at the American Chamber of Commerce, Baku, Azerbaijan, 1 June 2009.

79. For example, FDI in Armenia comes from Russia (27%), Greece (27%), Canada (11%), and the United States (10%), with companies from several EU countries also major investors. Likewise, major investors in Azerbaijan include American, British, and Turkish companies, alongside a significant presence from Norway, Russia, Japan, France, Germany, and Italy. Canadian companies are the main investors in Kyrgyzstan, alongside substantial interest from US and Turkish capital.

80. FDI data calculated from United Nations Conference on Trade and Development, *Foreign Direct Investment Database,* www.unctad.org/, accessed July 2008. Data on the share of FDI in each sector of the economy from United Nations, Economic and Social Commission for Asia and the Pacific, *Foreign Direct Investment in Central Asian and Caucasian Economies: Policies and Issues,* Studies in Trade and Investment 50, ST/ ESCAP/2255, 2003, www.unescap.org/.

81. Michael Cohen, "The Effect of Oil Revenues on Transition Economics: The Case of Azerbaijan," *Geopolitics of Energy* 28, no. 6 (June 2006): p. 13.

82. "US Senior Advisor on Caspian Energy Speaks at Jamestown Forum," Press Release, PR031005, United States–Azerbaijan Chamber of Commerce, 10 March 2005, http://usacc.org/. For joint investments by Western and Chinese companies, see "CNODC Acquires Interest in Azeri Fields," *Rigzone News,* 24 January 2002, www .rigzone.com/.

83. Testimony of Leonard L. Coburn, Director, Russian and Eurasian Affairs, Office of Policy and International Affairs, Department of Energy, at hearing "US Energy Security: Russia and the Caspian," Senate Committee on Foreign Relations, 30 April 2003, p. 2, www.senate.gov; Energy Information Administration, *World Production of Crude Oil, NGPL, and Other Liquids, and Refinery Processing Gain,* 24 August 2007 update; Energy Information Administration, *World Petroleum Consumption: Most Recent Annual Estimates, 1980–2006,* 11 February 2008 update. Figures for 2007 compiled from Energy Information Administration, *Country Analysis Briefs: Kazakhstan,* updated February 2008, and *Country Analysis Briefs: Azerbaijan,* updated November 2007.

84. Energy Information Administration, *Country Analysis Briefs: Kazakhstan,* February 2008 update.

85. International Monetary Fund, "Azerbaijan: 2008 Article IV Consultation, Preliminary Conclusions of the IMF Mission," 12 March 2008, www.imf.org/; Energy Information Administration, *Country Analysis Briefs: Azerbaijan,* updated December 2007.

86. World Bank, *Making Transition Work for Everyone: Poverty and Inequality in Europe and Central Asia,* August 2000, pp. 1–3, http://web.worldbank.org/.

87. World Bank, *Growth, Poverty and Inequality: Eastern Europe and the Former Soviet Union,* October 2005, pp. 5–6, http://web.worldbank.org/.

88. See, for instance, Farangis Najibullah, "Central Asia: Tajikistan, Kyrgyzstan Making Efforts to Reform Health-Care Systems," *Eurasia Insight,* 29 March 2003; Jeremy Bransten, "As World Marks Literacy Day, What of USSR's Legacy?" *Eurasia Insight,* 8 September 2003, both at www.eurasianet.org/.

89. Yelena Kalyuzhnova, *The Kazakhstani Economy: Independence and Transition* (London: Macmillan, 1998), pp. 146–50.

90. US State Department, "Kazakhstan," *Congressional Budget Justification for Foreign Operations,* FY 2007, p. 501.

91. UNDP Kazakhstan, *Poverty in Kazakhstan: Causes and Cures,* 2004, pp. 3–5, www.undp.kz/; "Kazakhstan: Poverty Persists Despite Impressive Economic Growth," *IRIN News,* 13 May 2004, www.irinnews.org/.

92. Asian Development Bank, *Country Gender Assessment: Azerbaijan,* December 2005, pp. 1–4, www.adb.org.

93. Amy Myers Jaffe and Martha Brill Olcott, "The Geopolitics of Caspian Energy," in Yelena Kalyuzhnova and Dov Lynch, eds., *The Euro-Asian World: A Period of Transition* (London: Macmillan Press, 2000), p. 75.

94. Svetlana Tsalik, *Caspian Oil Windfalls: Who Will Benefit?* Caspian Revenue Watch, Open Society Institute, 2003, http://archive.revenuewatch.org/; Richard Auty, "Natural Resources, Governance and Transition in Azerbaijan, Kazakhstan and Turkmenistan," in Shirin Akiner, ed., *The Caspian: Politics, Energy and Security* (London: Routledge, 2004), pp. 109–25.

95. Christopher Walker and Jeannette Goehring, "Petro-Authoritarianism and Eurasia's New Divides," in *Nations in Transit 2008: Democratization from Central Europe to Eurasia* (Washington, DC: Freedom House, 2008), pp. 25–35.

96. Richard Pomfret, *The Central Asian Economies since Independence* (Princeton: Princeton University Press, 2006), pp. 40–60. Azerbaijan's presidency did change hands in 2003, but from father to son in an election widely condemned as neither free nor fair.

97. Walker and Goehring, "Petro-Authoritarianism and Eurasia's New Divides," pp. 25–35.

98. Human Rights Watch, "Azerbaijani Parliamentary Elections Manipulated," *Human Rights Watch Backgrounder,* October 2000, and Human Rights Watch, "Bush Must Press for Human Rights Reform in Azerbaijan," Press Release, 24 April 2005, both at http://hrw.org/.

99. Martha Brill Olcott, *Revisiting the Twelve Myths of Central Asia,* CEIP Working Papers, Number 23, September 2001, p. 13, www.carnegieendowment.org/.

100. Fiona Hill, "Central Asia: Terrorism, Religious Extremism, and Regional Stability," testimony before the House Committee on International Relations, Subcommittee on the Middle East and Central Asia, 23 July 2003, www.brookings.edu/; Pauline Luong Jones, "The Middle Easternization of Central Asia," *Current History,* October 2003, pp. 333–40.

101. International Crisis Group, *Radical Islam in Central Asia: Responding to Hizb ut-Tahrir,* Asia Report 58, 30 June 2003, www.crisisgroup.org/.

102. Hizb ut-Tahrir, *The American Campaign to Suppress Islam,* Al-Khalifah Publications, 1996, www.hizbuttahrir.org/.

103. Strobe Talbott, "A Farewell to Flashman: American Policy in the Caucasus and Central Asia," Address at the Johns Hopkins School of Advanced International Studies, 21 July 1997, www.state.gov/.

104. Energy Information Administration, *International Energy Outlook 1998*, p. 32; White House, *A National Security Strategy for a New Century*.

105. Jonathan Cohen, "Southern Caucasus: Struggling to Find Peace," in Paul van Tongeren, Hans van de Veen, and Juliette Verhoeven, eds., *Searching for Peace in Europe and Eurasia: An Overview of Conflict Prevention and Peacebuilding Activities* (London: Lynne Rienner, 2002).

106. See, for instance, "Hostage Rescue Operation in Kyrgyzstan," *BBC News*, 26 August 1999, and "Kyrgyz Army Pursues Rebels," *BBC News*, 13 August 2000, both at http://news.bbc.co.uk/.

107. US State Department, "Declaration on the Strategic Partnership and Cooperation Framework between the United States of America and the Republic of Uzbekistan," 12 March 2002, www.fas.org/.

108. White House, "Joint Statement by President George W. Bush and President Askar Akayev."

109. Ariel Cohen, "Bush Administration Backs Uzbek Response to March Militant Attacks," *Eurasia Insight*, 14 April 2004, www.eurasianet.org/.

110. Testimony in front of hearing on "Balancing Military Assistance and Support for Human Rights in Central Asia," Subcommittee on Central Asia and South Caucasus, Senate Committee on Foreign Relations, 27 June 2002.

111. US Department of Defense, "Secretary Rumsfeld Joint Press Conference in Kazakhstan," 28 April 2002, www.defenselink.mil/.

112. Core US funding has increased almost fourfold since 9/11, whilst Kazakh defense spending in 2007 saw a 74% rise on 2006 levels. Nathan Hodge, "Kazakhstan Unveils Modernisation Plans," *Jane's Defence Weekly*, 25 April 2007. This has included plans to build up its naval force in order to guard oil platforms on the Caspian Sea. "Kazakhstan to Expand Its Navy," *Financial Times*, 25 October 2007.

113. James Doran, "Americans Covertly Training Kazakh Troops," *The Times*, 30 March 2002; John J. Lumpkin, "US Will Help with Kazakhstan Security on the Caspian, Rumsfeld Says," *Associated Press*, 25 February 2004; James Murphy, "Kazakhstan Boosts Defence Spending," *Jane's Defence Weekly*, 12 October 2005.

114. Lumpkin, "US Will Help with Kazakhstan Security on the Caspian, Rumsfeld Says"; John D. Banusiewicz, "Rumsfeld Visits Kazakhstan for Talks on Strengthening Relationship," *American Forces Press Service*, 25 February 2004, www.news.navy.mil/.

115. US State Department, "Kazakhstan," *Congressional Budget Justification for Foreign Operations*, FY 2005.

116. US State Department, *Congressional Budget Justification for Foreign Operations*, FY 2010, p. 515.

117. US State Department, *Congressional Budget Justification for Foreign Operations*, FY 2009, FY 2010, p. 312.

118. US State Department, "Azerbaijan," *Congressional Budget Justification for Foreign Operations*, FY 2007.

119. See questions by representatives Brad Sherman, Grace Napolitano, and Adam Schiff as well as Colin Powell's responses in "The President's International Affairs Re-

quest for Fiscal Year 2005," Hearing before the Committee on International Relations, House of Representatives, 11 February 2004, serial no. 108-88, pp. 53, 82–83, www .foreignaffairs.house.gov/.

120. David Pugliese, "Baku Builds Up, Warns Armenia, Warms NATO Ties," *Defense News,* 3 September 2007.

121. NATO Parliamentary Assembly, "NATO Parliamentarians Debate Central Asian Security," Press Release, 12 March 2008, and "The Protection of Critical Infrastructures," Committee Report, 162 CDS 07 E rev 1, 2007, both at www.nato-pa.int/.

122. John C. K. Daly, "NATO Weighs Protection of Kazakh Oil Facilities," *Eurasia Daily Monitor* 5, no. 71 (15 April 2008), www.jamestown.org/.

123. Joshua Kucera, "US Helps Forces, Gains Foothold in Caspian Region," *Jane's Defence Weekly,* 25 May 2005.

124. General Charles Wald, Deputy Commander, EUCOM. April 2004, www.aei.org/.

125. Jeremy Scahill, *Blackwater: The Rise of the World's Most Powerful Mercenary Army* (London: Serpent's Tail, 2007), p. 238.

126. "Concerns Are Rising," *Oil and Gas Journal,* 27 January 2003; John Roberts, "Georgia Falls Victim to Pipeline Politics," *BBC News,* 12 August 2008, http://news.bbc .co.uk/; Nihat Ali Özcan and Saban Kardas, "Energy Security and the PKK Threat to the Baku-Tbilisi-Ceyhan Pipeline," *Terrorism Monitor* 6, no. 18 (22 September 2008), www .jamestown.org/. Georgian defense spending was set to rise from $400 million to $600 million over the course of just one year. Guy Anderson, "Georgia Looks to Boost Its Defence Budget for 2007," *Jane's Defence Industry,* October 2007.

127. US Department of Defense, "Georgia 'Train and Equip' Program Begins," Press Release, No. 217-02, 29 April 2002, www.defenselink.mil/; P. W. Singer, *Corporate Warriors: The Rise of the Privatized Military Industry* (Ithaca: Cornell University Press, 2003), p. 17.

128. Nick Paton Walsh, "US Privatises Its Military Aid to Georgia," *The Guardian,* 6 January 2004.

129. Foley Hoag LLP, *Human Rights and Security External Monitoring Assessment of the AGT Pipeline Projects in Georgia,* May 2007, pp. 22–31, www.bp.com/.

130. Robert G. Lawson, "BTC Pipeline Completed, Ready to Move New Crude Supplies," *Oil and Gas Journal,* 27 June 2005.

131. Foley Hoag LLP, *Human Rights and Security External Monitoring Assessment,* pp. 17–18.

132. US Department of Defense, "Georgia 'Train and Equip' Program Begins"; Ian Traynor, "US Targets al-Qaeda Hideout in Georgia: America Wants to Train Forces on Ground to Root Out Islamists," *The Guardian,* 15 February 2002; Jim Garamone, "US Troops to Begin Counterterrorism Training," *American Forces Press Service,* 30 April 2002, www.news.navy.mil/; US Embassy, Georgia, "Briefing on Georgia Train and Equip Program at Georgian Ministry of Defense," 2 May 2002, http://georgia.usem bassy.gov/; US Embassy, Georgia, "Press Briefing on the Georgia Train and Equip Program at Georgian Ministry of Defense," 7 May 2002, http://georgia.usembassy.gov/; Office of the Coordinator for Counterterrorism, US Department of State, *Patterns of Global Terrorism 2003,* 29 April 2004. For details on the Turkish link, see *Armed Forces Monthly,* August 2002.

133. This region, 100 miles from Tbilisi and on the border with Chechnya, is under extremely limited control by the Georgian government and houses thousands of

Chechen refugees and, according to Russian officials, hundreds of Chechen fighters. As the Bush administration sought funding for GTEP, Phillip Ramler (acting US ambassador to Georgia) claimed that "a few dozen mujahedin fighters from Afghanistan have appeared in the Caucasus region" and that "we know that several mujahedin have taken cover in the Pankisi gorge and are in contact with the Arab terrorist Khattab, who in turn has contacts with bin Laden." As details of the proposed assistance program became clear, senior Pentagon officials were stating that "we have a clear connection between Chechens and al Qaeda. They clearly fall under the potential targets of the global war on terrorism." This was confirmed by President Bush himself. As Washington formally dispatched military advisors to Georgia, Bush told reporters: "As long as there is al Qaeda influence anywhere, we will help the host countries rout them out and bring them to justice." Asked whether he believed fighters in the Pankisi Gorge were influenced by al Qaeda, Bush replied: "I do." See "US to Help Train Troops in Yemen," *Miami Herald,* 12 February 2002; Vernon Loeb and Peter Slevin, "US Begins Anti-Terror Assistance in Georgia; Al Qaeda–Linked Rebels Find Haven in Mountains," *Washington Post,* 27 February 2002; Nicholas Kralev, "US Takes War on Terrorism to Guerrillas," *Washington Times,* 28 February 2002.

134. US Department of Defense, "DoD News Briefing: ASD PA Clarke and Gen. Pace," 27 February 2002, www.defenselink.mil/.

135. US Embassy, Georgia, "Briefing on Georgia Train and Equip Program," 2 May 2002; US Department of Defense, "Media Availability with Rumsfeld and Georgian Defense Minister," 7 May 2002, www.defenselink.mil/.

136. Cited in Nick Paton Walsh, "Oil Fuels US Army Role in Georgia," *The Observer,* 12 May 2002.

137. CBC-TV, "The Pipeline," documentary aired 28 July 2004, www.cbc.ca/.

138. US Department of Defense, "Joint Press Conference with Georgian President Eduard Shevardnadze," News Transcript, 4 August 1999, www.defenselink.mil/; Linda D. Kozaryn, "Cohen Talks Security with Ukrainian, Georgian Leaders," *American Forces Press Service,* 2 August 1999, www.news.navy.mil/; US Embassy, Georgia, "Briefing on Georgia Train and Equip Program," 2 May 2002; Linda D. Kozaryn, "US Considers Train and Equip Program for Georgia," *American Forces Press Service,* 27 February 2002, www.news.navy.mil/.

139. US State Department, *Congressional Budget Justification for Foreign Operations,* FY 2010, p. 339.

140. US State Department, *2007 Country Reports on Human Rights Practices,* March 2008, www.state.gov/.

141. Amnesty International, "Europe and Central Asia: Summary of Amnesty International's Concerns in the Region: January–June 2007," 1 December 2007, AI Index: EUR 01/010/2007, www.amnesty.org/.

142. Human Rights Watch, "Crushing Dissent: Repression, Violence and Azerbaijan's Elections" (January 2004): p. 2.

143. US State Department, "Armitage-Aliyev Phone Call," Taken Question, 20 October 2003, www.state.gov/; White House, "President Bush Welcomes President Aliyev of Azerbaijan to the White House," Press Release, 28 April 2006, http://georgewbush-whitehouse.archives.gov/.

144. According to Bush, for example, the two governments shared a "desire to defeat extremism and . . . to support the forces of moderation throughout the world."

With complete disregard for the political reality on the ground in Kazakhstan, Bush spoke of Nazarbayev's "commitment to institutions that will enable liberty to flourish" and stated that he had "watched very carefully the development of this important country from one that was in the Soviet sphere to one that is now a free nation." White House, "President Bush Welcomes President Nazarbayev to the White House," 29 September 2006, http://georgewbush-whitehouse.archives.gov.

145. The CSF had allocated more than $53 million to Georgia and $38 million to Uzbekistan by FY 2005. The MAP provided $12 million to Georgia in FY 2002. The "Partners Fund" was created as part of the FY 2005 supplemental budget request and included $2 million for Kyrgyzstan as part of an effort to "provide economic assistance for America's partners in the War on Terror." See White House, "Fact Sheet: Request for Additional FY 2005 Funding for the War on Terror," 14 February 2005, http://george wbush-whitehouse.archives.gov/. For amount destined for Kyrgyzstan, see Center for Public Integrity, www.publicintegrity.org/.

146. Data up to FY 2005, and including $1.2 million to Georgia, $786,000 to Azerbaijan, and $615,000 to Kazakhstan (of a total of nearly $4 million worth of training provided).

147. DOD-CD (Department of Defense–Counterdrug) is otherwise known as Section 1004/1033 funding. See 2007 *Defense Authorization Act,* PL 109-364. Initial authorization for the program came from Section 1033 of the *National Defense Authorization Act* FY98, PL 105-85.

148. Joshua Kucera, "One Year after Andijan: US Lawmakers Take Action to Punish Uzbekistan," *Eurasia Insight,* 11 May 2006, www.eurasianet.org/.

CHAPTER FIVE: West Africa

1. This has not wholly been the case, of course, and southern Africa in particular became the scene of numerous proxy low-intensity conflicts during the Cold War, leading to enormous devastation across the region (with, in just one example, over 100,000 people alone killed by apartheid South African–backed insurgents fighting the nationalist government in Mozambique). Chester Crocker, Assistant Secretary of State for African Affairs, "Summary of Mozambican Refugee Accounts of Principally Conflict-Related Experience in Mozambique," 1988, http://pdf.usaid.gov; James Brooke, "Visiting State Department Official Condemns Mozambique's Rebels," *New York Times,* 27 April 1988.

2. Bryan Bender, "Pentagon Plans New Command to Cover Africa," *Boston Globe,* 21 December 2006.

3. Office of the Spokesman, US Department of State, "Secretary of State Madeleine K. Albright: Remarks at Chevron's Takula Oil Drilling Platform," Cabinda, Angola, 12 December 1997, www.state.gov/.

4. White House, *A National Security Strategy for a New Century,* October 1998, p. 55, http://clinton2.nara.gov/.

5. British Petroleum, *BP Statistical Review of World Energy 2008,* p. 6, www.bp.com/.

6. Angola and Nigeria hold proven reserves of 45.2 billion barrels, out of a regional total of 51.9 billion barrels. In 2006, the two countries produced 3.9 mbpd, out of a regional total of 4.8 mbpd. In 2004, Angola and Nigeria exported 3.2 mbpd, out of a regional total of 4.2 mbpd. Figures do not include North African states. See British Petroleum, *BP Statistical Review of World Energy,* June 2007, p. 6; Energy Information Ad-

ministration, *World Production of Crude Oil, NGPL, and Other Liquids, and Refinery Processing Gain, Most Recent Annual Estimates, 1980–2007*, 21 April 2008 update, www.eia .doe.gov/; Energy Information Administration, *World Petroleum Supply and Disposition, 2004*, 6 August 2007 update, www.eia.doe.gov/.

7. Based on 2007 data. Energy Information Administration, *World Production of Crude Oil, NGPL, and Other Liquids*, 21 April 2008 update.

8. In 2004, 4.2 of the 4.4 mbpd were exported. Overall, 43.2 mbpd were released onto the world oil market in 2004, representing just 52% of production. We see, then, that West Africa exports a far higher proportion of its oil than most producers. Production-export ratios are derived from 2004 data. Energy Information Administration, *World Petroleum Supply and Disposition, 2004*, 6 August 2007 update.

9. Energy Information Administration, *International Energy Outlook 2007*, Table G1, p. 187, www.eia.doe.gov/; Energy Information Administration, *International Energy Outlook 2002*, p. 35, http://tonto.eia.doe.gov/; Energy Information Administration, *Country Analysis Briefs: Nigeria*, April 2007 update, www.eia.doe.gov/; Energy Information Administration, *Country Analysis Briefs: Angola*, January 2007 update, www.eia.doe .gov/.

10. Energy Information Administration, *Country Analysis Briefs: Chad and Cameroon*, January 2007 update, www.eia.doe.gov/.

11. These figures have been calculated from data presented at Energy Information Administration, *International Energy Outlook 2007*, Table G1, p. 187.

12. Michael Klare, *Blood and Oil: How America's Thirst for Petrol Is Killing Us* (London: Penguin, 2004), p. 121.

13. White House, "Secretary of State Powell Discusses President's Trip to Africa," Press Briefing, 10 July 2003, http://georgewbush-whitehouse.archives.gov/.

14. George Bush, Remarks in Roundtable Interview with African Print Journalists, "President Bush Discusses Upcoming Africa Trip with Reporters," 3 July 2003, http:// georgewbush-whitehouse.archives.gov/.

15. Cited in Mike Crawley, "With Mideast Uncertainty, US Turns to Africa for Oil," *Christian Science Monitor*, 23 May 2002.

16. Paul Michael Wihbey and Barry Schutz, eds., *African Oil: A Priority for US National Security and African Development*, Proceedings of a Symposium Held by the Institute for Advanced Strategic and Political Studies in Washington, D.C., on 25 January 2002, Published as Research Papers in Strategy No. 14, May 2002, p. 11, www .israeleconomy.org/.

17. Ed Royce, "Pentagon Imperative: A Spotlight on Africa," *Christian Science Monitor*, 14 November 2006; Wihbey and Schutz, eds., *African Oil*, pp. 5, 8; Keith Somerville, "US Looks to Africa for 'Secure Oil,' " *BBC News*, 13 September 2002, http://news.bbc .co.uk/.

18. African Oil Policy Initiative Group, *African Oil: A Priority for US National Security and African Development*, pp. 6, 17–18, www.iasps.org/.

19. Cited in ibid., p. 5.

20. US Department of Defense, *EUCOM's Strategy in Africa*, reprinted at www.aei .org/.

21. General Charles Wald, Deputy Commander, US European Command, Address to a Conference at American Enterprise Institute, www.aei.org/, p. 16. See also the declassified Pentagon report, cited in African Oil Policy Initiative Group, *African Oil*, p. 5.

22. Jon Lee Anderson, "Our New Best Friend: Who Needs Saudi Arabia When You've Got Sao Tome?" *New Yorker,* 7 October 2002. See also the comments by Robert Murphy (Bureau of Intelligence, State Department), cited in Wihbey and Schutz, eds., *African Oil,* p. 29.

23. US State Department, *Congressional Budget Justification for Foreign Operations,* FY 2010, p. 136, www.state.gov/.

24. Phillip Carter, "US Policy in Africa in the 21st Century," Africa Center for Strategic Studies, 9 February 2009, www.state.gov/.

25. See US State Department, *Congressional Budget Justification for Foreign Operations,* FY 2002–2007, www.state.gov/.

26. US State Department, *Congressional Budget Justification for Foreign Operations,* FY 2007, www.state.gov/.

27. See, for instance, US State Department, *Congressional Budget Justification for Foreign Operations,* FY 2002–2007, www.state.gov/; US Department of Defense, Security Cooperation Agency, *Foreign Military Sales, Foreign Military Construction Sales and Other Security Cooperation Historical Facts,* 30 September 2007 update, www.dsca.mil/.

28. Office of the Press Secretary, White House, "Memorandum for the Secretary of State and Secretary of Defense: Determination to Authorize the Furnishing of Emergency Military Assistance to the Government of Nigeria," Presidential Determination No. 2002–16, 19 April 2002, www.whitehouse.gov/.

29. Karen Kwiatkowski, cited in Wihbey and Schutz, eds., *African Oil,* p. 27. This burgeoning military relationship is not limited to the two largest oil producers: to a lesser extent in absolute terms, but equally significant in terms of percentage rises, aid to other oil-rich countries in the region has also accelerated as the value of their oil deposits has become clearer. On Chad, for example, see Center for Defense Information, *US Arms Exports and Military Assistance in the "Global War on Terror": 25 Country Profiles,* pp. 31–36, www.cdi.org.

30. "Ward Testifies before Senate on US Africa Command," AFRICOM, 17 March 2009, www.africom.mil/. Figures compiled from US State Department, *Congressional Budget Justification for Foreign Operations,* FY 2010, pp. 6–136.

31. Michael Klare and Daniel Volman, "The African 'Oil Rush' and US National Security," *Third World Quarterly* 27, no. 4 (2006): pp. 609–10; Daniel Volman, "The Bush Administration and African Oil: The Security Implications of US Energy Policy," *Review of African Political Economy* 30, no. 98 (December 2003): p. 581. Emphasis added.

32. Energy Information Administration, *Country Analysis Briefs: Nigeria,* April 2007 update; David L. Goldwyn and J. Stephen Morrison, "A Strategic Approach to Governance and Security in the Gulf of Guinea: A Report of the CSIS Task Force on Gulf of Guinea Security," CSIS, July 2005, p. 5, http://csis.org.

33. Chris Alden, *China in Africa* (London: Zed Books, 2007), pp. 8–9.

34. See, variously, "Gabon: Oil Pact with China Aims to Boost Falling Reserves," *IRIN News,* 5 February 2004, www.irinnews.org/; Don Lee, "China Barrels ahead in Oil Market," *LA Times,* 14 November 2004; Le Tian, "Ties with Chad Gather Momentum," *China Daily,* 21 September 2007, www.chinadaily.com.cn/; "China's CNPC Invests in Oil Refinery in Chad," *Forbes,* 7 October 2007; Chris Hogg, "China Oil Firm Buys into Nigeria," *BBC News,* 9 January 2006, http://news.bbc.co.uk/; "China and Nigeria Agree Oil Deal," *BBC News,* 26 April 2006, http://news.bbc.co.uk/; Dino Mahtani, "Nigeria Turns to China for Defence Aid," *Financial Times,* 27 February 2006; Rory Carroll,

"China Extends Its Reach into Africa with $1bn Deal for Nigeria's Railways," *The Guardian*, 23 May 2006.

35. US Department of Defense, "General Jones Briefs on European Command and NATO," 10 October 2003, www.defenselink.mil/.

36. Eric Schmitt, "Threats and Responses: Expanding US Presence; Pentagon Seeking New Access Pacts for Africa Bases," *New York Times*, 5 July 2003.

37. As Kenneth Mooreland, US ambassador to Gabon (and therefore the key US diplomatic link with Sao Tome and Principe), stated: "There are different ways of assuming a strategic presence. It doesn't necessarily have to be a base or a port with all the commitment and investment that implies. You have to build the damned thing, and then, God knows, you have to protect it. But if you believe that this is an area of enhanced strategic importance, and I do, then the U.S. must adopt a new level of relationship with the region. If you see that fifteen per cent of our oil comes from this area, and this could soon be thirty per cent, then x plus y makes z. It doesn't take a genius to work that out." Anderson, "Our New Best Friend."

38. Including Cameroon, Gabon, and Equatorial Guinea, with further attempts to secure access in Nigeria, Benin, and the Ivory Coast. Martin Plaut, "US to Transfer Troops into Africa," *BBC News*, 17 September 2003, http://news.bbc.co.uk.

39. Anderson, "Our New Best Friend"; Alex Belida, "US General: Sao Tome Possible Site for 'Forward Operating Location,'" *Voice of America*, 4 September 2003, www.voanews.com/; Institute for Security Studies, "Situation Report: Sao Tome and Principe Update," 9 November 2004, p. 11, www.iss.co.za/.

40. Alex Belida, "US Moving Quickly to Cement Security Relations with Sao Tome," *Voice of America*, 6 May 2004, www.voanews.com/.

41. "US Naval Base to Protect Sao Tome Oil," *BBC News*, 22 August 2002, http://news.bbc.co.uk/.

42. US State Department, *Congressional Budget Justification for Foreign Operations*, FY 2010, p. 136.

43. Carter, "US Policy in Africa in the 21st Century."

44. On defense attachés, see Karen Kwiatkowski, cited in Wihbey and Schutz, eds., *African Oil*, p. 28. On US naval activity, which increased from almost nothing in 2004 to 130 "ship days" in 2005, and even more in 2006, see Donna Miles, "US Increasing Operations in Gulf of Guinea," *American Forces Press Service*, 5 July 2006, www.news.navy.mil/.

45. General Jones, quoted in Julian Borger, "Oil and Terrorism Drive the US Presidential Tour," *The Guardian*, 7 July 2003; Admiral Harry Ulrich, Commander, US Naval Forces Europe, cited in "Framework for Action Plan Adopted at Ministerial Conference," *Commander, US Naval Forces Europe/Commander, US 6th Fleet Public Affairs*, 16 November 2006, www.news.navy.mil/.

46. Office of the Press Secretary, White House, "President Bush Creates a Department of Defense Unified Combatant Command for Africa," 6 February 2007, http://georgewbush-whitehouse.archives.gov/.

47. General James Jones, cited in Greg Mills, "World's Biggest Military Comes to Town," *Business Day*, 9 February 2007.

48. Samantha L. Quigley, "EUCOM Leader Calls Africa Global Strategic Imperative," *American Forces Press Service*, 8 March 2006, www.news.navy.mil/.

49. Donna Miles, "US Must Confront Terrorism in Africa, General Says," *American Forces Information Services*, 16 June 2004.

50. Belida, "US General: Sao Tome Possible Site"; US Department of Defense, "Special DOD Briefing with Gen. Ward and Admiral Ulrich from the Pentagon, Arlington, VA," 15 October 2007, www.defenselink.mil/.

51. This was reflected in one of the slides used in his presentation to the American Enterprise Institute conference, which pictured large arrows from the oil fields in the Gulf of Guinea to both North America *and* Europe as part of the overall "strategic opportunities" for Africa. Speech and presentation at www.aei.org/.

52. Thomas J. Christensen, Deputy Assistant Secretary of State for East Asian and Pacific Affairs, and James Swan, Deputy Assistant Secretary of State for African Affairs, "China in Africa: Implications for US Policy," Statement before the Senate Foreign Relations Committee, Subcommittee on African Affairs, 5 June 2008, www.state.gov/. Emphasis added.

53. James Swan, Deputy Assistant Secretary of State for African Affairs, "China's Expanding Role in Africa: Implications for the United States," Remarks at the Center for Strategic and International Studies, 8 February 2007, www.state.gov/.

54. Theresa Whelan, Deputy Assistant Secretary of Defense for African Affairs, Statement before House Committee on Oversight and Government Reform, Subcommittee on National Security and Foreign Affairs, "AFRICOM's Rationales, Roles and Progress on the Eve of Operations," 15 July 2008, www.africom.mil/.

55. United Nations Economic Commission for Africa, *Economic Report on Africa 1998* (Addis Ababa: UNECA, 1998).

56. US State Department, *Congressional Budget Justification for Foreign Operations,* FY 2007, p. 336.

57. White House, "President Proposes $5 Billion Plan to Help Developing Nations," Remarks by the President on Global Development, Inter-American Development Bank, 14 March 2002, http://georgewbush-whitehouse.archives.gov/.

58. Including the degree of state intervention in the economy (and any subsidization of "uncompetitive industries"); the "efficiency" of the tax system (including the presence or otherwise of "pro-investment tax policies"); the development of employment law which "provides for flexibility in hiring and firing"; investment attractiveness (including, crucially, any "legal restrictions on ownership of business and equity by non-residents"); and the "participation of the private sector in infrastructure projects" (including the "openness of the public sector contracts to foreign investors"). Millennium Challenge Corporation, *Guide to MCC Indicators and the Selection Process: Fiscal Year 2008,* pp. 26–28, www.mca.gov.

59. Ibid.

60. George Monbiot, "Africa's New Best Friends," *The Guardian,* 5 July 2005.

61. *African Growth and Opportunity Act 2000,* Section 102 (3) and (8); Section 104 (a) (1) (A)–(D); Office of the US Trade Representative, *2003 Comprehensive Report on US Trade and Investment Policy Toward Sub-Saharan Africa and Implementation of the African Growth and Opportunity Act,* May 2003, pp. 26–27, http://agoa.gov/.

62. *African Growth and Opportunity Act 2000,* Sections 111 and 112.

63. Statement of Matthew T. McManus, Acting Director of International Energy and Commodity Policy Office, Economic and Business Affairs Bureau, US Department of State, Testimony before the Senate Foreign Relations Committee, Subcommittee on International Economic Policy, Export and Trade Promotion, 21 October 2003, p. 14, www.senate.gov/.

64. UN Conference on Trade and Development, "FDI Inflows to Africa Doubled over Two Years, Led by Investments in Natural Resources," Press Release, 16 October 2007, UNCTAD/PRESS/PR/2007/031, www.unctad.org/.

65. With Equatorial Guinea the site for 31% of all investment in the region, and Angola, Chad, and Nigeria cumulatively representing another 22%. Danielle Langton, *US Trade and Investment Relationship with Sub-Saharan Africa: The African Growth and Opportunity Act and Beyond,* CRS Report, RL31772, 12 September 2007 update, p. 9, http://italy.usembassy.gov/. Export data for oil-rich states gathered from Energy Information Administration, *Country Analysis Briefs: Nigeria,* April 2007 update; Organisation for Economic Co-operation and Development, *African Economic Outlook 2007,* p. 108, www.oecd.org/; Energy Information Administration, *Country Analysis Briefs: Equatorial Guinea,* October 2007 update, www.eia.doe.gov/. Other trade data gathered from International Trade Administration, US Department of Commerce, "US-African Trade Profile," March 2007, and Bureau of Census, US Department of Commerce, "US–Sub-Saharan Africa Trade Statistics: 2006," both at www.agoa.gov/.

66. International Trade Administration, "US-African Trade Profile," p. 1.

67. Whilst the primary beneficiary of the AGOA trade regime has been capital invested in the oil sector (fully 93% of all AGOA imports into the United States in 2006 came from the oil sector). For trade data, see International Trade Administration, "US-African Trade Profile," p. 1; Office of the US Trade Representative, *2007 Comprehensive Report on US Trade and Investment Policy toward Sub-Saharan Africa and Implementation of the African Growth and Opportunity Act,* May 2007, www.ustr.gov/.

68. Energy Information Administration, *Country Analysis Briefs: Nigeria,* April 2007 update; Organisation for Economic Co-operation and Development, *African Economic Outlook 2007,* p. 108, www.oecd.org/; Energy Information Administration, *Country Analysis Briefs: Equatorial Guinea,* October 2007 update.

69. Freedom House, *Freedom in Sub-Saharan Africa, 2007: A Survey of Political Rights and Civil Liberties,* p. i, www.freedomhouse.org/.

70. International Action Network on Small Arms, Oxfam International and Saferworld, *Africa's Missing Billions: International Arms Flows and the Cost of Conflict,* October 2007, www.oxfam.org/.

71. In 2005, for instance, the region's score was 0.493, as compared to 0.691 for the developing world overall (where 0 is the least developed and 1 is the most developed). See UN Development Programme, *Human Development Report 2007,* data retrieved from http://hdr.undp.org/ (accessed August 2008).

72. UN Conference on Trade and Development, *Economic Development in Africa: From Adjustment to Poverty Reduction; What Is New?* 2002, UNCTAD/GDS/AFRICA/2, p. 3, www.unctad.org/.

73. Asad Ismi, *Impoverishing a Continent: The World Bank and the IMF in Africa,* July 2004, www.halifaxinitiative.org/.

74. UN Conference on Trade and Development, *Economic Development in Africa,* pp. 3–7.

75. All figures from UN Development Programme, *Human Development Report 2007/2008,* pp. 229–84, http://hdr.undp.org/.

76. Cited in Garry Leech, *Crude Interventions: The United States, Oil and the New World (Dis)Order* (London: Zed Books, 2006), p. 92.

77. Sharon LaFraniere, "As Angola Rebuilds, Most Find Their Poverty Persists," *New York Times,* 14 October 2007.

78. See, for instance, Christopher Thompson, "'Curse of Oil' Sees Corruption Soar in Nigeria," *The Independent,* 31 January 2007; Human Rights Watch, "Some Transparency, No Accountability: The Use of Oil Revenue in Angola and Its Impact on Human Rights," 12 January 2004, www.hrw.org/; Human Rights Watch, "Angola: New OPEC Member Should Tackle Corruption Not Critics," 14 December 2006, www .hrw.org/.

79. Human Rights Watch, "Nigeria's Delta Blues," 20 July 2008, www.hrw.org/.

80. Human Rights Watch, *World Report 2007,* http://hrw.org/.

81. Paul Brown, "Chad Oil Pipeline Under Attack for Harming the Poor," *The Guardian,* 27 September 2002.

82. Amnesty International, "Chad," *Annual Report 2004,* http://web.amnesty.org/; Friends of the Earth, *Broken Promises: The Chad-Cameroon Oil and Pipeline Project; Profit at Any Cost?* June 2001. www.foe.org/; Stephan Faris, "Fool's Gold," *Foreign Policy,* July 2007; Bank Information Center and Catholic Relief Agency, *Chad's Oil: Miracle or Mirage? Following the Money in Africa's Newest Petro-State,* February 2005, www.bicusa.org/.

83. Kelly Campbell, *Bringing Peace to the Niger Delta,* US Institute of Peace Briefing, June 2008, www.usip.org/.

84. Jonathan Brown, "Niger Delta Bears Brunt after 50 Years of Oil Spills," *The Independent,* 26 October 2006.

85. See, for instance, Justin Pearce, "Poverty and War in Cabinda," *BBC News,* 27 October 2002, http://news.bbc.co.uk/.

86. MOSOP was created in the early 1970s but adopted its Bill of Rights for autonomy and against repression in 1990. For full text, see www.mosop.net/.

87. See, for instance, Richard C. Paddock, "Protester Testifies about Nigeria Troops Shooting Him at Chevron Facility," *LA Times,* 31 October 2008.

88. The Kaiama Declaration, reprinted at www.ijawcenter.com/.

89. International Crisis Group, *The Swamps of Insurgency: Nigeria's Delta Unrest,* Africa Report No. 115, August 2006, p. 15, www.crisisgroup.org.

90. Human Rights Watch, "The Warri Crisis: Fueling Violence," November 2003, pp. 17–18, http://hrw.org/; "Nigeria Delta General Moved Out," *BBC News,* 8 March 2006, http://news.bbc.co.uk/.

91. "Nigeria's Shadowy Oil Rebels," *BBC News,* 20 April 2006, http://news.bbc.co .uk/.

92. Simon Robinson, "Nigeria's Deadly Days," *Time,* 14 May 2006.

93. International Crisis Group, *Fuelling the Niger Delta Crisis,* Africa Report No. 118, 28 September 2006, pp. 3–5, www.crisisgroup.org.

94. Daniel Howden, "Shell May Pull Out of Niger Delta after 17 Die in Boat Raid," *The Independent,* 17 January 2006.

95. "Chevron Confirms Damage to Nigerian Oil Pipelines," *The Guardian,* 13 June 2009.

96. International Crisis Group, *Fuelling the Niger Delta Crisis,* p. i; CSIS Task Force on Gulf of Guinea Security, *A Strategic Approach to Governance and Security in the Gulf of Guinea,* July 2005, p. 2, http://csis.org.

97. Cabinda is properly considered an *exclave,* given that it is separated from the rest of Angola by a thin strip of the Democratic Republic of the Congo.

98. "Congo: Interview with Roman Catholic Priest Father Jorge Congo," *IRIN News,* October 2003, www.irinnews.org/.

99. See, for instance, "Angola Separatist Group Says Holding Portuguese," *BBC News,* 13 March 2001, http://news.bbc.co.uk/.

100. João Gomes Porto, *Cabinda: Notes on a Soon-to-Be-Forgotten War,* Occasional Paper 77, Institute for Security Studies, August 2003, www.iss.co.za/.

101. Jendayi Frazer, "Keynote Address: Maritime Safety and Security, Gulf of Guinea Ministerial Conference," 15 November 2006, www.state.gov/.

102. Statement of John R. Brodman, Deputy Assistant Secretary for International Energy Policy, Office of Policy and International Affairs, US Department of Energy, before the Subcommittee on International Economic Policy, Export and Trade Promotion, Senate Committee on Foreign Relations, 15 July 2004, www.senate.gov/.

103. *Voice of America,* 24 July 2002, www.globalsecurity.org/. The Pentagon has been deeply involved in policy forums within the "independent" think tank community, where a greater US military engagement in the region has been continually advocated for the express purposes of securing access to oil and providing a stable environment for investment. The Pentagon has also co-hosted several intergovernmental and interagency conferences on regional security, wherein securing internal dynamics and the maritime environment for the purposes of oil extraction and investment are key themes. See, for instance, Pentagon involvement in the African Oil Policy Initiative Group; the congressionally mandated Africa Policy Advisory Panel (published through the Center for Strategic and International Studies [CSIS], *Rising US Stakes in Africa,* May 2004); a CSIS conference, "Promoting Accountability and Transparency in Africa's Oil Sector"; a CSIS task force, "Gulf of Guinea Security" (published as *A Strategic Approach to Governance and Security in the Gulf of Guinea,* July 2005); American Enterprise Institute conference, "Leave No Continent Behind: US National Security Interests in Africa," April 2004; CSIS Conference, "The Niger Delta: Prospects for Elections and the Future Reform Agenda," 14 March 2007.

104. White House, "President Bush Creates a Department of Defense Unified Combatant Command for Africa," 6 February 2007, http://georgewbush-whitehouse .archives.gov/.

105. US Department of Defense, "DoD News Briefing with Mr. Henry and Lt. Gen. Sharp from the Pentagon," 7 February 2007, www.defenselink.mil/.

106. General Charles Wald, Address to a Conference at American Enterprise Institute, p. 16.

107. Ed Royce, House of Representatives, contribution to Wihbey and Schutz, eds., *African Oil,* p. 7.

108. General Charles Wald, Address to a Conference at American Enterprise Institute. Emphasis added.

109. US Department of Defense, "DoD News Briefing with Mr. Henry and Lt. Gen. Sharp from the Pentagon." On the role of PMCs in the running of ACSS, see Deborah D. Avant, *The Market for Force: The Consequences for Privatizing Security* (Cambridge: Cambridge University Press, 2001), pp. 121–22.

110. Details of the 2005 energy security training course can be found at http:// africacenter.org/.

111. US State Department, *Congressional Budget Justification for Foreign Operations,* FY 2004–2007.

112. William D. Hartung and Frida Berrigan, *Militarization of US Africa Policy, 2000 to 2005*, World Policy Institute, March 2005, www.worldpolicy.org/.

113. Daniel Volman, *US Military Programs in Sub-Saharan Africa, 2001–2003*, Association of Concerned Africa Scholars, February 2003, www.prairienet.org/.

114. CSIS Conference, *The Niger Delta: Prospects for Elections and the Future Reform Agenda*, 14 March 2007. An audio recording of Whelan's speech can be found at www .csis.org/.

115. Wihbey and Schutz, eds., *African Oil*, p. 7.

116. Greg Jaffe, "In Massive Shift, US Is Planning to Cut Size of Military in Germany," *Wall Street Journal*, 10 June 2003, cited in *Africa Command: US Strategic Interests and the Role of US Military in Africa*, CRS Report, July 2007, www.fas.org/.

117. Hector Igbikiowubo, "US Offers Nigeria Military Aid to Protect Offshore Oil," *All Africa*, 25 July 2004, www.energybulletin.net/.

118. Ian Garrick Mason, "A Growing Source for Oil Is Also a Target: West Africa, a Big Exporter to the US, Demonstrates the 'Paradox of Plenty,'" *San Francisco Chronicle*, 19 September 2004.

119. CSIS Conference, *The Niger Delta*.

120. Nico Colombant, "US Helps West African Navies," *Voice of America*, 1 February 2005, www.voanews.com/; "US Military Commander to Visit African Oil Producers," *IRIN News*, 23 August 2004, www.irinnews.org/.

121. Amnesty International, *World Report 2008*, http://thereport.amnesty.org/.

122. Amnesty International, "Contracting Out of Human Rights: The Chad-Cameroon Pipeline Project," September 2005, AI Index: POL 34/12/2005, http://web.amnesty.org/.

123. See the various annual reports on the situation in Chad throughout the 1990s from Amnesty International and the State Department. Also see Amnesty International, "Chad: The Habré Legacy," AI Index: AFR 20/004/2001, 16 October 2001, http:// web.amnesty.org/; Amnesty International, "Contracting Out of Human Rights."

124. Friends of the Earth, *Broken Promises*.

125. Amnesty International, "Contracting Out of Human Rights."

126. Porto, *Cabinda*.

127. United Nations, *Civil and Political Rights, Including Questions of Torture and Detention: Report of the Special Rapporteur*, Sir Nigel S. Rodley, Submitted Pursuant to Commission on Human Rights Resolution 1998/38, UN Commission on Human Rights, 55th Session, 12 January 1999, E/CN.4/1999/61, para. 42, http://documents-dds-ny.un.org/.

128. "Rebels on the Run, Villagers Flee into Jungle," *Edmonton Journal* (Alberta), 17 March 2003.

129. Porto, *Cabinda*.

130. Radio France Internationale, "Angolan Defence Minister Says Cabinda War 'Has Been Practically Resolved,'" *BBC Monitoring International Reports*, 15 December 2003.

131. Porto, *Cabinda*.

132. Human Rights Watch, "Angola," *World Report 2005*, http://hrw.org/.

133. "Angola," Country Reports on Human Rights Practices 2002, US State Department, www.state.gov/; Zoe Eisenstein, "Angolan Army 'Abuses Cabindans,'" *BBC News*, 2 February 2005, http://news.bbc.co.uk/.

134. "Cabinda, One of Africa's Longest, Least Reported Conflicts," *IRIN News*, October 2003, www.irinnews.org/.

135. For detailed cases, see Human Rights Watch, *Angola: Between War and Peace in Cabinda,* Briefing Paper, 2004, http://hrw.org/; plus the various State Department human rights reports.

136. Human Rights Watch, "Angola," *World Report 2005;* US State Department, "Angola," *Country Reports on Human Rights Practices 2004,* www.state.gov/.

137. "UN Reports Angola 'Torture' Abuse," *BBC News,* 28 September 2007, http://news.bbc.co.uk/.

138. "Angola: Military Blames Church for Cabindan 'Banditry,'" *Africa News,* 14 May 2004.

139. "Angolan Forces Break Up Human Rights Group Launch: Organisers," *Agence France Presse,* 5 February 2004.

140. See, for instance, the continued calls it makes for an immediate and unconditional truce between FLEC and Luanda, often during peace marches which it has organized. "15,000 March for Peace in Angola's Troubled Cabinda Enclave," *Agence France Presse,* 12 July 2004; "Angola's Oil-Rich Cabinda Province Rallies for Self-Rule," *Agence France Presse,* 31 January 2005.

141. Radio France Internationale, "Angola: Civic Rights Leader Says Situation in Cabinda 'Tense,'" *BBC Monitoring International Reports,* 22 March 2004.

142. Amnesty International, "Angola: Human Rights Organisation Banned," public statement, 4 August 2006, AI Index: AFR 12/006/2006, www.amnesty.org/.

143. Human Rights Watch, "Angola: Events of 2006," *World Report 2007,* http://hrw.org/.

144. Amnesty International, "Nigeria: Are Human Rights in the Pipeline?" 9 November 2004, www.amnesty.org/.

145. Human Rights Watch, *The Price of Oil: Corporate Responsibility and Human Rights Violations in Nigeria's Oil Producing Communities,* January 1999, www.hrw.org/.

146. John Vidal, "Shell Settlement with Ogoni People Stops Short of Full Justice," *The Guardian,* 10 June 2009.

147. International Crisis Group, *The Swamps of Insurgency,* pp. 7–11.

148. Human Rights Watch, *World Report 1994,* www.hrw.org.

149. Human Rights Watch, *The Price of Oil.*

150. Unrepresented Nations and People Organisation, "Nigerian Government to Use Armed Force against People," Press Release, 29 April 1994, www.cwis.org/.

151. "Nigeria's 'Drilling Fields,'" *Multinational Monitor,* January/February 1995, www.multinationalmonitor.org/.

152. Amnesty International, "Ten Years On: Injustice and Violence Haunt the Niger Delta," November 2005, http://www.amnesty.org/.

153. Kenneth C. Omeje, *High Stakes and Stakeholders: Oil, Conflict and Security in Nigeria* (London: Ashgate, 2006), p. 145.

154. Xan Rice, "Civilians Killed in Nigeria Fighting, Claims Amnesty," *The Guardian,* 22 May 2009.

155. Wihbey and Schutz, eds., *African Oil,* p. 6.

156. Barry Schutz, "veteran African analyst" for the State Department (where he was senior analyst in the Africa Office of the Department's Bureau of Intelligence and Research and co-chair of the influential African Oil Policy Initiative Group, cited in Anderson, "Our New Best Friend."

157. Human Rights Watch, Letter to Secretary of State Powell, "Africa: Use Trade Law for Human Rights," 25 October 2001, and "Bush Trip to Africa, July 2003," *Human Rights Watch Backgrounder,* undated, both at http://hrw.org/.

158. CSIS Conference, *The Niger Delta.* Emphasis added.

CHAPTER SIX: Latin America

1. David Harvey, *A Brief History of Neoliberalism* (Oxford: Oxford University Press, 2005), p. 88.

2. Kelly Hoffman and Miguel Angel Centeno, "The Lopsided Continent: Inequality in Latin America," *Annual Review of Sociology* 29 (2003): p. 372.

3. 2007 figures. When Mexico is included in the figures as a Latin American state (some analysts, unlike us, refer to it as part of North America), the region holds 123.4 billion barrels. British Petroleum, *BP Statistical Review of World Energy 2008,* June 2008, p. 6, www.bp.com/.

4. Together, Mexico, Venezuela, and Colombia are known to be sitting on proven reserves of 100.7 billion barrels of oil, out of a regional total of 123.4 billion barrels. In 2007, the three countries together produced 6.7 mbpd, out of a regional total of 10.8 mbpd. In 2004, they exported 3.9 mbpd to markets, out of a total from the region of 4.9 mbpd. See British Petroleum, *BP Statistical Review of World Energy 2008,* June 2008, p. 6; Energy Information Administration, *World Production of Crude Oil, NGPL, and Other Liquids, and Refinery Processing Gain, Most Recent Annual Estimates, 1980–2007,* 21 April 2008 update, www.eia.doe.gov/; Energy Information Administration, *World Petroleum Supply and Disposition, 2004,* 6 August 2007 update, www.eia.doe.gov/.

5. National Energy Policy Development Group, *National Energy Policy,* May 2001, 8-10.

6. Peter Pace, *Advance Questions for Lieutenant General Peter Pace: Defense Reforms.* US Senate Committee on Armed Services, 2000, www.senate.gov/; Admiral James G. Stavridis, *The Posture Statement of United States Southern Command before the 110th Congress,* 21–22 March 2007, www.southcom.mil/.

7. "Interview with Anne Patterson, US Ambassador to Colombia," *El Tiempo* (Colombia), 10 February 2002, www.ciponline.org/.

8. George H. W. Bush, "Statement on Trade Initiatives for the Andean Region," 1 November 1989, http://bushlib.tamu.edu/.

9. US State Department, *Summary of Principal Provisions of NAFTA: North American Free Trade Agreement,* 30 August 1993.

10. All GDP figures are in current US dollars for 2006 and are calculated from data presented at World Bank, *Key Development Data and Statistics,* http://web.worldbank .org/.

11. Also known as the Dominican Republic–Central America Free Trade Agreement (DR-CAFTA). See "Central American Trade Deal Done," *BBC News,* 28 May 2004, http:// news.bbc.co.uk/.

12. The deal eliminated more than 80% of existing duties on US manufacturing exports to the region as well as 50% of US agricultural exports. As a consequence, US exports to participating states expanded by 16% in the first full year of the agreement's operation (2006) when compared to the previous year, with parallel imports *from* the region rising just 3%: overall figures which hide larger discrepancies in particular

cases. For instance, exports to El Salvador rose more than 16% during this period, whilst imports fell more than 6%. Overall, this allowed the United States to post a trade surplus to the region, as the removal of trade barriers led to the opening up of previously protected sectors within Central American economies. In the key agricultural sector, for instance, exports to Honduras were up 31% as US-based capital made use of the new opportunities, with parallel imports from the Central American country into the US down 1%. A similar picture has been emerging in the agricultural sectors of El Salvador and Guatemala. Office of the US Trade Representative, "US Trade with the CAFTA-DR Countries," *CAFTA Policy Brief,* July 2007, www.ustr.gov/.

13. David de Ferranti, Guillermo E. Perry, Francisco Ferreira, and Michael Walton, *Inequality in Latin America: Breaking with History?* World Bank, February 2004, http://worldbank.org.

14. Hoffman and Centeno, "The Lopsided Continent," p. 369.

15. Tom Gibb, "US Praise for Brazil's Reforms," *BBC News,* 24 April 2003, http://news.bbc.co.uk/.

16. SOUTHCOM is the Pentagon's Unified Combatant Command responsible for providing contingency planning, operations, and security cooperation for Central and South America (not including Mexico) and the Caribbean as well as ensuring the defense of the Panama Canal and surrounding area. See www.southcom.mil.

17. Pace, *Advance Questions.*

18. James T. Hill, *Posture Statement,* US Southern Command, House Armed Services Committee, March 12, 2003, www.house.gov/.

19. Stavridis, *Posture Statement.*

20. Figures peaked at a staggering 23,000 in 2003, as aid to Colombia under Plan Colombia gathered speed.

21. Posture Statement by General James T. Hill, Commander, US Southern Command, before the House Armed Services Committee, 12 March 2003, www.ciponline.org/.

22. Center for International Policy, *Blurring the Lines: Trends in US Military Programs with Latin America,* September 2004, http://worldbank.org.

23. US Southern Command, "Fuerzas Comando," www.southcom.mil/.

24. General James T. Hill, Commander, US Southern Command, testimony before the House Armed Services Committee, Washington, March 24, 2004, www.house.gov/.

25. "Secretary Rumsfeld Remarks at Roundtable during the Central American Ministerial in Miami, Fl.," 12 October 2005, www.defenselink.mil/; Stavridis, *Posture Statement.*

26. The new focus of US-trained militaries was made clear by the Argentine Defense Minister: "The vision of the United States and Canada (for the role of the military) is one of policing or internal control. Our vision is diametrically opposed to that." This was clearly the case in Guatemala in 2005, as popular resistance to the then-upcoming ratification of CAFTA, underpinned by discontent with the agreement by 65% of the population, was crushed by Guatemalan security forces. These developments, which saw the feared military back on the streets to impose order, met with little US opposition. In contrast, the US State Department certified that the military no longer played a role in internal defense, thus removing established constraints on military aid to the country. Rumsfeld visited Guatemala the week after the protests to for-

mally announce the shift in policy, stating: "I've been impressed by the reforms that have been undertaken here in the armed forces [and] I'm very pleased that the United States has been able to release the $3.2 million of military assistance funds." The Guatemalan Defense Minister, Carlos Aldana, said that Rumsfeld had visited in order to support a retransition of military focus back toward meeting domestic threats and agreed that "the armed forces need to become more involved in internal security." See Amnesty International, "Guatemala: Fear for Safety," 13 May 2005, AMR 34/021/2005, www.amnesty.org/; Matthew Kennis, "Despite Ratification, Anti-CAFTA Protests Continue in Guatemala," IRC Americas Program, International Relations Center, 13 April 2005, http://americas.irc-online.org/; "Press Conference with Secretary Rumsfeld and Honorable Oscar Berger Perdomo, President of Guatemala," 25 March 2005, www .defenselink.mil/.

27. "Deadly Clashes in Peru's Amazon," *BBC News,* 5 June 2009, http://news.bbc.co .uk/.

28. Admiral James Stavridis, *US Southern Command: 2009 Posture Statement,* p. 15, www.southcom.mil/.

29. Center for International Policy, *Below the Radar: US Military Programs with Latin America, 1997–2007,* March 2007, www.ciponline.org; Center for International Policy, *Blurring the Lines.*

30. In 2006, oil accounted for $3.1 billion out of total exports of $8.8 billion. US International Trade Commission, *US-Colombia Trade Promotion Agreement: Potential Economy-wide and Selected Sectoral Effects,* December 2006, www.usitc.gov/. For FDI data, see US State Department, "Background Note: Colombia," May 2009, www.state .gov/.

31. By 2006 Colombia had become the United States' largest agricultural export market outside NAFTA and the fifth largest export market overall, representing a stunning success for the interests of foreign companies wishing to export to the country. US State Department, "Background Note: Colombia," March 2008.

32. Government of Colombia, *Plan Colombia: Plan for Peace, Prosperity, and the Strengthening of the State,* 1999. Reprinted at US Institute of Peace Library, www.usip .org/.

33. US International Trade Commission, *US-Colombia Trade Promotion Agreement.*

34. Garry Leech, *Crude Interventions: The United States, Oil and the New World (Dis) Order* (London: Zed Books, 2006).

35. Energy Information Administration, *Country Analysis Brief: Colombia,* September 2007 update, www.eia.doe.gov/.

36. "Colombia President Welcomes China to Invest in Oil," *People's Daily,* 8 April 2005, http://english.peopledaily.com.cn/. The relationship between China and Colombia's oil sectors was sealed when both China's Sinopec and India's Oil & Natural Gas Corp. concluded an $850 million investment for a 50% stake of Colombia's oil giant Omimex de Colombia with further key investments in the future. "Oil PSUs Look for More Blocks in Colombia," *The Hindu,* 7 September 2008, www.hindu.com/.

37. Tony Avirgan, "World Bank, IMF Threw Colombia into a Tailspin," *Baltimore Sun,* 4 April 2002; Mario Novelli, "Globalisations, Social Movement Unionism and New Internationalisms: The Role of Strategic Learning in the Transformation of the Municipal Workers Union of EMCALI," *Globalization, Education, Societies* 2, no. 2 (July 2004): pp. 161–90.

38. USAID, "Colombia," *Congressional Budget Justification for Foreign Operations,* FY 2006, www.usaid.gov/.

39. Two groups in particular pose a significant challenge to the Colombian state: the FARC and the smaller ELN. For a spotlight on the opposition of these groups to neoliberal reforms, and the revolutionary agenda adopted in this light, see the interview with (since-assassinated) FARC commander Raul Reyes. Garry Leech, "Interview with FARC Commander Raul Reyes," *Colombia Journal,* 12 July 2007, www.colombia journal.org/.

40. For a recent example, see the occupation of the Pan-American Highway in Colombia in the autumn of 2008 by over 20,000 civilians opposed to the US-Colombia Free Trade Agreement and demanding unmet legal entitlements to land. See "Indigenous Peoples of Colombia Flex Their Muscles," *Semana,* 28 October 2008, www.semana .com/.

41. Luis van Isschot, "The Siege of Barrancabermeja: Human Rights, Urban Armed Conflict and the Dirty War in Colombia's Oil Capital," paper presented at the annual meeting of the ISA's 49th Annual Convention, 26 March 2008.

42. Bill Weinberg, "Terror in Colombia: An Instrument of 'Free Trade Policy?" *The Nation,* 23 March 2004.

43. A total of 170 attacks. Connie Veillette, *Plan Colombia: A Progress Report,* CRS Report RL32774, 22 June 2005 update, p. 11, www.fas.org/.

44. Testimony of Lawrence P. Meriage, Vice President, Executive Services and Public Affairs, Occidental Oil and Gas Corporation, before the House Government Reform Subcommittee on Criminal Justice, Drug Policy and Human Resources Hearing on Colombia, www.house.gov/.

45. Garry Leech, "Plan Petroleum in Putumayo," *Colombia Journal,* 10 May 2004, www.colombiajournal.org/.

46. Such ties are not limited to the oil sector. There is significant evidence that both the Ohio-based banana company Chiquita Brands International and the Alabama-based coal company Drummond have had direct links with the largest paramilitary group, the AUC. Such links have included the financing, arming, and equipping of AUC units and complicity in the murder of union leaders. "US Companies Tied to Colombian Labor Activist Murders at House Hearing," *International Herald Tribune,* 28 June 2007; Juan Forero, "Colombia May Seek Chiquita Extraditions: Eight Executives Targeted in Paramilitary Payment Scandal," *Washington Post,* 21 March 2007.

47. Michael Gillard, Ignacio Gomez, and Melissa Jones, "BP Hands 'Tarred in Pipeline Dirty War,'" *The Guardian,* 17 October 1998.

48. Thad Dunning and Leslie Wirpsa, "Oil Rigged," *Resource Center of the Americas,* February 2001, www.globalpolicy.org/.

49. Garry Leech, "Colombia's Economic Growth Fuelled by Repression," *Colombia Journal,* 19 May 2008, www.colombiajournal.org/.

50. For an in-depth discussion of the US-supported CI war in Colombia during the Cold War, see Doug Stokes, *America's Other War: Terrorizing Colombia* (London: Zed Books, 2004), pp. 57–83.

51. The first Bush administration compiled a $2.1 billion, heavily militarized package under the Andean Initiative. Not least, this package accelerated IMET and FMF programs to Colombia from $8 million in FY 1989 to over $70 million twelve months later. Congressional Budget Office, *The Andean Initiative: Objective and Support,* March

1994 (Washington, DC: CBO), pp. 18–19, 42, 54. Likewise, the Clinton administration's support for Plan Colombia led to a predominantly military focus (75% of the $860 million initially allocated by Congress to Plan Colombia was for military aid, making it the third largest global recipient of US security assistance). Ingrid Vaicius and Adam Isacson, *Plan Colombia: The Debate in Congress,* April, 2000, www.ciponline.org/. General Charles Wilhelm, CINC of SOUTHCOM, summarized the primacy of the military component of Plan Colombia when he stated: "While I share the widely held opinion that the ultimate solution to Colombia's internal problems lies in negotiations, I am convinced that success on the battlefield provides the leverage that is a precondition for meaningful and productive negotiations." General Charles Wilhelm, Statement before the House Committee on Government Reform, Subcommittee on Criminal Justice, Drug Policy, and Human Resources, 15 February 2000, http://usregsec.sdsu.edu/.

52. Amongst various sources, see US Department of Justice, Drug Enforcement Administration, Intelligence Division, *Insurgent Involvement in the Colombian Drug Trade,* June 1994, www.gwu.edu/; "Statement by James Milford," *DEA Congressional Testimony,* House International Relations Committee, Subcommittee on the Western Hemisphere, July 16, 1997, www.usdoj.gov/; "Statement of Donnie R. Marshall," *DEA Congressional Testimony,* Senate Caucus on International Narcotics Control, February 28, 2001, www.usdoj.gov/. On Uribe and drugs, see "US Intelligence Listed Colombian President Uribe among 'Important Colombian Narco-Traffickers' in 1991," National Security Archive, 2 August 2004, www.gwu.edu/. For a full discussion, see Stokes, *America's Other War.*

53. Ingrid Vaicius and Adam Isacson, "The 'War on Drugs' Meets the 'War on Terror,'" *International Policy Report,* February 2003, http://ciponline.org/.

54. Thus, the US embassy in Colombia received private "assurances from the Colombian Ministry of Defense that these aircraft will be primarily used in counternarcotics *and counterterrorism* operations." US Embassy of Colombia cable, "Colombia UH-60 Helicopter Purchase: Exim Bank Financing," 26 April 2000, unclassified, www.gwu.edu/. Emphasis added.

55. Interview conducted by Doug Stokes, 26 June 2002.

56. Making Supplemental Appropriations for Further Recovery from and Response to Terrorist Attacks on the United States for the Fiscal Year Ending September 30, 2002, and for Other Purposes, Section 601, P.L. 107–117.

57. US State Department, "Colombia," *Congressional Budget Justification for Foreign Operations,* FY 2005, www.state.gov/.

58. Figures from Center for International Policy, *US Aid to Colombia: Summary Tables,* www.ciponline.org/.

59. In a recent example, the peaceful occupation of the Pan-American Highway discussed earlier has been met by widespread police violence, including shooting into the crowd by masked riot police. See "Video May Show Colombian Police Firing Shots during Protest," *CNN News,* 22 October 2008, www.cnn.com/.

60. See the vast amount of data compiled on this subject from a variety of sources and presented in the annual State Department Country Reports on Human Rights, as well as the annual Human Rights Watch *World Report.*

61. Amnesty International USA, "Human Rights and USA Military Aid to Colombia II," January 2001, http://web.amnesty.org/.

62. Human Rights Watch, *The "Sixth Division": Military-Paramilitary Ties and US Policy in Colombia* (New York: Human Rights Watch, 2001), p. 1.

63. Human Rights Watch, *Colombia's Killer Networks: The Military-Paramilitary Partnership and the United States* (London: Human Rights Watch, 1996).

64. In a visit to the region in 2001, Human Rights Watch obtained "extensive, detailed and consistent evidence showing that the Twenty-Fourth Brigade maintained a close alliance with the paramilitaries, resulting in extrajudicial executions, forced disappearances and death threats." Human Rights Watch, *The "Sixth Division,"* p. 17. For relations between the First CN Battalion and the 24th Brigade, see US Embassy of Colombia cable, "Part of the 1st CN Battalion Deployed to Southern Putumayo; Logistical Support from 24th Brigade," 26 June 2000, confidential, www.gwu.edu/.

65. State Department cable, "Approach to MOD on 24th Brigade," 5 July 2000, secret, www.gwu.edu/.

66. Nearly 2,000 noncombatants were killed by paramilitaries between June 2000 and June 2001, and well over 1,000 in both 2002 and 2003. US State Department, "2002 Country Reports on Human Rights Practices," 31 March 2003; "2003 Country Reports on Human Rights Practices," 25 February 2004. Both at http://www.state.gov.

67. Human Rights Watch, "Colombia's Checkbook Impunity," September 22, 2003, http://hrw.org/; UN High Commissioner for Human Rights Bogotá Field Office, *Observaciones al Proyecto de Ley Estatutaria que trata sobre la reincorporacion de miembros de grupos armados* (Bogotá: UNHCHR, 2003); Amnesty International, "Colombia: The Paramilitaries in Medellín; Demobilization or Legalization?" http://web.amnesty.org/.

68. The UN concluded that throughout this period "the paramilitary groups, despite their declared cessation of hostilities . . . continued their expansion and consolidation, including social and institutional control at the local and regional levels, as well as close links with drug trafficking." Organization of the Work of the Session, Report of the High Commissioner for Human Rights on the Situation of Human Rights in Colombia, E/CN.4/2005/10, 28 February 2005, www.hchr.org.co/. See also Amnesty International, *Report 2008: Colombia* (London: Amnesty International, 2008). In particular, the capture in 2007 of a laptop computer from a leading paramilitary commander revealed evidence that unemployed peasants had posed as paramilitaries during the demobilization process, whilst the real fighters continued to massacre civilians (killing 558 individuals in one region of northern Colombia during the "ceasefire"). See "Colombia's Ex–Spy Chief Charged," *BBC News,* 23 February 2007, http://news.bbc.co.uk/; Toby Muse, "Colombian Won't Resign Despite Scandal," *Washington Post,* 16 February 2007.

69. Leech, *Crude Interventions,* pp. 160–62.

70. "Oil Inflames Colombia's Civil War: Bush Seeks $98 Million to Help Bogota Battle Guerrilla Pipeline Saboteurs," *Christian Science Monitor,* 5 March 2002.

71. House Appropriations Committee, Secretary of State Colin Powell before the Foreign Operations Subcommittee, 13 February 2002. Excerpts available at www.ciponline.org.

72. "Interview with Anne Patterson, US Ambassador to Colombia," *El Tiempo* (Colombia), 10 February 2002, www.ciponline.org/.

73. Assistance funding compiled by the Center for International Policy's Colombia Program, www.ciponline.org/; George Bush, *President's Budget Message on Andean Counterdrug Initiative,* Washington, DC, US Department of State, 4 February 2002, http://usinfo.state.gov/.

74. US State Department, *Foreign Military Training: Joint Report to Congress, Fiscal Years 2003 and 2004,* June 2004, Section IV, p. 259, www.state.gov; Jeremy McDermott, "Green Berets Move into Colombia's Oil Fields," *Daily Telegraph,* 12 October 2002; Vaicius and Isacson, "The 'War on Drugs' Meets the 'War on Terror.'"

75. Amnesty International, "Colombia: Trade Unionists and Human Rights Defenders Under Attack," 27 August 2003, AI Index: AMR 23/058/2003, www.amnesty.org/; Isabel Hilton, "Colombia's Oil Pipeline Is Paid for in Blood and Dollars: Trade Unionists are the Prime Target of the US-Funded 18th Brigade," *The Guardian,* 20 August 2004.

76. Michael Wimbish, "SOUTHCOM Commander Testifies before Congress," US Southern Command Public Affairs, 13 March 2008, www.southcom.mil/.

77. Stavridis, *US Southern Command,* p. 16.

78. Center for International Policy, "First Peek at the Obama Administration's 2010 Aid Request," 7 May 2009, www.cipcol.org/; Nadja Drost, "A Heightened US Military Presence in Colombia?" *Semana,* 5 June 2009, www.semana.com/.

79. Michael Camdessus, Managing Director, International Monetary Fund, "Press Conference," 3 October 1996, www.imf.org/.

80. James Bennet, "In Venezuela, Clinton Promotes Hemisphere Trade Zone," *New York Times,* 13 October 1997.

81. See Suzana Sawyer, *Crude Chronicles: Indigenous Politics, Multinational Oil, and Neoliberalism in Ecuador* (Durham, NC: Duke University Press, 2004).

82. Francisco Rodriguez, "Factor Shares and Resource Booms: Accounting for the Evolution of Venezuelan Inequality," in Giovanni Andrea Cornia, ed., *Inequality Growth and Poverty in an Era of Liberalization and Globalization* (Oxford: Oxford University Press, 2004), p. 327.

83. Steve Wiggins, Alexander Schejtman, George Gray, and Carlos Toranzo, "Institutions and Economic Growth in Bolivia," Research Programme Consortium on Improving Institutions for Pro-Poor Growth, IPPG Briefing Paper 6, November 2006, www.ippg.org.uk/.

84. Omar S. Arias and Magdalena Bendini, "Bolivia Poverty Assessment: Establishing the Basis for Pro-Poor Growth," World Bank, *En Breve* 89 (May 2006), http://site resources.worldbank.org/.

85. World Bank, *Ecuador Poverty Assessment,* April 2004, Report No. 27061-EC, p. xxxii, www-wds.worldbank.org/.

86. Douglas Farah, "A Tutor to Every Army in Latin America: US Expands Latin American Training Role," *Washington Post,* 13 July 1998.

87. Hill, testimony before the House Armed Services Committee, Washington, March 24, 2004.

88. Roger Pardo-Maurer, Deputy Assistant Secretary of Defense for Western Hemisphere Affairs, remarks before the Hudson Institute, 26 July 2005, www.ciponline.org/. Likewise, then–secretary of defense Rumsfeld was clear that "both Cuba and Venezuela have been involved in the situation in Bolivia in unhelpful ways." "Secretary Rumsfeld Media Availability Enroute to Paraguay," DoD News Transcript, 16 August 2005, www.defenselink.mil/.

89. US State Department, "Bolivia," *Congressional Budget Justification for Foreign Operations,* FY 2006. See also Lisa Haugaard, Adam Isacson, and Joy Olson, *Erasing the*

*Lines: Trends in US Military Programs with Latin America* (Washington, DC: CIP, LAWGEF, and WOLA, 2005), www.ciponline.org/.

90. "New Law Sparks Venezuela Oil Row," *BBC News,* 1 December 2001, http://news .bbc.co.uk/.

91. James Ingham, "Nationalisation Sweeps Venezuela," *BBC News,* 15 May 2007, http://news.bbc.co.uk/, and "Venezuela Raises Foreign Oil Tax," *BBC News,* 16 April 2008, both at http://news.bbc.co.uk/.

92. The largest share of the vote received by any candidate in the country since democracy was restored in 1980.

93. "Morales Inaugural Speech: Excerpts," *BBC News,* 22 January 2006, http://news .bbc.co.uk/.

94. Paulo Prada, "Bolivian Nationalizes the Oil and Gas Sector," *New York Times,* 2 May 2006.

95. Energy Information Administration, *Country Analysis Briefs: Ecuador,* April 2008 update, www.eia.doe.gov/.

96. "Ecuador 'Expels World Bank Envoy,'" *BBC News,* 26 April 2007, http://news .bbc.co.uk/.

97. Greg Morsbach, "Venezuela Basks in Oil 'Bonanza,'" *BBC News,* 17 February 2006, http://news.bbc.co.uk/; Juan Forero, "US Aid Can't Win Bolivia's Love as New Suitors Emerge," *New York Times,* 14 May 2006. The full text of the People's Trade Agreement is reprinted at www.pcusa.org/.

98. White House, "President Bush Discusses Democracy in the Western Hemisphere," 6 November 2005, http://georgewbush-whitehouse.archives.gov/; Elisabeth Bumiller and Larry Rohter, "Bush Targets Venezuela's Chavez in Tough Speech," *New York Times,* 6 November 2005.

99. Frank C. Urbancic, Principal Deputy Coordinator for Counterterrorism, State Department, "Venezuela: Terrorism Hub of South America?" Statement before the House Committee on International Relations, Subcommittee on International Terrorism and Nonproliferation, 13 July 2006, www.state.gov/. Likewise, Carl Ford, when assistant secretary of state for intelligence and research, spoke of the threat posed by Chavez "joining with Castro in several occasions in voicing concerns about the US." Although Ford claimed that it "doesn't bother me so long as it's just words," he was clear that the anti-US rhetoric masked real action: "There are also indications that he is sympathetic and helpful to the FARC in Colombia and various other groups." Testimony of Carl W. Ford, Assistant Secretary of State for Intelligence and Research, "Current and Projected National Security Threats to the United States," Senate Select Committee on Intelligence, 6 February 2002, www.fas.org/. Such claims have been reinforced by the Uribe administration in Colombia, although they have yet to be confirmed by any independent source. "Dead Rebel's Laptop Shows Chavez Is Funding Rebels, Colombian Police Say," *International Herald Tribune,* 3 March 2008.

100. White House, *The National Security Strategy of the United States of America,* March 2006, p. 15, http://georgewbush-whitehouse.archives.gov/.

101. Testimony of George Tenet, Director of Central Intelligence, "Current and Projected National Security Threats to the United States," Senate Select Committee on Intelligence, 6 February 2002, www.fas.org/.

102. Steve Holland, "What's in an Obama-Chavez Handshake?" *Reuters,* 20 April 2009.

103. Andy Webb-Vidal, "US Military Sees Oil Nationalism Spectre," *Financial Times,* 25 June 2006.

104. Hill, testimony before the House Armed Services Committee, Washington, March 24, 2004.

105. Testimony of Admiral James Stavridis, CINC-SOUTHCOM, before Senate Armed Services Committee, 6 March 2008, www.southcom.mil/.

106. "Venezuela: Not Fully Cooperating with US Anti-Terrorism Efforts," Taken Question, State Department Daily Press Briefing, 15 May 2006, www.state.gov/.

107. US State Department, *Congressional Budget Justification for Foreign Operations,* FY 2010.

108. "Bolivia Tells US Envoy to Leave," *BBC News,* 11 September 2008, http://news .bbc.co.uk/.

109. "Hugo Chavez Departs," *New York Times,* 13 April 2002.

110. US Department of State and the Broadcasting Board of Governors, Office of Inspector General, *A Review of US Policy toward Venezuela, November 2001–April 2002,* Report No. 02-OIG-003, July 2002, http://oig.state.gov/.

111. Juan Forero, "Documents Show CIA Knew of a Coup Plot in Venezuela," *New York Times,* 3 December 2004.

112. Ed Vulliamy, "Venezuela Coup Linked to Bush Team: Specialists in the 'Dirty Wars' of the Eighties Encouraged the Plotters Who Tried to Topple President Chavez," *The Observer,* 21 April 2002.

113. Duncan Campbell, "American Navy 'Helped Venezuelan Coup,'" *The Guardian,* 29 April 2002.

114. "Energy Focus for Chavez in China," *BBC News,* 22 August 2006, http://news .bbc.co.uk/.

115. For recent details of Venezuelan-Russian and Venezuelan-Chinese relations, see Rory Carroll and Luke Harding, "Russia to Build Nuclear Reactor for Chavez," *The Guardian,* 19 November 2008; Rory Carroll, "President's Latin American Tour Cements Beijing's Trade Clout," *The Guardian,* 19 November 2008.

116. Roger F. Noriega, Assistant Secretary for Western Hemisphere Affairs, Statement before the House Subcommittee on the Western Hemisphere, 6 April 2005, www .state.gov/.

117. Energy Information Administration, *Country Analysis Brief: Mexico,* December 2007 update, www.eia.doe.gov/.

118. Luis Téllez Kuenzler, "Latin America," in Jan H. Kalicki and David L. Goldwyn, eds., *Energy Security: Toward a New Foreign Policy Strategy* (Washington, DC: Woodrow Wilson Center Press, 2005), pp. 387–88.

119. Such as the systematic blocking of loans or spare parts to the sector throughout the Cold War. See Gabriel Kolko, *Confronting the Third World: United States Foreign Policy, 1945–1980* (New York: Pantheon Books, 1988), p. 38.

120. Gary Gereffi and Martha A. Martinez, "Mexico's Economic Transition Under NAFTA," in Russell Crandall, Guadalupe Paz, and Riordan Roett, eds., *Mexico's Democracy at Work: Political and Economic Dynamics* (London: Lynne Rienner, 2005), p. 120.

121. By the end of the 1990s there were only 200-odd state-owned firms in existence (down from 1,100 in 1982).

122. See, for example, International Monetary Fund, "IMF Approves US$17.8 Billion Stand-By Credit for Mexico," Press Release No. 95/10, 1 February 1995, www.imf.org/.

123. Gereffi and Martinez, "Mexico's Economic Transition Under NAFTA," pp. 119–20.

124. J. W. Russell, "Mexico's Rising Inequality," *Monthly Review* 49, no. 7 (December 1997): pp. 28–33.

125. Harvey, *A Brief History of Neoliberalism*, p. 104.

126. John J. Audley, Demetrios G. Papademetriou, Sandra Polaski, and Scott Vaughan, *NAFTA's Promise and Reality: Lessons from Mexico for the Hemisphere* (Washington, DC: CEIP, 2004), pp. 6–7.

127. See Laura Carlsen, "'Deep Integration': The Anti-Democratic Expansion of NAFTA," Americas Policy Program, 30 May 2007, http://americas.irc-online.org.

128. Council on Foreign Relations, *Building a North American Community: Report of an Independent Task Force*, 2005, www.cfr.org/.

129. "SPP Prosperity Working Groups," Security and Prosperity Partnership of North America, www.spp.gov/.

130. Hector Tobar, "Calderon Seeks an Overhaul of Mexico's Oil Firm," *LA Times*, 9 April 2008.

131. "Oil Debate Stirs Mexico Passions," *BBC News*, 19 March 2008, http://news.bbc .co.uk/.

132. Mario Gonzalez and Rey Rodriguez, "Mexico Opens Pemex to Private Investment," *CNN News*, 29 October 2008, http://edition.cnn.com/.

133. See, for instance, Kenneth C. Shadlen, "Neoliberalism, Corporatism and Small Business Political Activism in Contemporary Mexico," *Latin American Research Review* 35, no. 2 (2000): pp. 73–106.

134. Timothy A. Wise, Hilda Salazar, and Laura Carlsen, *Confronting Globalization: Economic Integration and Popular Resistance in Mexico* (Bloomfield, CT: Kumarian Press, 2003). See also "The Mexican Presidency, 2006–2012: Neoliberalism, Social Movements and Electoral Politics" in the special issue of *Latin American Perspectives* 33, no. 2 (March 2006): pp. 5–140.

135. "Mexico Congress Oil Row Deepens," *BBC News*, 15 April 2008, http://news .bbc.co.uk/.

136. Kate Doyle, "Official Report Released on Mexico's 'Dirty War': Government Acknowledges Responsibility for Massacres, Torture, Disappearances and Genocide," National Security Archive Electronic Briefing Book No. 29, 21 November 2006, www .gwu.edu/.

137. Human Rights Watch, *World Report 1995*.

138. Human Rights Watch, *World Report 1994*.

139. Human Rights Watch, *World Report 1995*.

140. US Army Intelligence and Threat Analysis Center, *Army Country Profile— Mexico*, Part I, April 1993, Secret, pp. 1-1, 1-3, www.gwu.edu/.

141. US State Department, "Mexico," *Country Reports on Human Rights Practices—2007*, 11 March 2008, www.state.gov/.

142. Human Rights Watch, *Implausible Deniability: State Responsibility for Rural Violence in Mexico*, 1 April 1997, www.hrw.org; Amnesty International, "Mexico: Fear for Safety/ Paramilitary Attacks," 16 August 2000, AI Index: AMR 41/42/00, www.amnesty.org/.

143. Michael W. Foley, "Southern Mexico: Counterinsurgency and Electoral Politics," United States Institute of Peace, Special Report No. 43, 27 January 1999, www.usip.org/.

144. Robert Collier, "US Offer Raises Sticky Questions," *San Francisco Chronicle,* 10 December 1996.

145. "Joint Statement by President Bush, President Fox, and Prime Minister Martin: Security and Prosperity Partnership of North America," 23 March 2005, http://georgewbush-whitehouse.archives.gov/.

146. For details, see David T. Johnson, Assistant Secretary for International Narcotics and Law Enforcement Affairs, statement before the Subcommittee on Border, Maritime and Global Counterterrorism of the House Homeland Security Committee, 5 June 2008, www.state.gov/.

147. Colleen W. Cook, Rebecca G. Rush, and Clare Ribando Seelke, *Merida Initiative: Proposed US Anticrime and Counterdrug Assistance for Mexico and Central America,* 18 March 2008, Congressional Research Service, RS22837, p. 2, http://fpc.state.gov.

148. Office of the Press Secretary, White House, "Fact Sheet: US-Mexico Discuss New Approach to Bilateral Relationship," 16 April 2009, www.whitehouse.gov/; Center for International Policy, "Mexico Aid in the 2009 Supplemental," 20 May 2009, www.cipcol.org/.

149. For details, see Johnson, statement before the Subcommittee on Border, Maritime and Global Counterterrorism of the House Homeland Security Committee.

150. Manuel Roig-Franzia, "Calderon's Offensive against Drug Cartels: Use of Mexican Military Increasingly Criticized," *Washington Post,* 8 July 2007.

151. US State Department, "Mexico," *Country Reports on Human Rights Practices—2007.*

152. Ken Ellingwood, "Army's Role in Mexican Drug Seen as Crucial Yet Risky," *LA Times,* 3 June 2008.

153. Ioan Grillo, "Mexico's Narco-Insurgency," *Time,* 25 January 2008.

154. US Department of Defense, *Merida Initiative: Program Description Reference Document, Mexican Security Cooperation Plan,* 29 February 2008, http://americas.irc-online.org/.

155. April 2008 speech to the Council of the Americas. Cited in Laura Carlsen, "A Primer on Plan Mexico," Americas Policy Program Special Report, 5 May 2008, p. 3, http://americas.irc-online.org. Emphasis added.

156. See, for instance, the extensive report of the fact-finding mission by the International Civil Commission on Human Rights, as a result of its visit to Mexico in February 2008, http://cciodh.pangea.org/.

157. John Gibler, "Why We Oppose Plan Mexico," www.globalexchange.org/.

158. US State Department, "Mexico," *Country Reports on Human Rights Practices—2006,* 6 March 2007, www.state.gov/.

159. Human Rights Watch, "Mexico: Events of 2007," *World Report 2008,* http://www.hrw.org/.

160. Michele Heisler, Alejandro Moreno, Sonya DeMonner, Allen Keller, and Vincent Iacopino, "Assessment of Torture and Ill Treatment of Detainees in Mexico: Attitudes and Experiences of Forensic Physicians," *JAMA* 289, no. 16 (23–30 April 2003): pp. 2135–43.

161. Traci Carl, "Police 'Torture' Videos Cause Uproar in Mexico," *Associated Press*, 2 July 2008, http://edition.cnn.com/.

162. Carlsen, "A Primer on Plan Mexico"; Amnesty International, "Mexico: General José Francisco Gallardo Should Be Released Immediately," 9 June 1998, AI Index: AMR 41/28/98, www.amnesty.org/.

CONCLUSION: The Futures of American Hegemony?

1. "Comprehensive Analysis of Polls Reveals Americans' Attitudes on US Role in the World," World Public Opinion, 3 August 2007, www.worldpublicopinion.org/.

# Index